GW00482883

The Growth of a Profession:
Nursing in Victoria,
1930s–1980s

The Growth of a Profession:

Nursing in Victoria, 1930s–1980s

Judith Bessant and Bob Bessant

La Trobe University Press
Australia

First published in 1991 by
La Trobe University Press
La Trobe University
Bundoora Victoria Australia

Copyright © Florence Nightingale Committee of Australia,
Victorian Branch

Cover and book design by Lauren Statham, Alice Graphics
Typeset in 11/13 Sabon by Bookset, Melbourne
Printed in Australia by Brown Prior Anderson Pty Ltd,
Melbourne

National Library of Australia
Cataloguing-in-Publication data:

Bessant, Judith C.

The growth of a profession: nursing in Victoria 1930s–1980s.

Bibliography.
Includes index
ISBN 1 86324 411 5

1. Nursing — Victoria — History. I. Bessant, B. (Bob). II.
Title.

610.7309945

All rights reserved. Apart from any fair dealing for the
purpose of private study, research, criticism or review, as
permitted under the Copyright Act, no part may be reproduced
by any process without written permission. Enquiries should
be made to the publisher.

The dedication of a history of the nursing profession in Victoria is very difficult, because such a book should include the names of all those who have steadfastly carried out their duties with great love and devotion to their colleagues, no matter what conditions prevailed at the time.

Leaders are necessary and good leaders should be praised for their skill and wisdom, but down the line we must remember those who provide the day to day commitment of caring for the sick.

This book is thus dedicated to the unsung and unnamed nurses at all levels, who did their best at all times, often in daunting situations.

The publication of this book was made possible by the following donors:

Florence Nightingale Committee of Victoria, Victorian Branch

Alfred Hospital Professional Development Fund

Alfred Hospital Medical Staff

Alfred Hospital Nurses League

Melbourne School of Nursing Past Trainees Association

Prince Henry's Past Trainees Club

Associate of Directors of Nursing Victoria Incorporated

Special Interest Groups:
   Geriatrics
   Maternal Child and Health Nurses
   Occupational Health
   Nurse Administrators
   Operating Nurse Group

Principal Teachers Association

Australian College of Midwives Incorporated

In memory of Marjorie Connor

Contents

Acknowledgements

Many people have helped in the production of this book and it is not possible to list them all. Nevertheless, it would not have been produced at this time but for the drive and enthusiasm of the late Miss Marjorie Connor. Her devotion to the history of nursing in the State of Victoria together with the willing assistance of the members of the Victorian Branch of the Florence Nightingale Committee made this book possible.

Thanks are due to the numerous people who read the various draft chapters of the book and especially to Miss Rae Lockey whose detailed knowledge and understanding of the period proved invaluable. The comments of Dr Margaret Bennett, the late Miss Pat Slater and Dr Richard Trembath who read most, if not all, of the final draft proved of great assistance and encouragement.

It was a pleasure to work on the archives of the RVCN at the University of Melbourne Archives where the archivists were always interested and helpful. This was also the case when working with the research officers at the ANF, Victorian Branch headquarters.

One of the regrets has been the lack of time to interview the many nurses who participated in the events described in the book. Those we did interview brought refreshing insights to the history, especially from such strong and dynamic people as Pat Slater and Irene Bolger. In this respect one person deserves particular attention. Miss Ruth Henderson, whose work in recording the experiences of trainee nurses in the 1930s and 1940s and collecting them in a monograph which she herself published, was of great help in the writing of the third chapter.

Our thanks go also to all those not mentioned above who assisted in the production of this book. It was an enlightening experience and one we will never regret.

J.B.
B.B.

Foreword

As the late Marjorie Connor indicated in her Foreword to the companion volume of this present book, *All Care and Responsibility* by Trembath and Hellier, 'A book like this is the result of the efforts of many people'. The words are true for this book also. However, all those involved would agree that the driving force behind both books was Marjorie herself. It was a great disappointment that she did not live to see the publication of this volume. The recording of the history of nursing in Victoria from 1850 to the 1980s was her passion, and is her final gift to the profession that she loved and helped to shape. She was the impulse that initiated and influence that sustained the recording of this history. Trembath and Hellier acknowledge her as 'guide and mentor' and describe her as 'indeed an outstanding lady'. And so she was.

During the creation of this volume, Marjorie, an octogenarian, and slowing down physically, was still mentally active and had more than sufficient enthusiasm and dynamism to drive all those associated with the book. Her unflagging energy ensured its completion, especially through the innumerable vicissitudes associated with its writing.

The present authors have included an oral history from Marjorie, and her stentorian voice looms large through these pages. For almost three decades (1945–1973) of the time covered in this book, (that is, the 1930s to the 1980s), Marjorie, as executive secretary of the Royal Victorian College of Nursing, was influential in the shaping of nursing. It is a fitting tribute to her that the authors have recorded accurately her significant contribution to the nursing profession, and have captured her caring attitude, her warmth and energy.

For both volumes of this history, Marjorie ensured the early drafts were scrutinised carefully. Included in her team of readers was Patricia Slater. As described in this book, Pat Slater was one of those leaders who exerted considerable influence on the nursing profession. The present authors had the benefit of an oral history and both sets of authors received substantial support and guidance from her. Pat, too, did not live to see the completion of this book, but, like Marjorie, her contribution to the profession has been captured faithfully, and her voice speaks eloquently and with conviction through these pages.

This book brings to the reader many outstanding women who have exerted their influence on the development of nursing as a profession. They speak clearly, and through them, the reader understands how nursing developed over this period. However, there are many others who have played a part in the shaping of the profession and who are not named here. For these people, Marjorie had a deep concern and in typical fashion, has ensured that this book is dedicated to them. This book is also, however, a fitting tribute to Marjorie.

It has been my privilege to write for Marjorie, on behalf of the Florence Nightingale Committee, Australia, Victorian Branch, to commend this history to the reader. Like the companion volume, it is both enjoyable and instructive. Within the six decades of this book considerable change has occurred within the profession of nursing. Old images have been shaken off and new ones adopted. The authors have captured the turmoil of the era and shown how 'The Growth of the Profession' occurred during that time — growth in both quality and quantity for the profession of nursing in Victoria.

Margaret J. Bennet,
Ph.D., R.N., R.M., F.R.C.N.A.

Chronology and Abbreviations

1899	Foundation of International Council of Nurses	ICN
1901	Victorian Trained Nurses Association	VTNA
1904	Royal Victorian Trained Nurses Association (formerly VTNA)	RVTNA
1921	Trained Nurses Guild TNG registered as an industrial organisation with federal Arbitration Court	TNG
1924	Nurses Board — control over training, qualifications and registration of Victorian nurses	
1924	Australian Nursing Federation	ANF
1929	Hospital Employees Federation	HEF
1934	Royal Victorian College of Nursing (formerly RVTNA)	RVCN
1936	Hospital Nurses Board (Wages Board) — control over wages and conditions of Victorian nurses	
1937	ANF affiliated with ICN	
1943	RCVN Employees Association	
1945	TNG re-activated	
1946	National Florence Nightingale Memorial Committee	NFNMC
1949	Australian United Nurses Association (formerly TNG) — concerned with economic interests at national level. ANF looking after professional area.	AUNA

1949	College of Nursing, Australia	
1953	ANF, Employees Section (formerly AUNA)	ANFES
	ANFES, Victorian Branch	
	ANF and ANFES administered at RCVN office.	
1956	Victorian Nursing Council (formerly Nurses Board)	VNC
	Royal Australian Nursing Federation (formerly ANF)	RANF
1960	ANFES, Victorian Branch and RCVN Employees Association merge to become ANFES, Victorian Branch.	
1970	Integration of RANF and ANFES to form Australian Nursing Federation	ANF
	ANF, Victorian Branch (formerly ANFES, Victorian Branch)	ANF, VB
1971	Royal Australian Nursing Federation (formerly ANF)	RANF
	Royal Australian Nursing Federation, Victorian Branch (formerly ANF, Victorian Branch)	RANF, VB
1975	RANF, Victorian Branch and RVCN merge as RANF, Victorian Branch	
1989	Australian Nursing Federation (formerly RANF)	ANF
	Australian Nursing Federation, Victorian Branch (formerly RANF, Victorian Branch)	ANF, VB
	Royal College of Nursing, Australia (formerly College of Nursing, Australia)	

Other Abbreviations

Australian Army Nursing Service	AANS
Australian Council of Trade Unions	ACTU
Australian Labor Party	ALP
Australian Medical Association	AMA
Health Commission of Victoria	HCV
Industrial Relations Commission	IRC
New South Wales Nurses Association	NSWNA
Preliminary Training School	PTS
State Enrolled Nurse	SEN
Victorian Institute of Colleges	VIC

Introduction

THIS book is about nurses and nursing in Victoria from the 1930s to the 1980s. A previous work, *All Care and Responsibility. A History of Nursing in Victoria 1850–1934* by Richard Trembath and Donna Hellier, covers the earlier period.[1] However, for those who have not read that work this introduction will provide an outline of the history of nursing in Victoria prior to the 1930s.

When Florence Nightingale sent out her emissaries to the far flung corners of the British Empire, they arrived with a message for the colonials: Raise the status of nursing by employing women of impeccable character who will be able to command respect and who are willing to make sacrifices in the care of the sick; in charge of these women place a leader of women:

> Though vested in all the duties of an ordinary nurse, she should, in social degree and in culture of the mind, be very much superior to an ordinary nurse; otherwise she should not have the power of commanding respect and obedience from her subordinates. Refined and educated persons have always a strong moral influence over their inferiors in station, and the latter will submit willingly — nay almost involuntarily — to those in whom they recognize a superior intelligence.[2]

Florence Nightingale sought to take nursing out of the hands of domestic servants and at the same time introduce an awareness of the need for cleanliness, hygiene and sound diet. She saw nursing as being more than simply the administration of medicines and the application of poultices:

It ought to signify the proper use of fresh air, light, warmth, cleanliness, quiet, and the proper selection and administration of diet — all at the least expense of vital power to the patient.[3]

She also believed a nurse should be a person possessing special skills — one who would be able to carry out a doctor's instructions faithfully and efficiently and who could observe and record results for reporting back to him. At the same time she did not see nurses simply as the handmaidens of doctors. The work of nurses complemented that of doctors, but it also had its own field of experience and expertise.

For proficiency in their tasks the nurses had to undertake a suitable period of training in a hospital. They were also to live on the hospital premises, for Miss Nightingale regarded this as an essential part of their moral training. Her early trainee nurses were not necessarily drawn from the upper class however, but were more likely to come from the solid urban middle class and rural yeomanry, with the stress always on high moral character, rather than on educational achievements. Closely linked with this was the belief that the trainees should be as chaste as the members of any religious order and subject to strong discipline and constant supervision.[4]

Many of Florence Nightingale's ideas were not new; but her strength came from the publicity she had received during the Crimean War and her ability to use the position she had established in British society to further the cause of nursing. She was able to establish a training school for nurses at St Thomas's Hospital, London in 1860, and from this school nursing sisters went out as ambassadors of the new nursing ethic. Although six arrived in Sydney in 1868 to work at the Sydney Hospital, it took many years for the Nightingale reforms to be put into practice in Victoria.

Victorian hospitals were regarded as 'charitable institutions', though in 1882 well over half of their costs for building and maintenance came from the Government.[5] Even so, they jealously guarded their independence from government interference and were administered by hospital committees who appointed their own staff and managed their own finances. Until the 1930s when they began to admit fee-paying patients, the public hospitals were intended for the poor and for accident cases.

In these hospitals both wardsmen and nurses attended the sick. They were untrained and their work, like their pay and conditions, was mostly akin to domestic service. The standards of care varied considerably between and even within hospitals largely depending on the sympathy and competency of the particular nurses or wardsmen. The number of men working in the wards declined in the later part of the nineteenth century until, by 1900, caring for the sick was almost solely a female occupation.[6]

The first direct influence of the Nightingale reforms in Victoria came with the arrival of Haldane Turriff as the matron of the Alfred Hospital in 1871. She had been one of the sisters brought out by Henry Parkes, colonial secretary, three years earlier. It was not until 1880 however, that the first training school along Nightingale lines was established in Victoria, at the Alfred, when Turriff was no longer matron.

It seems that the enthusiasm and support of mainly physicians and surgeons was instrumental in the establishment of the many training schemes that developed in Victorian hospitals during the 1880s and 1890s. This was partly a reaction to the need for trained assistance in the wards with the increasing sophistication of medical practice, but was also intended to give the medical profession a strong influence in what went into the training of nurses. Demarcation lines had to be established between the work of nurses and doctors, and doctors made sure that nurses did not take over any of their functions. Doctors were prepared to accept nurses as handmaidens of the sick and injured, but they would not tolerate any challenge to their authority. They made sure that the training schools taught trainees to be obedient to doctors at all times. This established a pattern which was to survive for at least 100 years.[7]

> The early Nightingale nurses were superior, nineteenth-century housewives. The medical profession was the husband and ruler of the house (the hospital). Proper servants, scrubbers, wardsmen, porters, cooks, laundresses and gardeners were engaged to do the heavy work, as they were in any well-run mid-Victorian household, while the nurses themselves supervised, coordinated, inspired, 'poured tea' (administering the prescribed medicine), and above all saw that the wishes of the head of the house were fully carried out.[8]

The model nurse was expected to be the epitome of the model Victorian woman. A woman dedicated, self-sacrificing, honest, trustworthy, totally committed to her work, who would be always cheerful and uncomplaining, at the same time as she was efficient, dutiful and demure. These personal qualities were continually stressed in the training hospitals together with much attention to physical appearance:

> The office of nurse is too high and too holy for any woman called to it to wish to devote much time to the adornment of her person. Her one object as regards herself should be, to be clean, simple, neat, modest, sweet-tempered and to know how to mind her own business.[9]

The emphasis in the 1880s and 1890s then, was on getting the 'right type' of person into nursing.

The burden of selecting these women and ensuring that they upheld the standards expected of them fell to the matrons of the hospitals. Matrons had won the fight to establish themselves as the commanding officers over the nurses in their charge within a structure which owed much to Florence Nightingale's success on the battlefield. The matron took her orders from the hospital board of management, but in the day-to-day running of the hospital she was in command. Below her developed a hierarchy of head nurse, sisters and probationers (the privates).

Within the context of the uncomplaining, dedicated and professional nurse menial labour took on a new meaning. It was no longer domestic work, but part of the professional duties of a nurse. It was part of the aura surrounding the ministering to the sick and as such became an important part of the training. Florence Nightingale herself believed a nurse should know how to keep the sick room clean and tidy, and scrub and disinfect walls.[10] Those trainees who could cope with the domestic service side of nursing were seen by some matrons as more likely to survive as good nurses. As it so happened this suited the hospital administrators admirably at a time when domestic servants were scarce, particularly in the urban areas, and were also demanding wages significantly higher than those paid to trainee nurses.[11]

One of the problems which arose with the setting up of training schools in the hospitals was the lack of uniform standards of training, examination and registration. To those doctors and nurses who wished to see nursing developed as a profession, uniformity in these areas was regarded as essential. Only those who had passed the necessary examinations and registration procedures could be classified as nurses, thus separating the trained from the untrained and ensuring not only that the qualified person practised nursing, but also that person was acceptable to other members of the profession and could be expected to conform to the profession's ethics.

The hospital committees were also interested in uniformity because it had become very difficult to compare applicants for nursing positions who had been trained in different hospitals. As a result hospitals, doctors and nurses combined in 1901 to establish the Victorian Trained Nurses Association (VTNA; RVTNA from 1904), although most of the actual organisation was done by the doctors. Similar associations had already been set up in Britain and the United States.

For the first 20 years of its existence the RVTNA was controlled by the doctors, matrons and proprietors of trained nurses homes, with the doctors holding most of the executive positions. Although there were only four representatives of sisters and nurses in 1911, this state of affairs did not seem to worry anyone, for there existed a sincere belief that all were acting in the interests of nursing.[12]

The association began registering nurses in 1901, basing their registration on three years training in a public hospital. It began examinations for trainees in hospitals of less than 40 beds at the same time, incorporating the larger hospitals in 1905. Altogether it was a remarkably successful operation. The RVTNA had within a very short space of time established itself as the recognised voice of the nursing profession in Victoria. In 1903 it also produced its own journal, *UNA*, which survived until 1976. American nurses praised the achievement:

> Apparently all the older countries can only hope to secure through bitterly contested legislation what the Victorians have been able to achieve by voluntary agreement between the hospital and the nursing organisation. The smoothness and excellent results of the uniform system of training and experience established by the 40 state hospitals in response to the representation of the organisation of nurses are beyond all question. The adoption of this uniform system

and standard may well be called a triumph for the principles of voluntary cooperation. There is nothing else like it in nursing history.[13]

Nevertheless, there was one important qualification to this success that few seemed to recognise at the time. It has always been a particular feature of professional organisations that they are controlled by members of the profession. This was clearly not the case with the RVTNA. Nurses were subservient to doctors and lacked the confidence to pursue a separate identity. Indeed, it was ten years before a nurse became president of the RVTNA.

From the outset the RVTNA rejected any suggestion that the association was a trade union or in any way connected with trade unionism. This was not surprising since both employers and employees were represented on its council. The association refused to be drawn into any activity which might be seen as seeking an improvement in the wages and conditions of hospital nurses, for this was clearly a trade union concern. Trade unionism was too closely connected with the working class, especially domestic servants and hospital orderlies, above whom the nurses hoped to rise. However, this did not prevent the RVTNA from spending considerable time in debating private nurses' pay; establishing its own fees was seen as a legitimate function of a professional association. Hospital nurses and sisters were a different matter, especially as most were not registered. Their wages and conditions, it was argued, were not the concern of the RVTNA. Apart from any other reason nursing leaders must have realised that for the RVTNA to launch into the industrial arena on this matter would have split the organisation asunder. This meant that for 20 years the RVTNA turned a blind eye to the exploitation of nursing trainees in the hospitals.

Part of the explanation for this lack of concern lies in the fact that the great majority of RVTNA members were private nurses, most of whom were residents of private nurses homes.[14] Before the Great War private nursing had a certain status and prestige which was much sought after by the graduates of the training schools; it was probably the closest they would ever come to being independent professionals.

Nurses homes were first set up in the 1880s and by the mid-1890s were well established as the main providers of private nurses in Victoria. Nurses paid rent and board to the management of the homes and retained the fees paid by the private patients, although some paid the homes a fee and stayed in other accommodation. The homes were centres which could be approached by the public and were also where work schedules could be arranged. In these ways they aided private nurses. They also had links with doctors who recommended nurses to their patients. In 1904 the RVTNA set the scale of fees for private nurses.

In most cases the homes were close to the centre of Melbourne or in the southern and eastern suburbs and large provincial towns where those who could afford to pay lived, and where most of the main hospitals were situated. Living conditions in the homes varied and even here nurses were subject to the authority of the superintendents because the latter knew full well that a nurse on her own could not obtain private work.

Private nursing was popular in a time when public hospitals were essentially for the poor and there were few private hospitals. When nursing was required the middle and upper classes turned to the private nurse. While this nurse was also expected to perform domestic tasks in the home, the work did not have the same rigour and discipline associated with hospital nursing. There were certainly long hours, broken sleep and problems of coping with the family as well as the patient, but there was a certain independence and prestige which hospital nurses did not enjoy. A private nurse could also expect to earn more, with a minimum income of £57 per annum before 1914.[15] It was this apparent independence which attracted nurses. It was somewhat similar, dare it be said, to that of the female factory workers who preferred to work long hours in poor conditions rather than go into domestic service.

Between 1904 and 1912 hospital administrators had pursued the policy of taking on greater numbers of trainees, rather than trained sisters, since they were much cheaper to employ. First year trainees in 1912 received anything from no payment to £15 per annum and in the third year a maximum would have been £25, compared with trained staff whose salaries ranged from £35 to £75 per annum. In 1915 there were 158 trained nurses in Victorian hospitals and 650 trainees.[16]

Like the Second World War, the Great War (1914–1918) did much to raise the public's appreciation of the work of nurses and this increased with the influenza pandemic that followed. The war brought home how much the community depended on nurses, especially when by 1916 somewhere between one-third and one-half of the trained nurses in Victoria had joined the Australian Army Nursing Service (AANS). The hospitals were denuded of trained staff and with two major epidemics, meningitis in 1915 and influenza in 1919, the strain on existing staff and resources highlighted the need for reform of nurses' working conditions.

The press gave much publicity to the long hours worked by trainees under sweated labour conditions. In 1918 to the horror of the RVTNA, nurses at the Melbourne, Children's and Homoeopathic hospitals acting quite independently of the association, took a deputation to the State Treasurer seeking a wages board for nurses, and received a sympathetic hearing. A special inquiry into working conditions was held which supported a reduction in nursing hours to eight hours per day. While nothing specific resulted from this, it did focus attention on working conditions and revealed the unwillingness of the RVTNA to act in any serious way to bring about change.[17]

Also of great interest to nurses at this time was the establishment of a nurses' registration board in which the RVTNA was heavily involved. Registration with the RVTNA did not prevent untrained, unregistered nurses from engaging in private practice, even if at reduced rates. State registration of nurses was seen as the answer to this problem and for about 13 years the RVTNA had campaigned for this. After numerous failed attempts an Act was finally assented to in 1923. A nurses' board took over the control of the training, qualifications and registration of Victorian nurses from 30 March 1924. The RVTNA was well represented on the board with five members of seven.[18]

It was almost inevitable that the question of an industrial role for the RVTNA would again arise. After the return of the 1 000 Victorian members of the AANS, the association was forced to show more interest than had previously when trainees had tried to improve their conditions. A new body, called the Trained Nurses' Guild (TNG), was formed in January 1921 at a meeting of some 200 nurses and took over from where the trainees had left off, seeking the improvement of conditions in hospitals through a wages board or the Federal Arbitration Court. Even though it at no stage aimed at supplanting the RVTNA, the guild came up against bitter and formidable opposition, including the matrons of public hospitals as well as the owners of private hospitals. They outlawed the guild and warned nurses against having anything to do with it. The guild failed to get any backing from where it mattered most, trainees and trained staff in hospitals; nevertheless, its formation had an immediate and salutary effect on the RVTNA.

For the first time the RVTNA acted to improve nurses' salaries in hospitals. Dr W. B. Vance, president, and Mr R. G. Fincham, RVTNA council member and president of the Country Hospitals Association, persuaded the Country and Metropolitan Hospitals Associations to accept significant rises in nursing salaries using the threat that they would be faced with Arbitration Court proceedings from the guild if they did not comply. Even though the RVTNA had taken the initiative out of the hands of the guild the latter still had its main card to play. In November 1921 it applied to the Arbitration Court for registration as an industrial organisation and gained approval in February 1922, in spite of objections raised by counsel for the RVTNA, Mr R. G. Menzies.[19]

When the Melbourne *Herald* wrote in support of the guild that the RVTNA had revealed itself 'as an intensely conservative organisation designed to serve the interests of the doctors and hospitals which employ them', it was expressing what many nurses had known for a long time.[20] The representation on the RVTNA Council had changed little in 20 years. In 1921 there were 27 representatives of doctors, managers and nurse employers and only nine from nurse employees. Although nothing further came of the guild's efforts and the organisation faded away, it left one gift to posterity — it had been approved as the nurses' industrial organisation for the whole of Australia. Many years later when this issue arose again the guild was to be exhumed from the grave in order to institute Arbitration Court proceedings.

Throughout the 1920s there was a persistent shortage of

trained nurses. This continued over the next 60 years, except for a brief period during the 1930s depression. The middle class had accepted nursing as a respectable occupation for a middle class girl, and a brief career as a trained nurse before marriage had become the ambition of many young women and their parents. But the pool from which to select trainees had grown smaller, especially in the 1920s when other avenues offering more attractive working conditions, such as in teaching and office work, were opening up.

By the 1920s many of the problems and conflicts which were to be the concern of nurses over the next 50 years had already emerged. The reluctance of the RVTNA to interest itself in industrial issues other than under extreme pressure, could not be explained simply by the presence of both employers and employees on its council. Any association with industrial trade unionism was seen by nursing leaders as undermining the quest for professional status. Professional people eschewed the tactics of the trade unions which were seen not only as working class organisations, but, especially in the 1920s and 1930s, were considered tainted with socialism and Bolshevism. Nursing had only recently shed its associations with the working class and the nursing leaders had no wish to undermine the acceptance of nursing as a respectable middle class occupation by engaging in unionistic activities.

Nurses in the RVTNA and later the RVCN, were to face the constant dilemma of maintaining a shopfront devoted to the display of professionalism, while in the rear rooms grappling with problems associated with wages and conditions. While increasing numbers of nurses became convinced that better pay and conditions were important in raising the status of nursing, the dilemma was how to achieve this without resorting to the tactics of a trade union?

Many nurses saw nursing as a vocation where questions of pay and working conditions were irrelevant to the main task of helping the cause of suffering humanity. Above all else they were there to help the sick. They were not working simply for the money. Even though in the 1920s some challenged this approach, it continued to dominate the thinking of the leading nurses in Victoria for many years after the 1920s, and to directly affect the organisation of nurses in the State.

Professional status could not be separated from training and education, and it was quite consistent for nursing leaders to place so much emphasis on gaining State registration, for without that safeguard the untrained nurse was a constant threat to the status of the whole profession. It is probable that many nurses also considered the RVTNA a bulwark against the untrained. Nor was the problem of the untrained nurse solved by the *Nurses Registration Act 1923*. As the hospital system expanded over the next 30 years the rift between trained nurses and nursing aides (also nursing assistants) was maintained, with the latter persistently seen as undermining all efforts to attain true professional status.

Another theme which will recur in the chapters to come is also directly associated with this quest for professional status. The leaders of the nursing organisations were concerned not only with maintaining high standards in the initial training of nurses, but also with furthering the education of trained nurses. The full recognition of nursing as a profession was seen to be largely dependent on as many nurses as possible gaining post-graduate training and credentials. This would raise the public image of nursing and also improve the quality of care for patients. Credentials helped create the mystique surrounding the physicians and surgeons, why not also for nurses?

But this question was related to another problem which recurred over the next 50 years: How was nursing to be defined? What were the parameters of a nurse's work? Was it possible to distinguish a body of knowledge which was specific to nursing? How was this affected by the relationship of nursing to medicine; the nurse to the doctor? These are the themes which will be explored in this book, but this history is also about people and organisations. It is about the training and work of nurses with the emphasis on hospital training because the majority of nurses worked in hospitals during the period covered. A few outstanding nurses are given special mention, and our selection will not please everyone because there were so many from which to choose.

This is not a history of the RVCN/RANF, VB, but as this organisation has had a significant role in the history of nursing in Victoria, some (but only some) of its activities have been given prominence. Histories of the VNC, bush nursing and the nurses in the wars have been admirably covered elsewhere, and so these areas are not looked at in detail here. There are many other facets of nursing that are not covered. These could be the subjects of many books or monographs, and we hope that one day this will be the case. This history is essentially an introduction to the general trends in nursing in Victoria from the 1930s to 1986. As such we hope it will inspire others to fill out the story, to build on what we have written — there are many rich and vital histories yet to be researched and recorded.

Endnotes

[1] Richard Trembath, Donna Hellier, *All Care and Responsibility. A History of Nursing in Victoria 1850–1934*, Florence Nightingale Committee, Australia, Victorian Branch, Melbourne, 1987.

[2] Quoted in Beverley Kingston, *My Wife, My Daughter and Poor Mary Ann. Women and Work in Australia*, Thomas Nelson, Melbourne, 1975, p. 83 from *New South Wales V & P*, 1899, vol. 5, Fourth Report of the Royal Commission on Charities, Minutes of Evidence, p. 32.

[3] Florence Nightingale, *Notes on Nursing. What it is, and What it is Not*, D. Appleton-Century, New York, 1946, p. 8.

[4] See Brian Abel-Smith, *A History of the Nursing Profession*, Heinemann, London, 1982, pp. 19–22.

[5] Trembath, Hellier, op. cit., p. 11, 6.

[6] ibid., pp. 14–15.

[7] Monica Mackay, 'Handmaidens of Medicine — A History of Nursing in Colonial Victoria', M.Ec. thesis, Monash University, 1982, pp. 106–9.

[8] Kingston, op. cit.

[9] E. A. M. Storey, *Practical Points in Nursing*, Philadelphia, 1899, p. 18 quoted in Mackay, op. cit., p. 102.

[10] Nightingale, op. cit., pp. 87–9.

[11] See Mackay, pp. 160–83 for details of hours, wages and working conditions of nurses in Victoria in the late nineteenth century.

[12] Trembath, Hellier, op. cit., pp. 46–8.

[13] Quoted in *UNA*, 30 May 1907 from *American Journal of Nursing*, April 1907.

[14] For details of nurses homes in this period see Trembath, Hellier, op. cit., pp. 87–93.

[15] ibid., p. 93.

[16] ibid., pp. 94–5.

[17] ibid., pp. 115–19 for details of these developments.

[18] See Maureen K. Minchin, *Revolutions and Rosewater. The Evolution of Nurse Registration in Victoria 1923–1973*, Hart Hamer, Melbourne, n.d., ch. 3.

[19] Trembath, Hellier, op. cit., pp. 127–141.

[20] ibid., p. 142.

1

The RVCN
1934–1950

THE ordinary working people of Victoria were used to times of unemployment between periods of work even in the 'prosperous' years of the 1920s. People in government positions or in relatively prestigious and seemingly secure private employment in banks, hospitals, private schools and insurance offices, were looked on with envy by the majority of workers who knew that unemployment could be just around the corner. Even when unemployment began to rise significantly from 1927 and industrial output began to decline in 1928, together with dramatic falls in prices of Australia's staples, wool and wheat in 1929, the seriousness of the economic situation was not generally realised. People were out of work, but that was not unusual. They were used to the upturns and downturns of the economy.

But when money became too expensive on the London money market, thus halting the flow of long term loans and leading to severe cuts in public works programs in 1930, there was even doubt that Australia would be able to meet the interest on existing debts. Then people began to realise that what was upon them was more than just a temporary decline in the inevitable progress of a nation.

In 1930 the economy deteriorated rapidly. Unemployment soared, businesses went bankrupt, farmers walked off their farms and pressures for a drastic downward adjustment in government expenditure began to develop. State Governments were unable to borrow money and even workers in seemingly secure positions lost their jobs. Unemployment rose to 30 per cent in 1932, and the unemployed roamed city and country in search of work or sustenance. There were numerous charitable institutions working to help them, but in the cities many were kept alive by relief schemes run by the government, such as the Great Ocean Road and the Yarra Boulevard developments. In the country many resorted to living off the land.

All State Governments and the Federal Government made substantial reductions in their expenditures in 1931. In Victoria hospitals had their budgets cut by 20 per cent. At the same time contributions from private charities to hospitals fell sharply. The result was not only cuts in the salaries of hospital staff in line with the general reduction of 10 per cent which the Arbitration Court sanctioned in 1931, but also the beginning of a long period of cost-cutting in hospital administration in areas such as medical supplies, catering, linen and the employment of staff.

With the supply of cheap trainees already dominating the hospital labour forces, it was not surprising that managements sought to decrease still further the proportion of fully trained staff compared with those in training, as they had done in previous periods of economic stringency. They were encouraged by the large numbers of young women now seeking to train as nurses. It was also encouraging for the matrons, who could now could afford to be much more selective. They saw it as an ideal opportunity to raise nursing standards. With so many young women knocking at hospital doors, the matrons kept up the pressure on trainees with the ever present threat of instant dismissal.

The Great Depression accelerated what was to be a major change in the employment pattern of trained nurses in Victoria, from an emphasis on employment as private nurses to the employment of nurses in hospitals. It has been estimated that in 1920 between one-half and two-thirds of RVTNA members were practising as private nurses, and this proportion almost certainly continued throughout the twenties.[1] Two trends in the 1930s, however, drastically reduced the number of private nurses — the drop in the demand for their services and the growth of inter-mediate wings in public hospitals. Many of the clients of private nurses in the 1920s no longer had the means to employ them in the 1930s. They faced long 'slack' periods. They were undercut by untrained women willing to work for less than the prescribed fees who were desperate to obtain work at any price. Fee reductions were debated in the RVTNA but rejected, yet even if fees had been reduced it is doubtful that this would have created more work for trained private nurses.[2]

The most significant long term development was the growth in the number of fee-paying patients in the intermediate wards of public hospitals. The public hospital system established in the nineteenth century was for the poor and deserving members of the community. Hospitals were firmly based within the charitable institution network and were controlled by boards dominated by middle and upper class charity workers. For those who did not qualify for public hospital admission, there were the private nurses and the private hospitals. However, the growth of the middle class in Victoria meant that increasing number of people could not afford private care or treatment, but also could not use the public hospitals. The problem was aggravated in the 1920s by an increasing shortage of beds in public hospitals. People at this time also appreciated the fact that the public hospitals provided the highest standard of care available, especially surgical, and a diverse range of services. Consequently, they began to demand that public hospitals be allowed to admit fee-paying patients. The Charities Board which supervised the administration of public hospitals supported this in the late twenties, especially after a report by Dr Malcolm T. MacEachern, a visiting American hospital expert. This report recommended the addition of pay-wards, 'particularly intermediate, to public hospitals throughout the State of Victoria, in order to provide proper medical and hospital service for the middle class group'.[3]

In 1929 the regulations allowing fee-paying patients into public hospitals were gazetted. The fee paying wards were to be quite separate from the public wards and no charitable funds were to be used for their upkeep.[4] In spite of the depression, there followed a significant increase of fee-paying patients in Victorian country hospitals over the next decade. Between 1933–1934 and 1937–1938 the number of fee-paying patients rose from 2 971 to 9 816. Ten years later this figure had grown to 37 169, over 4 000 more than public patients. The metropolitan hospitals were much slower to enter this field and by 1947 there were only 9 407 fee-paying patients compared with 64 274 in the public wards.

This discrepancy between city and country was probably due to the large number of private hospitals in Melbourne — over 200 in the 1930s.[5]

Since it was a common practice to employ a greater proportion of trained nurses to trainees in the fee-paying wards, from 1930 a whole new avenue of employment opened up for trained nurses at the same time as the demand for private nurses declined. While the fee-paying hospitals deprived private nurses of their patients, they did offer prospects for alternative employment. This had far reaching implications for the nursing profession as a whole, and in particular for the RVTNA.

The Emergence of the RVCN

IN 1934 the RVTNA changed both its name and its constitution to become the Royal Victorian College of Nursing (RVCN). The events which brought about this change were symptomatic of a problem that leading nurses were to face within their organisation for the next 40 years. This was the resolution of the conflict between the quest for genuine professional status for nursing and day-to-day demands of a trade union. Despite attempts which became quite desperate at times to strike a happy balance between these two endeavours, the cutting edge of the sword of professionalism was always there militating against any lasting resolution of the conflict. Nursing and professionalism will be discussed in detail in the next chapter. It is sufficient to point out here that it was an important factor in the events leading to the establishment of the RVCN.

Some members of the council of the RVTNA had been active during the late 1920s in seeking the establishment of a post-graduate diploma course for nurses at the University of Melbourne. While this attracted little interest on the part of nurses or the university, it was very close to the heart of Miss Jane Bell, matron of the Melbourne Hospital 1910–1934 and a member of the RVTNA Council. Miss Bell was not one to give up easily. She became president of the RVTNA in 1932 and not long after, in 1933, the opportunity came to gain the support for post-graduate courses for nurses from outside the nursing profession.

In April 1933 'several ladies of high standing in the community' including Miss Stella Pines and Mrs Herbert Brookes ('active charity workers'), placed before the council of the RVTNA a proposal for the establishment of a college of nursing similar to those they had seen during their recent travels around Britain, Canada and the United States.[6] Many universities in these countries offered diplomas in nursing. The outcome of this was the setting up of an executive committee representing a variety of medical, hospital, nursing and women's organisations, as well as and the University of Melbourne, to establish a college as part of the Victorian centenary celebrations.[7]

The course proposed for the diploma was modelled on the University of London course consisting of two parts, one on the scientific bases and general principles of nursing (elementary physics, chemistry, anatomy, histology, physiology, hygiene, bacteriology, psychology) and the other on the history of the profession together with a special study in one branch of nursing.[8] It was aimed at attracting trained nurses who wished to take on teaching and administrative positions in hospitals, such as matrons or sister tutors.

However, the university would not agree to the diploma because the proposed course was not up to the standard of other university diplomas, nor were there any existing courses appropriate to nursing studies. The university favoured the college of nursing running its own courses with the university strongly represented on the college board. There is also evidence to suggest that some members of the medical profession opposed the diploma because they had not been consulted, and because they were not happy about raising the educational standards of nurses.[9]

Meanwhile the executive committee went ahead with plans for a college of nursing and a draft constitution was proposed which contained clauses which the RVTNA Council found impossible to accept. It became clear to nurses that what medical men and lay charity workers had in mind was a very different organisation from the one they themselves envisaged. Once again nurses could have found themselves under-represented on their own governing body, which would also have allowed untrained persons to join on payment of a guinea per annum. For Jane Bell and other RVTNA council members this would have amounted to a loss of control over what they envisaged as the main role of a professional organisation — the further education of its members.[10] Not only would this have been a step backwards, but it would also have given lay persons a say in what that education was to be. Moreover, taking away its professional functions would have left the organisation with an imbalance towards the industrial side, a situation which was to be resisted at all costs.

The RVTNA withdrew from the executive committee and immediately announced that it would form its own college of nursing which would be firmly under the control of the nurses themselves.[11] A draft constitution was drawn up and early in 1934 an appeal was launched for £15–20 000 to fund the new college to be called the Victorian Centenary College of Nursing:

> The building up of a powerful self-governing organization is placed in the hands of all trained, registered nurses in Australia — a grand opportunity and a great trust![12]

It was not long before it became apparent that the appeal, launched during the worst depression Australia had known, would be a failure. Whether or not this was the catalyst for the RVTNA Council's decision in April 1934 to incorporate the college in a revamped RVTNA, will probably never be known. However, by taking this course the council effectively ended the attempts by some nurses (notably Miss Grace Wilson, matron of the Alfred Hospital, and the remnants of the original executive committee which set the college move in motion) to establish a series of post-graduate courses. Rivalry between the Alfred and Melbourne Hospitals, which had existed for many years, was another complicating factor in these developments. There was open hostility between Grace Wilson and Jane Bell, and a perusal of those who made donations to the appeal would probably reveal that there were few from what was then the second largest hospital in Victoria.

It was decided to register the new organisation as a company to be known as the Royal Victorian College of Nursing. This was approved by an overwhelming majority in a ballot of RVTNA members. The new organisation came into existence on 28 August 1934. Hopes were high that the new college 'in the immediate future ... will have the same status with the University of Melbourne as the Medical School has at present'.[13]

It would be wrong however, to see the founding of the new organisation as simply the result of the events surrounding the attempt to get the college under way. An examination of the new constitution reveals two major changes from that of the RVTNA. Nurses were to be in full control of the new organisation and there was a clear recognition that a trade union role could no longer be avoided. In many respects the new title was a mis-nomer. It reflected aspirations which were never realised by that body, while the real day-to-day business of the organisation became increasingly like that of other semi-professional associations or trade unions.

The new constitution established a council consisting of 24 members, of whom at least 18 were to be nursing members, plus one midwifery member, a president ('who shall be a nursing member'), two or more vice-presidents, an honorary treasurer and an honorary secretary. The remaining members were to be elected by medical and honorary members. One-third of the council members retired each year. The composition of the new council contained a clear message to the medical profession and other bodies such as the Hospitals Association which had taken an active role in the old RVTNA: nurses were now in control, and while they welcomed the advice of benevolent medicos, in the future they were going to make their own decisions.[14]

As mentioned, the other major departure from the RVTNA was the clear recognition that the new association that it would have an industrial role. It was to represent members in connection with wages boards or proceedings for conciliation and arbitration. It was to recommend minimum salary scales for nurses and nurses in training. It was to obtain free legal advice for members, work towards the setting up of a superannuation scheme, assist nurses in old age, ill health and adversity, and prescribe uniforms and badges to be worn by members. While many other objectives reflected the professional aims of the association, this was the first time that nursing leaders had recognised that professional aims had to be linked with industrial aims. But herein was a problem that beset all such associations seeking professional status. How did you marry the two without sullying the profession?[15]

The burst of enthusiasm that went with the formation of the new organisation quickly waned as it became apparent that nurses were not really in a position to undertake further study. Further, the growth of membership that was confidently predicted did not occur. At the end of 1935 only half of registered nurses in Victoria belonged to the RVCN. Of these little over one-quarter bothered to vote in the council elections.[16] An impassioned plea in *UNA* (probably from the new president, Miss Ethel Simons) revealed the frustration often felt by hard-working officials of an organisation whose members were apathetic.

> Will members earnestly consider the retrograde step which must occur if the College ceases to pay its way and therefore goes out of existence. The *general public* has not fought every inch of the way to raise nursing and nurses to the present high standard ... To combat injustice and error and abuse every body of workers must unite and the bigger the body the better the argument, the stronger the chance of satisfactory conditions. Everything is made out of small pieces to form the unity of strength ... Why should nurses be weary vessels of indifference?[17]

A plea that any union leadership might endorse.

The post-graduate classes for nurses consisted of a two year part-time course for those wishing to train as sister tutors or for administrative positions in hospitals. They began in March 1936 as the result of co-operation between the RVCN, the University of Melbourne, the Teachers College and the Melbourne Technical School. The fees varied from one guinea to nine guineas for a course of lectures in chemistry, physics, psychology, anatomy, methods of teaching, bacteriology, physiology and hygiene. The response was poor and very disheartening for leading members of the RVCN. In 1938 there were no applicants and other courses arranged by the college in dietetics, industrial nursing and public speaking eventually also had to be abandoned. Nurses found it difficult to find the finance for further education, particularly during a period of economic depression. Nor did they have the time and energy to devote to study after working full time in their jobs.[18]

A Wages Board for Nurses

IN March 1936 in a pamphlet distributed to nurses in hospitals, the Hospital Employees Federation (HEF), a union which included nurses (hospital asylum attendants) in its membership, issued a call to other nurses to join its ranks. This event foreshadowed an approach to the Government to create a wages board for nurses.[19] Under the Victorian system of industrial arbitration wages boards had been established for trades and industries not covered by awards of the Federal Arbitration Court. These were made up of equal numbers of employee and employer representatives with a government appointee acting as chairperson. These awards had the force of law. In April 1936 the HEF announced that it would apply for a wages board for nurses, and, by so doing, galvanised the RVCN into action. It was a crisis situation, for if the HEF was successful the RVCN could be excluded from future wage negotiations, thus opening the way for the HEF to represent and recruit a significant number of nurses. A wages board could be promulgated by regulation by the Minister of Labour, and even though a minority Country Party government ruled Victoria at the time, it did so with Labor Party support.

The RVCN called a hasty meeting of members to discuss the situation and determine which way the organisation should go in response to the HEF challenge. Again, as they had done in the past, they turned to the medical men in what was essentially an industrial issue. Fortunately the medicos who addressed the general meeting urged the RVCN to file for a wages board. Even so, some nurses remained wary of anything associated with the Victorian Trades Hall Council. The resolution which was finally passed by the 150 members present favoured regulation of nurses' conditions by a legally constituted body, though not necessarily a wages board.[20] Nevertheless, the council had little alternative and in June 1936 a deputation to the Assistant Minister of Labour urged the establishment of a wages board for 'trained certificated nurses and nurses in training, and the proportion of trainees to trained nurses employed on the staffs of public, intermediate and community hospitals'. The matters of particular concern at the time were hours, wages and the surplus of trained nurses.

When the deputation arrived in the Minister's office they found the representatives of the HEF already there, and, in spite of attempts to have their case heard separately, both unions were heard together. Miss Simons who was offering strong leadership on the question of nursing conditions, put it to the Minister:

> There were instances where nurses in public and private hospitals had to work 60 hours a week exclusive of time allowed for meals, and in the case of trainees much off duty time had to be given up to attend lectures. After 3 to 5 years of training a general trained nurse was offered £70 per annum ... the result ... frequently meant a permanent impairment of health ... Another important matter ... was the proportion of trainees to trained nurses, and the founding of more intermediate and community hospitals was likely to increase the present position of an oversupply of trained nurses.

Miss Simons was concerned that the increasing number of fee-paying wards in the rural areas would be used as an excuse to employ more trainees rather than trained nurses, thus exacerbating the oversupply problem.[21]

The Minister commended the 'excellent' case put forward by the nurses and they went back to begin work on drawing up a detailed submission for an award which would 'give substantial increases to trainees and registered nurses' (staff nurses, sisters, matrons) plus a 48-hour week with at least one day off per week or two in a fortnight. Special duties and uniform allowances, as well as increased annual leave, were also sought.[22]

After an amicable meeting between the RVCN and the Metropolitan and Country Hospitals Associations (the employers), agreement was reached to support a wages board for nurses. It was only a matter of time before this was established.[23] On 23 November 1936, the Governor-in-Council created a Hospital Nurses Board and on 10 February 1937 the *Government Gazette* announced the composition of the board with five representatives each from employers and employees. Much to the horror and consternation of nurses two of the employees were members of the HEF. One of these, Mr G. R. A. Beardsworth, Victorian secretary of the HEF, was appointed under that section of the Act which allowed one representative of employees to be an officer of the trade union concerned. The RVCN, in protest, immediately took another deputation to the Assistant Minister of Labour stating that they would rather have the wages board delayed than be associated with a representative of the Trades Hall. Miss Sage from the RVCN Council, declared:

> I wish to protest against an officer of a trade union as a representative of nurses on the wages board ... practically the general body of nurses is in accord with the objection raised, and would rather that a wages board were not established than to have it formed on a wrong basis. As a professional body of women we do not wish to bring nursing into an industrial sphere.

But the RVCN had already brought nurses well and truly into the industrial sphere by seeking a wages board and drawing up an application for an award. The Minister threw the contradiction in their position back at them when he replied to their request:

> Your organisation is not a union and the Hospital Employees Federation is, consequently it is the union concerned. Its constitution has been extended to cover nurses ... If it only had the smallest membership it would still be the union concerned and entitled to have its secretary sit on the Board.[24]

The nurses were hoisted on their own petard. Indeed, they were so incensed by their representation on the board that at an extraordinary general meeting later in the year they discussed taking political action against the Government. The president, Miss Grace Wilson, suggested that if they used their votes wisely they should be able to obtain help from Members of Parliament. Another speaker wanted every nurse to write to Members of Parliament. In the end a compromise was reached with the Government. Beardsworth remained as the HEF representative, but the other four employee nominees were from the RVCN.[25]

At the 1937 general meeting of the RVCN consideration was given to the position of matrons representing nurses on the board. Up until this time matrons had played a leading role in the affairs of the RVTNA and the RVCN. Their dominant role in the hospitals was carried through to the affairs of the college. However, their ambivalent role in acting as employees came into question at the general meeting. The vice president, Miss Gwen Jones, who chaired the meeting in the absence of Miss Grace Wilson who was away at the coronation of King George V, said she felt 'that matrons were more employers than employees', and that 'the time might come when the position might become very difficult for matrons'. On the other hand, one speaker suggested that the trainees should be represented on the board and 'there could be no more suitable representative of trainees than a matron.'[26] At a later meeting Miss Wilson refused nomination to the board on the grounds that matrons should not sit on it because of their position in the hospitals.[27] The situation was analogous to that of school principals who were responsible for carrying out the employer's directions (the Education Department) but who also had a dominant role in the Victorian Teachers Union at the time.

During the presidencies of Miss Simons and Miss Wilson (1936–1938) industrial matters had come to the fore in the RVCN. Much of the activity around the wages board had occurred while Miss Jane Bell was overseas in 1935–1937, and clearly she did not approve. She wrote from England to *UNA* early in 1938 criticising the RVCN log of claims because it made no mention of the 'educational side of nursing', which was of course the main reason for establishing the RVCN. She pointed out that the discontent amongst nurses was due to the 'persistent overcrowding of the larger city hospitals with consequent overwork and curtailment of leisure time for their nurses'.[28] For her the nurses' wages board was a mistake, and she returned to Australia determined that both professional and industrial matters be put under the control of the Nurses Registration Board, which was a 'professional' rather than an industrial organisation. At the 1938 RVCN annual elections Miss Bell defeated Miss Wilson for the presidency, and the matrons reasserted their strength and took five of the seven positions. The two others were a sister and an assistant director of infant welfare. On taking office Miss Bell reiterated her determination to turn the RVCN away from industrial matters, and even spoke again of bringing it under the aegis of the University of Melbourne. The reaction against the brief period of nurse militancy had set in.[29]

On the whole the hospitals emerged from the depression economies more quickly than most other public and private institutions. This was partly due to increased funds as a result of the Totalisator Act of 1930 which provided for a percentage of the takings of the Totalizator Board to be paid into the Charities Board for the running of the hospitals. This meant a return to late 1920s conditions was hastened, but it did not bring about any significant improvement in hospital conditions in general. Nurses' salaries were restored to pre-depression levels by the mid-1930s in many hospitals.

The first award of the Hospital Nurses Board operated from 1 December 1938. It covered all certificated nurses in public, private, intermediate or community hospitals, convalescent homes and trainees in hospitals which were recognised as registered training schools. It gave nurses a substantial pay rise, and laid the basis for a general improvement in their working conditions throughout the State. A comparison between the award and the submission by the RVCN to the board, shows that on the major items the board agreed with the RVCN and in some cases went beyond the RVCN's proposals.

The RVCN did not make any proposal on the weekly hours of work for trained nurses, possibly because these varied so much from hospital to hospital, and also because there was a strong view, especially amongst matrons, that nurses should be required to finish their duties, even if it meant working overtime. The

Table 1   The 1938 Hospital Nurses' Board award

Rank of nurse	Average salary p.a. 1926–27*	RVCN submission	1938 award
Trainee — first year	23	26	28
Trainee — second year	31	39	41
Trainee — third year	36	52	54
Sister — third year out	119	156	156
Matron	180	250**	250**

*   Trembath, Hellier, op.cit. p. 154
** 66–100 bed hospital

board set a 50-hour week which was considerably less than that worked by nurses in many hospitals. Instead of time off for overtime, as the RVCN had requested, the board set payment of time and a half for work in excess of 50 hours per week spread over a period of four weeks. The RVCN asked for three weeks annual leave for staff nurses and trainees and four weeks for sisters, and the board agreed.[30]

The Second World War

W HEN Britain declared war against Germany in September 1939, Australia followed as a matter of course, as it had done in 1914. The Prime Minister, R. G. Menzies, declared, 'Britain is at war, and as a result, Australia is at war also'. Britain was the motherland, and it was Australia's duty to go to her defence. Miss Bell echoed these sentiments when she wrote in *UNA*:

> Our foe is not a people of the same Nordic race as we ourselves are but a system whose god is force, whose ideal is brutality and arbitrary action towards weaker nations, whose power is gained by a ruthless crushing of the individual and his thought.
> Our Prime Minister (Mr Menzies) said in one of his very finest speeches 'There can be no doubt that where Britain stands, there stand the people of the entire British world'.
> The British Empire and France are fighting for the right of civilization to enjoy peace and fair dealing, to maintain Christian principles; fighting against dishonoured promises and crass brutality.[31]

Nurses were no less patriotic than other sections of the Australian middle class in the 1930s and 1940s, but hospital matrons seem to have been particularly responsive to the call of Empire. Many had been involved in the Great War, which was still a vivid memory for the older generation of nurses. It was a time when the old colonial ties were revivified, and when most Australians could still easily trace their British origins. Britain still continued to dominate Australia's economic, trade and foreign policies, and British cultural traditions prevailed in schools, churches, literature and the law. A sea voyage back to the 'old country' was an ongoing middle class ambition, realised by many, even if not until their retirement.

When the call went out for nurses to join the Australian Army Nursing Service (AANS), there was no shortage of volunteers. The Nurses Registration Board encouraged enlistment by deciding that all members of the AANS would be retained on the register without cost during their service.[32] The waiting list had grown to 4000 when the first nurses sailed out of Sydney Harbour in January 1940 bound for Egypt. Miss Grace Wilson, who was matron-in-chief of the AANS before the war, remained in that position for the first two years of the war. The story of the involvement of Australian nurses in the Second World War has already been told.[33] The main concern here is to fill in the background of those who remained in Australia.

In the period of the 'phoney war' (to mid-1940) in spite of suggestions from the RVCN, no arrangements were in hand for setting up a special nursing service for a civil emergency except by the Red Cross and local councils. Nothing was done to overcome the extreme shortage of nurses that accompanied the loss of nurses to the AANS. It was only with the bombing of Darwin in February 1942 that the Victorian State Government took action. It proclaimed the Emergency Nursing Services Order in March that year which obliged registered nurses and midwives to comply with any direction or regulation made by the Chief Health Officer, assisted by his Nursing Service Advisory Committee.[34]

So the war accentuated a problem which had already become evident in 1938–1939 — the growing shortage of trained nurses. While there had been an increase in the number of trained nurses in the 1930s, demand had been stepped up by the growth of fee-paying wards and intermediate hospitals. One measure was considered as a long term solution to this problem was to shorten the training period required in the smaller general base hospitals, where trainees had to go elsewhere to complete their training in order to gain wider experience than could be offered by their base hospital. At a conference in May 1939, which included the matrons of 20 metropolitan and country training schools, the Minister of Health, Sir John Harris, and representatives from the Health Commission, it was agreed that the period of training should be three years for hospitals with a daily average over 40 beds and reduced from four and a half years to a maximum of three and a half years for those under 40, with provision for affiliation of the latter with larger hospitals. Affiliation meant that the trainees spent part of their time in another hospital or hospitals designated by the board. The affiliation arrangements envisaged then were between the larger country based hospitals and the smaller hospitals, and did not involve the larger city hospitals, which had always vigorously resisted this arrangement. With the onset of war, however, their opposition disappeared and they became involved in affiliation when it was introduced in 1941.[35]

Some members of the RVCN saw all this as a lowering of standards, which war time emergencies tended to cultivate. When it was announced in June 1940 that the Nurses Registration Board had agreed to allow student midwives to sit for their qualifying examination after they had completed only ten of their 20 cases of labour, and assisted in another five, the RVCN became convinced that their worst fears of a war time dilution of the educational standards and training of nurses was under way. Members were angered that they had not been consulted, and immediately sought the rescission of the change.

The war also created a shortage of doctors, of course, and this was felt particularly in the rural areas. It was argued that midwives would be more likely to be called to difficult births unassisted. Miss Bell was adamant that experience of only ten labour cases was completely inadequate:

> Under the law midwives are required to deal only with uncomplicated cases, but, notwithstanding, many nurses expressed the view that even at the end of 20 cases they were only just beginning to feel a slight degree of confidence ... but with 10 cases only, they felt absolutely without confidence at all.[36]

This measure had been approved not long before a new board consisting mostly of elected members was due to take over, one of whom was Miss Jane Bell. As soon as she became a member she gave notice to rescind the new regulation, but the Minister stood firm, and even a request from the board met with refusal.[37] It was a Country Party government and the shortage of doctors and midwives was acute in the country.

Fears of a lowering in nursing standards were further accentuated by the fact that partly trained women recruited were being recruited into the Australian Army Women's Auxiliary Services. Many had hospital experience and on demobilisation could expect to obtain work in hospitals. As noted, there had always been partly trained women working as nurses; they were usually drawn from those who had some hospital training but had failed their examinations or had not completed their training due to ill health, unsuitability or marriage. Prior to the war many obtained work as semi-trained nurses in private hospitals or took on private nursing. The RVCN had never really faced up to this issue, although it was certainly one reason behind their endeavours to turn nursing into a profession.

The problem came to the fore when it was raised by Miss Gwen Burbidge, the matron of Fairfield Hospital and well known for her handbook on nursing, at a general meeting of nurses held in September 1943. What was going to happen to these partly trained women after the war?

> When these women are demobilised thousands who have had hospital experience will be available for caring for the sick, and the public will accept them. They can afford to offer their services at a lower rate than our trained nurses, they will still have the glamorous service behind them, and, in fairness to our nurses training today and in days to come, we who can see ahead must move and *move now* to define the position of this great army of women that will pour into the hospital world.

Miss Burbidge wanted a committee formed to find some suitable term to describe these women and to draw up conditions under which they could work. She believed there was a place for nursing assistants in the nursing service, 'Useful work can be done by nurses who are not State registered but in a well defined sphere, not in competition with the fully qualified'.[38]

Such sentiments were akin to sacrilege to the older members of the RVCN, especially Miss Bell, who at a later meeting described Miss Burbidge's proposals as 'the negation of all that trained nurses had stood for in the last forty years'. To implement such proposals would be nothing less than 'professional suicide'. For senior nurses and matrons who had spent their lives in training nurses, 'this proposal came as a shock'. As far as they were concerned, 'There was no such thing as a semi-trained nurse, a nurse was either qualified or she was not'. But Miss Burbidge was not deterred by such opposition, and gained much support from the meeting, including that of Miss Grace Wilson, who was very much aware of the potential problem due to her work in the AANS. As was customary at the time Miss Burbidge referred to the British precedent, for, in many spheres of life if an advocate of change could cite a British example, this would go a long way towards acceptance of change in Australia.[39]

In Britain a Nurses Act had been passed to control the flood of semi-trained nurse onto the market. Under the scheme full particulars of a nurse would be taken when she enrolled at a registered office or agency and that agency would be responsible to the patient and to the doctor to see that the nurse sent was suitable for the duties she was to perform. Miss Burbidge pointed out that this system had been approved by trained nurses in Britain and already 12 000 nursing assistants had been registered.[40] Ultimately Miss Bell succeeded in having the issue deferred, but it was a problem that was not going to go away.

The shortage of nurses had become so acute by 1943 that it became an important topic of comment and discussion in the press, on radio and in the weekly journals. The topic was linked with the sinking of the hospital ship, *H.S. Centaur*, off the Australian coast on 14 May 1943. Eleven members of the AANS died in the incident, along with 257 others. Among the 63 survivors was a sister, Ellen Savage. The ship had been appropriately notified as a hospital ship and was suitably marked so that the Japanese action was seen in Australia as the act of a 'barbarian' nation.[41] Miss Bell wrote in *UNA*:

> Only a people of treachery, savagery and abomination could deliberately subject a boat's company defenceless and bound on a work of mercy to the sick, to the horrors of sudden explosion, fire and shark infested waters in the early morning hours. The answer, in cold anger, to these yellow-skinned and poisonous barbarians, is clear ... By dying gloriously, our nursing sisters have at least escaped a fate far worse than if they had fallen prisoners to the uncontrolled and licentious Japanese monsters.[42]

Five of the sisters killed had trained or worked in Melbourne. 'Avenge the Nurses' became the cry in the press, but a bitter Miss

Bell commented in the *Age* that the 'Australian nurses during this war had the most harsh treatment of any within our Commonwealth of Nations':

> let the avenging include fair justice for all nurses henceforward. In time of war, pestilence, or other public calamity they are always the first summoned to help, but alas, they are always the last to be considered.[43]

By the end of 1943 when the tide of war had turned in favour of the allied forces, there followed a period of concern about the changes which would come about in Australia at the end of the war. In 1944, 1945 and 1946 there was much talk and much optimism about the post-war world. (Although great plans were made, however, many never came to fruition as the malaise of the late forties and early fifties set in, with its labour and material shortages, witch hunts and political instability). In this brief period of hope there was much discussion among nurses and in the media about the future of nursing, and especially about the ongoing acute shortage of trained staff. At the forefront of this discussion was Miss Burbidge who had become the spokeswoman of a new generation of nurses who were critical of the 'old guard', who they believed were unable to cope with the changes war had brought. The conflict between Miss Burbidge and Miss Bell over nursing assistants flared up again in June 1944. This time it was a public confrontation in the press caused by another refusal by the RVCN to take any action on the matter.[44]

A long editorial appeared in the *Age* based largely on material supplied by Miss Burbidge. After recognising that nursing conditions and wages had to be improved, it came out in support of the 'partly trained nurse':

> Many competent judges are persuaded that by controlling the activities of the nursing assistants — who are given the antiquated and unsuitable designation of 'female attendant' in Victoria — the status and security of registered nurses would be enhanced.

It called for the setting up of a sub-committee of Cabinet to prepare legislation.[45] An immediate rejoinder from Miss Bell was published next day. It reiterated her opposition and appealed to medical men for support:

> The medical profession has more to lose than almost any other section of the community by the setting up of an inferior class of nurse, and we can only hope, as in the past ... a sufficient number of medical men will throw their weight on the side of trained nurses.[46]

Whether medical men did come to the aid of Miss Bell is not clear, but at the next conference of the RVCN with the Minister of Health, which had been specifically called to discuss the improvement of conditions and salaries for nurses, no mention was made of the problem of nursing assistants. Similarly, on the Nurses Registration Board, despite attempts by the chairman, a lawyer, and some of the younger nurses, the influence of Miss Bell ensured that nothing was done about nursing assistants.[47]

Separation of Industrial and Professional Matters

THE representation of the RVCN on the wages board continued to cause concern in the early forties. In 1942 an amendment to the Act enabled the college to be represented by a salaried officer of the RVCN, but instead of replacing the salaried HEF officer with RVCN secretary, Miss M. Anderson as the RVCN had anticipated, the Government allowed the HEF officer to remain. A strong note of frustration at this development was expressed in *UNA* and this was to have its repercussions in 1943:

> Until nurses shake off the apathy with which so many of them seem to be afflicted and make a strong stand for their just claims, expressing this through their votes for members of Parliament, it seems almost hopeless to expect reform in the profession. Nurses are the last people to decry or belittle any form of labour if properly done, and the marshalling of its forces into powerful organizations, but they do resent the officials of these trying to split nursing unity.[48]

In May 1943 full control over nursing was transferred to the Manpower Directorate, established in January 1942 under the Commonwealth's defence powers. The directorate was set up to implement the full mobilisation of the country's people and resources. It directed people from 'non-essential' occupations to bolster the fighting services and war production.[49] The Deputy-Director of Manpower in Victoria set up a committee to advise him on matters relating to the registration and control of nursing personnel. This committee was chaired by a doctor and included two army matrons and the matron of the Women's Hospital. Miss Burbidge was given leave to help organise the new authority. She had been particularly active in the state Nursing Service Advisory Committee set up in April 1942. This committee had already established procedures for the registration of nursing personnel which were taken over by the new commonwealth committee.[50]

At first the RVCN welcomed the new arrangements as it had been very critical of the State committee's secrecy and had found it 'utterly futile' in dealing with the problems of nurses.[51] However, it did protest about the poor representation of civilian nurses on the new committee, and indeed it was not long before Miss Bell was declaring that the manpower regulations were 'the most retrograde step in nursing since the day of Florence Nightingale':

> The document entitled Control of (Nursing) Hospital Personnel, issued to civil hospitals by this Authority, showed such a want of psychological insight and understanding, not only of the nurse, but of everything for which nursing stood. It cut at the root of every principle of Hospital discipline and control of nurse training and showed no realization that the patients with whom nurses are dealing are human beings and not inanimate objects turned out by ordinary industry.[52]

It was a time of crisis, however, and Miss Bell's objections went unheeded.

The underlying contradiction in the membership of the RVCN and its council, whereby it acted as a union and yet allowed employers both as members and on its Council, was once again called into question in 1943. The catalyst this time was the infant welfare nurses who were seeking a determination under the Hospital Nurses Wages Board. The Government had agreed that these nurses should come under the wages board, but they could not gain separate representation. The HEF, again on the sidelines actively seeking to recruit these nurses, must have been able to mount quite a persuasive case. It had representation on the board and able to represent their interests as a union, unlike the RVCN which was not a union and included employers on its council.

As a result of these events members of the RVCN petitioned the RVCN in July 1943 to hold an extraordinary general meeting to discuss the formation of an employees' branch of the college. It was one of the largest meetings for some time. It was pointed out that the RVCN under its present constitution could not be recognised by the Federal Arbitration Court, nor was it recognised in the industrial world as a union. Until the college had a branch composed of employees only it would not achieve full representation on the wages board. An employees' section was seen as the solution to this problem because it would come under the general supervision of the RVCN Council, but act independently on matters of salaries and conditions.[53] The alternative was to make the RVCN an employees only association. There is no evidence that this was considered, however, for it would have meant not only terminating the membership of employers (some of whom were leading members of the RVCN), but also placing full emphasis on the industrial side of the RVCN's activities.

At the annual general meeting of the college in August 1943 Miss Bell moved a motion for the establishment of the Royal Victorian College of Nursing Employees Association 'to control salaries, wages, emoluments and working conditions' of members of the RVCN classed as employees and to make representations to the wages board. It was passed, but only after the deletion of a section suggesting that this would also be the body to seek Federal Arbitration Court recognition if the Australian Nursing Federation so decided.[54]

The Move into the Federal Arena

WHILE the shortage of nurses received much sympathetic comment in the media in the mid-1940s, the RVCN found it difficult to capitalise on this sentiment because another dilemma had presented itself — whether to persist with the State wages board or to go all out for registration under the Federal Arbitration Court. To make matters worse 'great consternation and indignation' was aroused when in January 1946 an award for hospital domestic workers and 'so-called assistant nurses' placed them on higher salaries than staff nurses. This award had been gained by the HEF.[5] The RVCN had again been caught unprepared, especially as it did not even have a request for a new award before the wages board at the time. This matter was resolved when the board brought down a new award which granted a 44-hour week and an all-round one pound pay increase for all trained staff.

Miss Bell saw federal arbitration as the lesser evil when compared with the wages board and as a means of gaining significant improvements in the salaries and conditions of nurses. But in a referendum in 1943 members had voted three to one against applying for an award in the Federal Court.[56]

Early in July 1945 the HEF succeeded in getting the federal Minister for Labour to refer the question of conditions and remuneration of nursing and domestic workers in hospitals to the Federal Arbitration Court, with a preliminary sitting set down for 1 August. At this sitting the judge ruled that claims on behalf of interested parties would be received up until 28 August.[57] This was of direct concern to both the RVCN and the Australian Nursing Federation (ANF). The latter body had formed in 1924 and in the 1940s was strongly under the influence of the RVCN. It had a very limited role since nursing organisations in Australia were essentially State organisations, working under State awards and State health departments. The RVCN and the ANF had four weeks to work out an appropriate course of action. They turned to the Trained Nurses Guild (TNG).

The TNG had already been recognised by the Federal Arbitration Court in 1922 and had been revived by the RVCN when the HEF had made moves towards challenging the Guild's recognition. Nevertheless, it had a very small membership and really only existed because of its federal registration. It was decided that a joint log of claims should be made by the guild and the ANF. It was also necessary to increase the guild's membership and RVCN members were urgently requested to join. The Tasmanian Nurses Union had recently affiliated with the guild, and there had also been a conference between its representatives and the New South Wales, Western Australia and Tasmanian Nurses Associations.[58] Despite all this, on 14 November 1945 Judge Kelly of the Arbitration Court ruled that:

The regulation and reference in question were not available for him to make an Award . . . It is not within the jurisdiction of the Court to decide whether or not nursing is an industry.[59]

Here the matter rested for the time being. The only recourse available to the nurses was to appeal, but they had neither the finances nor the unity on the question to carry this through. The whole episode once again showed up the members of the RVCN as babes in the industrial woods. The HEF continued to make the running, with the RVCN going from one crisis to the next in their endeavour to keep up.

Late in 1946 the TNG approached the ANF with the suggestion that the two bodies unite in order to retain the guild's registration in the Arbitration Court. At the ANF Conference in January 1947 it was decided that the affiliation should take place if all legal difficulties could be overcome. Before anything further was done, however, two developments threatened to upset the whole nursing industrial arena. The federal Minister for Repatriation decreed that all nurses, other than ex-service nurses, employed by the Commonwealth Government, could only have the benefit of awards made by the Public Service Arbitration if they were members of an organisation registered with the Federal Arbitration Court. The other development was an affidavit lodged against the TNG by the HEF in the Arbitration Court asking the guild to state reasons why it should not be deregistered on the grounds of industrial inactivity. It also claimed that the guild was competing for members because it had applied for benefits for its members under an award gained by the HEF for Repatriation nurses.[60] This posed another crisis for the TNG, the ANF and the RVCN. It was not difficult to foresee control of the industrial side of nursing passing to the HEF if the guild was deregistered. As Miss Jane Muntz, president of the guild, told an extraordinary general meeting of the RVCN in September 1947:

> This threat of de-registration by the Hospital Employees Federation is a very real one, so real that I think it is a matter of life and death to nurses in Australia if it succeeds, and I do not know how we can stop it from succeeding under our present set up.

Miss Muntz saw the solution in the nurses supporting the motion that was before the meeting. This motion, which was passed without dissent, supported changing the name of the guild to the Australian Nursing Federation and merging of the two organisations.[61]

On the day after this meeting, however, there was an interstate conference called by the TNG in Melbourne to which all the main nursing organisations in Australia sent representatives. A list of these organisations shows the disparate nature of nursing organisations in Australia in September 1947:

Trained Nurses Guild
Trained Nurses Guild (WA Branch)
Australian Nursing Federation
Australasian Trained Nurses Association (delegates from NSW, Qld, SA, WA, Tasmania)
Royal Victorian College of Nursing
NSW Nurses Association
WA Nurses Association
Tasmanian Nurses Union

The recommendations of this conference included a decision to unite as one organisation with branches in each State to be known as the United Australian Nurses Association, formerly the TNG, and to open membership to 'all persons engaged in the profession of nursing in Australia as registered trained nurses, trained nurses, student nurses and assistants in nursing employed in and in connection with the calling or profession of nursing'.[62] For a time it looked as though a strong, unified federal body representing nurses would emerge from these developments, but it foundered on the question of admitting nursing assistants to membership. Another extraordinary general meeting of the RVCN in October refused to accept this vital recommendation of the earlier conference.[63]

Following these events a successful effort was made to increase the guild's membership which resulted in the HEF withdrawing its application for deregistration. During 1948, the guild prepared a draft constitution which was put to an interstate conference of delegates from nursing organisations in November the same year. Here the views of the RVCN prevailed and nursing assistants were excluded from the proposed new federal body. As a result the three State nursing unions left the meeting leaving the ANF and the TNG to try to reach agreement. Even this proved difficult when the ANF delegates demanded that in all future negotiations acceptance by the ANF would be contingent, among other things, upon the International Council of Nurses (ICN) giving approval to the registration of an affiliated body under the *Commonwealth Conciliation and Arbitration Act.*[64] The ANF, which was virtually under the control of the RVCN, was not interested in compromising principles it had held for many years in order to achieve national unity of nurses.

Over 12 months from March 1948 to March 1949, negotiations between the ANF and the TNG continued, with the latter changing its name to the Australian United Nurses Association (AUNA). This resulted in a plan which satisfied the RVCN's principles and worries about ICN affiliation, and which could also bring nursing assistants into a federal organisation. The RVCN president, Miss Helene Grey, outlined the proposals at an extraordinary meeting of nurses in December 1949. The ANF was to remain as the professional organisation affiliated with the ICN, and AUNA was to become the body looking after the economic interests of nurses:

> it could not be seen [that there is] any reason why Assistant Nurses, Short Term Trained Nurses, such as Mental, Midwifery, T.B. and Mothercraft could not be admitted to membership of AUNA which would not affect our affiliation with the ICN.[65]

A nurse joining ANF would automatically become a member of AUNA, with the onus on the ANF to pay the agreed percentage of her subscription to AUNA.

A structure committee consisting of representatives of the ANF and AUNA met several times from May to August 1950 to work out how Miss Grey's plan should be implemented. But the early optimism of these meetings soon evaporated. Queensland found the proposal unacceptable, and the New South Wales branch of AUNA threatened to call together the many NSW nursing organisations to form a united front against the plan. Moreover, AUNA representatives were raising new problems at each meeting. The unity of nurses at the federal level appeared as remote as ever, and the structure committee referred the whole matter back to the parent bodies. Negotiations had come to an impasse over AUNA refusing to agree that nurses would have to first join the ANF to become members of AUNA. The AUNA representatives wanted joint membership and this then raised the old question of allowing nursing assistants to join which the ANF could not accept.[66]

Negotiations continued sporadically for another two years, until AUNA finally agreed in 1953 to change its name to the ANF, Employees Section. The arrangements were similar to those originally proposed by Miss Grey at the meeting of nurses in December 1949. In each State there was to be a branch of the ANF catering for nurses who were qualified for membership of the various organisations, as well as a branch of the ANF, Employees' Section, being part of an organisation registered with the Federal Arbitration Court, functioning as an integral part of the State branch of the ANF. The ANF and the ANF, Employees Section were to share offices with the RVCN. A challenge from the HEF to the change of name by AUNA was rejected by the Industrial Registrar of the Court.[67]

As a consequence of these new arrangements it was agreed that 'short-term trained nurses' should not be admitted 'at present' to membership of the ANFES, Victorian Branch, but should be offered assistance to organise themselves into groups for the purposes of affiliation along the same lines as the Victorian Mothercraft Association.[68]

Apart from the Employees Association, during the war years various other groups had been set up within the structure of the RVCN and under the general supervision of the council. These catered for specific interests which the council was unable to attend to, were largely under the influence of the matrons and preoccupied with more general concerns. A Sister Tutors' Section was formed late in 1939 as was a Private Nurses' Section. The first meeting of the Matrons Section was held in November 1941. An Industrial and Insurance Nurses Association was formed in 1942, with an Infant Welfare Section following in December that year. Early in 1944 a Student Nurses' Association was established.

After the war came a Visiting Nurses' Section in 1949, a Ward and Departmental Sisters' Section in 1950, an Obstetric Sisters' Section in 1951 (changed to Midwives Section in 1955), a Theatre Sisters' Section in 1957 and a Psychiatric Tutors' Section in 1959. Although these sections met regularly and elected office bearers who conveyed their concerns to the RVCN council when necessary, they were seen by the council to have a specifically educational function. They did not send resolutions to the council for discussion as was the practice of many other associations and unions. They entertained visiting speakers and guests, and planned social activities.

In 1954 four country branches of the RVCN were formed — Bendigo, Geelong and District, Ballarat and District and West and South Gippsland. These branches were founded with the help of matrons at the base and district hospitals and were aimed specifically at involving country members in the RVCN. Although allowed to send resolutions to the council, their emphasis, like the sections, was to be on the promotion of 'the professional, educational, technical and recreational interests of the nurse'.[69]

Miss Jane Bell

ON 1 January 1947 Miss Jane Bell resigned from her position as president of RVCN. She had been president from 1932 to 1934 and from 1938 to 1946. During those 12 years she was the dominant figure in the organisation. She had retired in 1934 after 24 years as Lady Superintendent of the Melbourne Hospital. Her work there has been well documented.[70] When she became 'full time' president in her 'retirement', she came to the position with some very clear ideas about the future direction of the RVCN. She was devoted to the cause of building nursing to the level of a profession as highly regarded as the medical profession. She saw this happening by raising the qualifications of trained nurses through post-graduate diplomas and degrees conducted by the University of Melbourne. She hoped this could be achieved through the RVCN, which she had helped to fashion to that purpose as a college.

Closely associated with this was an unwavering determination to resist any dilution of training standards and to adhere to her belief that *all* types of nursing should be preceded by three years general hospital training. Hence her vehement resistance to recognising or even mentioning the 'assistant nurse', whom she regarded as one of the most serious threats to nurses gaining professional status. It also sparked her opposition to any question of reducing midwifery training.

Anything which threatened the road to professional status was to be resisted at all costs. Number one threat was any association with the trade union movement. She was certainly not opposed to improving the salaries and conditions of nurses, but these could not be separated from professional issues, such as training, ethics, and further education. For Jane Bell, unions were concerned only with economic matters, and seldom with a broad perspective or the common good. This explains her opposition to the RVCN becoming involved with the wages board and the Arbitration Court. Once caught up in these matters, she believed the RVCN would become just like any trade union and lose its professional perspective.

But during her time as president much of what she stood for was undermined, due largely to circumstances outside her control. The composition of the nursing membership of the RVCN had changed since the days of the RVTNA in the late twenties. Private nurses were no longer a significant and influential group; hospital nurses now dominated. The group that came closest to Miss Bell's ideal of independent professionals was in fact disappearing. The RVCN also faced constant pressure from the HEF, and in order to maintain the organisation as the leading Victorian nurses' organisation, it was forced to give prominence to industrial matters. The Employees Association was a compromise that worked for a while, but was never really a satisfactory solution. In practice industrial questions could not be ignored and left to the various sections of the RVCN. They frequently surfaced at council meetings where the crucial decisions had to be taken.

Miss Bell saw nurses and their organisations in the years immediately following the war as in a state of 'disunity and division', and desperately wanted them to show the unity which characterised the medical profession:

> the solid base on which the strength of the sisterhood of nursing must rest is the fact that they have all been trained as nurses and after much and prolonged opposition from interested sources have obtained statutory status under State Registration with all the imposition and discipline this had entailed. The solidarity of the medical and other professions in the industrial spheres are before their eyes as examples of what they can accomplish if they only achieve unity in their ranks.[71]

Jane Bell became increasingly disillusioned as her years as president came to a close.

> I get so tired of the continual bickering going on ... I would willingly give it all up [but I] do not want to see all our efforts over the last fifty years to advance the profession brushed aside by ignorant people. Without any nursing ideals or standards, ethics are non-existent now.[72]

In November 1947, no longer president, she somewhat hesitantly re-entered the arena to oppose the move to unite the RVCN and other State organisations with the guild. Here she made her position quite clear, but her words were tinged with despair:

> We have not only the industrial side of nursing to consider ... To my mind, the educational, cultural and economic side of nursing are one and indivisible. If you are going to have good training schools with every modern facility for training nurses, that means you are going to have very highly qualified women in the nursing schools getting very good salaries. You are going to set up much more expensive equipment than we have today, because, except in one or two hospitals, facilities do not exist for nursing education as I understand it. I maintain the Arbitration Court is not a suitable body to have control of nursing. We want something quite different altogether if we are to get anywhere ...
>
> These are my suggestions to you, Ladies. There is no need for haste. If the Trained Nurses' Guild is de-registered, I do not think that would be a great tragedy. I am told that many nurses would not care either way.[73]

Endnotes

1 Trembath, Hellier, op. cit., p. 156.
2 ibid., pp. 158–9.
3 VPP, vol. 2, 1926, report by Dr Malcolm T. MacEachern on the Hospital System of the State of Victoria, p. 6.
4 VPP, 1929, report of the Charities Board of Victoria, June 1929, p. 4.
5 VPP, 1935, report of the Charities Board of Victoria, June 1935, p. 9; VPP, 1939, report of the Charities Board of Victoria, June 1939, pp. 8–9; VPP, vol. 2, 1949, report of the Hospitals and Charities Commission, June 1949, pp. 11–12.
6 Letter from M. Anderson, RVTNA secretary to Mrs D. A. Skene, Organising Secretary, Women's Centenary Council, 17 June 1933. Box 35, UM archives.

[7] Letter from provisional organising secretary to chancellor, vice-chancellor and members of the council of the University of Melbourne, 19 June 1933. Box 35, UM archives.

[8] J. A. Williams, R. D. Goodman, *Jane Bell, O.B.E. (1873–1959): Lady Superintendent, the Royal Melbourne Hospital (1910–1934)*, Royal Melbourne Hospital Graduate Nurses' Association, Melbourne, 1988, p. 114.

[9] ibid., p. 116.

[10] Letter from M. Anderson, RVTNA secretary to the secretary of the Temporary Conjoint Committee for the proposed College of Nursing, August 1933. Box 35, UM archives.

[11] Minutes of the council of the Royal Victorian Branch of the Australian Nursing Federation, 24 August 1933.

[12] *UNA*, March 1934, p. 87.

[13] *UNA*, June 1934, p. 172.

[14] See memorandum of association of Victorian College of Nursing, *UNA*, June 1934, pp. 174–5; Articles of Association of Royal Victorian College of Nursing, 25 May 1934, Box 35, UM archives.

[15] *UNA*, op cit.

[16] *UNA*, November 1935, p. 323.

[17] ibid., p. 324.

[18] *UNA*, October 1938, p. 300.

[19] *To Victorian Nurses*, ps. issued by the Hospital, Dispensary and Asylum Employees' and Allied Government Officers' Federation, Professional and Nursing Division, 6 March 1936. (G. Roy A. Beardsworth, Victorian Branch secretary). Box 88, UM archives.

[20] *UNA*, May 1936, pp. 131–8. Full report of the meeting of RVCN members.

[21] *UNA*, July 1936, pp. 204–5. Report of the deputation.

[22] RVCN minutes, July 1936. Report of sub-committee appointed to deal with improved conditions and salaries for nurses. See also ibid., 22 March 1937, May 1937.

[23] ibid., report of conference re proposed wages board for nurses.

[24] RVCN minutes, report of deputation to the Minister of Labour, 23 March 1937.

[25] *UNA*, November 1937, pp. 325–30. Full report of an extraordinary general meeting of RVCN members.

[26] *UNA*, October 1937, p. 305.

[27] *UNA*, November 1937, p. 330.

[28] *UNA*, February 1938, p. 36.

[29] *UNA*, October 1938, pp. 301–5.

[30] ibid., p. 292.

[31] *UNA*, October 1939, p. 292.

[32] Minchin, op cit., p. 40.

[33] See Rupert Goodman, *Our War Nurses, the History of the Royal Australian Nursing Corps 1902–1988*, Boolarong Publications, Brisbane, 1988.

[34] Minchin, op. cit., p. 41.

[35] ibid., p. 42.

[36] *UNA*, October 1941, p. 222.

[37] Minchin, op. cit., p. 48.

[38] Transcript of an address given by Miss Gwen Burbidge at an open meeting of nurses, 7 September 1943. Burbidge papers.

39 *UNA*, December 1943, p. 241–50. Report of a meeting of RVCN members, 16 November 1943.

40 ibid., p. 245.

41 Goodman, op. cit., p. 195.

42 *UNA*, June 1943, p. 98.

43 *Age*, 2 June 1943; *UNA*, July 1943, pp. 124–7.

44 *Age*, 16 June 1944.

45 *Age*, 21 June 1944.

46 *Age*, 22 June 1944.

47 Minchin, op. cit., p. 49.

48 *UNA*, December 1942, p. 263. Probably written by Jane Bell.

49 See Ann Curthoys, A. W. Martin, Tim Rouse (eds), *Australians from 1939*, Fairfax, Syme, Weldon, Sydney, 1987, p. 23.

50 'The Position of Civil Nursing in Victoria', G. N. Burbidge, July 1942. Burbidge papers.

51 *UNA*, April 1943, p. 59.

52 *UNA*, August 1943, p. 151.

53 ibid., pp. 154–7. Report of an extraordinary general meeting to discuss the formation of an Employees Branch of the RVCN.

54 *UNA*, October 1943, p. 198.

55 RVCN minutes, 10 January 1946.

56 *UNA*, September 1945, p. 234.

57 ibid., pp. 234–5.

58 RVCN minutes, 2 August, 23 August, 25 August 1945.

59 ibid., 15 November 1945.

60 Mary G. Armstrong, 'A Brief History of the First 50 Years of the Royal Victorian College of Nursing 1901–1951', *UNA*, Jubilee Issue, 1951, p. 213.

61 *UNA*, October 1947, pp. 299–307. Report of the extraordinary general meeting, 29 September 1947.

62 Proceedings of the Conference of Interstate Nursing Organisations, Melbourne, 29 September 1947. Box 40, UM archives.

63 *UNA*, November 1947, pp. 333–44, Report of the extraordinary general meeting, 27 October 1947.

64 *UNA*, March 1950, pp. 83–9, Report of the extraordinary general meeting, 7 December 1949.

65 ibid., p. 85.

66 Proceedings of the structure committee of ANF and AUNA, May–August 1950. Box 40, UM archives. See also 'General Explanation About Negotiations between ANF and AUNA' October (?) 1950. Box 46, UM archives.

67 Business for extraordinary general meeting, 14 October 1953. Box 46, UM archives.

68 Minutes of the joint committee, RVCN and ANFES, Victorian Branch (third meeting), 30 April 1954. Box 40, UM archives.

69 Rules for Sections and Branches, Box 24, UM archives.

70 See Williams, Goodman, op. cit.

71 Letter to Miss E. P. Evans, General Secretary, ANF from Miss Jane Bell, 31 October 1946. Box 32, UM archives.

72 Williams, Goodman, op. cit., p. 123.

73 *UNA*, November 1947, p. 336.

2

The Training and Work of Nurses in Victoria, 1930s–1940s

B Y the 1930s the pattern of nurses' training and work in Victorian hospitals had been well established. It was firmly based on principles of obedience, seclusion, celibacy and service which were enforced within a rigid hierarchical structure, with the matron at the top and the most recent batch of trainees at the bottom. The system owed much to its military, religious and domestic service origins.

This chapter is concerned with the training of nurses within this system in the 1930s and 1940s in Victorian hospitals. For the most part the situation will be described through the eyes of the trainees, and in doing this a picture will emerge of the general pattern of work and life in the hospitals for all nurses. The conditions under which nurses worked in the training hospitals during this time were exacting — long hours, poor pay, rigid discipline and exhausting work — yet they were much better off than their predecessors in the 1880s and 1890s. Some description will be given here of those conditions, not only to give some historical perspective on the later years, but also because they were within the living memory of the older and/or retired nurses of the 1930s. Some were leaders of their profession. They knew progress had been made along lines with which they fully approved, and this may help to explain some of their approaches to the problems of the later period.

In the 1880s and 1890s in Victoria nursing was still only emerging from its close association with domestic service. With the possible exception of the Alfred Hospital, nurses little more than domestic servants during this period. They performed the work of domestic servants for much of the time, had little or no training as nurses and lived under conditions which many domestic servants would not tolerate. While the hospitals were already trying to attract young middle class women, they could not provide them with the conditions they expected. One of these ladies at the Melbourne Hospital in 1886 complained that too many of her fellow nurses wore earrings, used bad grammar, and dropped their aitches. The meals were poor, the accommodation dreadful, she was paid almost nothing, and 'she worked mostly as a charwoman for over seventy hours a week'.[1] At the Alfred they had two classes of trainee nurses, A and B. A class nurses were charged an entrance fee of 12 guineas and a guinea per month for board and were absolved from certain cleaning duties. They could also go home at weekends. B class nurses did little more than domestic work. Much of their time was taken up with 'scrubbing', that is, waxing the ward floors and then polishing them with large brooms, which involved shifting the lockers and beds.[2]

One witness before the 1890 Royal Commission on Charitable Institutions described her work in the tents set up to cope with typhoid cases who were kept in isolation from the rest of the Alfred hospital. Her day commenced at 6.00 a.m. carrying the heavy matting out of the tents and sweeping it. Before 8.00 a.m. she also had to have sponged and prepared between eight and 16 patients for breakfast. After breakfast she had to carry food from the hospital kitchens to the tents and prepare the midday meals on site, after which she started the sponging process all over again. The same procedures were repeated for the evening meal. Her final duty was sorting the laundry before going off duty at 8.30 p.m. or 6.30 p.m. on alternate days.[3]

In 1890, following complaints to the Board of the Homoeopathic Hospital (later Prince Henrys) from 19 nurses about their work and hours, a sub-committee of the Board concluded that the work was not at all difficult and that 65 hours a week for day nurses and 74 for night nurses was reasonable. It was 'regrettable', the committee thought:

> that some nurses should fail to recognize the high nature of their profession and to realize that no work in connection with it can be considered as menial, or any slight sacrifice of time in carrying out their onerous and responsible duties as a breach of their privileges.[4]

The reality of course was that it was cheaper to employ nurses to do domestic work than to employ domestic servants, and it was also easier to obtain them. In 1890 domestic servants could expect between £35 to £45 per annum with keep, while trainee nurses received no pay in their first year, £15–20 in their second and £30 in their third. A qualified nurse in a large public hospital could expect to receive £35 per annum.[5] Like teaching, where large numbers of women were employed as pupil teachers on minimal wages, sometimes for most of their teaching careers, trainee nurses were used as a form of cheap labour which hospital boards seized upon as an answer to their problems in running hospitals as charitable institutions. There was no shortage of applicants in the late 1880s and 1890s because nursing was becoming an increasingly popular vocation for women. It is difficult to tell whether this was the result of newspaper publicity on the desirability of 'respectable' women becoming nurses, or simply that there were many more young women seeking jobs due to the onset of economic depression at this time. There were also very few employment avenues open to females in spite of the growing number of occupations considered 'acceptable' for women.[6]

Domestic work apart, the actual nursing done by nurses in the 1880s and 1890s consisted of sponging, bathing and positioning patients and giving them the correct medicines when required. There were also poultices to be made up and applied and temperatures to be taken. As few nurses were trained the this nursing tended to vary enormously from ward to ward and from hospital to hospital. In 1890 even a matron with training was rare. At the 1890 Royal Commission it was revealed that most of matrons of the larger Melbourne hospitals had received no training.

Nurses could be rude and insulting, disorderly and apparently often under the influence of alcohol, which was widely used for medicinal purposes. This is hardly surprising given that nursing was not only underpaid and dirty, but also a very dangerous job in those days. Back injuries were common, as were other physical disabilities. Illness and early death were also not unusual among nurses, and many were forced to resign because of ill health and tuberculosis. Very few nurses were willing to comment openly on conditions before the 1890 Royal Commission, but one, Alice Martelli, former head nurse at the Children's Hospital in the 1880s, gave her opinion on submitting her resignation:

> I must recall to you that during my period of office (three years) typhoid fever attacked seven nurses, two of whom died while in your service. Within the last few days another of our number has been seized with the same terrible fever and now lies dangerously ill. I would ask you to realize what a day's work and a night's watching in the wards mean: to come and witness our labours there and to remember that for such sources of twelve and fourteen hours a day most of us receive less wages than you offer a house or kitchen maid.[7]

In 1895 it was estimated by medical authorities that when she became a nurse a woman shortened her life by ten to 15 years.[8]

Nurses were required to live in, although living conditions were generally appalling. The Alfred offered what was regarded as good accommodation for nurses — wooden houses lent to the hospital by the Public Health Department for the typhoid season. This was dormitory style accommodation, with up to 12 per room. When the new hospital had been designed and constructed in the 1880s, no special provision for nurses had been made.[9] At the Melbourne hospital the nurses called their home 'Ratland', and at the Homoeopathic they had to put up with bed bugs which dwelt in the walls and floors. These were very difficult to get rid of, and one of the rooms was so bug-infested that it was referred to as 'the buggery'.[10]

Food was poor, and it was leftovers for nurses in most hospitals. They often ate anything they could find on the run. The staple was bread and butter and mutton stew. At the Melbourne one ward attendant sent a sample of his food to the Public Health Department for analysis. It was found to be diseased, and he was dismissed for his trouble. At the Homoeopathic meat served to nurses was found to contain tubercular ulcers and hydatids.[11]

There was no recognised and standard form of training in the 1880s in Victoria, although the Nightingale system with its emphasis on on-the-job training was favoured. In 1890 Miss Isabella Rathie, Lady Superintendent at the Melbourne Hospital who had trained at Edinburgh Infirmary during the time of Miss

Pringle, began training nurses. Soon most of the Melbourne and provincial hospitals had developed two year training courses and awarded their own certificates of competency. Few of the country hospitals ran training schemes, and standards varied greatly. At the leading hospitals nurses attended regular lectures. In the smaller hospitals they learnt what they could from bedside talks with the doctors.[12]

As outlined in the introduction to this book, over the next 30 to 40 years the training and work of nurses in Victorian hospitals was to become much more uniform and systematised. A job closely associated with domestic service in the 1880s had become a much sought after vocation by the 1920s and 1930s. While it had still not thrown off all the shackles of domestic service, for those who could remember conditions in the 1880s the changes had been monumental.

The prospective trainee who with much trepidation faced the matron of a Victorian training hospital for an interview in the 1930s, most likely came from a middle class family background. Her parents would not necessarily be 'well off', but would at least come from that 'respectable' core of society, the solid farmers, the provincial shop keepers, the urban middle class who could afford the not inconsiderable outlay for the uniform which all trainee nurses were expected to purchase. If, by any chance, a daughter from the urban or rural working class slipped through the screening process, she would most likely be weeded out in the first year of training when many were eliminated.[13]

It is likely that there was a greater proportion of trainee nurses in Victorian hospitals from the rural areas compared with the urban areas, because the avenues for 'respectable' employment for young girls in the country were virtually non-existent outside teaching and nursing. In the cities girls had a wider, although still very limited choice, with the growth of clerical positions in offices. Apart from being an occupation with considerable status and prestige in the 1930s, nursing also had the attraction of providing an avenue of relatively secure employment once a girl had completed her three years training. This was a period when security in employment was sought over high salaries. A person with a secure job was envied in a society where thousands roamed the countryside looking for work.

The two most prestigious public hospitals in Victoria were the Alfred and the Melbourne. They were also much more difficult to enter for training. They expected trainees to have at least a merit certificate, and in the 1930s intermediate (level 10) or leaving (level 11) were essential. Since only a small proportion of the school population reached these levels and successfully completed the exams, trainees were being drawn from a smaller elite than ever before. Good references from clergy and head teachers were also required, and much depended on the matron's assessment of the letter sent applying for an interview, as well as the appearance and decorum of the girls who actually reached this stage. The waiting period for an interview was anything up to two years for the Melbourne or the Alfred.

Some other metropolitan hospitals were almost as prestigious as the Alfred and the Melbourne, and in the 1930s all were able to be selective. But hospitals also attracted students for reasons other than prestige. It was said:

> Alfred — for the Presbyterians; Melbourne for the Anglicans; Prince Henry's for the Methodists; St. Vincent's for the Catholics and the Childrens' for parents who thought nursing adults was 'not nice'.

In the provincial cities such as Ballarat, Geelong, Bendigo and Warrnambool the training hospitals had standards and prestige commensurate with the main Melbourne hospitals.

One trainee of the period describes her interview at the Alfred thus:

> I was shown into a huge office where Matron was sitting, wearing an immaculately white uniform and veil. I can still remember her beautiful hands and nails as she picked up her desk calendar and said 'Come back and see me' on a certain date six months thence, writing in my name on the page — my first step! On the appointed date I went back, by myself this time, and she had all my references in front of her. 'I see you are interested in Guiding', she said, and read through my various letters, from Vicar, Guide Commissioner, school reports from Headmistress etc. 'Well now, I want you to bring me a Certificate of Invalid Cookery, and you'll need to have a medical examination. You could have that straight away as they are doing the medicals this afternoon'.[14]

Many girls came from Victorian public schools where nursing was regarded as a highly desirable occupation for young women (prior to marriage), and where special efforts were made to help them through their applications and interviews. The Hermitage, in Geelong, for example, had an honour board showing those students who had been successful as nurses.[15]

The uniform had become the most important piece of paraphernalia associated with the nursing ritual. It defined status and responsibilities. Its upkeep and appearance were subject to constant perusal and close inspection. The state of the uniform was not only important for the hospital's public image, but was seen by those in authority to measure the worth of the wearer. Indeed, a matron inspected the uniform of her nurses for much the same reasons as an army officers inspected his troops. It promoted discipline, defined rank and stressed order and precision.[16] Trainees were introduced to it even before taking up their positions, and instructions were explicit:

> 12 pairs of black stockings, 12 aprons to be made at Sister Susie's, 3 uniforms of Alfred Hospital special material, 2 pairs of shoes — black laced nurses' shoes to be obtained from Wallace's in King Street — 2 laundry bags, half a dozen collars and half a dozen pairs of white cuffs, a blue Alfred Hospital nurse's cape — all to be marked and laundered — studs, etc., and one cup and saucer.[17]

The first thing trainees learnt was the exactitude, the care and the endurance which was to be associated with the wearing of the uniform. The uniform, above all else (perhaps, even, the care of the patients) was to be worn exactly according to hospital requirements on pain of reprimand or severe disciplinary action:

> The temperature was 104 degrees F. but by 8 am we had managed to don the necessary apparel. We were to be instructed first in the intricate art of cap making converting the flat starched white shape into the evenly frilled model which discreetly covered our varying hair styles, before we could proceed to breakfast to make our debut — the new girls in the preliminary training school. I felt the heat, so by the time I donned the uniform, which came in seven parts all cruelly starched stiff, I was purple in the face. There were studs, pins and an extremely stiff collar and belt, a stiff much

pleated blue and white long sleeved heavy cotton dress, and enormous white heavy cotton apron, reaching exactly nine inches from the floor, heavy black woollen stockings and ghastly black rubber heeled and soled lace-up shoes weighing about five pounds each. One poor girl had to go to the sewing room to have her skirt lengthened as it was eleven inches from the floor, showing too much leg — someone had made an unforgivable mistake in measuring her, or she had grown meanwhile.[18]

The caps were the most significant part of the uniform. They designated the status of individuals in the nursing hierarchy, so particular care had to be taken with them:

> With our uniforms it was important how the frills on our caps were made. The caps came from the laundry as a flat piece of starched linen, a square with one half curved as if two corners were cut off. There was a draw string which drew the curve in, and there was a piece of material beyond the draw string which formed a frill. We made each curve of the frill the size of our fingers, and all curves had to be equal. There was great interest in our caps. Tutors sisters, Matron, and even the honoraries could stop you and tell you that your frill was not up to standard, and you would have to report each morning for a week or so and have your cap checked.[19]

Of course there was no jewellery, pocket watches only, very little if any make-up and hair had to be well above the collar.

As noted earlier, trainees 'lived in' accommodation close to the hospital. In the case of the larger hospitals, this was the nurses' home. Here a trainee was introduced to the discipline which would dominate her life for the next three years, if she survived. At the same time, however, she met the others in her intake (maybe 16 to 20 trainees), many of whom would become her lifelong friends.

The nurses' home was an integral part of the disciplinary structure of the hospital. The rules and regulations of the home were designed both to ensure the celibacy of its occupants as well as to aid the efficient functioning of the hospital. The hospital authorities, particularly the matrons, were very much aware that they were charged with the responsibility of guarding the honour and chastity of their trainees, many of whom were girls who had come to the 'big, bad city' from the country, and whose parents expected close supervision of their daughters. It has been argued that the 'high moral tone' was insisted upon by Florence Nightingale in order to counter the mid-nineteenth century image of the 'drunken whores' who were responsible for what 'nursing' was done in the poor houses of the time.

Trainees knew that if any of their number strayed from the straight and narrow path of 1930s middle class morality and entertained a male within the confines of the home, or visited the quarters of the resident medical officers and medical students, dismissal would be instant. Marriage incurred the same penalty. Even female visitors from 'outside' were not allowed in nurses rooms in most hospitals:

> One night, after a very hard day's work I was suddenly and rudely awakened at 3 am. Terrified when a torch was shone in my face I lay blinking with fright. The Night sister in a truly terrible rage, threw back my bedclothes and demanded to know how I had got undressed and into bed so quickly when she had just followed me in from the street? I flatly denied it, but she made me go and waken two of my friends I had been with at 10 pm for a cup of tea, then we had all gone to bed. She was finally convinced but of course there were no apologies. There never were. We did not tell on the culprit, whose room was not far from mine and whose boyfriend was due to go overseas any minute with the army.[20]

The discipline of the home was also directly related to the working hours and requirements of the hospital and the hospital hierarchy. At 5.30 a.m. in most homes the night sister or her assistant would awaken each nurse who was on morning duty, which commenced half an hour later:

> A memory every nurse must have is the doors banging at 5.30 in the morning. Much earlier if you were in the wing where the assistant night sister started her round. The door flew open — she said '5.30 Nurse' and waited until she saw a movement in response. The door then went bang. A few minutes later it happened next door. I can remember lying in bed and listening to the bangs coming closer and closer, then finally my door would fly open. Then I could hear the bangs receding down the corridor.[21]

All the door banging happened again at 10 p.m. when there was a thorough check to see that everyone who should be was in bed. Late passes were not granted readily. Usually these allowed a trainee to remain out to midnight. Most trainees were so tired after their work that they had little energy left for a social life. Besides, it was in the interests of the efficient running of the hospital and as well as the patients that every nurse get a good night's sleep.

By the 1930s the accommodation provided for nurses by the major hospitals in Melbourne and the large provincial towns had improved immensely. Even if the regime was strict, hospitals such as the Melbourne and the Alfred provided each nurse with her own room, adequately furnished, and to which she could add her own small luxuries such as a radio and bed lamp. But these conditions did not apply in many of the smaller hospitals, particularly in the country, where nurses still shared rooms and there was little in the way of amenities.

In some of the large hospitals there was even a nurses' lounge, usually tastefully decorated at the matron's behest, where nurses could relax, talk and perhaps even play the piano. The Alfred provided a smoke room — the only place where smoking was allowed in the nurses' home:

> No room could have been more bare. As far as I can remember it was furnished only with lino and chairs, and the walls were discoloured, but many a story was told there! All the happenings of the hospital went the rounds from the Smoke Room. Looking back, probably most of the hospital extroverts congregated there — and extroverts usually have a good sense of humour. To poke one's nose in would be to hear comments such as 'silly bugger', 'poor kid', 'the old so-and-so', or shrieks of laughter, and probably it was good psychologically for some, to get things off their chests — recount the dramas, have everyone join in with comments, have a good old swear — and then take off for a bit more swotting or do some laundry and sit and watch it dry on bits of string stretched across the verandahs.[22]

By now nurses' uniforms were laundered by the hospital and fresh bed linen was provided each week. House maids serviced the rooms and in some homes there were small pantries where food, tea and hot water were readily available. The connection between good food and a healthy nurse was well established, and it was in the hospital's interests to ensure that this was so. Patients in the hospital itself would have been a constant reminder to trainees that in many respects they lived a sheltered and privileged existence, compared with other members of the community. Their work was hard, however, and their conditions were well deserved.

Prior to the introduction of Preliminary Training Schools (PTS) a trainee went straight into the wards:

> I started in the Women's Surgical Ward, I was scared to death ... you didn't get any instructions. You had to ask, if you had a nice Senior nurse you were all right ... if you got snags they'd say — find out for yourself. Generally speaking they were pretty good.[23]

The first PTS in Australia was begun in 1927 at the Melbourne Hospital by the Lady Superintendent, Miss Jane Bell. The aim was to give trainees a short period of preparation before they entered the wards. The Alfred followed with its PTS in 1933. In the thirties and forties these courses usually lasted about six weeks, during which the trainees learnt basic tasks such as how to present a bed pan, the various methods of sponging patients, bandaging, the making up and application of foments and poultices, giving enemas, applying leeches and the prevention of bed sores. They were also instructed on taking temperatures, reading pulses, the use of hot water bottles and bags, bladder washouts, eye and mouth toilets, and that most important of operations, correct bed making:

> For eight long weeks a sweet patient tutor sister instructed us daily in everything from decorum to table manners to bed making. From a truly memorable Text Book we read daily, discussing the contents of each chapter, after which we digested such pearls of wisdom as 'Refuse tips' (to be interpreted not as in rubbish, but reward of cash or kind), 'Doctors' — no nurse is to have intercourse (to be interpreted as in friendly conversation we learned with interest) with any resident doctors.
>
> Anatomy we learned by close inspection of poor skeleton 'Ella' in the corner. I used to wonder who she really was, as she certainly was not a plastic girl ...
>
> Unfortunately the weekly 'test day', conducted under the strictest examination conditions, usually fell on a Friday, coinciding with a day when we were imbibing as much 'free fluid' as we could chart and eliminate. This embarrassing exercise was designed to help us understand how patients felt.
>
> We took each others' respirations, temperatures, pulses

etc., charting everything we could lay our hands on, then bandaged each other. At the end of eight weeks those who survived the 'acid test' were deemed fit to be gently introduced to THE WARDS. Yea, prepared by two hours every morning for the shock ahead for our innocent systems.[24]

They would most likely have been introduced to the first handbook for nurses, published in 1935 and written by Miss Gwen Burbidge, matron of the Fairfield Hospital. It became very popular in the training schools and soon trainees were learning its chapters by rote. In her book Miss Burbidge made it clear that training nurses was not simply about the practical problems of poultices and bed sores. It was also about inculcating habits which are 'ways of action or behaviour which have been learnt and practised until they have become almost automatic'. In particular trainees had to be introduced to behaviour such as kindness, tact, discretion, resourcefulness and adaptability and endurance, especially when things go wrong. A sense of responsibility which 'grows with experience' should also be engendered, as should observation, memory and attention to detail, and obedience to the rules and regulations of the hospital:

> Nursing gives opportunity for the expression of all the finest womanly attributes — tenderness, gentleness, cheerfulness, motherliness, and a graciousness to all. Tact and discretion, a broad tolerant outlook on life, and a well developed sense of humour help the nurse through many a difficult situation.[25]

Miss Burbidge paid special attention to the development of a sense of loyalty in trainees towards patients, doctors, fellow nurses and the profession in general. For her a nurse was 'to remember at all times that the nurse's first consideration is for the patient'. However, a nurse was also to be aware that her experience and expertise could never match the doctors:

> The little knowledge you will have gained during your years in the hospital in no way fits you to diagnose disease or to prescribe treatment, nor does it place you in a position to criticize the doctor and his methods.[26]

As well as this a nurse had to remember that her conduct in and out of the hospital, for good or ill, would reflect upon the profession and her training school. At all times she was to conform to the established patterns of behaviour common to the group of nurses she was working with, 'Failure to adhere to the accepted customs of the group is a failure in responsibility to the professional group'.[22] Matrons such as Miss Burbidge demanded high standards from their trainees and staff, which extended far beyond their conduct in the wards of the hospital.

Trainees fresh from the PTS soon learnt that they were the very lowest in the hospital hierarchy, and it was here that the military and religious origins of nursing were most apparent. There was no place in the system for a nurse who showed any inclination to question the authority structure, or in any way to challenge the traditional procedures and relationships. Those who did faced swift dismissal:

> When being addressed by Matron or Senior Sisters the nurse stood to attention, her sleeves rolled down, starched cuffs on wrists and hands behind her back — one felt a salute would not have been out of order.[28]

At one hospital in the early thirties nurses still whispered about the nurse who had dared to write a book about the endless hard work, the unduly strict discipline, and the strange hospital hierarchy. Of course she was instantly dismissed for her trouble and 'as a warning to others'. In the depression years the threat of dismissal was a powerful deterrent.

One incident which changed the whole direction of a trainee who had had her life planned around becoming a nurse and then a missionary, illustrates the importance attached to any circumstance which might question authority:

> She had to do the cleaning and was using lysol. There was a hole in her gloves and she burnt her finger with the lysol. She took off the glove and put her finger to her mouth, burning her lips, she put some vaseline on her lips. She had a full mouth and her lips looked shiny red. She went to the sister of the ward, to speak about something, and the sister told her to go and wash off the lipstick before she addressed her. The girl came and told me about it and the only thing to do was to go and explain to the sister, but we were scared of her, obviously she was more scared than I was, but she finally went back. Before she could open her mouth, she was told to obey at once, to go and wash her mouth and report back immediately, and this in very forceful terms. The poor girl was now in tears. We discussed the situation, and there was nothing to do but stay in front of the sister until she

listened. So off she went again. Without giving her time to say anything, Sister told her to report to the Matron immediately. She thought the Matron would give her time to explain ... weeks later we met in the city. She told me Matron was angry and started telling her straight away that they did not want girls who defied orders and she could leave at once.[29]

The rationale behind this unquestioning obedience to orders from above was directly related to the army life where many of Florence Nightingale's ideas were nurtured. In emergencies one does not have time to think. Instant discipline with everyone working as a team, obeying orders without question, was seen as essential for hospital emergencies. It was not only Florence Nightingale's influence which operated here, however, for this type of authority structure could be found in many other institutions at the time. Schools were run on similar lines. Private company managers issued orders down the line to workers on the factory or office floor who did what they were told.

It was also believed that this type of authority structure would help everyone to cope with the crises of hospital life without displaying emotion, which was considered detrimental to nursing. Nurses could not afford to show emotion, and it was not uncommon for a trainee to be dismissed over emotional displays which erupted, for example, when a patient whom she had been nursing died. 'Nothing would have induced me to show any emotion about anything on duty. I wanted to be a good nurse!'[30] Miss Ruth Henderson recalled that after nursing a young man who died of pneumonia:

> My friend and I went into the linen room and were crying, when sister found us there. She said 'You two get to work, there are 40 other patients out there who need you'. I thought she was unfeeling, but she was so right, and I never became emotionally involved like that again. Maybe nursing makes one hard, but I learnt then how to be a professional nurse.[31]

No member of the hierarchy would be blamed for the death of a patient. As a group working within an authoritarian line of command the ultimate authorities (the matron and the medical personnel), who in theory could have been blamed, were so remote from the scene of operations for most of the time, that it would have been pointless to call them to account. Even if there had been a clear case of incompetence, the system protected its own through professional solidarity.

When trainees first entered the wards they were immediately introduced to the domestic service origins of their occupation. There were always domestic tasks, varying from hospital to hospital, which had to be completed, for example collecting jugs and drinking vessels, emptying and cleaning sputum mugs, urinals and bedpans, squeezing oranges and lemons for drinks, cleaning locker tops, tables, window sills. A particular horror was cleaning the brass pan steriliser with Brasso or acetic acid and salt, and also the enamel spittoons:

> The wards we cleaned, till our fingers were raw, everything from lockers to walls, bed pans, bed pan rooms, skirting boards, cupboards, tops of doors, false teeth, glass eyes, toe nails and last but not least, people who were at our mercy in their beds. We made thousands of beds and on the way learned about care of patients — an incidental I feel, second only to the cleaning.[32]

The morning duty had to set up the breakfast trolleys, which included heating up milk, boiling eggs, serving porridge, spreading bread and butter and trundling them down to the wards where they would help the charge sister with feeding where necessary. Later the trays and trolleys had to be collected and handed over to the pantry maid who, as one nurse commented, 'did not seem to do much in those days'.[33] Similar procedures were observed at other meal times. Even on night duty spare moments were occupied, 'we cut the toilet paper, we used the *Sun* or the *Age*. I always used the *Sun* because the page divided into nice blocks ... we put a string through, to hang it up'.[34]

Once the domestic tasks were done the trainee nurse would have to face up to her first enema or perhaps a sponging or a simple dressing, in between handing out bed pans and screening off patients. She soon discovered the tyranny of the ward clock — how could she possibly get everything done? Nurses learnt to do the work which was the most important in the eyes of the ward sister, 'If I don't do that I will be caught and reprimanded'. 'I knew which children would tell the sister if I had not got around to bathing them'. It was 'a tough way to learn', but it was all vital knowledge for survival. 'Slowly I realised what nursing could perhaps be.'[35]

In the larger hospitals there was usually a highly ritualistic lunch or afternoon tea where trainee nurses would be reminded again of their low place in the hierarchy:

> Formal dinner at midday was supervised by Matron who reigned supreme at the top table. Down the dining room and in order of magnitude from greatest to least followed Ward Sisters in cream, Staff Nurses in blue, third year nurses, second year nurses and first year nurses, then inside the door, on their own for all to inspect were the Preliminary Training School, the most humble being taught protocol, respect, humbleness and manners. All were to be in place, standing with hands at sides with cuffs on, backs to chairs, forming a guard of honour for Matron to make her grand entrance, take her place, signal all to be seated with a quick thankful shuffle of chairs then the babble of voices. To be late for dinner was a criminal offence, punishable by having a battery of censuring eyes turned on while 'walking the plank' to stand at attention before Matron, waiting to be excused, hoping there would be a seat amongst one's own peer group, or one at all in fact. It was really much easier to miss the meal, making do with piece of toast and cup of tea in the Nurses' Home.[36]

Food was 'plentiful, fattening and filling'. Lots of bread, butter, biscuits and tea.

Generally, in the large hospitals, wards had about 30 patients divided into two sections, male and female. The staff of each ward for each duty roster (shift) consisted of one charge sister, one or two staff nurses plus one senior and one junior nurse. New trainees quickly learnt that each of these grades could be recognised by their uniform, for example at the Melbourne Hospital a first year nurse had a series of pleats at the back of her cap, in the second year a frill, but no spoke stitching, and in the third year a frill as well as a row of spoke stitching around the head band. Even within the first year those who entered training last had always to defer to other trainees, for example in holding doors open, entering lifts, at luncheon with the matron and when the medical staff swept through the wards on their inspections. This latter ritual was usually headed by the senior honorary physician or surgeon followed by the registrar in charge of two or more wards and the resident medical officer who was probably a last year medical student who needed lots of help from those next in line, the charge sister and the staff nurse.

Nurses' work in the 1930s placed much emphasis on nursing patients back to health. This meant constant nursing of patients who spent long periods in hospital, often six to 12 weeks. For many illnesses there was little that could be done except to ensure that the patient was comfortable, clean and well fed so that his or her strength could be built up enough to combat the ailment. There were no antibiotics to cope with infections, so any injuries which became infected could lead to many days or weeks of nursing to clear them up. Sulphonamides were new in the late thirties. There were still many fatalities from tuberculosis, pneumonia, typhoid fever and erysipelas, and from diphtheria, whooping cough and scarlet fever in children. Often, especially where fever was present, constant nursing was needed until the crisis was reached, when the patient either pulled through or died.

Under such circumstances, an enormous responsibility was placed on the shoulders of trainee nurses who far outnumbered the trained sisters in the major hospitals. On top of this, the general wards coped with all types of cases, including emergencies, post-operative, psychiatric and infectious diseases:

> When I think back — those terribly serious cases we had in those General Wards, as well as all your other patients and you had to give them so much extra attention. There was a young man with tetanus ... he had to have someone with him *all* the time ... there were *three* of us for *forty* patients ... there were injuries and emergency operations that had to be prepared, taken to the theatre, brought back and looked after until they were out of the anaesthetic. Really and truly you were running![37]

Junior nurses found that what they learnt at the PTS was quite inadequate to help them cope with the many and varied crises and demands of the wards, but somehow they managed:

> A patient named Irene, who was admitted from 'Hollywood', a boarding house in St Kilda. Irene wore three coats with mangy fur collars, every finger was adorned with cheap

rings from Coles, all according to Irene given her by various film stars, e. g. Clark Gable. She said her hair was just like heaven — no parting. It was also crawling with pediculi as was the rest of her. I was the 'lucky' one to give her an admission bed bath, and check all her clothing seams for money. I felt I needed an admission bath myself before returning to the Home.

We sent to the children's ward for comics as she could neither read nor write, but she was kept amused looking at the pictures and telling her own story. Irene was adept at voiding into the drinking bottle from her locker. She would do this repeatedly, despite being told it was wrong, and never a mess — no wet sheets.[38]

Life, to me, seemed to consist of 'fluids and urines'. It was the Junior's job to make up orange drinks for all patients on copious fluids. In Ward 12 nearly all the patients had been ordered a fluid and urine chart. This meant charting all fluids taken and all urine passed each 24 hours. We had to see that each one consumed at least 200 oz per day, an equivalent of about 10 lemonade bottles full of fluid.[39]

Urine testing was a nasty and tedious job. Many different solutions were used, some boiled in a test tube over a bunsen burner. Sometimes, if it boiled too quickly, it exploded up to the ceiling. It was a hazardous and smelly test which could often go wrong.

There was also the frequent monitoring of patients' temperatures. The rituals varied between hospitals. In some, all charts stayed on the sister's desk so the nurse would take three or four patients' temperatures at a time and then return with the results. There were also the pulses, respirations and bowel actions to be entered Poultices and other counter irritants were very popular in the thirties and nurses had to make up and apply them. Linseed poultices were used for relief of pain in pneumonia and pleurisy, bread poultices for minor infections, mustard paste and turpentine stupes to relieve distension and methyl salicylate foments were applied to relieve deep seated inflammations.

One of the innovations of the mid-1930s was the introduction of inverted thermos flasks to administer continuous rectal saline as treatment to combat shock, loss of blood or dehydration. The flask had a rubber cork with two holes holding a short and a long glass tube. Rubber tubing, a clip, a glass connector, more rubber tubing and a fine rubber catheter completed the apparatus. This was all assembled and administered by the nurses who were also required to constantly monitor the drip. If it became disconnected by a restless patient the bed would be saturated. In severe cases blood transfusions were given, but there was no blood bank and a donor such as a relative or friend had to be found. Blood was transferred directly from donor to patient.

Even though nurses led a somewhat cloistered existence their patients would never let them forget the real world outside where ignorance of elementary sanitary procedures flourished and where poverty was widespread. It must have been quite traumatic at first for these middle class girls to come face to face with people and problems quite beyond their realm of experience:

> My first encounter in the ward with a real 'unclean'. Joan and I were sent to do an admission bed-bath. The patient literally 'crawled', from head to toe, and being unused to any kind of cleaning process the woman yelled loudly all the time as though in pain. It was a female medical ward, 12. She didn't have hands and feet but claws, nails so long and curved under that bone cutters were used in the effort to trim them. I think we were given extra assistance by more senior staff when it was realised we were unable to cope. But we did have to do the cleaning up afterwards.[40]

> I went with the doctor and he explained that he did not want a junior nurse, because what I was about to do might put a junior nurse off her nursing career for life. We went into a cubicle. There sat a dear little couple in their seventies, holding hands. There was a terrible stench, the little old man had his head bandaged as if he had ear trouble. The dressing had not been changed for weeks, that was obvious. We sat the little old lady outside, with some difficulty as she did not want to leave her husband. We took off the bandage. The whole ear was fly blown, enormous maggots. Syringing with kerosene they just fell away, the wound was beautiful but at what a price. That is a memory hard to forget. The little old man had been in such torment, and he was so grateful. I was glad that I was the one to help him.[41]

> Mr Gordon, far left bed in corner 4 poster fracture bed, plaster from waist to toes — my first Saturday morning — Sister Ems said 'Mr Gordon is to have an enema'. I duly gathered my tray and in trepidation approached the bed, screened same and wondered how I would accomplish

something which seemed impossible. The dummy we used in the school wasn't surrounded with all these obstacles, besides, it was female. Mr G. was co-operative and quite used to this weekly attack on his person. Finally all was done, and his bed restored to normal. Going to the sluice I was half way down that long ward, when Mr G's voice reached me and beyond. 'That new nurse has given me the best enema I've ever had, and wipes your bum better too.' I was so embarrassed, but a small glow of satisfaction stole over me. My first task and I had made it.[42]

It was unlikely that any were attracted to nursing by the pay and working conditions (refer back to chapter 1). While on day duty time off was generally one day or one and a half days each week. For night duty there was significant variation of conditions between hospitals. For example the Alfred had 12 weeks on in the first year, 14 in the second and third, with one day off for each week at the end of the period of duty. Melbourne had a five night on and one off system.[43] At the Alfred day duty began at 6.30 a.m. with either morning hours off (9.30–12.30), or afternoon hours (2.00–5.00), finishing at 8p.m. Night duty was from 8 p.m. to 6 a.m., except for one night a week when it commenced at 9.30 p.m. In reality the hours were much more 'flexible', in that the finishing times were often extended where tasks had to be completed or emergencies occurred. It is impossible to generalise about the actual total working hours in hospitals in the 1930s. The variation was probably between 48 to 66 per week. Annual holidays were also significantly different between hospitals — from one to three weeks — and also according to the level of training.

After the completion of PTS each trainee in the major hospitals had to sign a declaration of loyalty to the hospital management. At the Melbourne Hospital the document declared among other things:

> I agree to submit and conform cheerfully and without demur to all rules and regulations of the Hospital for the time being, whether the same have been made before or after my admission.
> I also agree at all times and in all things to obey the orders and conform to the wishes of the Lady Superintendent or other officer for the time being in charge.

> And I hereby recognise the right of the Hospital Commit-
> tee or Sub-Committee in the event of my committing any
> breach of this agreement, or conducting myself in a manner
> disapproved of by the Hospital authorities, to dispense with
> my services at once.

It ended with the words 'I am, Gentlemen, Yours obediently ...'.[44]

As a nurse progressed through her training, if she was in one
of the larger hospitals, she would probably have had some
experience in the operating theatre. 'Scrubbing up' with nail
brush and carbolic soap was one of the rituals of a hospital,
especially before doing a dressing. But before an operation it was
a far more important occasion:

> In fact it could be a social event. There was a row of basins
> at which everyone who was taking part in the operation
> would scrub up for twenty minutes. Our masks would first
> be put on and sleeves well rolled up, a theatre cap tied on
> with *no* hair showing, and we would get to it at the scrub up
> basins, all in a row. One tall and lanky resident was in the
> middle of his scrubbing up when the surgeon burst in,
> furious that his operating pants weren't in his cupboard. Of
> course silly Normie, on his first day, thought he could pop
> on any old pair, so we had to get him off quickly to change
> while pretending to hunt for the pants, then smuggle them
> back into the Honoraries' room for the Surgeon.[45]

After scrubbing up a sterile gown was put on, taking care not to
touch anything that was not sterile. A nurse was at the beck and
call of the honorary surgeon as was everyone else in the theatre:

> Mr Trumble was always extremely careful and insistent on
> asepsis, sterility during every operation no matter how big
> or small. He also made quite a few of his instruments or had
> them made to his design and also named them to suit
> himself, and the theatre staff just had to know what he
> meant. Two of his favourites were a trephine for cutting
> through the skull which he called a 'jigger' and a 'thing-
> ummy' which was a small instrument for feeling if he was
> through bone on to the brain covering ... Each surgeon had
> his own particular special instruments he preferred and the
> theatre staff had to know which surgeon liked what kind of
> forceps or retractor.[46]

Instruments, which were kept in glass cases when not in use,
were boiled and set on a trolley before an operation in the order

they would be used, together with an array of suture needles. Catgut for sutures was sterilised in spirits, while horse hair, thread and silk were boiled in water for at least ten minutes. An instrument nurse was ready with the threaded needles for the surgeon as the operation progressed.

A swab nurse had a trolley on the opposite side of the surgeon where there were large and small packs of gauze and cotton wool swabs, sterilised like the linen by autoclave. These packs were all counted and checked before the operation and again before the final sewing up to make sure none were left inside. After the operation it was nurses who did the cleaning up:

> Lots of fun as theatre nurse dodging the night sister, cunningly polishing and putting away some of the instruments whilst leaving enough to look like a full setting. A wrong instrument count at the end of the night always caused panic. We used to send the old porter to go through the rubbish bins while we searched the theatre and sterilizing room. With three theatres to clean one often left the masks boiling on the gas ring in one theatre, and proceeded to work in another theatre. Panic — Panic, when one remembered. Supposing the hospital burned down. Were we all neurotic? I don't think so. We were young, overworked, anxious for our patients, and at the same time anxious for our own survival. In the depression years of the early thirties, one could not afford to be the object of several bad reports.[47]

Trainees who survived the three years and became registered nursing sisters generally looked back on those years with warmth and affection towards their fellow trainees, who often became life-long friends. Indeed trainee reunions are regular features of any nurse's or retired nurse's calendar. The sisterhood engendered during those years of hard work and education was an experience that was to be relived, rather than forgotten as quickly as possible. And, of course, 'only the devoted girls made it — it was *too* hard — you had to be very determined and *very* devoted'.[48] You had very good reason to rejoice if you were a survivor. Again the military analogy is relevant. Nurses continued to meet in much the same way as returned soldiers (the survivors) remember their experiences and reunite with their former comrades-in-arms each year on Anzac Day. They too had shared an experience where survival depended on trust, loyalty and humanitarian bonds over a relatively long period of time. For the trainee nurses:

> The hospital and those participating seemed a small world of its own ... we formed close friendships, we shared so many experiences. We spent so much time in each other's company. I think it was this bonding and the comfort we received from it that helped many of us put a protective shell around to enable us to cope with a lot of the trauma and strain of our training and eventually finish the course.[49]

Trainees became dependent on their colleagues for emotional support, for knowledge, for fun and relaxation. There was no-one else to cry your heart out to if something went wrong. It was not the sisters who taught trainees on the job but their own immediate seniors, that is, the *next* most senior nurse to you. It was rare for a sister to go out of her way to explain something to a trainee. Most of her concerns related to checking on jobs done and reprimanding when appropriate. The camaraderie was associated with a special sense of humour and a language which would not readily be understood by outsiders:

> Nurses have a different outlook on life, they have a special sense of humour, some of our jokes would shock the outside public. We handled life and death and we had to prevent ourselves from being shattered by it, and still care and be gentle.[50]

The fun came with going out with your fellow trainees on days off or taking short cuts and not being caught, at the small parties and celebrations in the nurses' home or simply talking and joking with your companions — relating experiences, giving advice, helping each other survive:

> Most of our leisure was the companionship with those we trained with — you could talk problems over you wouldn't dream of talking about outside the hospital. Nursing life was fun. We made friends, life-long friends.[51]

The wastage rate from the rigorous training was extremely high. Many left in the first few months when they realised the real nature of the work, others simply could not cope with the pressures and broke down and left, some were dismissed, others failed their examinations and marriage claimed many. You had to be a dedicated person to see it through and this was what the new breed of matrons were aiming at.

The three most influential matrons of the 1920s and 1930s were Miss Jane Bell at the Melbourne 1910–1934, Miss Louisa Mann 1912–1928 and Miss Grace Wilson 1933–1940, both at the Alfred. All were strong disciplinarians whose arrival in a ward would be greeted with fear and trepidation by the nursing staff:

> The Matron, Miss Grace Wilson of World War I fame was always a handsome sight, in starched white from the tip of her pointed toe to her flying captail. But the sight of supreme authority coming into the ward sent us all scampering into panrooms, lavatories, out of one balcony door and in the other, for the hospital rule was that the first nurse to see Matron enter, must go forward to her until Sister came. 'Going forward' meant pulling down one's sleeves, putting on one's cuffs, and usually being asked questions to which one did not know the answers. So one somehow avoided seeing Matron enter.[52]

Nevertheless, they commanded respect and loyalty in much the same way as outstanding officers in the military forces. They were used to unquestioning obedience and inspecting the nurses/troops was their forte:

> We were in awe of Miss Bell — she was very strict but I'd call her a just woman. We saw her every day but not at the same time, you could never say — it might be one o'clock in the morning or eight o'clock at night. Miss Mann (Alfred 1912–1928) was present always ... she'd pull you up ... she wouldn't reprimand you loudly ... but she'd pull you up. There was great rivalry — terrific rivalry over standards — I think that was why the standards were so high in both hospitals, the two of them weren't going to let the other get one better.[53]

A matron had control over all the domestic and nursing arrangements within a hospital. She had the power to engage or dismiss the nursing and domestic staff. She was responsible for all domestic and nursing properties within hospital — the inventories, the requisitions and the distribution. Each day she or the sub-matron was required to visit 'all wards, kitchen, laundry, and nursing and domestic quarters, and all other offices and buildings as often as necessary, seeing that cleanliness and order are everywhere observed'. She was also responsible for the supply, preparation and cooking of food as well as the education of the nurses and a register of their performance and duties while at a hospital.[54] She was required to confer with the medical superintendent on all matters of her department affecting the welfare of patients or the general functioning of the hospital. Her area of command was clearly defined in the rules and regulations related to the particular act under which the hospital was established. Together with the medical superintendent, she was effectively in control of the day-to-day functioning of a hospital.

Endnotes

[1] K. S. Inglis, *Hospital and Community. A History of the Royal Melbourne Hospital*, Melbourne University Press, 1958, pp. 96–7.

[2] Ann M. Mitchell, *The Hospital South of the Yarra. A History of Alfred Hospital Melbourne from Foundation to the Nineteen-forties*, Alfred Hospital, Melbourne, 1977, pp. 79–80.

[3] *VPP*, vol. 4, 1892–3, report of the Royal Commission on Charitable Institutions, Minutes of Evidence, Q7358–80.

[4] Jacqueline Templeton, *Prince Henry's. The Evolution of a Melbourne Hospital, 1869–1969*, Robertson and Mullens, Melbourne, 1969, p. 127.

[5] Monica Mackay, 'Handmaidens of Medicine — A History of Nursing in Colonial Victoria', M.Ec thesis, Monash University, 1982, p. 171.

[6] ibid., p. 125.

[7] Quoted in Monica Keneley, 'Handmaidens of Medicine: Working Conditions for Nurses in the Late Nineteenth Century', *Journal of Australian Studies*, no. 22, May 1988, p. 67.

[8] Mackay, op. cit., p. 180.

[9] ibid., p. 178.

[10] Templeton, op. cit., p. 129.

[11] Mackay, op. cit., p. 180.

[12] ibid., p. 197.

[13] The matrons preferred the respectable middle class girl, but actual figures on the background of trainees in the 1930s will have to wait on a detailed survey of hospital records. Interviews with Miss Marjorie Connor (21 February 1989), Miss Jean Hanna (12 March 1989), Miss Pat Slater (26 February 1989).

[14] Ruth Henderson (ed.), *Alfred Hospital Reminiscences (1927–1947)*, 1990, Virginia Kircher (trainee from September 1935), pp. 69–70.

[15] Interview, Miss Pat Slater, 26 February 1989.

[16] The use of the uniform as an aid to discipline was not confined to nurses and

the armed forces. It was used in schools and for shop assistants, domestic servants, clerical workers etc.

17 Henderson, op. cit., p. 69.
18 Henderson, op. cit., Aileen Schofield (trainee from December 1938), p. 140.
19 Henderson, op. cit., Ruth Henderson (trainee from September 1934), p. 61.
20 Henderson, op. cit., Aileen Schofield, p. 149.
21 Henderson, op. cit., Ruth Henderson, p. 54.
22 Henderson, op. cit., Virginia Kircher, p. 90.
23 Ribecki, 'Memories of Training to be a Nurse at the Alfred and the Royal Melbourne Hospitals 1920–1940', N.D., JEAN HANNA, P. 5.
24 Henderson, op. cit., Aileen Schofield, pp. 140–1.
25 Burbidge, op. cit., p. 10.
26 ibid., pp. 12–14.
27 ibid., p.xx.
28 Henderson, op. cit., Ruth Henderson, p. 46.
29 Interview, Pat Slater, 26 February 1969.
30 Henderson, op. cit., p. 52.
31 Henderson, op. cit., Aileen Schofield, p. 142.
32 Interview, Rae Lockey, 24 January 1989.
33 Ribecki, op. cit., Betty Lawson, p. 6.
34 Interview, Slater, op. cit.
35 Henderson, op. cit., pp. 142–3.
36 Ribecki, op. cit., Jean Hanna, p. 13.
37 Henderson, op. cit., June Pierce (trainee July 1940), pp. 153–4.
38 Henderson, op. cit., Virginia Kircher, p. 77.
39 For the significance of this ritual in nursing see Virginia H. Walker, *Nursing and Ritualistic Practice*, Macmillan, New York, 1967.
40 Henderson, op. cit., Susan Willoughby, p. 66.
41 Henderson, op. cit., Ruth Henderson, pp. 53–4.
42 Henderson, op. cit., June Pierce, p. 153.
43 Ribecki, op. cit., Jean Hanna, p. 14.
44 'Training of Nurses in the Melbourne Hospital', Conditions of Appointment, 1932. This included a loyalty declaration addressed to the committee of the hospital.
45 Henderson, op. cit., Virginia Kircher, p. 91.
46 Henderson, op. cit., Ruth Dale (trainee from 1936), p. 107.
47 Henderson, op. cit., Ruth Ogden (trainee from May 1934), pp. 38–9.
48 Ribecki, op. cit., Jean Hanna, p. 5.
49 Henderson, op. cit., Susan Willoughby, p. 67.
50 Henderson, op. cit., Ruth Henderson, p. 60.
51 Ribecki, op. cit., M. Orton, Jean Hanna, p. 15.
52 Henderson, op. cit., Ruth Ogden, p. 36.
53 Ribecki, op. cit., Jean Hanna, p. 10.
54 *Victorian Government Gazette*, no. 399, 6 December 1939, pp. 5–6.

Building Nursing as a Profession

Florence Nightingale's intervention in the organisation of the nursing profession in the middle of the nineteenth century both created nursing as a profession for women, and lumbered it with some of the most repressive notions of ladylike behaviour ever to emerge from nineteenth-century drawing-rooms ... nurses ... were ladies first, and for that doubtful privilege they paid very heavily indeed.[1]

IT seems that every profession endeavours to develop its own mystique, whether it be the legalese of lawyers, medicos with their knowledge of sickness and death, or the clergy with their special authority over spirituality and life after death. Training and knowledge isolates the members of a profession, and adds to the mystique which enhances their authority. For nurses Florence Nightingale had established the mystique of the caring, devoted woman with a loving heart, humble and docile, virginal and endlessly diligent, the 'lady with the lamp' flitting from bed to bed in the stillness of the night on her mission of mercy. Indeed, this image constituted the late nineteenth century male version of the ideal woman. For Miss Nightingale:

> What makes a good woman is the better or higher or holier nature — quietness, gentleness, patience, endurance, forbearance — forbearance with her patients — her fellow workers — her superiors — her equals. We need above all to remember that we come to learn, to be taught. Hence we come to obey. No one ever was able to govern who was not able to obey ... The best scholars make the best teachers — those who obey best — the best rulers ...
> Who does it best?
> As a mark of contempt for a woman is it not said, she can't obey? She will have her own way.
> As a mark of respect — she always knows how to obey. How to give up — her own way.[2]

But a mystique does more than separate off a profession from the rest of humankind and make those who follow it seem special in some way. It also helps bind the members of a profession together, who are just as much under its spell as the public. It helps them endure hardships and cope with demanding situations to know that they are doing a very important and highly regarded job. This is in some respects similar to the farmer who faces fire, flood, drought and the ravages of pests, but is sustained by the myth that he is the backbone of the country, that without him the city people would starve, and the nation would collapse.

Florence Nightingale's achievement was to convince nurses that nursing could become a profession and a worthy vocation. But this was done in the context of late nineteenth century middle class morality. What emerged was the nurse as the epitome of the perfect Victorian lady — an image which was to persist well into the twentieth century.

While Florence Nightingale's contribution to nursing has been well documented, it would be worthwhile here to briefly outline her main achievements as they related to the enhancement of nursing as a profession.[3] She had an unshakeable belief in adequate training for nurses, midwives and all other workers in the health field. At the Nightingale School at St Thomas's Hospital, London, which she established in 1860, probationers were admitted for one year's training, with doctors and the Lady Superintendent giving them lectures in anatomy and other subjects. Closely associated with this was what went on in the nurses' home. She considered that the physical wellbeing and moral tone which could be created in a 'Home' was vital to the training of a nurse and was most important in attracting a 'better type' of woman to the work in the first place. With its strict regime it was a public message emphasising the change from 'hospital nurses as failed prostitutes' to women beyond suspicion of immorality. Superintending the home and hospital she saw a matron with exceptional qualities of leadership and insight.[4]

Another characteristic of Nightingale's approach to nursing which contributed to its professional status was her insistence on the observation and recording of all aspects of a patient's sickness. In this way she initiated a more scientific approach to nursing based on a holistic view of a nurse's work. After all, a nurse was the only person able to observe a patient over a prolonged period and much could be learnt from careful noting of that person's condition and her or his reaction to medical treatment. This meticulous observation also applied to the work of Nightingale's trainee nurses. A report was kept on the progress of each nurse on a 'Monthly Sheet of Personal Character and Achievements', which the matron filled in under various headings such as Moral Record and Technical Record. Nightingale used the grades 'excellent', 'good', 'moderate', and 'imperfect' at a time when few if any educational institutions gave such detailed attention to the progress of their students.[5]

In these ways Florence Nightingale helped to define two of the most important characteristics of a profession for nursing, that is a minimum training period leading to a recognised qualification, and a substantive body of knowledge which is unique to the profession. But signifying their importance was only the first step towards their achievement. Miss Nightingale did not believe that registration was necessary to help to enforce a minimum standard of qualification. She did not see that registration and a minimum training period were closely connected. However, in Victoria, the singular victory in establishing the RVTNA as a registering authority in 1901 was seen as the first step to establishing minimum standards of entry to the profession. But it was a much longer road in Victoria and elsewhere to achieving the second characteristic — a unique body of knowledge accepted by the public as unique to nursing.

Traditionally nurses agreed with the medical profession that it was doctors who were the source of scientific and medical knowledge. A nurse translated the doctor's orders into a 'discrete quota of work' assigning some to others and carrying out some herself.[6] But she also had many other duties where she used her skills as a nurse and in which she carried full responsibility. For nurses at the beginning of the twentieth century the unique body of knowledge they had to offer as true professionals was that which they built up by the holistic observance of patients and which had at its core the practice of 'tender, loving care' or as some would have described it, 'knowledge of the heart'. Patients required this special care and during the long periods that many spent in hospital or in their beds at home, it was just as important for recovery as a doctor's prescriptions. But this was not a body of knowledge like medicine or law which could be set down in textbooks and learnt off by rote. Neither could it be clothed in jargon which would shield it from public criticism and help maintain its mystique. It took a long time to overcome the assumption that any 'good woman' could be a nurse. Nursing was built on a relationship between nurse and patient and there was no textbook which could prescribe how this should be handled since every such relationship was different. There was no set of rules to which a trainee nurse could refer to guide her in her everyday contact with the patients.

The 'tender loving care' image which Florence Nightingale bequeathed to nurses was at once a strength and a weakness in their struggle for professional status. It provided the basis for the nursing mystique, but at the same time confined nurses to what were considered menial tasks which had no association with a profession in the public's mind, and which restricted them to being the handmaidens of medical men. The caste system of the hospital created an unbridgeable gap between nurse and doctor. For many in the medical profession a nurse was a 'non-person' to whom orders were issued, but with whom knowledge was not shared.[7] In order to build a profession of the male medical, legal kind, many nurses believed they had to break away from these 'menial' tasks and to build a body of knowledge which was unique to their calling, but which was consistent with the generally acceptable view of a profession. This led to a preoccupation with raising the post-graduate qualifications of nurses, for post-graduate credentials were seen as contributing to the professional standing of other occupations, as well as helping to build up a body of knowledge through teaching and research.

The Shortage of Nurses

IT was stressed in chapter 1 just how dedicated Miss Jane Bell was to the establishment of nursing as a profession. She fashioned the RVCN with the specific aim of developing post-graduate courses for nurses in conjunction with the University of Melbourne. Not only was she unable to get the university to incorporate the courses in its diploma programs, but when the courses were launched under the auspices of the RVCN, few nurses enrolled. This is not to suggest that in the period before the Second World War notions of developing nursing into a profession on a par with the medical profession were confined to the leading nurses. In fact, the RVCN became increasingly pre-occupied with industrial matters during the 1940s, and professional issues, although never forgotten by leaders of the college, were forced into the background.

The reality was that wartime exigencies accentuated the many problems the nursing profession had faced in the previous decade, so that by 1945 it was becoming increasingly difficult to separate professional and industrial issues. Any talk of building up a 'profession' was lost in the general concern over the acute shortage of trained nurses and the generally very poor working conditions. In this situation to talk of a nursing 'profession' rang very hollow. It was simply an irrelevancy for most nurses struggling to cope with day-to-day problems. Indeed, some nursing leaders were by now convinced that drastic improvements in salaries and conditions were the first step towards achieving that elusive professional status.

All this was emphasised in the report of a committee established early in 1945 by the Minister for Defence, John Curtin, to inquire into the shortage of nurses and the means of alleviating this.[8] Miss Gwen Burbidge was one of the two nurses on the committee of seven. The committee concluded:

> For years there has been a growing dissatisfaction among trainees and trained nurses as to their present salaries and conditions and also an increasing awareness of the inevitable poverty that awaits them at the end of many years of service.
> More and more trained nurses have been leaving the profession and taking up other avocations ... the number of well educated suitable applicants to commence nursing training has been dwindling. This was less apparent in major metropolitan training schools than in country schools. Country training schools, however, play a considerable part in maintaining the annual total output of trained nurses, and in the care of the sick.[9]

The committee found that apart from the poor conditions other factors more directly related to the war had intervened.

A large number of nurses had joined the armed services for example, and there had been a greater number of trained nurses employed in private and country hospitals owing to the shortage of trainees. There had also been a general increase in the number of hospital beds. These factors, combined with the high marriage rate of the later war years, had exacerbated the crisis. Further, the committee did not expect many nurses in the services to return to civilian nursing due to the consequent drop in salary and conditions that this would entail. 'At the present rates of pay and conditions Service personnel are receiving they regard a nursing career as economic retrogression'.[10] On inspection of many hospitals throughout Australia committee members were appalled at the salaries and working conditions of nurses, 'The remuneration now paid to qualified nurses is so inadequate that to secure their future they must leave the profession'. They were also 'disgusted' at the staff accommodation in many hospitals:

> Young women cannot be expected to leave good homes and go into unsatisfactory nurses' homes; forced to live three or four in a room; in obsolete structures converted into cubicles with most inadequate ventilation; in dark sub-basement bedrooms; quarters with insufficient sanitary and bathing accommodation; insufficient recreation rooms; insufficient places for study and insufficient facilities for sport and health exercises away from nursing.[11]

Girls of the 'right type' would not be attracted back to the profession until the accommodation improved.

It could be argued that whereas in the 1920s and 1930s nursing was regarded as a very suitable vocation for middle class girls, at the end of the Second World War it had become 'the last thing for girls to adopt as a career'.[12] Nursing conditions had not improved during the war, but there were two other factors which would have had some influence here. For some years after the war there was a general shortage of labour. The long boom period of the 1940s, 1950s, 1960s and early 1970s had begun with very low levels of unemployment. For most of the time employees were able to pick and choose jobs. At the same time the war had helped to open up other avenues of employment for women in clerical, retail and commercial occupations. As well, there were now scholarships available which paid all fees and provided living allowances for students doing university degrees. Teaching, which had in the past attracted many middle class girls, offered very generous scholarships to take trainees through college or university from 1950.[13]

Senior nurses and matrons who could remember conditions in the first years of the century were perplexed at the decline in the popularity of nursing. They argued that training conditions 'as a whole' were 'very satisfactory':

> Student nurses are provided with board, lodging and tuition; and nursing is the only profession whose students are paid for the work they do while obtaining the practical experience necessary for their qualification.[14]

But they were unable to understand that young women since at least the 1920s had shown a strong tendency to favour jobs which gave them full freedom outside working hours. Middle class girls probably turned away from nursing for much the same reasons as working class girls preferred the dirty, noisy, and ill-ventilated factories of the 1920s and 1930s to domestic work.

The failure of nursing to retain its attractiveness was a subject of some concern in the media in the immediate post-war years. In 1946 the *Sun* asked 'What is wrong with the nursing profession? Why is it so difficult to attract nurses to it and why ... do so many leave it before or immediately after graduation?' To conclude an article which raised many of the issues surrounding nursing conditions, one writer asked, 'Why, in addition to being underpaid, must nurses also be subjected to conditions which workers in other walks of life would not tolerate?'[15] At a large meeting of nurses the State Labor Health Minister, W. P. Barry, referred to this poor publicity, 'in fact, it had been enough to frighten girls away from nursing'. 'But', he asked, 'what better could a young girl do than help to protect humanity? Nursing was a vocation not a job'.[16] Clearly for Mr Barry and many others at the time, a vocation was associated with poor conditions and hard work. These people considered a vocation, not simply as an occupation or a profession, but as a call, possibly divine, to a person to devote a life's work to a special purpose, which might also mean foregoing many of the pleasures experienced by ordinary mortals. The joy of being a nurse had to be earned. The poor conditions were akin to penance for being privileged enough to minister to the sick. Herein lay one of the problems with the mystique surrounding nursing as a vocation. It could be used by both politicians and the public to justify poor conditions and low pay. For nursing leaders nursing was both a vocation *and* a profession which, for some outsiders, appeared to be a contradiction in terms when comparing the professions of law and medicine with nursing. But the mystique associated with these professions was of a very different kind from that of nursing.

The RVCN and Post-graduate Courses

NEVERTHELESS, at the end of the war the RVCN returned to the problem of building the profession by distancing it from the wages board system and developing post-graduate courses for nurses. In 1946 they considered a proposal which Jane Bell had put forward a number of times before asking for a commission with a composition the same as a wages board to fix salaries and conditions of both hospital and private nurses under the Nurses Act. The proposal also called for the RVCN to be recognised as the controlling body of nurses in Victoria, except in respect to those matters dealt with by the Nurses' Registration Board, which would include the social and cultural interests of nurses, post-graduate training, a placement bureau for private nurses and a superannuation scheme.[17] Perhaps Miss Bell and others believed they had more hope of achieving their aims because the newly elected Labor Government had granted teachers a Teachers' Tribunal in 1946. This had a similar composition to a wages board, but was established under a different Act from that covering the wages boards. Teachers, however, had taken very effective political action to achieve this by campaigning against the previous conservative government, a course of action which nursing leaders did not contemplate.[18]

In 1946 there were a series of conferences convened by the Minister of Health which actually went a long way to recommending what Miss Bell had been advocating. The RVCN, the TNG, the HEF, the Australian Auxiliary Nursing Service and the British Medical Association agreed that the powers of the Nurses' Board should be widened to enable it to prescribe minimum living conditions for trainees and trained staff in hospitals, to set out conditions of training and the duties of trainees and trained nurses, and to set a minimum scale of fees for private and visiting nurses, thereby taking over many of the functions of the Nurses Wages Board. But, instead, a Hospitals and Charities Commission was created and the recommendations were never implemented.[19]

As we saw in Chapter 1, the post-graduate courses begun by the RVCN before the war were not very successful. RVCN leaders attributed this to the long hours nurses were required to work and its own inability to provide the infrastructure to run the courses because of the shortage of funds and staff. There were constant negotiations between the University of Melbourne and the college and many deputations were taken to the Government in order to obtain finance, with little result. Some nurses who had begun courses were able to complete them during the war, but otherwise the only war time course offered was one in industrial nursing. Like the others this was modelled on the course run by the Royal College of Nursing in London. It extended over one year if taken full time. As well as this the RVCN agreed to run a short intensive course over three months as a 'war emergency measure'.[20]

Overall, the numbers who successfully completed RVCN post-graduate courses by 1949 were small: Diploma of Nursing — 3, Sister Tutors' Certificate — 8, Diploma of Dietetics — 7, Occupational Therapy — 6 and Industrial Nursing — 44.[21] Nevertheless, it was a beginning in the face of government indifference and half-hearted support from the University of Melbourne, which was happy for individual staff members to participate in the courses, but would not contemplate giving them recognition, as was the case with other universities outside Australia.

The College of Nursing, Australia

WHILE the RVCN was wrestling with the future of its post-graduate courses, the ANF had formed the provisional committee of the National Florence Nightingale Memorial Foundation, whose main objective was also to provide post-graduate courses for nurses. A National Florence Nightingale Memorial Committee (NFNMC) was established in 1946, with branches in all states and with representatives of the Australian Red Cross Society sitting on their committees.[22]

The Florence Nightingale International Memorial had been established in England in 1934 to commemorate the life and work of Miss Nightingale, and took the form of an endowment for post-graduate nursing education to provide facilities for nurses throughout the world to undertake study beyond their initial training. This memorial took up the work of the League of Red Cross Societies which in 1920 had arranged for facilities to enable outstanding nurses, on the recommendation and support of the national Red Cross Societies, to undertake study. The memorial resulted from an arrangement between the League and the ICN whereby both organisations participated in its activities through the Florence Nightingale International Foundation Committee.[23]

Before the war, associations had been established in three States (Victoria, Western Australia and South Australia) to promote post-graduate education of nurses, but these all had lapsed. After the war the Florence Nightingale International Foundation Committee had asked the ANF to establish an Australian National Committee of the foundation, and at the ANF council meeting in 1946 it had been decided that a federal council should be set up, consisting of delegates appointed by the State committees of the foundation. The Australian Red Cross Society had made 3600 available for post graduate nursing scholarships which were to be awarded by the Australian National Committee.[24] Muriel Knox Doherty, as convener of the education sub-committee of the NFNMC, had recommended in a report that a college of nursing be set up to service the educational needs of nurses throughout Australia. At the second annual meeting of the

NFNMC in 1947, it was decided that a post-graduate nursing college be established.[25]

Miss Doherty had trained at the Royal Prince Alfred Hospital, Sydney, studied at the Sister Tutor Diploma course at Kings College, University of London, held positions as matron during the war and later had worked for the United Nations Relief and Rehabilitation Administration.[26] In January 1947 she outlined her ideas of how a college of nursing would develop to an open meeting of nurses in Melbourne. She saw the college as providing 'unity and uniformity' of nursing courses in Australia by a 'complete reconstruction of the training of nurses'. She envisaged an Australian College of Nursing as standing side by side with the Royal Australasian College of Surgeons and the Royal Australasian College of Physicians:

> The College would not only deal with the educational side, it could also deal with recommendations regarding provision of social and economic security of nurses. Because I think if we can offer the young girl ... some security for the future, we must attract more girls to the profession. In a college, we should make provision for nursing experimentation, and research. We could supervise nursing conditions in all branches. We would provide courses for post graduate education ... we could develop and encourage very much the social and cultural side of nursing, by the establishment of clubs, dramatic societies and so on.

Miss Doherty wanted the college to be the instrument by which nurses would remain in control of their profession, 'to safeguard our whole efforts, to protect the public, to keep pace with the rapid advances in medical science'.[27]

Her proposal was not greeted with much enthusiasm from the RVCN, even though it was endorsed by the federal council of the ANF in January 1947.[28] The idea required that the be nationally unified, and in 1947 that was certainly not the case. The RVCN Council did not discuss the proposal and went ahead with its own plans for post-graduate nursing courses. The State Government was again approached, and there looked to be some hope from that quarter when the Hospital and Charities Commission was established under the *Hospital and Charities Act 1948*, which included a clause requiring the commission to promote the post-graduate education of nurses.[29] In fact the Charities Board which the Commission replaced had been advocating schools for the post-graduate education of nurses for some time, and had been awarding a small number of scholarships to nurses for further study.[30]

Late in 1948 a joint meeting of the executive of the NFNMC, the ANF and the TNG decided to seek finance from the Federal Government to establish an Australian College of Nursing. But at this time relations between nursing organisations in Victoria and New South Wales were at a very low ebb (refer to chapter 1). The RVCN remained lukewarm to the idea of a national body taking over the post-graduate training of nurses, and saw local State branches of a national body as a more viable proposition. Earlier in the year the federal Labor Minister of Health had offered to consider the establishment of an Australian post graduate school of nursing as part of a federal health plan with a grant of 5 000 per annum, partly to pay the salaries of the director and the assistants. This was unacceptable to the RVCN because it would have given control to the federal health ministry.[31] The RVCN leaders were very keen for post-graduate education to be controlled by nurses, since they believed this was one of the characteristics of a profession.

Early in 1949 it was revealed that the chairman of the recently established Hospital and Charities Commission, Mr McVilly, had promised Miss Hughes-Jones and Major-General Kingsley Norris 3–4 000 towards establishing a post-graduate school for Victorian students.[32] Miss Edith Hughes-Jones had trained at the Alfred Hospital, and was matron and owner of the 'Windermere' private hospital in Melbourne. She was one of the founders both of the War Nurses Memorial Centre and the NFNMC, and secretary of the National Committee from 1946 to her death in 1976.[33] Major-General Kingsley Norris told the RVCN Council in April 1949 that despite further efforts to involve the Federal Government in plans for a college, there had been no response and as a result 'very active interested people decided it was time something was done'. A constitution was drawn up. The first council was to consist of nominees from the NFNMC, the ANF and the TNG. The State branches would be constituted along the lines of the federal body. To enable Victoria

Helene D. Grey, OBE,
Foundation Fellow CNA

Betty C. Lawson, OBE

Mona Menzies, AM

Marjorie Connor, MBE, RN,
FRCNA

Jane Bell, OBE

Left to right: Jean Headberry, FNM; Annie Sage, CBE, Hon. FCNA;
Patricia Chomley, MBE

Jane Muntz, OBE, Foundation
Fellow CNA

Edith Hughes Jones, OBE,
Hon. FCNA

Nurses Memorial, Nurses
Memorial Centre, Melbourne

Patricia Violet Slater, OBE,
FCNA

Leitha Mavis Avery, FCNA

Mary E. Patten, FCNA

Irene Margaret Bolger

to take advantage of the funding from the Hospital and Charities Commission, the State committee would also include representatives from the metropolitan teaching and non-teaching hospitals and one from the country hospitals. The RVCN Council was told that the new College of Nursing, Australia, would not be supported by the Australian Trained Nurses Association, New South Wales.[34] The name, as one might expect, was chosen because it was similar to the Royal College of Nursing, London. Meanwhile in early 1949 in New South Wales, the representatives of the four nursing organisations in that State had formed the New South Wales College of Nursing which remained separate from the College of Nursing, Australia, for nearly 30 years.

The formation of these two quite separate colleges almost simultaneously was as much a product of the traditional rivalry between New South Wales and Victoria (Sydney versus Melbourne) as the ongoing divisions between nurses in the two states which hindered the national unity of nurses in the decades to come. The irony of these events was that the RVCN, which had shown the way with its post-graduate nursing courses, was so completely preoccupied at this time with the machinations of a new national nursing body, that it was the NFNMC and a number of individuals who pioneered the establishment of the College of Nursing, Australia, with its headquarters in Melbourne. The college was modelled on the lines of other professional colleges in Australia and Britain and was seen by all involved as a step towards building the nursing profession in Australia. The first director was Miss Patricia Chomley, with senior lecturers Miss Pat Osborne and Miss Jean Murray.

The Official Recognition and Training of Nursing Aides

THE acute shortage of trained nurses persisted into the late forties and early fifties. By the end of 1950 it was apparent to the Hospital and Charities Commission that the existing number of trainee nurses was not going to alleviate the shortage in any way. The number of nurses in training in 1951 compared with 1948 had increased by only four, from 2797 to 2801! The commission had undertaken a significant modernisation and expansion of hospital accommodation throughout the State, and there was a real likelihood that much of this would be left unused if more nurses could not be found. Moreover, it was estimated in 1951 that 1193 additional beds would be made available in the near future.[35]

To solve this problem, the commission chose a course of action which was to have long term implications for nursing in Victoria and for the future of nursing as a profession. It decided to classify nurses into two divisions, those who undertook highly-skilled nursing treatments and those who did 'routine nursing care which does not require a high degree of professional knowledge'. The first division referred to State registered and student nurses,and the second to qualified and student nursing aides. The Commission argued:

> The introduction of the nursing aide will widen the field of recruitment by drawing upon those who, although keen to serve in nursing, have previously been excluded because of failure to meet the entrance standards demanded of the general nurse, or who, for economic reasons, have entered other employment.[36]

The commission established two avenues for training nursing aides. The first was to tap into the supply of cheap labour provided by the large number of immigrants (called 'new Australians' in this period) arriving in Australia, many of whom were refugees from the war. The second was to cater for existing Australian citizens. A nursing aide school was opened on 3 October 1950 for girls selected from migrant camps, who were given a two month intensive course in English and, in the second month also took a course in simple nursing duties. Their training was completed by a further ten months in a hospital. Nearly 100 were admitted in the first intake. A one year training school for Australian girls, mainly from rural areas, was also started in 1950 in Toorak, a suburb of Melbourne.[37] By June 1953 the commission was able to report that there were 16 nursing aides training schools — eight in the metropolitan area and eight in the country, and 220 nursing aides were already employed in hospitals.[38]

Training nursing aides was only legitimising what had been the situation in hospitals for many years. In 1953 there were 1 348 'unqualified assistant nurses' in Victorian hospitals and institutions compared with a total of 5 768 — 2 932 trainee nurses and 2 836 trained nurses.[39] There is no record of any public comment on this by the RVCN, but its council did decide to send a letter to the Nurses Board suggesting it make representations to the Nursing Adviser to the State Minister of Health urging that power be vested in the board to regulate the training and State enrolment of nursing aides.[40] It was not simply the dilution of training standards and the inherent threat to the professionalism of nursing which bothered the RVCN. Nursing assistants were already taking over, in some hospitals, many of the tasks which were considered the fundamental activities of nursing, while trained nurses were required to be more specialised and skilled in particular areas. Often the tasks performed by nursing aides were those which brought them into closer contact with patients. Under the *Nurses Act 1956* registration of nursing aides became the responsibility of the Victorian Nursing Council from 1 March 1958.[41]

The labour market in the late forties and fifties was highly competitive and the Hospitals and Charities Commission had taken measures to try to attract more young girls into nursing. By the middle of 1958, 3 919 £50 nursing bursaries had been awarded to girls in secondary schools to induce them to train as general nurses.[42] The recipients were encouraged to stay at school in order to be eligible for entry to nursing schools. Many metropolitan hospitals required a higher entry level than the minimum requirements, as laid down by the Nurses' Board. The girls were obliged to work for one year in a hospital after training. A nursing recruitment officer was employed to address students in schools, talking to some 10 000 students in 1956 to 1957, particularly in the rural areas where hospitals were still very short-staffed.[43]

An Experiment in the Training of Nurses

D URING the late forties the training of nurses was coming under increasing scrutiny as part of the growing media interest in nursing and in health care more generally which characterised this period. Nurses returned from North America, Britain and Europe having seen radically different schemes in operation from the standard form of training offered in Victoria. In Australia's hospitals training was basically on the job, supplemented with lectures by specialists in various fields. Apart from what the trainees learnt in the preliminary training period (usually six to eight weeks), most of their knowledge came from observation and practice in the wards with help from more senior trainees, rather than trained staff, over the three year training period. Lectures often took place during off duty hours and simply keeping awake seemed to be the main obstacle to learning under these circumstances, especially given that nurses worked up to 60 hours a week. The deficiencies in this system were well known, but until the post-war years there were few vocal critics.

One of the first hints of change came with a paper printed in the Annual Report of the Royal Melbourne Hospital in 1945/6 by Dr John H. Lindell, the Hospital's Medical Superintendent. Dr Lindell advocated revision of 'the whole system of nursing training to embody new procedures'. He wanted:

> an extension of the preliminary period of lectures and demonstrations before entry to the wards, the introduction of the 'block' system, whereby most of the lectures and demonstrations are done when the nurse is not working in the wards or departments, and the transfer of certain aspects of nursing training to the post-graduate sphere.[44]

Dr Lindell and Miss Gwen Burbidge, matron of the Fairfield Hospital, worked out a scheme which had as its ultimate aim the setting up of a central training school for the Fairfield and the Royal Melbourne Hospitals. While this did not come to fruition, it did lead to the matter to be taken up by the Hospital and Charities Commission in 1949.[45] The commission had been working on a new approach to nurses' training in Victoria. It was proposed to divide the State into regions each with a school of nursing to provide a training base for the hospitals in the area. While only two of these schools were actually established — the Northern School of Nursing, Bendigo and the Melbourne School of Nursing — the commission lost no time in getting them underway.

In Melbourne the participating hospitals were the Royal Melbourne, the Womens', the Fairfield, the Queen Victoria and the Children's. From the outset the Royal Melbourne (with its two year waiting list of applicants) was a reluctant participant in the scheme. Nursing and medical staff were concerned that what they saw as a successful training school with a long history of initiatives in the area had been closed. It was also unfortunate that the traditional antagonism between the Alfred and the Royal Melbourne was not taken into consideration in the appointment of staff to the school. There were no Royal Melbourne trained staff, but the Alfred was well represented.[46] The school's program which began in 1950 provided for 1176 lectures, demonstrations and the like over the training period (double the normal requirement), which were held for the most part in a teaching centre separate from any hospital and taken during study blocks of four or six weeks each year.[47] This meant that the trainees were able to concentrate on their studies without the worries and exertions of their work in the wards. They were also able to live at home during these study block periods.

It soon became apparent that this method of training had its opponents, notably Miss H. D. Grey, the Lady Superintendent at the Melbourne Hospital and president of the RVCN from 1947 to 1952. From her viewpoint the scheme was a radical diminution of the power of matrons. Trainees were students of the Melbourne School of Nursing and graduates of that school. They applied to and were selected by the school, and were rotated around the participating hospitals to vary their clinical experience. All this meant that matrons were no longer closely involved in the selection, general supervision and discipline of trainees. Miss Grey also had numerous organisational problems which for her meant that the 'student establishment was in a constant and maddening state of flux and over which she had only the minimum of control.'[48] She believed trainees lost the sense of 'belonging' to a hospital and needed to be at a hospital like the

Melbourne for a much longer period than the school provided. She also considered the movement of trainees between hospitals disruptive to hospital routines and that in these circumstances nurses became irresponsible because they had no loyalty to any one institution.[49]

This general opposition from the Royal Melbourne, would probably not have been enough to put an end to the new training school. However, in the late 1950s the school failed to attract sufficient recruits to keep up an adequate supply of trainees. The Queen Victoria had already withdrawn from the scheme, and its opponents used this fact along with its failure to attract recruits as reason for its abolition.[50]

It would seem though that this opposition was primarily related to the fear that theory and practice would be separated. Miss Bell did not favour the off-campus block scheme because of the 'removal of practical contact with patients and continuity of observation for varying periods'. For Miss Grey, who was an admirer and disciple of Miss Bell, practical experience also had to be directly linked with theory in time and place. Both were the adherents of an 'apprentice type' training system such as used in law (articles) and medicine (clinical practice). They seemed to ignore the fact, however, that the 'apprenticeship' was under-taken only after a significant period of theoretical preparation in both these professions. It is a matter of debate whether their opposition was really directed towards building nursing as a profession, or towards maintaining the power and the authority of the lady superintendent in the hospital.

Miss Gwen Burbidge

DURING the initiatives concerning the block training scheme, in endeavours to get the RVCN to face up to the problem of nursing aides, and in general media coverage of the acute shortage of nurses during the mid and late forties, one name keeps popping up — Miss Gwen Burbidge. Miss Burbidge did her training at the Melbourne and the Women's Hospitals. In the latter she was appointed staff nurse and ward sister. During this period she was awarded the Sister Madge Kelly Memorial

Prize for the best practical nurse in the State. She was appointed sister tutor at the Preliminary Training School established in 1927 by Miss Bell at the Melbourne Hospital. After three years she went to the Alfred to establish their PTS, where she also wrote her nursing handbook, *Lectures for Nurses* (1935). The book had many editions and became prescribed reading for trainee nurses. It was also used during the war by the army in its scheme for training medical auxiliary personnel.

In 1935 she went to England where she obtained a Hospital Housekeeping Certificate, a Sister Tutor Diploma, and a Diploma of Nursing (distinction) at the University of London. On her return to Australia in 1939 she became matron of the Queen's Memorial Infectious Diseases Hospital at Fairfield (later known as the Fairfield Hospital), where she remained until her retirement in 1960. At Fairfield she introduced several innovations such as a training course for trained nurses to become ward sisters, a two year infectious diseases course for nurses, the appointment of a nursing recruitment officer (the first in Australia), the introduction of daily visits by relatives to patients with infectious diseases (also the first in Australia), the reduction of nurses' working hours and lessening the amount of students' leisure time taken up with lectures, and study and development of a ward manual giving clear instructions on all procedures to make things easier for nurses who moved from one ward to another.

She became the first president of the NFNMC (1946–1949), and the first Censor-in-Chief, College of Nursing, Australia (president in 1961). She was a member of the Nurses Board (later Victorian Nursing Council) for 19 years and in 1954 became a member of the National Health and Medical Research Council. She was also the first Australian nurse to be offered a scholarship by the Rockefeller Foundation to study nurse training courses in university schools of nursing in the United States. On her return she was able to convince the chairman of the Hospital and Charities Commission to set up training courses for nursing aides. She was appointed as chairwoman of the management committee. In 1950 Miss Burbidge was awarded the Florence Nightingale Medal by the NFNMC, and in 1955 the OBE.[51]

The Nurses' Board and the VNC

MISS Bell and her contemporaries saw the establishment of the Nurses' Board in 1924 as the most significant step towards building the profession achieved in Victoria up until the early 1950s. It did firmly establish one of the most important characteristics of a professional organisation, that being the registration of its members according to recognised qualifications and minimum standards of training. However, compared with law and medicine, which the leaders of the RVTNA aspired to emulate, they had no legal control of their registration body, although for most of its existence they did exercise considerable influence over the Nurses' Board.

A full history of the Nurses Board and its successor, the Victorian Nursing Council, will not be given here since this has been well covered up to 1973 by Maureen Minchin in *Revolutions and Rosewater*.[52] Nevertheless, since it played an important part in building the nursing profession in Victoria some aspects of its history will be mentioned. After the formation of the RVCN in 1934, members of that body pressed for more direct representation of nurses on the board, and this led to changes in 1940 which gave nurses the right to elect five representatives and midwives to elect one. This meant that in theory, though not in practice, there could be no matrons on the board.[53]

One of the important tasks of the board was the establishment of uniform standards of training. It continued the administration of the final year trainee nurses' examinations in 1924 following the pattern set up by the RVTNA. In 1940 it instituted examinations at the end of the first year of training as a prerequisite for entry into the second year.[54] This was to ensure that trainees received a uniform basic instruction in their first year, and also to eliminate those who were not up to standard at the end of that year, rather than allowing them to continue until the final examination.

As was noted in chapter 1, one of the main concerns of the RVCN during the war years was the dilution of training standards, because this was seen to undermine the professional status of nurses. Many battles were fought on the Nurses Board which was under pressure to recognise the experience of women who had served in the voluntary auxiliary detachments or had worked in military hospitals. In 1943 the board rejected the proposal that these women should be given exemption from the first year of nurse training. But in the long term the board was forced to grant concessions to women who had worked as nurses in the Australian Army Medical Women's Services or the Women's Australian Auxiliary Air Force, especially as male nurses and orderlies who had worked in the armed forces were awarded registration if they passed the State final nursing examinations.[55]

But these measures provided only temporary respite for the board. The Nurses Board was basically a 1920s invention functioning in the 1950s in a manner that was no longer appropriate and with little administrative backup. There was also a great deal of dissension at the board level between the new breed of nurses epitomised by Miss Burbidge and the 'old guard' who found it difficult to cope with the changing conditions of the post-war years. Added to this were the changes occurring in nursing practice and the consequent demands made upon staff. Nursing was undergoing a revolution, not just in medical and technical developments, but in its scope and diversity. The board was ill-equipped to handle this, especially as many of the problem areas were outside its jurisdiction.[56]

By 1953 there was a general consensus in the Ministry of Health, the Hospital and Charities Commission and the RVCN that the Nurses' Board had to be reconstituted. Miss Jane Muntz, president of the RVCN, played a leading role in the discussions which followed, and which resulted in the creation of the Victorian Nursing Council (VNC) in 1957. Miss Muntz had been appointed as the first Nursing Adviser to the Minister of Health in 1951, a position she held until 1968. She had trained at the Melbourne and sat on the council of the RVCN from 1946 to 1967, and was president from 1953 to 1958. She was also president of the RANF for five years from 1961. During that time she led the RANF delegation to ICN congresses on two occasions, and served both on the Grand Council and the Board of Directors of the ICN. In 1965 she was a keynote speaker at the Thirteenth Quadrennial Congress in Frankfurt. She had been actively associated with the formation of the College of Nursing,

Australia, and a member of its Council and Executive Committee. She received an OBE in 1957.

It was her 'tireless and conscientious service on committees' where she 'always paid meticulous attention to detail' while 'never losing sight of the main objectives', and her 'brilliant and provocative, yet constructive' contributions to debates, which made her an outstanding spokesperson for nurses in Victoria in the 1950s and 1960s.[57] Miss Muntz was the real driving force behind the setting up of the VNC. As Nursing Adviser to the Minister and president of the RVCN, she was able to bring the many and varied nursing interests together as a united body; no mean achievement considering the lack of unity which characterised the post-war period. She was able to gain fairly quick agreement that the new Nursing Council should be a policy-making body with control over all nursing matters.

Miss Muntz was able to report to a general meeting of the RVCN that a series of discussions had been held on the initiative of the RVCN with the Matrons Association of Victoria, the Victorian Committee of the College of Nursing, Australia, and the Victorian branch of the NFNMC, and that details of legislation required to reorganise nursing in Victoria had been worked out. For the first time in many years leaders of the various nursing organisations in Victoria were able to present a united approach to the Government. The general principles were:

(a) that there be one Act — to incorporate relevant aspects of all existing Nurses' Acts — to provide for education and training and all other matters concerned with all branches and aspects of nursing education, training and service.

(b) there should be a Council with very wide representation of the community which we feel should be represented and that nurse majority should be maintained as on the present Nurses' Board.

(c) that provision be made for the authority to formulate control and direct all policy relating to all nursing matters in this State. This will include experimental training schemes, research, promotion of all branches of nursing for all types of nursing personnel in order to provide an adequate and efficient nursing service for the community.[58]

A deputation to the Minister of Health, Mr E. P. Cameron, in the new Bolte Ministry gained a favourable and sympathetic response, and a detailed proposal was sent to the Minister in August 1955. In April 1956, Cameron accepted most of the proposals and assured nurses that a Bill would be brought before Parliament before the end of the year.[59]

In the months before the presentation of the Bill in October 1956, nurses lobbied members of parliament to gain support. Many would have remembered the previous long and drawn out efforts to get changes to the Nurses' Board and the lack of interest from politicians. However, in this situation, where nurses were united and clearly determined, the Bill passed all stages without opposition. The Victorian Nursing Council came into operation on 1 March 1957.

The *Nurses' Act 1956* was a milestone in building the nursing profession in Victoria. A new council which replaced the Nurses Board was set up to administer the Act. The council included 16 nurses in its 28 members — three from the RVCN, one each from the Matrons Association, the Victorian branch of the FNMC, the College of Nursing, Australia and the Private Hospitals Association. A further six were to be elected from registered general nurses, one by registered midwives, two by registered mental nurses and two were to be appointed by the Minister representing mothercraft nurses and nursing aides. Of the ten remaining members two were doctors nominated by the BMA, one a barrister or solicitor, an 'expert in education', plus one each from the Hospital and Charities Commission, the Chief Health Officer, Department of Health, the Mental Hygiene Branch, Department of Health, the Metropolitan Hospitals Association, the Country Hospitals Association and the Victorian Bush Nursing Association. The entire spectrum of interests connected with nursing in Victoria had been brought together on this one Council.[60]

Of fundamental significance for the nursing profession was a provision in the Act making it unlawful for persons to practise for gain in any branch of nursing unless they were registered with the council and in possession of an annual practising certificate.[61] A person who did practise without a certificate would have no legal claim for any expenses incurred. This was much tighter than that in the original 1923 Act, which simply made it unlawful for an unqualified person to use the name, badge or head-dress of a nurse.[62]

Apart from taking over the registration functions of the Nurses Board which were extended to include mothercraft nurses and nursing aides, the new council was largely concerned with the training of nurses. Whereas the previous board was essentially a registration authority which also conducted the annual examinations, the council was charged with investigating and researching all matters related to the education and training of nurses. This included the educational standards for entrance, the standards of instruction in training courses, the approval of hospital nursing schools and the regular inspection of any places where nurses were trained.[63]

Jane Bell, who died in 1959 not long after the Victorian Nursing Council had been established, would have been pleased with its formation, for it was structured along lines which she herself had so often advocated in the thirties and forties. However, she would have deplored the fact that it lacked any role in the determination of the salaries and conditions of nurses. It also gave full recognition to nursing aides which she would have found very difficult to countenance. Nevertheless, it was a most important step towards building the nursing profession in Victoria.

The ICN and the 1961 Conference

FOR nursing leaders in the thirties, forties and fifties the International Council of Nurses (ICN) was of crucial importance in establishing standards of professional practice. They looked to the ICN for guidance on many issues, but especially on questions concerned with the training and qualifications of nurses.

The ICN had its origins in the international feminist movement which began with the establishment of the International Council of Women in Washington in 1888. This council was made up of middle class women concerned mainly with questions of suffrage, equality and justice for women. An active participant in the organisation when it met in London in 1899, was Mrs

Bedford-Fenwick. She had been matron of St Bartholomew's Hospital, London, and was the founder of the British Nurses' Association in 1887. Like Florence Nightingale she regarded a minimum training period for nurses as important, but unlike Miss Nightingale she saw registration of all qualified nurses as the main avenue to creating a profession. Unlike Florence Nightingale she was also an ardent feminist and a personal friend of Mrs Emmeline Pankhurst.[64]

At the meeting of the Matrons Council of Great Britain which followed the 1899 conference, Mrs Bedford-Fenwick proposed the establishment of an international council of nurses:

> The nursing profession above all things requires organisation: nurses, above all other things, require to be united. It depends upon nurses, individually and collectively, to make their work of the utmost possible usefulness to the sick, and this can only be accomplished if their education is based on such broad lines that the term 'trained nurse' shall be equivalent to that of a person who has received such an efficient training, and has proved to be also so trustworthy that the responsible duties which she must undertake may be performed to the utmost benefit to those entrusted to her charge.
>
> To secure these results two things are essential: that there should be a recognised system of nursing education; and control over the nursing profession. The experience of the past has proved that these results can never be obtained by any profession unless it is united in its demands for the necessary reform, and by union alone can the necessary strength be obtained.[65]

The next day, 2 July 1899, a provisional committee of the International Council of Nurses (ICN) was formed. Two nurses representing Australia were present, Miss S. McGahey, Lady Superintendent of the Prince Alfred Hospital, Sydney and Miss M. Farquharson, Lady Superintendent, Melbourne Hospital. By the mid-1920s when the RVTNA became interested in affiliation with the ICN, there were 18 national nursing organisations affiliated. It was by then a well established organisation holding regular conferences. Its constitution in 1925 showed a strong commitment to the advancement of nursing as a profession, and one of the main objectives was the:

self-government by nurses in their associations, with the aim of raising ever higher the standards of education, professional ethics, and public usefulness of their members.[66]

The ICN took a particular interest in encouraging national licensing and accreditation laws for nurses, raising of the admission standards for nurse training and increasing the periods of training. All these things were closely aligned to establishing an international professional nursing model.

Although Australian nurses attended various ICN conferences, there were no formal links with Australia. In the late 1920s and the early 1930s formal links were sought, but attempts foundered because there was no united national nursing organisation in Australia. It was too much of a drain on the finances of the RVTNA for that organisation to pay the bulk of the affiliation fees. Later, in 1937, when the Australian Nursing Federation had been reorganised into a truly national body, the way was open for affiliation with the ICN. That year a delegation from Australia led by Miss Jane Bell went to an ICN conference as the members of an affiliated nursing organisation, the Australian Nursing Federation.[67]

The links established with the ICN were considered crucial by RVCN leaders. Its foundation was a British initiative, and for Victorian nurses who were patriotic supporters of King and Empire this was extremely important. The pages of *UNA* and other nursing journals in the late forties, fifties and early sixties were full of reports of nursing developments in Britain, and they remained the yardstick for nursing practice and reform in Australia.

Another preoccupation of nursing leaders in this period was reciprocity of Australian nursing credentials with other countries because of the large number of nurses who took overseas working holidays. Here the ICN was important in providing information on developments in member countries, and provided the opportunity for informal networks to be created at the international conferences. It also facilitated access to study courses in various countries.

A very successful regional conference of nurses was organised by the RANF in May 1955 in Melbourne with nurses attending from New Zealand, Thailand, Indonesia, Korea and India. The main speaker other than the Governor General, Sir

William Slim who opened the conference, was Miss D. C. Bridges, executive secretary of the ICN. She was obviously impressed with her reception and the organisation of the conference. This must have had a very positive influence on the ICN's decision to accept the RANF's invitation to hold the Twelfth Quadrennial Congress of the ICN in Melbourne in 1961.[68] By then the ICN had 36 affiliates. Each Australian State branch was required to support the congress, but much of the organisation was done by members of the RVCN, the College of Nursing, Australia, the Hospital Matrons Association and the Victorian Branch of the Florence Nightingale Committee, who were on hand in Melbourne. Finance was raised in each State towards congress expenses and surveys of private and hospital accommodation in Melbourne to house the visitors were undertaken. The organisation involved a great many nurses in Victoria. Ships and planes had to be met and transport arranged. There were excursions and social events for the 2 300 visitors from 40 countries. Every section of nurses played a role in what was an event to be remembered.[69]

The Twelfth Quadrennial Congress of the ICN was opened by the Governor, Sir Dallas Brooks, in the Exhibition Building, Melbourne on 17 April 1961. After a two day meeting of the Grand Council of the ICN the congress divided into four sections — nursing education, nursing service, economic welfare and public relations — with keynote speakers in each. Nine new member associations were admitted with due ceremony. Many countries contributed to an exhibition of material. Visits to hospitals were arranged and there were trips to the country and numerous social functions.[70]

Much of the discussion at the congress centred on building nursing as a profession and one of the most controversial items related to the definition of a 'registered professional nurse'. An attempt to write a definition into the constitution was deferred because the definition proposed would have eliminated many of the member nations, including Australia. It would have required all nurses to have had a general training in an approved school of nursing, thus excluding specialist areas such as psychiatric and paediatric nursing.[71]

In many respects the ICN Congress in Melbourne (the

headquarters of both the RANF and the RVCN) was a watershed in the growth of the nursing profession in Victoria. Nursing in Australia, but particularly in Victoria, gained international recognition, and this was something that nursing leaders had always cherished and valued highly. Victorian nurses believed they had achieved much for the profession in Victoria, and that this was comparable with the efforts of their sisters in other countries. The profession had gone a long distance since the 1880s, but there was still a rather bumpy road ahead.

Endnotes

[1] Beverley Kingston, *My Wife, My Daughter and Poor Mary Anne. Women and Work in Australia*, Thomas Nelson, Melbourne, 1975, p. 81.

[2] Letter from Florence Nightingale, 6 May 1881, quoted in *UNA*, April 1956, p. 100.

[3] There is an excellent select bibliography on Florence Nightingale in F. B. Smith, *Florence Nightingale. Reputation and Power*, Croom Helm, London, 1982, pp. 205–11.

[4] See Lucy Seymer, *Florence Nightingale's Nurses, The Nightingale Training School 1860–1960*, Pitman Medical, London, 1960, pp. 32–3.

[5] ibid., pp. 94–5.

[6] Fred. E. Katz, 'Nurses', in Amitai Etzioni (ed.), *The Semi Professions and their Organization*, Free Press, New York, 1969, p. 61.

[7] ibid., pp. 69–70.

[8] Edgar H. Ward (secretary to committee of inquiry) to Miss G. N. Burbidge, 28 March, 1945. Burbidge papers.

[9] Report of sub-committee to committee of inquiry, 5 May 1945, p. 1. Burbidge papers.

[10] ibid., p. 3.

[11] ibid., p. 2.

[12] Report to W. P. Barry, Minister of Health, (Victoria), from G. N. Burbidge, 13 March 1946, Burbidge papers.

[13] See B. K. Hyams, B. Bessant, *Schools for the People? An Introduction to the History of State Education in Australia*, Longman Cheshire, Melbourne, 1972, pp. 173–4.

[14] J. Cole, SRN, 'In Defence of Training Schools', in *UNA*, January 1947, p. 3.

[15] 'Prudence' (regular columnist) 'What is Wrong with the Nursing Profession', *Sun*, 16 August 1946. See also *Age*, 11 April, 23 April 1946.

[16] *Age*, 23 April 1946.

[17] *RVCN minutes*, 27 March 1946.

[18] See B. Bessant, 'A Moment of Unity : The Establishment of the Victorian Teachers' Tribunal', in *Melbourne Studies in Education 1967*, R. J. W. Selleck (ed.), pp. 28–101.

[19] Maureen K. Minchin, *Revolutions and Rosewater. The Evolution of Nurse*

Registration in Victoria 1923–1973, Hart Hamer, Melbourne, n.d., pp. 56–7. See also Jane Bell to E. P. Evans, General Secretary, ANF, 31 October 1946. Box 32, UM archives.

[20] Report of education sub-committee, RVCN, 28 February 1941. Box 10, UM archives; RVCN minutes, 6 June 1946.

[21] Box 10, UM archives.

[22] *UNA*, May 1946, p. 147.

[23] *UNA*, May 1934, p. 132.

[24] *UNA*, May 1946, p. 147.

[25] NFNMCA minutes, 30 August 1947.

[26] Bartz Schultz, 'Founders of the College', *The Seventh Patricia Chomley Oration*, College of Nursing, Australia, 1983, p. 5.

[27] *UNA*, February 1947, pp. 38–9.

[28] *UNA*, April 1947, p. 99.

[29] Vic. no 5300. *An Act to establish a Hospital and Charities Commission and to amend and consolidate the Law relating to Hospitals and Charities, and for other purposes.* 31 August 1948.

[30] VPP, 1947–8, vol. 2, Twenty Fifth Report of the Charities Board to June 1930, 1948, p. 9.

[31] RVCN minutes, 1 January 1949.

[32] RVCN minutes, 10 January 1949.

[33] Schultz, op. cit., pp. 11–12.

[34] RVCN minutes, 7 April 1949.

[35] VPP, 1951, vol. 2, Hospital and Charities Commission Report to 30 June 1951, p. 8.

[36] ibid.

[37] ibid., pp. 8–10.

[38] VPP, 1952–3, vol. 2, Hospital and Charities Commission report to 30 June 1953, p. 10.

[39] ibid., pp. 9–10.

[40] RVCN minutes, 7 June 1951.

[41] Vic. no 6035. *An Act relating to the Nursing Profession, and for other purposes.* 7 November 1956.

[42] VPP, 1958–9, vol. 2, Hospital and Charities Commission report to 30 June 1958, p. 26.

[43] VPP, 1956–8, vol. 2, Hospital and Charities Commission report to 30 June 1957, p. 18.

[44] Quoted in Norman J. Marshall, *The Melbourne School of Nursing 1950–1963. A Chapter in the History of Nursing in Victoria*, The Melbourne School of Nursing Past Trainees Association, 1985, p. 11.

[45] ibid., p. 13.

[46] Pat Slater to Marjorie Connor, 2 November 1989.

[47] Marshall, op. cit., p. 18.

[48] ibid., p. 26.

[49] ibid., p. 36.

[50] Jane Bell to E. P. Evans, General Secretary, ANF, 31 October 1946. Box 32, UM archives.

[51] Most of the material on G. N. Burbidge from the Burbidge papers. See also *UNA*, March 1961, pp. 73–4 on her retirement.

[52] op. cit.

[53] Minchin, op. cit., p. 37.

[54] ibid., pp. 43–4.

[55] ibid., pp. 49–50.

[56] ibid., p. 71.

[57] *UNA*, September 1970, p. 22.

[58] *UNA*, September 1955, p. 280.

[59] *UNA*, August 1956, p. 230. See also 'Summary of Recommendations to the Minister of Health of the Working Committee on Re-organization of Nursing in Victoria, August 1955'. Box 101, UM archives.

[60] *Nurses Act*, no. 6035, 1956.

[61] ibid., section 31(1)(2).

[62] *Nurses Act*, no. 3307, 1923, section 17(b)(2)(3).

[63] *Nurses Act*, no. 6035, 1956, section 9(1)(a-k).

[64] Daisy Caroline Bridges, *A History of the International Council of Nurses 1899–1964. The First Sixty-Five Years*, Pitman Medical, London, 1967, pp. 1–7.

[65] ibid., pp. 7–8.

[66] ibid., pp. 233–4.

[67] *UNA*, October 1937, p. 299.

[68] *UNA*, May 1955, pp. 129–42. Report of opening session.

[69] *UNA*, March and April 1961.

[70] *UNA*, April 1961. See also *ICN Congress News* (daily Congress news sheet).

[71] Bridges, op. cit., p. 213. The addresses by keynote speakers were published separately and also in *UNA* during 1961.

4

Changes in Nurses' Work and Working Conditions

T HE post-war decades of the fifties and the sixties in Australia were characterised by full employment in an expanding economy. Between 1946 and 1974 unemployment fluctuated between only 1 and 2 per cent, with an average annual economic growth of 4.5 per cent.[1] The population increased rapidly due to the baby boom in the late 1940s and early 1950s and the immigration programs initiated by the Federal Labor Government in the immediate post-war years and sustained during the Menzies era (1949–1966).

There was an enormous expansion in building activity during these years, both in the public and private sectors. This was closely associated with the growth in urban development. In Victoria, major building programs were undertaken, including multistorey flats for the poor in the inner city and the spread of housing to the satellite towns and outer suburbs of Melbourne. At the same time the provincial towns were expanding. Whereas in 1947 only four provincial towns in Victoria had more than 10 000 people, by 1971 there were 17.[2]

Wage earners benefited because of the labour shortage and were able to gain significant increases in wages and reductions in hours, however this was not achieved without many strikes and a high level of industrial unrest. The standard 40-hour week was introduced in 1947 and the Federal Arbitration Commission and the State wage fixing bodies gave regular basic wage increases. Women joined the workforce as never before — one married woman in eight worked outside the home in 1954 compared with one in three 16 years later.[3]

In the fifties and sixties consumerism came to Australia. People had more money in their pockets and they spent it on all the trappings of a consumer society. Home ownership increased dramatically, and homes became filled with the furnishings, the electrical gadgetry, the radios and television sets of the new society. With these developments, which were to place an enormous strain on health services, came the use of the automobile as a form of mass transport. For the first time owning a car was within the reach of most families. When the war ended there was only one car for every 14 Victorians. By 1960 this had risen to one to five. Motor bikes also became popular, and, like cars, helped fill the casualty wards and mortuaries of the hospitals.[4]

Another less obvious change which was also to have a significant impact on health care and nursing, was a general increase in awareness of matters relating to health. The higher education levels of the fifties and sixties and the wider dissemination of materials relating to health through the media and the schools was producing a more informed clientele. Patients were much more likely to have some knowledge of medical treatments and what to expect from hospitals. He or she might even ask a doctor or nurse questions.

While this was a prosperous era, it was also a time of bitter political and social divisions associated mainly with the Cold War and the two real wars in Korea and Vietnam in which Australians were involved. The Labor Party underwent a disastrous split in Victoria as the Cold War spilled over into local politics. All these wars created tensions in public and private life over issues such as national service and conscription, industrial unrest and political dissent. To add to this was the discovery that 7.7 per cent of Melbourne's population lived in poverty.[5]

Needless to say these developments placed a great strain on existing health services, but they also helped produce a revolution in approaches to health care, so that by the end of the 1960s the pattern of public health services had changed dramatically. The trend towards the growth in fee-paying patients in the public hospitals, which was first apparent in the 1930s, was accentuated in the 1950s and 1960s. While 33 per cent of in-patients treated in 1951 were in the fee-paying wards, by 1961 this had risen to 47 per cent. Put another way, while the number of public beds in

Table 1   Public hospitals from 1951–1971

	1951–1952	*1961–1962*	*1970–1971*
	Total number of in-patients treated		
Metropolitan	89 740	148 409	218 356
Country	82 613	122 431	163 430
Total	172 353	270 840	381 786
	Intermediate and private patients		
Metropolitan	13 649	42 505	79 938
Country	44 038	85 432	119 135
Total	57 687	127 937	199 073
	Number of beds available (public)		
Metropolitan	4 106	5 492	5 557
Country	2 956	2 957	2 845
Total	7 062	8 446	8 402
	Number of beds available (intermediate and private)		
Metropolitan	462	1 151	1 949
Country	1 713	2 979	3 563
Total	2 175	4 130	5 512

Table 2   Private hospitals 1951–1971

	1951–1952	*1961–1962*	*1970–1971*
	Number of hospitals		
Metropolitan	144	175	224
Country	97	87	93
Total	241	262	317
	Number of beds available		
Metropolitan	3 126	4 210	6 659
Country	1 069	1 351	1 941
Total	4 321	5 561	8 600

country hospitals remained stable between 1951 and 1970, the number of fee-paying beds doubled, and in the city an increase of 35 per cent in public beds was accompanied by a four-fold increase in fee-paying beds.

The increased number of in-patients treated in 1970 compared with 1951 was not simply a result of the increase in the number of beds available. A much more significant factor was the average length of stay of patients, declining from 14.2 days in 1951 to 9.4 days in 1970.[6]
This trend was to have repercussions throughout the health services. Hospitals had become primarily places for medical service rather than places of custodial care. Overall the increase in the number of public hospital beds by nearly 40 per cent during these 20 years reflected the results of a sustained hospital building, extension and renovation program. In the main period of expansion between 1950 and 1960, the number of metropolitan public hospitals increased from 21 to 31 and in the rural areas from 73 to 106.[7]

Compared with the thirties the large modern hospital of the early sixties was a greatly improved institution. The wards were much smaller and the backup services provided a form of specialisation which could not have been anticipated 30 years previously. In the 1930s a large hospital would have had pathology and radiology departments with perhaps one or two an almoner but social workers were unheard of. By the 1960s there were units or departments specialising in areas such as allergies, arthritis, cardiology, dermatology, diabetes, gastroenterology, geriatrics, gynaecology, neurology, neurosurgery, ophthalmology, orthopaedics, paediatrics, plastic surgery, urology and psychiatry. There were also ancillary services provided in anaesthetics, pathology, biochemistry, haematology, radiology, electrocardiography etc. and other services available from dentists, occupational therapists, physiotherapists, psychologists and social workers.[8]

This specialisation produced an ever-increasing division of labour, with a multitude of specialists representing different facets of their respective disciplines, with different value systems and different behaviour. Coupled with the increased size of most hospitals, this led to the growth of a new hospital bureaucracy intent on extending its power and intruding in the decision-making process at every level. This had a dehumanising effect on relationships between staff. The real decision-makers seemed to become more and more remote from the wards and were preoccupied with efficiency and balancing their books. Ward nurses not only had to cope with this new bureaucracy, but with a large number of specialists as well.

The Chronic Shortage of Trained Staff

IN the midst of this expansion and specialisation during a long boom period, were chronic problems, not the least being a shortage of trained staff, especially nurses. This was the subject of numerous reports and investigations, but no simple solutions were found. It is well to remember that apart from a brief period in the 1930s, a shortage of trained nurses had been the rule rather than the exception since nurses were registered in Victoria. As noted earlier, part of the problem was that only a fairly small number of middle class girls wanted to go into nursing, especially when there were other alternatives. Even if a girl did decide to try for nursing, she had to be acceptable to a matron who may not have been easy to please. The quite deliberate attempt to exclude girls from working class backgrounds in the 1930s and 1940s had not helped. When these 'lower class' workers did creep in as auxiliaries and nursing aides in order to alleviate the persistent shortage, they were not always welcome, to say the least.

Two background statistics were at the crux of the problem in the 1950s and 1960s. The thirties and early forties had been a period of low birth rates. This meant that the pool of women available for nursing was at a low level in the following two decades. To confound the problem the amount of nursing care required by patients was increasing. In 1930 the ratio of nurses to patients in Victorian hospitals was 1:2.23. By 1953 it was 1:1.8 and in 1960 it was down to 1:.91. It was not as if young women were not going into nursing in increasing numbers. In 1932 1 397 nurses were in training compared with 2 932 in 1953 and 4 140 in 1960.[9] The difficulty was one of supply from a small pool for which there were serious competition from other occupations such as teaching and clerical work.

For some the problem would have been alleviated by reducing the wastage rate. In 1952 to 1953 nearly 1 000 trained nurses left public hospitals and other institutions in Victoria for a variety of reasons, such as marriage (194), to go to private hospitals (130), to go overseas (90), to return home (66), to do midwifery training (81), because they wanted a change (21) etc. Trainees left to be married (79), because they failed (50), they were found 'unsuitable for nursing' (44), they did not like nursing (24), they returned home (22), were medically unfit (20) etc. But there was no ready solution here.[10]

Dr John Lindell, chairman of the Hospital and Charities Commission, did not consider for tackling the wastage rate the answer to the problem. For him 'too much emphasis was laid upon wastage. Young women will continue to marry and make homes ... unless the proposed reform included a radical alteration in the social structure':

> Nor should the restlessness which springs primarily from this urge be wrongly interpreted so that it appears under many guises on the list of causes of wastage —
>
> 'To return home'
> 'To go overseas'
> 'Dislike of work'
>
> and so on. Any reform which suggests an attack on the 'wastage' factor as a solution to the problem is neither physiologically nor psychologically sound.[11]

During the Australian Nursing Congress held in May 1955 a debate was held on the question of training nurses in universities. The debate brought out the link between the problems of recruitment and the work of nurses. It was argued by Miss F. M. Peterson, the principal of the Nursing Division, Commonwealth Department of Health, that:

> The public perception of nurses' training as a narrowly applied type of education involving hard physical work and a preponderance of routine with little intellectual content or stimulating teaching has caused many parents and vocational guidance officers to think that nursing is not a suitable occupation. In other words, the nursing profession does not offer the same educational opportunities, job satisfaction and professional status as other professions.[12]

In response, a sister tutor from the Royal Adelaide Hospital quoted from the *Nuffield Report*:

> Technical skill is now an essential part of Nursing, yet to insist that it is the basis is to destroy the original meaning of the word and turn the nurse into a medical technician

and asked:

> Is not the basic skill to be learnt at the patients' bedside? Are not those who are to be the leaders in our profession to have received their initial experience in hospital training schools, in constant contact with human beings?[13]

The problem of recruitment was seen to be directly related to the nature of nurses' training and work.

Throughout the fifties and sixties the Hospital and Charities Commission continued to be concerned at the shortage of trained nurses, especially in the country hospitals. The wastage rate was raised again in 1966 when a survey was taken of the wastage of trainee nurses. Over a three year period a wastage rate of 31 per cent was recorded, with half the total loss occurring in the first year of training and with a significantly greater loss from country hospitals. It was also found that the loss decreased as the educational standard at intake increased. This explained the high attrition rate for country hospitals since their entry standards were much lower than for city hospitals. In 1967 the decision was taken to raise the entry standard from intermediate (level 10) to leaving certificate (level 11), even though there was still a shortage of trained nurses.[14]

But the persistent shortage of trained nurses was due to a combination of contradictory phenomena whereby in the 1960s nursing was still associated in the public mind with domestic tasks in hospitals, even though the occupation demanded of the nurses high levels of training and specialisation. The chronic shortage of nurses was in no small measure due to the failure of nurses themselves to resolve the question of what was their job. What were non-nursing duties and what were the duties of nursing aides and registered nurses? For parents and young people interested in nursing, the distinctions between those people who called themselves 'nurses' were far from clear. In practice it would seem that the demarcation lines were very blurred indeed and varied significantly from one institution to another.

As emphasised above, there was a limit to the number of

well educated young women who would persist with all the routine, non-skilled tasks associated with nursing. There were also limits to what hospitals and governments were prepared to pay trained nurses who were seen to be carrying out duties considered more suited to lower paid staff. This made it difficult for nurses to obtain higher salaries, which could attract younger women and entice older women back into the profession. In 1970, the Report of the Hospital and Charities Commission noted that:

> There is a growing need to examine the use of nursing staff in health services to ensure that we are making the best use of people in this, the largest group of trained people engaged in the hospital field. The community has expressed its appreciation of nursing skills but has often obliged these highly trained nurses to waste their skill and engage in non-nursing duties which should not be required of them.[15]

The problem which was intimately linked with recruitment, was to define the work of trained nurses as well as the type of training trainees underwent. This will be taken up in chapter 6 where the training of nurses in the fifties and sixties will be looked at in detail.

The Problem of Nursing Aides

LINKED with the shortage of nurses in this period was the employment of nursing aides, who were taken on initially to assist nurses by taking over some of their responsibilities (see chapter 3). By 1970, nearly 20 years after the official recognition of nursing aides in Victoria, 23 per cent of the nursing workforce in public hospitals was made up of nursing aides (this includes student nursing aides) and student nurses.[16] We have seen how war time exigencies and the shortages of the immediate post-war years gave official recognition to nursing aides, thus creating a second tier of nurses whose work and responsibilities were similar to those of student nurses in their first year of training.

Similarly, the one year training program for nursing aides had many features in common with the trainee nurses' program. It included ward and personal hygiene, care of hospital equipment, care of patients' effects, bed-making, sponging, prevention of bed sores, feeding, bedpan techniques, hot water bags and care of pathological specimens. However it also included urine testing, sterilisation, temperatures, poultices, bandaging and nutrition.[17] Nursing aides were quite clearly expected to perform many basic nursing duties, although in practice these varied between hospitals in direct proportion to the amount of hostility which they engendered from particular matrons and trained nurses and/or the availability of trained staff. While the acceptance of nursing aides was never assured, and in many hospitals, it would seem, attempts were made to confine them to tasks of a more simple, domestic nature, practical day-to-day problems associated with the shortage of trained nurses intervened. So while nursing aides were not allowed to perform simple dressing or to give medications in a general hospital ward, they did both in geriatric institutions because of the shortage of registered nurses. A similar phenomenon occurred with nurses and doctors. Nurses would not perform certain technical procedures during the day when resident medical officers were available (unless specially trained or supervised), but at night the same procedures were performed by the registered nurse who happened to be in the ward.[18]

Opposition to nursing aides was so strong from RVCN council members that they were not admitted to the RVCN until 1974. Even when a definite attempt was made in 1961 to admit them as associate members (similar to student members), this failed at the council level. In 1961 the RVCN membership committee noted that there were 2 304 nursing aides registered with the Victorian Nursing Council as well as 1 494 mothercraft nurses. Over the years members of both groups had indicated an interest in joining the RVCN, although many already belonged to the HEF. The RVCN membership committee recommended that associate membership be offered to these nurses and that they have direct representation on the RVCN Council. It was suggested that they be organised into groups known as the nursing aide division and the mothercraft nurses division and that they be helped in the administration and organisation of these groups, which would include both the educational and economic aspects of their interests and concerns. Nothing resulted from this initiative.[19]

The continuing hostility was symptomatic of the problem of defining the work of nurses referred to previously. The expansion of the scope of nursing in the post-war period had forced the creation of this second tier of less qualified nurses but there was no inclination on the part of hospital managements or governments to staff hospitals with fully trained nurses to cover all nursing duties, even if there had been sufficient young women available to make this possible.

But for many trained nurses and matrons nursing aides were dilutees and were seen as a threat to all that they had fought for over the years. They were women with only one year of training doing nurses' work. If they were allowed to take over the basic caring aspects of nursing, trained nurses would become nothing more than technicians. They were not seen as freeing trained nurses to perform these technical duties as well as educational and administrative functions, but as less qualified people doing nurses' work for less pay. No other aspect of nursing more readily highlighted the ongoing problem of what constituted nurses' work than the role of nursing aides. They brought into sharp focus the contradiction between the quest for professional status and the desire to retain those aspects of nursing directly related to patient care within the work pattern of trained nurses. For nursing leaders those aspects were as essential to the professional training of nurses as the more technical and administrative tasks. The public and governments, however, did not see it this way. They were seen as domestic duties which could be performed by lower paid staff, and which were not associated with the public's perception of the work of a profession. Besides, they were the very same tasks performed for sick persons in their own homes by unqualified relatives and friends (where, of course, much of the care of the sick was carried out). The public might well ask why these tasks should be done by 'highly paid' professionals when carried out in a hospital.

In 1953 Dr John Lindell envisaged the nurse of the future as undertaking only 30 per cent of her 'present duties, the higher skills of nursing':

> she will learn how to supervise her assistants ... she will learn enough of management to enable her to run a ward efficiently and with economy ... She will have secured not

only her status, but her future, for she will occupy a key position in the nursing service, acting as colleague and assistant to the doctor at the same time as she directs and supervises her team of assistants.

He urged the trained nurse not to cling 'to her traditional right to perform unskilled jobs' for 'the status or professional standing of any person is not given to her own assessment, but according to the value which the community places upon her prowess; upon her worth to the people'.[20] The scenario which Dr Lindell outlined was exactly what many nurses in the sixties and seventies feared if they gave up the 'unskilled' tasks. They would not only become simply technicians, but would also be acting largely as supervisors of nursing aides and students. Nurses in Australia had watched the lowering of standards of bedside nursing in many hospitals in England which resulted from a deliberate policy that most of this care be provided by enrolled nurses with registered nurses acting largely as supervisors. This perpetuated the problems of the earlier period when most of the care was given by nursing students with registered nurses acting mainly as supervisors. Vocal Victorian nurses did not want this to continue, or even to become more of a problem by having nearly all the care provided by nursing students *and* nursing aides.[21]

Changes in Medical Practice

IN the early 1950s some leading nurses and members of the medical profession were well aware of the changes occurring in medical practice and nursing which would bring radical changes in health care over the next 20 years. The Second World War focused considerably more attention on medical research than would have been the case in more peaceful times, although it would be wrong to assume that all the new developments resulted from the demands of war. Many were well underway in the 1930s. The war speeded up their widespread application on the civilian front in the immediate post-war years. In the late thirties sulphonamides had brought a whole new approach to the treatment of disease. Instead of killing bacteria, which had been the aim of most treatments, these drugs were found to combine with and render unusable substances necessary to keep bacteria alive. They were very useful against pathogenic bacteria particularly the cocci group, and were most effective against erysipelas, peritonitis, mastoid infections, pneumonia and meningitis. The work of Sir Howard Florey meant that penicillin followed closely on the development of sulphonamides, though its genesis could be traced back to the work of Pasteur and Joubert in the 1870s and Dr Alexander Fleming in the 1920s. During the war strenuous efforts were made to produce it in large quantities, and this was finally possible in 1946. Penicillin was safer than the sulphonamides.[22] After sulphonamides and penicillin came a flood of various antibiotics and other specific drugs within a relatively brief period of time. Hormones, steroids and new vaccines followed. Therapeutics came into its own as a significant area of medical practice. Neuroleptic drugs, developed for use in mental disorders, were soon in widespread use.

Radiology, biochemistry, nuclear medicine, endocrinology, microbiology and electronics departments were by now considered essential for the functioning of a large hospital. One figure, often quoted at the time, highlighted the scope of change in one area. In 1948 in one Melbourne hospital 999 intravenous sets were issued from surgical supplies. In 1953 the figure was 4 400.[23] Major operations were now undertaken on the brain, the heart and the lungs. This went with improved methods of anaesthesia and asepsis and with advances in x-ray technology and interpretation.[24] In the thirties typhoid fever, scarlet fever, whooping cough, tetanus, diphtheria, pneumonia and tuberculosis claimed many lives. By the early fifties these diseases were well under control as a result of immunisation programs and the use of antibiotics. More attention was given to after-care, including mental and physical rehabilitation. Chronic diseases became of more interest to medical researchers. The extended life pattern which accompanied the advances in medical practice, as well as the improvements in public health services and general nutrition, focused attention on geriatric problems.

Increasingly a patient's survival was dependent on the proper application of a particular treatment, rather than on building up her or his strength over a long period of time, and relying on her or his inherent vitality to ensure survival. While this shortened the period of time spent in hospital, it did not lessen the work load on nurses. It led to wards full of acutely sick people needing elaborate treatments which required a high degree of skill on the part of staff. Nor did other advances in technology, proficient diagnosis, nutrition and early ambulation in any way reduce the demands on nurses. Indeed, the nursing load was considerably increased.[25] Antibiotics for example required trained nurses to supervise the preparation of drugs and the use of syringes, especially as trainees were usually involved in this work in the early days of their training. Moreover, constant observation of patients was necessary in case of possible side effects and incompatibilities related to medication.

The increasing knowledge of the importance of diet for recovery from illness (not simply 'good food' as in the thirties), required nurses to supervise the preparation of specific meals for patients. Early ambulation required considerable nursing skills to gain the patient's confidence, and to judge when he or she was attempting too much in hospitals which were not built to cope with ready patient access of patients to toilet and shower facilities.[26]

In 1955 Miss F. M. Petersen from the Commonwealth Health Department summed up these changes in nurses' work:

> Almost overnight we expect our nurses to cast aside poultices and foment bowls and to adapt themselves to highly technical nursing procedures — to be responsible, for instance, for the administration of powerful and dangerous antibiotics, without any knowledge of the symptoms and dangerous complications that can and do arise ... Let us briefly compare present day post operative treatment against that of the pre-specialist era. The latter consisted chiefly of basic nursing care, prolonged rest for the patient, sutures removed by the doctor on a certain day and perhaps foments for an infected wound. Today our nurses must be equipped to nurse patients severely shocked by extensive operation, to be responsible for intravenous therapy, to operate a Wangensteen's suction, to administer antibiotics.[27]

And this was only the beginning. Many more changes were to sweep through hospitals and health care over the next 20 years, which exacerbated the problem of defining the role of nurses.

A sociologist, Dr Jean Martin, saw the situation very clearly in 1961:

> ... the nurse well knows about the unity of the individual, the interdependence of *all* the individual's needs. But at the same time, specialisation is being forced upon her; her professional equipment is becoming more specialised and her contacts with patients are becoming more fragmented, shorter in duration, more in the nature of isolated technical services. She has less, not more, opportunity to react to the patient as a whole person.[28]

Changes in Health Care and the Work of Nurses

AS noted earlier, the late 1960s and early 1970s was a period of intense political, social, cultural and intellectual ferment associated mainly with student unrest and the Vietnam War. Changes in the public's expectations of the health system and health workers had been occurring since the Second World War, but by the early seventies these changing social demands were much more readily identifiable. Consistent with new expectations in areas such as education and with the emergence of ethnic and feminist pressure groups, people demanded full health care as a right and not a privilege. Consumers were now interested in participating in the planning of health services so that discrimination based on wealth, gender, ethnicity, age and disability could be removed.

These demands went with very different problems in the approach to health care. The generally high standard of living during the period of the long boom, together with increasing urbanisation and rapid advances in medical practice, had dramatically changed the entire health care scene. In summarising the changes since the war, Ruth White noted in 1972 that:

> No longer are infectious diseases a major source of morbidity but on the other hand, attempted suicide, the increasing evidence of degenerative ailments, trauma through traffic accidents, mental illness, and 'low-level wellness' require prolonged periods of treatment, advice and care.[29]

The increases in alcoholism, smoking, drug abuse, child abuse, and suicide rates could have been added. These new problems demanded a much more personal approach to health care. At the same time the demand for specialists with different skills and expertise to provide complete health care was increasing. Many more people were suffering from psychiatric and psychological problems, and groups with specific health needs required attention. These included:

> young children with congenital and other handicaps, youth whose needs predominantly were conditioned by self destructive behaviour and alternate life-styles; women of child bearing age and men in the workforce with stress-related problems; the aged with problems of chronic illness or adaptation; ethnic and indigenous groups having difficulty coping with the hazards and remoteness of their social, economic and physical environments; the socially incompetent families requiring long-term care.[30]

The new emphasis on health care highlighted the changes in terminology which came with the broadening of health and medical problems and increasing specialisation. There was now a clear distinction between medical care and health care. While medical care was associated with illness and disability, health care was concerned with total health and illness services (diagnosis, prescription, treatment of problems, health education and maintenance, prevention and restorative services).[31] This shift towards total health care with an institutional base represented a fundamental change. In the 1930s most of the health care was undertaken in the home. Those areas of care which in the 1970s required professional expertise, (for example psychiatric care, counselling and nutrition) were often performed by relatives and friends away from institutional care, albeit with the aid of private nurse if the family could afford it.

The net results of these developments were two-fold: increasing criticism of the health care system in Victoria in the late sixties and early seventies, and the accentuation of the problem which had been apparent for at least a decade — what was the role of nurses as a result of these changes? This revolution in health care firmly established the work of the nurses within institutions. In 1975 81.5 per cent of nurses employed in nursing were working in hospitals and geriatric homes. Included in the remaining 18.5 per cent were 4.5 per cent in community and public health (including infant welfare nurses), 2.9 per cent in doctor/dental clinics, 2.3 in district nursing, 1.8 per cent in nursing education and 1.2 per cent in occupational health.[32]

As medical care became more specialised and involved the use of technology and equipment which in itself was extremely expensive to purchase and maintain, institutions grew in size. Hospitals in the early 1950s were designed with 3–400 square feet per bed for all services. By the early 1970s this figure was 1 100–1 200 square feet.[33] The role of the nurse became more diverse. Doctors delegated many of their tasks in the wards to nurses, although still maintained their role as directors of medical care. At the same time, nurses themselves were moving into specialist areas where they were taking responsibility for decisions without direction from doctors. They were assuming a role which was more in accordance with the standards established by male professionals, and which lay outside the caring, nurturing functions of nurses in the wards. (This is not to suggest that these specialist nurses abrogated their caring functions in their specialist work.)

In a study carried out in the early 1970s a list of new activities performed by trained nurses was developed. They were divided under five headings:

1. **Preventive care** — immunisation, vaccination, case finding, screening and assessment, antenatal and post-natal classes, assessment of health status of the community, teaching, advising, counselling, health campaigns.
2. **First contact** — observation and measurement, screening, history taking, assessment, physical examination, interpretation of physical signs and symptoms, interviewing, diagnosis, referral, emergency treatment.
3. **Follow up** — management of minor illness — medical and surgical, identification of problems, modification of treatment, referral, counselling, advising, supporting.
4. **Treatment** — collection of specimens, venepuncture, cervical smears, wound swabs and throat swabs, measurement and interpretation of results in some tests, inhalation therapy,

fitting apparatus and appliances, dressings, immunisation and vaccination, ECG, exercises, occupational therapy supervision.

5. **Co-ordination** — work of health team members, services and treatments ordered.[34]

These tasks were not taken on overnight, but had been gradually assumed over 20 years. However, the level of knowledge and sophistication required of nurses was now much higher.

While the above list is comprehensive it does not indicate the real increase in the measure of responsibility given to the trained nurses because the tasks were performed across a wide range of conditions from minor medical and surgical to emergency situations. The degree of responsibility given also varied between hospitals and doctors. Most of the tasks had previously been performed by doctors, and some by relatives and friends of the patients. That doctors were unable to cope with the ever-increasing demand for health care was used by the medical profession to explain this change in nurses' work. Nurses themselves displayed little reluctance in taking over these tasks, often in situations where they were left with no alternative, and possibly because some felt the tasks were more in line with what people generally regarded as the work of professionals.[35] Their action was quite consistent with other occupations where, in an endeavour to enhance its public image and self-image, an occupation takes on prestigious tasks from a more respected occupation.[36]

Caring Nurse, Specialised Technician, or Both?

HEREIN was the problem. Nurses in leadership positions, especially matrons, who saw the caring, nurturing aspects as central to the work of nurses, looked on askance as so many trained nurses moved into specialist fields. They regarded specialists as little more than technicians. 'Are we to grow as members of a profession or technicians within a trade?', they asked. Sister Mary Paulina in an address to the College of Nursing, Australia, in 1968 considered that:

the technological expertise of the nurse in a coronary care unit must be unrivalled, if she is to accurately interpret the 'beep' of the cardiac monitor and to report the slightest change in a patient's physiological condition. But the entire structure of professional nursing care rests on the ability of the nurse to individualize care.[37]

The Reverend Mother Alphonus, Mother Rectress at St Vincent's Hospital, agreed:

In our days of training, the nursing team was a relatively small one, and we were happy to follow simple instructions of the medical officer and the sister-in-charge. There was a firm basic foundation. We knew our patients, the turnover was slower, there were fewer tensions, and no demands for psychiatrists.

Nursing tends nowadays to be regarded, by many, merely as a science. If a girl has a good basic education, she can, in a technical abstract way, learn practically all that is required to pass examinations. But our concept of nursing is as an art, that combines various skills, which, like most skills require practice. Our art of nursing also needs that indefinable quality of sympathy, which flourishes in an atmosphere where kindness, forbearance, and human understanding are found.[38]

For many trained nurses the caring side of nursing *was* the professional side. It was an essentially feminine approach in a world dominated by male ethics and it required just as much 'professional' expertise as any other profession. However, it was expertise which was gained largely through practical experience in a similar manner to teaching. Both professions dealt with the problems of individuals at a close, personal level, and often over a period of time. Every patient or pupil was different, every situation in a hospital or a classroom was different. There was no book which could be referred to to answer the question 'What do I do in this situation?' There were, of course, certain basic procedures to be followed, but the variety afforded by the human condition made the 'scientific', 'technical', or 'rational' approach to a patient quite irrelevant. For nurses like Sister Paulina and the Reverend Mother Alphonus nursing was very much about building relationships and rapport with patients through sympathy and understanding. They would have agreed with the German philosopher, Edith Stein, that the character traits required of nurse were germane to women:

> To nurse and shield, to help grow, is woman's natural motherly gift and skill ... Her nature tends more towards people than towards things — toward the concrete than towards the abstract, always towards the living, the personal and the whole ... It is her warmth of heart, her ability to devote herself to a cause, her natural patience, which make her able to endure, to partake in other people's lives and interests, to support and give strength to others.[39]

Nevertheless, while the preservation of the caring side of nursing was of real concern for many nurses, the actual practice in hospital wards left very little time for the nurse to pursue this caring role. Most wards in the early 1970s were organised on an efficiency basis whereby one nurse would give all the medications, another all the dressings, another all the treatments, etc., so that no one nurse was responsible for the complete care of a patient. This task-centred type of care defeated the all-round, patient-care approach.

Nurses looked towards the medical profession which was dominated by the male ethos and had little sympathy with this holistic, caring ideal. Medicine emphasised careerism by way of experience, plus credentials, and the latter became increasingly important in the 1950s and 1960s. And herein lay another dilemma. It was the doctors who were largely instrumental in delegating work to trained nurses and who required them to be increasingly efficient, informed and overworked. Yet, as Miss Mary Evans, Director of Nursing for the Royal District Nursing Service and Vice President of the RVCN pointed out in 1968, these were the same people who wanted nurses 'to remain unenlightened and consequently overly dependent upon the medical profession'. She believed professional nurses should free themselves from the handmaiden image:

> Whilst the nurse still performs technical tasks as required by the medical profession for the comfort and benefit of the patient, she can no longer be only a pair of hands and feet, if she is to provide the nursing service considered essential by the nursing profession itself for the well-being of patients today. Although the nurse must depend on the doctors for

information about medical diagnoses and the plan of medical care, she is also responsible for making her own assessment of the patient's nursing needs and how to meet these needs in terms of providing comfort and alleviation of suffering.[40]

The Work of Hospital Nurses in the 1970s

B UT what of the actual work and work situation of most nurses in the early 1970s? How did it compare with the 1930s? Had 40 years made any fundamental difference to the nurses' work? We have seen how hospitals became more specialised and how many routine medical tasks were delegated to the nurses. But apart from those nurses who gained expertise in specialised areas, for example, coronary care, neurosurgery, renal dialysis, thoracic and cardiac surgery, what occurred was a quantitative increase in the amount of work performed, and this within the reduced working hours. What Miss Jane Muntz said in 1954 still applied in the early 1970s:

> The truth is that we are consciously keeping our eyes averted from the fact that we increase the strain on the one hand by expecting the nurse to carry out effectively highly technical procedures, sometimes beyond the scope of her training and, on the other hand, expect the product of the same training to be satisfied with the job of carrying out tasks which could be successfully and happily done by personnel trained for less skilled but equally essential procedures.[41]

While it is very difficult to make generalisations about the nurses' work because of the significant variations between hospitals, certain fundamental characteristics of the work and the work situation remained similar to the 1930s. An overtly hierarchical structure still existed. Orders came down from above', whether from nursing superintendents (matrons) or physicians and surgeons. The authoritarianism of the regime described in chapter 2 had probably been modified in most hospitals by the 1970s. However, the socialisation process during and after training which ensured unquestioning obedience and discouraged nurses from participating in decision-making, was still part of this top down management structure, but by the late sixties it was under increasing challenge from the nurses and other members of the health care team.

The late 1960s and early 1970s was a period of great student unrest in North America, Europe and Australia with students everywhere demanding more say in the running of their colleges and universities. But little had changed in hospital training schools. Task-orientated nursing practice was still emphasised as it had been in the 1930s. It concentrated on the physical and technical aspects of care. Students were asked to make beds, administer medications, do dressings, attend to the ventilation and the lights and the ringing bells. This production line concept of care led to boredom, a loss of initiative and a diminished awareness of the individual patient's needs. 'The nurse does not care for a group of patients as individuals, but she performs the repetitive tasks that she has been assigned so that patients are seen in terms of a series of functions'.[42]

In 1970, however, the general atmosphere in the community was much more conducive to student nurses speaking out against the system:

> Our lack of dignity is what we are complaining about. If we are regarded as being capable of looking after people, why aren't we regarded as being capable of looking after ourselves? We are treated like somebody in an institution.

Students complained of invasions of personal privacy, archaic military-type discipline and insults. All this sounded very much like conditions forty years previously.[43]

Three nurses, one a ward sister, another a recently qualified nurse and the other a nursing aide, described what it was like working in a hospital ward in the 1970s. The *ward sister* describes a typical day:

> Started work at 7 am. I daren't be late. The night staff are tired so they must get off on time. I check the report of the night nurses and note changes in drugs, and fill out patient condition lists. Next are the orders for special diets for the day, arranging tests and X-rays. In order to be able to do this I have to keep locked in my head knowledge of a 100 odd blood tests, 20 types of X-rays and procedures in the nuclear medicine department. By this time all my day staff have arrived. If any are away I have to find a replacement. My staff includes sisters, third year and second year nurses,

nursing aides and ward helpers. Then the doctor appears. I tell him which patients need attention, others who have had a bad night. I frequently have to jog his memory. In these situations I have to know a lot about drugs — the doses, and for what period they are likely to be prescribed and to recognise adverse side effects. Doctors need to be pulled into line; their demands are excessive. Some are not courteous and this upsets me. Then there are the changes to be carried as a result of the doctor's visit, a break for coffee, and then an hours meeting with doctors who make all the decisions on the patient's treatment. Phones constantly ringing and staff and patients asking questions. I rarely sit down. I answer the phone for relatives of seriously ill patients — upsetting and exhausting. Lunch takes two hours — feeding staff and patients. I help in the feeding. This is a social occasion. The afternoon pace is slower — a report on each patient, doctors looking for X-rays, nurses asking for checks on injections. Time to tell the student nurses what to do and answer their questions. In between all this I see to the supplies of drugs, linen and soap. Finish at 3.30 pm.[44]

The newly *registered nurse* related her day:

I live in a nurses' home. Up at 6.30 am for a 7.30 start. I'm working in a 30 bed surgical ward. With a junior nurse I look after half the patients. First job is to read the nursing notes on all the patients. Then consult the order book — who has to have specimens collected, operated on, stitches out or who is going home or being transferred. Check 4 patients being fed intravenously. Check a road accident victim who is still unconscious. I give out the trays for breakfast. I help 10 patients to sit up. Three have to have food vitamised. It's like sitting on a hot seat. I'm thinking about everything else I should be doing or should have done 10 minutes ago. Whisk the breakfast trays away. The kitchen maids are yelling to us to hurry up. Today I've got three two-hourly, three four-hourly, one one-hourly and two half-hourly charts to keep — blood pressure, pulse, temperature and breathing of 9 patients, all within a few minutes of each other. My accident victim is still unconscious. Old Mr Perkins wants to sit out on a toilet chair, urgently. I don't make it in time. He bursts out crying. It is distressing for us both. I've not had time to pass the bottles and pans around after breakfast. Now they'll be calling for them all morning. Now 4 patients to prepare for the theatre. You are expected to know when a patient is worried. But what can you do about it when you haven't the time? I feel depressed. I feel I am not doing what a nurse should really be doing. I scuttle round giving out pills. I then do the rounds with the sister, giving injections. My junior nurse is too busy to help with the beds so I have to make them all, plus 4 baths. I remove all the rubbish. I can see if I can do 5 mouth washes in 5 minutes. Six patients need dressings. Lunch — 10 patients to get back in bed — then the same routine as for breakfast. Doctors have been issuing orders. I've had to wheel one patient to another floor, one has gone home, another in and 4 collected from the theatre. I gallop through lunch in 10 minutes, and spend the rest of the hour resting in my room. Back throwing out dead flowers, washing hair, oiling feet, checking the order book and the work of the junior nurse. 4.15 pm — time to leave.[45]

The *nursing aide* wrote:

6.55 am I'm on in a new ward. 7.05 reading the report. No other staff as yet. Night staff are ready to go off. I find a copy of the roster. Everybody has arrived for duty — me, just me! Well, I start breakfast. Who has what? Who is on a diet? Who is a diabetic? Who are feeds? I managed. 8.00 Ward Sister comes on duty. 9.00 am Another nurse arrives — two of us for 28 patients. We find most in wet and soiled beds. 8.15 — 10.00 we heave, and I mean heave, our patients out of bed on to a toilet chair; into the toilet, strip the bed; shower, dry and dress; clean teeth, comb hair; carry out dressings. 10.00 morning tea and back to tidying bathroom, emptying skips, etc. Now bed making until 11.30, then lunch. Sister serves out the meals, nurses clean up the dishes, kitchen maid watches. Will not touch dishes until they are stacked and clear of food. Wipe table tops, wash plastic feeders. 12.00 lunch. 1.00 make sure the toilets are clean and dry before the cleaners will clean them! Wash locker tops, overhead tables, ends of beds. Wash socks, dressing gowns, dresses, sheepskins. 2.00 Clean pan room and everything in it. 2.15 Patients now back in bed, are washed and have their backs rubbed. 3.00 Help prepare teas and go home.[46]

The Crisis in Health Care

BY the late 1960s it was common to hear talk of the 'crisis' in health care. This 'crisis' continued throughout the 1970s. The many government inquiries into the health care industry, including nursing, reflected this emergency. Inquiries were used by politicians to dampen public discontent and/or to put off making decisions, especially ones which would increase expenditure. In regard to nursing, there existed a general mystification in politics which caused people to wonder why nurses who in the past had been such pillars of the status quo, should have become so militant. As the seventies rolled into the eighties this level of militancy increased.

There were a number of factors which came together in the late sixties and seventies which provoked this militancy and began the long process of shedding the public view of nurses as 'handmaidens'. After all, handmaidens did not take part in political action; they did not demonstrate and march through the streets or go on strike as nurses did in the 1970s and 1980s.

The changes in medical practice and health care outlined in this chapter resulted in heightened stress and increased demands being made upon the nurses. Changes in technology meant that nurses, many with minimum academic qualifications, had to grasp concepts and knowledge for which they were not prepared. Not only was the use of this technology out of their control, but they were handed down the new tasks by the medical profession without consultation, and the power structures within hospitals meant that they could not reject them even if they had wished to do so.

The generally decreasing length of patient stay in hospitals took away the chance to learn about people, to discover their problems, to meet their relatives and to help them in a very personal way. It took away much of the caring side of nursing which, for many nurses, was why they were there in the first place. Nurses were expected to adjust to new situations and new traumas with little knowledge or understanding of the behavioural sciences, which had become essential for nursing practice and health care work in general.

By the early 1970s the need for nurses to be aware of the implications of nursing people from different cultural backgrounds was also being recognised. But nurses had been brought up in a profession which had very strong anglo-saxon roots. They had not been trained to cope with this situation. Now they were faced with nursing people whom they and their forebears had been taught were inferior to British stock.

Added to this were the implications of the women's liberation movement which was flourishing in the 1970s. While slow to permeate nursing, there was nevertheless sufficient influence to undermine the socialisation process of the hospital regime. Indeed, the hospital was a classic case of male institutional domination. The one area which had been traditionally the domain of women, the director/superintendent (matron) of nursing, was threatened by new career management structures in hospitals which were essentially male preserves.

All these factors contributed to the discontent of nurses in the 1960s and the 1970s. For nursing leaders raising the status of the profession was still the key to solving many of the manifestations of this crisis. While they recognised that improving salaries and conditions would help in this endeavour, they sought above all else higher educational qualifications, including some in other disciplines such as science, commerce, health and business administration. Many nursing leaders believed this could only be achieved by taking the basic training of nurses out of hospitals and by offering a greatly extended range of post-basic training courses to enable trained nurses to participate effectively in bringing about changes which were needed in the practice and administration of the health services.

Endnotes

[1] Tony Dingle, *The Victorians. Settling*, Fairfax, Syme, Weldon, Sydney, 1984, p. 221.
[2] Susan Priestley, *The Victorians. Making Their Mark*, Fairfax, Syme, Weldon, Sydney, 1984, p. 300.
[3] Dingle, op. cit., p. 225.
[4] ibid., p. 226.
[5] ibid., p. 240.
[6] VPP, vol. 2, 1951–2, report of the Hospitals and Charities Commission, 1952, pp. 16–17; ibid., 1962–3, report ..., 1961–2, pp. 25–6, 36; ibid., 1971–2, report ..., 1970–1, pp. 32, 38–9.
[7] VPP, vol. 2, 1951–2, report of the Hospitals and Charities Commission, 1951, p. 17; VPP, vol. 2, 1961–2, report ... 1960–1, p. 36.

8 For example see Jacqueline Templeton, *Prince Henry's. The Evolution of a Melbourne Hospital 1869–1969*, Robertson and Mullens, Melbourne, 1969, p. 186.

9 *VPP*, vol. 2, 1960–1, report of the Hospitals and Charities Commission, 1959–60, p. 25; John Lindell, 'Nursing, a Profession' in *UNA*, October 1953, pp. 295–305.

10 *VPP*, vol. 2, 1953, report of the Hospitals and Charities Commission, 1952–3, p. 9.

11 Lindell, op. cit., p. 297–8.

12 *UNA*, October 1955, pp. 302–3.

13 ibid., p. 303.

14 *VPP*, vol. 2, 1966–7, report of the Hospitals and Charities Commission, 1965–6, pp. 30–3.

15 ibid., 1970–1, report ..., 1969–70, p. 16.

16 ibid., pp. 18–19.

17 'The Training of Nursing Assistants', AUNA, Victorian branch, 1950. Box 148, UM archives.

18 Pat Slater to Marjorie Connor, 2 November 1989.

19 RVCN minutes, 1 August, 29 August 1961, 22 March 1962.

20 Lindell, op. cit., pp. 301–2.

21 Pat Slater to Marjorie Connor, 2 November 1989.

22 R. H. Shryock, *The History of Nursing: an Interpretation of the Social and Medical Factors Involved*, 1959, pp. 361–5.

23 G. N. Burbidge, 'Nursing Care and Nursing Education', Oration, NSW College of Nursing, 24 August 1954, p. 17. Burbidge papers.

24 Professor H. N. Robson, 'The Need for a Revolution in the Nursing Profession', in *UNA*, September 1954, p. 273.

25 F. M. Petersen, 'Scientific Progress and the Nurse', in *UNA*, January 1955, p. 19.

26 G. N. Burbidge, 'Trends in Nursing', in *UNA*, May 1954, pp. 131–5.

27 Petersen, op. cit., p. 20.

28 Jean I. Martin, 'Social Influences on the Nursing Profession', in *UNA*, September 1961, p. 280.

29 Ruth White, *The Role of the Nurse in Australia*, Tertiary Education Research Centre, University of New South Wales, 1972, p. 16.

30 Shirley Donaghue, *Goals in Nursing Practice. Trends within the Health Field and their Implications for Nursing Practice*, RANF, Melbourne, 1977.

31 ibid., p. 19.

32 *Facts*, Victorian Nursing Council, Melbourne, 1976.

33 *Nurse Education and Training, Report of the Committee of Inquiry into Nurse Education and Training to the Tertiary Education Committee* (Sax Report), Canberra, 1978, p. 73.

34 F. M. Katz, K. Mathews, T. Pyne, R. H. White, *Stepping Out. Nurses in their New Roles*, New South Wales University Press, Sydney, 1976, ch. 7.

35 ibid., p. 11.

36 Celia Davies, (ed.), *Rewriting Nursing History*, Croom Helm, London, 1980, p. 27.

37 Sister Mary Paulina, 'The Heart of Nursing', in *UNA*, June 1968, p. 178.

38 Rev. Mother Alphonus, 'Our Responsibility in Preserving the Essence of Nursing', in *UNA*, June 1965, pp. 182–3.

[39] Quoted in *UNA*, September 1959, p. 265.
[40] Mary Evans, 'Cooperation between Medical and Associated Professions in Health Care', in *UNA*, May 1968, p. 141.
[41] Jane Muntz, 'Nursing — Professional Responsibility', in *UNA*, November 1954, p. 342.
[42] *Sax Report*, op. cit., p. 44.
[43] *Gippsland Times*, 30 April 1970.
[44] Jean Munro, 'Eight Hours', in *Herald*, 13 May 1974.
[45] Mamie Smith, 'It's a Mad, Mad, Mad, Mad Whirl', in *UNA*, July/August, 1970, pp. 20–1.
[46] T. Eberius, 'A Day in the Life of a Nursing Aide', in *Australian Nurses' Journal*, August 1979, p. 14.

5

Integration and the RANF

I N 1951 when the RVCN celebrated the fiftieth anniversary of the founding of the organisation, its leading members could look back with some pride on its achievements. Compared with the problems faced by nursing organisations in other States and other countries, the RVCN's main achievement, apart from State registration and the provision for post-graduate nursing education, was the maintenance of a unified profession. Even though its membership figures left much to be desired, the RVCN was the undisputed leader of nurses in Victoria.

Executive officers of the RVCN had also succeeded in channelling what they regarded as non-professional issues (salaries and conditions) through the Employees Association, ostensibly leaving the RVCN to devote itself to professional matters. At the time this seemed a neat and tidy arrangement which the RVCN leadership also successfully applied to the RANF in the late 1950s, where there were to be separate State branches to be known as the ANF, Employees Sections (ANFES). The unity and strength of the nurses' organisation in Victoria contrasted with the divisions in New South Wales and Queensland and the relatively weak organisations in other states. While this situation continued the RVCN was able to steer the RANF along lines which maintained the dichotomy between the economic and professional issues at the federal level. However, by the late 1950s the inherent weakness of this dichotomy both in practical and philosophical terms was becoming apparent. Nursing leaders in the other States began to express their misgivings and to raise the question of establishing a genuinely national united nurses' organisation. This was not finally achieved until 1989.

In this chapter the struggle for national unity will be looked at up to the establishment of the RANF as a unified national organisation in 1970. It was a struggle in which the RVCN was a main player and which finally led to its merger with the RANF, Victorian Branch, in 1975.

The Problem of Two National Organisations

TO all intents and purposes a national nurses' organisation would seem to have had little attraction for rank and file nurses in the 1950s. Salaries and conditions were decided at the State level except where nurses worked in federal agencies. Conditions varied so much between the States and within hospitals that even State-wide perspectives were difficult to obtain. The post-graduate education centres — the College of Nursing, Australia and the New South Wales College of Nursing — were essentially state based.

The reality was that the two national organisations, the RANF and the ANFES, existed for three main reasons. Firstly, and above all else as far as RVCN leaders were concerned, to ensure there was a national body to represent nurses at the ICN. Secondly, to maintain registration with the Federal Arbitration Court in view of the ongoing challenge from the HEF, and thirdly so that nursing leaders could journey each year to confer and compare notes with their counterparts in other States.

Since 1943 when the Employees Association of the RVCN was formed, this group had been made up of RVCN members who were employees and who looked after the 'economic' interests of nurses in Victoria. In practice many of the more important issues relating to salaries and conditions were discussed on the RVCN council and links between RVCN executive officers and Employees Association personnel were always close.

When the Employees Association and the ANF Employees Section merged in 1960 the latter body took over the former's functions. To meet the requirements of the Federal Arbitration Court, the ANF was also required to enrol individual members.[1] As a result the RVCN undertook to pay one shilling to the ANFES out of its annual subscription of £2 10s for every member of the RVCN who also signed up with the ANFES (sixpence went to the national body, and sixpence to the Victorian branch). The small amounts involved are a clear indication that the ANFES was never considered anything more than an off-shoot of the RVCN and the RANF. The ANFES (VB) and the RVCN office were one and the same thing, with Miss Marjorie Connor, the RVCN executive secretary since 1945, acting for both.[2]

At the national level the RANF and the ANFES had moved closer together in 1959 when the Commonwealth Arbitration Court accepted a revised RANF constitution which provided for the ANFES to be a section of the RANF. However, even before these developments occurred there was considerable dissatisfaction within the RANF's State branches about the dual structure of the national organisation. At the ANFES annual meeting in 1958 branches reported that it would be difficult to maintain separate organisations due to the extra finance and personnel required. Both the Western Australian and South Australian branches indicated that they favoured making moves towards a single national nursing organisation.[3]

By 1961 it had become clear that simply transferring the Victorian situation to the federal sphere was not going to work. Two distinct federal bodies had been created and even though they worked closely together this was seen as confusing to both the public and the nursing profession. The Western Australian delegate to the 1961 ANFES annual meeting pointed out that the RANF had no control over the ANFES, and as a section working under its own constitution the ANFES could act at variance to the RANF. This could lead to an invidious situation. Again, there was strong support for the merger of the two bodies, but this was not easy to achieve, not only because of the problem of employer membership of some RANF branches, but also because the ANFES consisted of individual members as required by the Federal Arbitration Court, whereas the RANF was composed of autonomous organisations. A sub-committee was set up to examine the problem.[4]

The sub-committee reported that in all States except New South Wales where there were no ANFES members, ANFES members were members of an RANF branch with dual member-ship. Queensland operated the two organisations as one and Victoria, South Australia and Western Australia had separate branch committees. The sub-committee concluded that there was no future in this dual organisation, 'ANFES is economically too weak to carry out its purpose of wholly covering its members', for example, preparing a case for an award. The sub-committee recommended that either a modified ANFES constitution be incorporated into the RANF constitution or that the RANF give adequate financial support for the ANFES to carry out its objectives. Unless the ANFES was made a viable organisation in either of these ways, Mr Wild (WA), the convener of the sub-committee pointed out, there would be 'loss of membership to another organisation', and this could have 'grave' consequences.[5]

Much of this discussion hinged around ANFES members who were employed by the Commonwealth. Unless the ANFES could apply for an award on their behalf the HEF would step in to fill the breach. The 1962 ANFES annual meeting referred the question to the RANF Federal Council, supporting the incorpo-ration of the ANFES constitution into the RANF.

Opposition from the RVCN

AFTER the 1962 RANF council meeting it seemed only technical problems would delay the integration of the two organisations. The council had before it not only the recommen-dation of the ANFES annual meeting, but also a report from Miss Sheila Quinn, Director of the ICN Economic Welfare Division, which recommended amalgamation of the RANF and the ANFES. The council unanimously adopted as policy that the integration of the two organisations should proceed.[6]

The 1963 RANF council took integration one step further when it heard a report from an industrial adviser, Mr E. Behm, that the simplest approach to the problem was to disband the RANF, leaving the ANFES to function as the national organisa-tion. He stressed that integration would not endanger affiliation with the ICN, nor would the branches necessarily lose their autonomy. As a result of Mr Behm's report the RANF decided, again unanimously, to give its Economic Welfare Committee power to negotiate with the ANFES for the formation of a national organisation with federal registration. A draft constitution of the new organisation was to be prepared.[7]

It appeared to be 'all over bar the shouting'. A truly national organisation of nurses seemed assured. But RVCN leaders were worried. The thought of their own ANFES branch taking over the RVCN, which was the logical result of the RANF decision, cut across everything they cherished. It became apparent in 1964 that there were still many legal and industrial issues to be resolved before integration could take place. By the time of the RANF council meeting in October it was clear that the efforts of the Economic Welfare Committee to achieve integration had only highlighted the problems, to which no real solutions were offered. It would be another six years before integration was achieved and over ten years before the RVCN went out of existence.

It became obvious that State organisations which were not incorporated bodies under State arbitration law would have some difficulty becoming part of a national body. This was especially so in New South Wales where the New South Wales Nurses Association was registered with the State Arbitration Court for negotiating salaries and conditions, but had no association with the RANF. The New South Wales Australian Trained Nurses Association (ATNA) which was represented on the RANF had never formed a branch of the ANFES nor could it integrate with the ANFES, because of the conditions of its registration as a company in New South Wales. In Victoria the RVCN was also registered as a company and which had to be dissolved under the federal Arbitration Act. There appeared to be no legal problems in Queensland, South Australia, Western Australia and Tasmania.[8]

But the real problem which faced those who favoured integration was the strength of the opposition which had developed in Victoria. Victoria had always been numerically the dominant force in the RANF. It had contributed much to the RANF and had generally steered RANF policies along lines which were acceptable to the RVCN. As the RVCN was wont to do at such times, it consulted either the legal or the medical fraternity. In this case an opinion from legal counsel A. E. Woodward confirmed all the worst fears of RVCN leaders. Counsel concluded that:

> all decisions on changes of Rules must take place within the existing framework of the ANFES. The RVCN can only suggest how its members who are also members of ANFES should vote ... individual members of RVCN will have to decide whether to become or remain members of ANFES and acting as a corporate body they will also have to decide whether to wind up the College and transfer assets to the re-formed Federal body.
>
> If they do they will, on paper, be surrendering all control of their assets and a great deal of their autonomy — unless the Draft Rules are changed.

Woodward noted that the basic choice facing all RANF branches was whether to combine industrial and professional activities in the one organisation or to try to strengthen the ANFES without winding up the existing professional organisations. He doubted whether the full implications of the decisions taken by the RANF had been appreciated.[9] By the time of the 1964 October RANF federal council meeting the RVCN was firmly set on a course opposing integration.

RVCN opposition began with the assumption that economic and professional matters could be and indeed had to be clearly separated in two organisations. This assumption does not appear to have been questioned let alone debated in the RVCN, rather, it had developed over the years largely in response to the fear that if the RVCN was associated with salaries and conditions it would become tainted by trade union matters. For the very conservative and patriotic RVCN leaders trade unions were associated with the Labor Party and militant union tactics and strikes (there was much industrial unrest in the fifties and sixties), the very antithesis of what they believed a professional association should be about. Not only this, the fifties and early sixties were the years of the Cold War when the fear of communism was very real for many people. Communism and trade unions were often seen as synonymous and as a threat to the established order of society.

Apart from this, the RVCN leaders feared that the RVCN would lose much of its autonomy to a federal organisation. They could not see much to gain from national unity which they had not already achieved or could achieve with a strong RVCN in Victoria. They had built up an organisation which, although troubled with the occasional sorties of the HEF, enjoyed strong support from Victorian nurses, was recognised by official bodies and had acquired many assets. But there were other problems which provoked their concern. For example, if there was only one organisation less funds might be available to the State because it would be necessary to increase capitation fees but to limit the amount which nurses could be charged for membership. It was also feared that the energies of the limited number of staff that could be employed would be expended on industrial matters which were very time consuming, to the detriment of educational and professional activities. This was part of a general concern that establishing one professional organisation would result in the intrusion of industrial issues and tactics into the educational arena.[10] Some ANFES branches admitted nursing aides. Under a single organisation they would be associated with trained nurses, and as they would probably have full voting rights, they might even overshadow the trained nurses in the organisation. Moreover, many trained nurses who were members of the RVCN would no longer be eligible to join because of the Federal Arbitration Court rules. This would include nurses who were employers, self-employed private nurses and non-practising nurses.

When the RANF Federal Council met at Centaur House in Brisbane from 19 to 22 October 1964, it became obvious after a debate lasting over two days that Victoria was completely opposed to integration. One of the two Victorian delegates, Miss Edith Hughes-Jones (RVCN president) made it clear that she regarded integration as a threat to the development of nursing as a profession:

> I think it is the wish of every one of us to find the very best way in which nurses can be served both professionally and industrially. They cannot be served in their best interests in one organisation ... the integrated body ... would suffer on the professional aspect more than anybody else ... We must go ahead and work very hard for our professional aspects.[11]

The Victorian delegates were quite adamant that amendments to the rules would not change their position: 'It is on the question that members will be excluded, a great many members'. Miss Hughes-Jones was also concerned about each State having equal representation on the new body. She wanted proportional representation which would clearly favour the States with higher memberships.[12] She was concerned that Victoria should retain its dominant role in the organisation.

The president of the RANF, Miss Jane Muntz, found herself in a very difficult position. She clearly favoured integration, but also had much sympathy with the concerns of her own State over the issue. She saw no solution to the impasse:

> If the RVCN is of the opinion ... that the rules cannot be altered or amended to overcome their objection, then you have a clear indication that one State at least is not in favour of integration under any circumstances ... Well, the solution is as far away as ever ... I am sorry if I have wasted your time.[13]

Increasing Pressures towards a Strong National Body

THE appeal of a strong, national organisation was very persuasive, not simply from a political standpoint, but also on financial grounds. Two organisations at the federal level and two in each State were a drain on limited resources. Moreover, delegates to the RANF from Western Australia and Queensland argued very strongly that it was the only way to go given the general trend in Australian political, industrial and economic affairs since the second world war, towards investing power in federal organisations.[14] Miss O. E. Anstey from Western Australia was the only delegate at the conference to challenge the dichotomy between the industrial and professional areas:

> We do not consider that our professional activities can be split from economic welfare. They are both integrated in many ways, particularly [for example] regarding ... education. It is not just a matter of wages, salaries and hours, but forcing up the educational hours. We argued and asked for

lectures in the employer's time. There are many other facets that are so closely concerned with rights and status [that] to divorce the professional from the industrial organisation would be derogatory.[15]

While South Australia and Tasmania expressed some reservations, the RANF was moving towards a situation where Victoria would be the only state opposing integration. Later at the ANFES annual meeting, Mr Wild from Western Australia successfully moved notice of motion to rescind a motion from the 1963 annual meeting 'that it be the policy of ANFES not to commit itself in any way with any other organisation apart from the RANF. This was clearly a threat that unless the RANF did something concrete towards integration the ANFES might well look elsewhere.[16]

By the end of 1964 an assessment of the situation by the RVCN was that unless South Australia and Tasmania could be persuaded to stand firm against integration in March 1965, Victoria would be 'out on a limb'. The reality was that integration at the State level integration existed in all States except New South Wales and Victoria and that the ANFES was really only functioning effectively in Victoria. RVCN leaders had also come to realise that even if the existing situation continued, the ANFES would need to substantially increase capitation fees (as requested by the 1964 ANFES annual meeting) to carry out its functions, particularly in regard to those members who came under federal awards. While the ANFES could negotiate for nurses employed in four Federal Government departments — Repatriation, Social Services, Health, Territories — this involved no more than 2 000 nurses involved, of whom only a small number were ANFES members.[17]

Early in 1965 the Queensland Branch of the ANFES obtained a legal opinion on the three issues which seemed to be troubling the RVCN — the autonomy of State branches, the exclusion of some professional nurses and nursing aides. Counsel found that neither the autonomy nor the property of existing State bodies could be interfered with in any way by integration. The worry that nursing aides might dominate the organisation could be solved simply by excluding them from being office bearers. Existing members of an organisation retained the right of membership and this was established by legal precedents, while 'generally speaking a professional nurse who is employed by a hospital or a private patient, or an agency, would be an employee'. Much of this was at variance with legal advice obtained by the RVCN, nor did it help to allay the impression that Victoria was opposed to integration under any circumstances.[18]

By the March 1965 RANF federal council meeting there was open hostility from New South Wales and Queensland delegates to the stand taken by the RVCN. A motion of censure on the RVCN for 'unethical and irresponsible actions' in relation to integration 'whilst the Economic Welfare Committee was acting as instructed by the Federal Council and drawing up proposals to eliminate the causes of objection to the proposed constitution', was only defeated on the casting vote of the president.[19] The action which provoked this was the calling of a general meeting by the RVCN in February 1966 to discuss 'the inevitable loss by the RVCN of a great deal of its autonomy', the possible swamping of the RANF by such groups as nursing aides and the exclusion of some qualified nurses, if integration were to occur.[20] At the end of the March RANF council meeting the whole question of integration had become so confused by conflicting legal opinions that there was an equal split of delegates between those supporting immediate integration and those wanting to solve the legal difficulties first. The delegates passed it over to the ANFES for consideration.[21] Integration, which seemed just round the corner in 1964, was delayed once again.

But there was another issue which was guaranteed to keep the problem of integration before the RANF despite the fact that by now many wished it would simply go away. At the State level only South Australia did not recognise the HEF as a negotiating body on salaries and conditions. The HEF also had federal industrial registration and had previously unsuccessfully sought the deregistration of the ANFES. If the ANFES was to falter or was not built up sufficiently to cope with the demands of the federal arbitration system, a challenge from the HEF was seen as inevitable.

In the political context of the late 1960s where the possibility of a federal Labor government was no longer remote, there was also the prospect of increasing federal involvement and

control over health services. One of the concerns of the supporters of integration was that the position of nurses would be at risk
without a strong federally registered nursing organisation if a
'nationalised health scheme' was introduced at the federal level.[22]
This made the establishment of a strong national nursing organisation an urgent task, especially as there were also close links
between the Labor Party and unions like the HEF.

Victoria Maintains its Opposition to Integration

FOR the RVCN the battle over integration was not lost, and
the belief that eventually the other States would see the logic
of its arguments was boosted when those for integration received
a severe rebuff in the voting on the acceptance of an amended
ANFES constitution. In July 1966 the constitution containing the
amendments necessary to allow for integration with the RANF
was put to the branches — 76 members voted for and 145
against. The voting pattern revealed the weakness of all branches
except Victoria. No other branch could muster more than 28
members to a meeting; Victoria managed 130.[23] The strength of
the Victorian Branch was also reflected in the membership
figures as at 30 June 1966:

New South Wales	34
Northern Territory	58
Tasmania	86
South Australia	386
Western Australia	950
Queensland	1 378
Victoria	3 118

Victorian members made up more than half the Australian total
of 6 010.[24]

However, from the viewpoint of those supporting integration, the large vote of the Victorians was seen as an orchestrated
attempt to prevent any further steps towards integration. It was
viewed as another indication of Victoria's domination of the
RANF and as its unwillingness to agree to anything that might
threaten that domination.

By the September 1966 RANF council meeting a new peak of bitterness and hostility was reached in the struggle. The majority of States were opposed to even discussing the suggestions and proposals for reform of the ANFES constitution put forward by Victoria, claiming that 'Victoria's recommendations were intended to completely negate the present draft constitution'. It was alleged that:

> Victoria, having been largely responsible for the rejection of Council's recommendations to members ... was now seeking to structure the ANFES draft constitution in such a way as to prevent amalgamation of RANF and ANFES.[25]

To some extent these allegations were correct. Victoria still saw the way forward in building a strong ANFES, but keeping it separate from the RANF. This meant the Victorian efforts were centred on strengthening the ANFES constitution, rather than preparing it for a merger with the RANF. Marjorie Connor, Executive Secretary of the RVCN, commented:

> the sole reason for Victoria performing so much work [on the constitution] ... is derived from the view that an organisation such as ANFES should exist, and as such, should be clearly superior to any other organisation in the same field of operation.
>   Unfortunately the Constitution has become the instrument by which integration is being debated and presents a vital reason for clarifying issues.[26]

Those for integration wanted to go ahead and adopt a revised constitution which the RVCN and legal counsel saw as flawed and then correct it later. The RVCN wanted to correct it first, and in advocating this RVCN leaders were seen as engaging in delaying tactics.

Those for integration went ahead and passed a key resolution which formed the basis of future integration developments:

> That when the new constitution of ANFES is registered in the Federal Court of Arbitration and Conciliation, RANF consider the transfer of its assets to ANFES provided that ANFES guarantee to carry out all the functions of RANF and that an interim council consist of the executive officers of RANF and ANFES together with the federal councillors of RANF and ANFES.[27]

Later the secretary of the Victorian branch of the ANFES protested to its federal secretary:

> The Branch is concerned at the cavalier treatment given to the Victorian proposals ... the Branch is concerned that many proposals put forward by the Victorian Branch and by the honorary solicitor ... were not even discussed. This approach to the business of the Association is hardly calculated to inspire confidence in any proposals to concentrate greater power (and, in particular, rule-making power) in the Federal Council.[28]

Late in 1966, in a move which might have been seen as compromise but was more likely an attempt to show up the RVCN as being intransigent, the Queensland branch of the ANFES, with the support of the other branches, invited the Victorian branch to prepare a draft constitution for the ANFES. An assurance was given by a majority of the branches that such a constitution would be considered by the ANFES federal council in 1967.[29] The Victorian branch duly drew up a draft constitution at considerable expense but, of course, it was designed for an industrial body and not an integrated body in line with RVCN policy. As such was completely unacceptable to those who favoured integration. The success of the Queensland tactics became apparent at the RANF federal council meeting in March 1967 when a resolution was passed with Tasmania abstaining and Victoria voting against, 'that as the Victorian Branch does not wish to integrate RANF and ANFES ... the Victorian Branch be asked to withdraw from the Federation until such time as the Victorian Branch wishes to rejoin the Federation'.[30]

As the legal adviser to the RVCN, A. E. Woodward put it in a long memorandum, 'I think you have come to some sort of crossroads'. 'Some sort of showdown' was imminent:

> It would not take very much to convert that motion into a motion of expulsion and to have the necessary unanimous vote if Tasmania could be persuaded accordingly.

Woodward felt that all the work that had been done on the ANFES Constitution greatly improved the existing rules, but that eventually the Victorian superiority in numbers would be challenged by some intensive recruiting in the other States, and then you could 'go on blocking but sooner or later, I think you would find Victoria would be left alone'.[31] He devised what the RVCN saw as a compromise plan which, while still keeping the professional and industrial issues separate, provided for a professional committee to be based on the federal ANFES to which there would be direct representation from State professional bodies or alternatively from ANFES councillors serving in that capacity. This would enable the RVCN to retain its identity and link with the ICN through the professional committee of the ANFES. For Woodward the 'ultimate solution' was to allow for the fact that some States would finish with one body handling their professional and industrial problems and in other States there would be two. He could see no legal difficulties in this arrangement. He presented the RVCN with a detailed plan of how this might work at the federal level.[32]

Woodward's problem in devising this plan (which was also the problem of RVCN leaders) was that there existed a basic assumption that professional and industrial matters must remain separate. At no stage did he or the RVCN leadership attempt to argue this proposition, which was the inherent weakness in their position. Nursing leaders in the other States who considered his plan as well as the Victorian branch draft federal constitution, which retained this dichotomy, regarded them as unacceptable because from their viewpoint industrial and professional matters could not be separated.

The other States argued that even though they had given an undertaking to discuss the Victorian draft constitution at the September 1967 federal council meeting of the ANFES, this should not happen because the Victorian draft would not lead to integration. In fact it was discussed at the federal council meeting during the debate on the notice of motion that it should not be discussed. For the first time it became clear to everyone that the fundamental question distancing Victorian delegates from the rest was their insistence on separating industrial and professional matters. The whole debate was a long one, and centred around this problem. The Victorian delegates refused to make any compromise and when challenged to justify the separation of industrial and professional matters, were unable to do so. A motion was passed asking Victoria to give their objections to the inclusion of professional objects in the ANFES constitution.[33]

Early in 1968 the HEF applied to have a dispute declared under section 28 of the *Commonwealth Conciliation and Arbitration Act* (1904). This brought home to nursing leaders that their indecision over integration could not go on forever. The dispute related to a nursing matter and the HEF application was a clear challenge to the ANFES. Once again the HEF was forcing nurses to face up to the realities of industrial relations. As many other federally registered unions had found or were discovering, federal advocacy was an expensive business. It required a financially strong federal organisation, able to employ industrial relations experts and pay legal and travel expenses. The ANFES as constituted in 1968 was not in any sense able to act at this level. Its resources could not cope with the demands of federal advocacy and the HEF was there waiting to have a go.

The ANFES meeting in March 1968 adopted the amended constitution which cleared the way for integration and began the process of getting the new rules registered with the Federal Arbitration Court. But first they had to be accepted by a two-thirds majority of members in the State branches. Here again the Victorian branch was able to thwart the plans of the integrationists — 392 members voted against the amendments and 539 in favour — not the necessary two-thirds majority, but close.[34]

Later that year the RANF Federal Council rejected the RVCN's 'compromise plan'. It was then intimated that once the new ANFES constitution was registered, all ANFES branches would withdraw from the RANF, and, in this way, achieve an integrated federal organisation. This would leave the RVCN standing alone, and because the RANF would no longer be a federation, ICN affiliation could not be maintained by a single State. The RVCN delegates were unable to accept any alternatives to their 'compromise plan', even though it had been clear for many months prior to the meeting that it was unacceptable to most of the states. The Victorian delegates were left no room for negotiation. For them the only one positive outcome of the meeting was the decision to recommend to the ANFES that provision be made in its standing orders for the setting up of advisory committees to deal with industrial, professional and educational objectives respectively.[35]

After the failure to obtain the two-thirds majority to change the rules, those in favour of integration worked very hard in New South Wales, Queensland and Western Australia to increase the membership of the ANFES branches of these States. Not the least of their achievements was winning the support of the powerful New South Wales Nurses Association (NSWNA) which up to this time had stood aloof from RANF affairs.[36] The NSWNA had 15 000 members, made up of 8 000 trained nurses, 4 000 auxiliaries and 2 000 assistant nurses. This had a decisive influence on the voting figures when the amended ANFES constitution was put to members again in July 1969.[37]

Table 1   Amendments to ANFES Constitution 1969[38]

	Voting for	Voting against
Queensland	1 489 (123)	nil
New South Wales	1 269 (72)	nil
Victoria	7 (nil)	1147 (391)
Tasmania	10 (11)	nil (1)
South Australia	251 (136)	nil
Western Australia	743 (167)	nil
Northern Territory	38 (30)	nil
Total	3 807 (539)	1 147 (392)

1968 voting figures are given in brackets.

The result was a bitter disappointment to RVCN leaders, yet was hardly surprising in view of the intensive recruiting which had been done in all States (including Victoria). The new rules were duly lodged with the Industrial Registrar for approval.

The vote not only ensured that integration would take place in the near future; it also ended Victoria's numerical dominance over the ANFES. This augured well for the success of the new organisation. It remained to be seen whether the fears of RVCN leaders that the ANFES would 'deprive the state branches of the right to initiate projects and activities' and that all branches 'would become subservient to the Federal Council of ANFES irrespective of the requirements of the local branch' would be realised.[39]

Right to the end the RVCN maintained its opposition to the

dissolution of the RANF and its activities being taken over by the ANFES. At the March 1970 RANF federal council meeting the Victorian delegate, Miss M. Evans, declared that 'Victoria could not alter the principle behind their objection to a 'trade union' managing all nursing affairs'. This had always been the crux of Victoria's opposition to integration.[40] But this opposition was based on an attitude to industrial unionism which was the product of another era. Industrial action by professional groups had become commonplace by 1970, and increased throughout that decade. Professional and industrial questions had become so intertwined in many organisations that they could not be separated, and in any case professionalism depended on industrial action for its maintenance and sustenance. In much the same way, RVCN council meetings which were ostensibly devoted to professional affairs had always spent some time on industrial matters, especially in the late 1960s.

The Industrial Registrar accepted the amended ANFES constitution and in line with the 1966 decision of the RANF Federal Council, the 1970 March meeting became the last meeting of the RANF as such when it voted itself out of existence:

> That it is the intention of this Council, with the exception of the RVCN, that from 30 June 1970 the organisation known as the RANF will go out of existence by virtue of the fact that seven of its eight members will withdraw.[41]

The ANFES which took over from the RANF on 1 July 1970 became known as the Australian Nursing Federation (ANF), but assumed the 'Royal' prefix from October 1971 and became the RANF.

The RVCN and the RANF, Victorian Branch, 1970–1975

IN Victoria the RVCN and the Victorian branch of the ANF had worked out an agreement by the end of 1970 to establish the working parameters of the two organisations. Nursing service and nursing education remained the responsibility of the RVCN, while economic welfare was to be the responsibility of the ANF. The RVCN retained the right to act when an industrial question was of such importance that it could sufficiently affect the professional aspects of nursing. The RVCN became the agent to collect ANF subscriptions — $10 for each organisation.[42] But after 18 months many RVCN council members became convinced that these arrangements were not working, and that they would have to work towards a single organisation for Victoria.[43]

On 20 June 1972 a joint meeting of some 250 members of the RVCN and the RANF, VB was held where RVCN president, Miss Mary Evans, reported on the outcome of a review of the two organisations working together, which 'have the same members, the same staff, share the same subscription', but 'have two councils to govern the same business':

> Frustration and difficulties have increased as the national body has developed its professional and educational programmes and the RANF Victorian Branch has been required to formulate policies in relation to same, much of this work being referred to RVCN Standing Committees. This system is cumbersome, time consuming and can be abortive if the recommendations by the Standing Committee are not acceptable to the RANF.[44]

The working of the two organisations which shared office accommodation 'had not been an easy experience for all concerned with the actual working situation':

> Far too much energy and time has been spent channelling business through two bodies and it has been somewhat frustrating when the two Councils do not agree, which has happened on many matters of federal business: the RVCN having no direct voice to the federal body.
>
> It is recorded with deepest regret that the proposed course of action [dissolving the RVCN] seems the only responsible course open and it has been with considerable personal and professional distress that the Council has reached this conclusion.[45]

The industrial organisation was no longer simply an off-shoot of the RVCN, but a body in its own right with national connections and acting independently of the RVCN. While they were not merged, there was a real threat that the two organisations would go their own ways.

The RVCN Council had actually seriously considered complete separation of the two bodies, but came to the conclusion that the RVCN would then have no voice at all at either the national or international level, nor would it have any say in industrial negotiations. In fact, it must have been obvious to RVCN council members that under such circumstances the RVCN would have been most unlikely to have attracted many members. As Miss Mary Evans said:

> the RVCN Council is facing the sad and unpalatable fact that it believes the only rational course of action to recommend to its members is to dissolve the RVCN and have *one* organisation with *one* governing body.[46]

It took three years to achieve amalgamation. Negotiations proceeded very slowly because the majority of RVCN council members were still loath to submerge their organisation in the RANF, VB, even though that branch was rapidly taking over the leadership of nurses in Victoria. In April 1974 the RVCN Council voted three to seven against to confirm its own policy of working towards one organisation of nurses in Victoria, in spite of strong support from the RVCN president, Miss Shirley Jennings. However, at the same meeting the RVCN business adviser, Mr Leon Turner, suggested he would assist the RANF, VB, and RVCN leaders in carrying out an analysis of the structure and objectives of the two bodies.[47] This was accepted and in September 1974 a report from a sub-committee consisting of the presidents of the two organisations, the secretary of the RVCN and Mr Turner, was presented to the RVCN executive committee. The sub-committee had made a detailed examination of the functions of the RVCN and superimposed on them a similar examination of the functions of the RANF, VB. They concluded that 'a tremendous amount of duplication was evident', and that:

> Neither organisation is fulfilling the role it is supposed to fulfil because of the two bodies, especially in the matter of promoting nursing and improving health care. It is obvious that too many high calibre people are being put into things that they should not get themselves involved in.[48]

The sub-committee could see no basic difference between the two organisations except that the RANF, VB, had to conform federally. It had become obvious by 1975 that this did not mean any loss of autonomy within Victoria which had been one of the chief worries of the nursing leaders in the 1960s. In fact, none of the dire results predicted by those against integration had eventuated.

The sub-committee pointed out that the main areas of concern of the two bodies — the protection of nursing, improving health care, facilitating fellowship, improving status, influencing authorities, improving conditions, protecting rights and building membership — required the efforts of many highly skilled people, and that duplication could not be afforded in these tasks. The sub-committee recommended amalgamation on 1 July 1975 and that a committee be established to work out the structure of the new organisation.[49]

With this report the opposition to merging the two organisations collapsed, and early in 1975 the new rules of the RANF, VB, were agreed to by the councils of the two organisations and put to a referendum of members in May — 3 194 members voted in favour of one organisation and 73 voted against. All members of both councils resigned and a new council was elected under the provisions of the new rules. The affairs of the RVCN were to be limited to the administration of trust and special funds, but it effectively went out of existence on 17 October 1975 when it handed over its responsibilities to the RANF, VB.

The new RANF, VB, had a council of registered nurses elected by all members, with a maximum number of 24 and a minimum of 12. Two members were elected by student nurses. Elections were held every two years in accordance with federal rules. A finance committee was established, as were standing committees for education, nursing services and economic welfare. The branches and sections of the RVCN were to continue their functions as before. All assets and liabilities of the RVCN were transferred to the RANF, VB. In fact the day-to-day financing and organisation of the administration continued in much the same way as previously. Miss S. R. Jennings became the first president of the new organisation and Miss E. P. Orr and Miss R. M. McNair (former president of RANF, VB), the two vice-presidents.[50]

While it was a new and united organisation, it was also the old organisation rejuvenated. It was a merger of two wings of the same organisation which had worked closely together for 32 years, yet were separated by the belief that it was not the role of a professional organisation to be associated with industrial matters. It put an end to the charade that nurses should not sully their hands with the concerns of salaries and conditions, yet in those 32 years hardly a RVCN council meeting went by without some industrial question being discussed. In practice industrial matters had always been a concern of the RVCN, but the public image which RVCN leaders wished to convey was of a professional organisation which disdained trade union affairs. In the context of the 1970s this dichotomy was unnecessary and untenable when teachers, doctors, airline pilots and engineers did not hesitate to openly flex their industrial muscles.

For Miss Marjorie Connor, executive secretary of the RVCN for 27 years (1945–72), the incorporation of the RVCN in the RANF, VB was nothing less than a disaster. It represented a triumph for all she had fought against. She believed that industrial affairs would take over the work of the new organisation; that professional matters would be cast aside and that the pursuit of 'money' would become the overriding consideration:

> I gave away a professional body for it to become an industrial union which broke my heart, completely and utterly … We have got to have money, I suppose, but let us not suppose that money is the beginning and end of all things.[51]

The RVCN had become Miss Connor's bailiwick. Her long tenure in office, her astuteness and dedication, coupled with her unstinting devotion to the organisation, had placed her in a very powerful position, particularly during the 1960s when the RVCN was struggling to retain its professional leadership within the organisation of the RANF, and to maintain its autonomy. She had led the resistance to the merging of the professional and the industrial wings of the RVCN and the RANF, which successfully delayed the incorporation of the RVCN in the RANF, VB for many years. In this she had the strong support of the RVCN Council members, most of whom shared her ideals and loyalty to the organisation.

For Miss Connor nursing 'must be a vocation'. 'You are not doing it for what money you earn, ever'.[52] In these views she was reflecting the outlook of many of her contemporaries who were hostile and bewildered by the growing emphasis on salaries and conditions, and the submerging of what they believed to be the true aims of the nursing profession.

Miss Connor had trained at the Alfred Hospital from 1925 to 1928 and had worked for 15 years until 1945, for one of Melbourne's leading dermatologists. Other than during her training, she had never worked as a nurse in a hospital. As she said, 'I did not want to live in a hospital'. She prized her freedom too much. But she never regretted choosing nursing as her vocation and joining the RVCN, 'because I am part of a great family of friends'.[53]

Endnotes

1. *UNA*, August 1961, p. 240.
2. 'Draft of Proposed Agreement Between the RVCN and the ANF — Employees Section (Victorian Branch)', September 1954. Box 40, UM archives.
3. ANFES, minutes of annual general meeting, August 1958. Box 145, UM archives.
4. ibid., September 1961.
5. ANFES, report of the committee on 'How Better Integration between Royal Australian Nursing Federation and Australian Nursing Federation Employees Section can be accomplished'. Box 145, UM archives.
6. RANF, minutes of annual meeting of the federal council, September 1962, pp. 13–15. Box 3, UM archives.
7. ibid., October 1963, p. 6. Box 12, UM archives.
8. RANF, report of economic welfare committee, 1964. Box 169, UM archives.
9. RVCN, advice from counsel (A. E. Woodward), 19 September 1964. Box 169, UM archives.
10. Pat Slater to Marjorie Connor, 2 November 1989. See also Marjorie Connor 'Notes on RANF, AGM 1964'. Box 169, UM archives.
11. RANF, federal council meeting, October 1964, extract from verbatim minutes, p. 15. Box 169, UM archives.
12. ibid., p. 63.
13. ibid.
14. ibid., p. 9.
15. ibid., p. 15.
16. ANFES, minutes of annual federal council meeting, October 1964. Box 19, UM archives.
17. RANF, federal council meeting, October 1964, op. cit.
18. RANF, Queensland branch, 'Opinion', 29 January 1965. Box 24, UM archives.
19. RANF, federal council meeting, March 1965, p. 10. Box 3, UM archives.
20. *UNA*, December 1964, p. 380.

21 RANF, federal council, op. cit., p. 13.
22 Lorraine Jarrett, secretary RANF to Marjorie Connor, secretary RVCN, 13 October 1966. Box 13, UM archives.
23 Statement from Miss Jarrett, 29 July 1966, ANFES Constitution, Amendment to Rules Change. Box 19, UM archives.
24 Lorraine Jarrett to Marjorie Connor, 11 August 1966. Box 13, UM archives.
25 Quoted in document circulated to all ANFES committee of management members by Marjorie Connor as a result of 1966 ANFES federal council meeting, September 1966, p. 3.
26 ibid.
27 RANF, federal council meeting, March 1966, p. 13. Box 147, UM archives.
28 Marjorie Connor to Lorraine Jarrett, 10 October 1966. Box 13, UM archives.
29 Lorraine Jarrett to Marjorie Connor, 20 December 1966. Box 19, UM archives.
30 RANF, federal council meeting, March 1967, p. 3. Box 12, UM archives.
31 RVCN, executive meeting minutes, 20 March 1967, p. 2. Box 10, UM archives.
32 ibid., p. 2–14.
33 ANFES, annual general meeting, September 1967, pp. 14–18. Box 41, UM archives.
34 *UNA*, June 1968, p. 164.
35 RANF, federal council meeting, March 1968, pp. 12–15. Box 41, UM archives.
36 RVCN newsletter, 30 May 1969. Box 25, UM archives.
37 ANFES, minutes, committee management, 9 April 1969, p. 3.
38 *UNA*, June 1968, p. 164; June 1969, p. 2.
39 Leaflet issued by the RVCN, June/July 1968, to ANFES members. Box 13, UM archives.
40 RANF, federal council meeting, March 1970, p. 8. Box 41, UM archives.
41 ibid., p. 12.
42 *UNA*, September 1971, p. 7.
43 RVCN, executive committee minutes, 24 February 1972. Box 22, UM archives.
44 RVCN, RANF, VB. Report of joint meeting of members, 20 June 1972, ps, p. 2.
45 *UNA*, September 1972, p. 6. Annual report of the RVCN, to 30 June 1972.
46 RVCN, RANF, VB. Joint meeting, op. cit., p. 3.
47 RVCN Council, 4 April 1974, p. 6–7.
48 RVCN, minutes of executive committee, 26 September 1974, p. 2.
49 ibid., pp. 1–4.
50 RVCN Council, 5 June 1975, pp. 4–5; RANF, VB council minutes, 19 June 1975, p. 2; RVCN Council, 3 July 1975, p. 2; *UNA*, September/October 1975, p. 24.
51 Marjorie Connor interviewed by R. Ribechi, May 1987. Tape 2.
52 Marjorie Connor interviewed by J. Bessant, 21 January 1989.
53 Marjorie Connor interviewed by R. Ribechi, May 1987. Tape 2.

6

The Education and Training of Nurses, 1960s–1980s

B Y the mid-1950s the training of nurses in Victoria was coming under increasing criticism. The basic elements of the training system had been in operation for over 60 years and there was a general unwillingness among nurses to make any changes. The demise of the Melbourne School of Nursing (see chapter 3) was a very good indication of the general conservatism of nursing leaders. It died with little sign of protest or remorse from the profession, even though it appeared to have been singularly successful.

In 1953 Dr John Lindell, chairman of the Hospitals and Charities Commission, deplored the tardiness of nurses to adapt their training, and consequently their work, to the rapidly changing face of medicine. He asked:

> Has the significance of the medical revolutions which succeeded each World War been fully appreciated by nursing leaders?[1]

Over the next 30 years major changes occurred in the basic training and education of nurses, but it was a slow and often painful process, not only because of a strong resistance to change, but also because of the efforts that had to be made by the RVCN and others to put the problems of nurses high on the political agenda of successive Victorian State Governments.

The training system in the 1950s (apart from the two schools of nursing), was concentrated around either independent hospital training schools or affiliated hospital training schools. The probationer entered the hospital training school to be given a preliminary training period (usually six to eight weeks) during which she was introduced to the areas of junior general nursing, anatomy and physiology and the ethics (in reality the etiquette) of nursing. She would also visit the wards for half or whole days to become accustomed to the hospital routine. Once in the wards her training consisted of lectures taken during both on and off duty hours and what she could learn by the practices she saw around her. Some hospitals which could not give the trainee all the essential aspects of training in their own wards sent them to affiliated hospitals. For example, St Vincent's Hospital had no children's ward so their trainees went to the two affiliated hospitals, the Austin and the Royal Children's, to gain three months experience in paediatrics.[2]

This system has often been described as an 'apprentice' system, yet a more appropriate description would be 'on the job training'. It did not meet the generally accepted view of an apprentice system, in which a trainee learns from and experienced person. Trainee nurses normally did not learn from trained nurses, but from other trainees who had been on the job longer. The 91 lectures nurses were required to attend over the three years under the Nurses Act were usually given by members of the medical profession, rather than sister tutors (at least in the 1950s), so that nurses learnt much from trial and error and from their immediate colleagues, rather than from older, more experienced members of their own profession. This was not a system of education but of indoctrination. The trainees learnt precisely what to do in specific situations in a way that left little or no scope for individual initiative or thinking. In fact, any variation from the specified norm in clinical practice or in theoretical instruction was very quickly curbed.

When the report of a survey of nurses' work in England, carried out by the Nuffield Hospitals Trust, came out in 1953, it was seized upon by critics of the training system as being applicable to conditions in Victoria. The report covered nearly 16 000 hours of detailed observation throughout the day and night in 12 selected hospitals over a period of three years. The survey showed that, on average, trained nurses spent 4.5 hours on ward organisation and 4.5 hours on nursing duties each day.

The latter involved 40 minutes of personal contact with patients, 50 minutes giving instructions to staff and five minutes a day teaching trainees. One critic, referring to the report, commented:

> It is an interesting and amazing fact, that the public would be terrified to let a man learning to drive take a bus full of passengers for a run, and yet blandly accepts what is virtually a school girl dressed in a uniform while she learns her work , and allows her to take care of sick people, often alone … the great mass of basic care is left in the hands primarily of the most junior [trainee] nurses.[3]

Criticisms of the training system continued throughout the 1950s but were generally associated with the ongoing shortage of nurses and the significant wastage rate of trainees (see chapter 4) As Miss Jane Muntz put it, the most significant hindrance to any change in the training of nurses was that the 'educational function of a hospital is not remotely understood'. If hospitals were to keep their responsibility for training then they would have to face up to what it entailed:

> Nursing executives if they are completely honest will admit that their loyalties are acutely divided between the need for adequate training for the student nurse and the more pressing requirement of sufficient nursing staff for the wards. In the final analysis the latter will come first every time.[4]

In the 1950s, just as in the 1930s, the trainee nurses performed most of the basic nursing functions in the training hospitals. They were still a source of cheap labour, and so were indispensable in a system where finance was always a problem. The inherent contradiction between providing trainees with adequate training while at the same time requiring them to take the burden of nursing duties was to bedevil the efforts of the reformers in the 1960s and 1970s, and to lead to the final solution, that is, taking training out of the hands of hospitals. In the fifties and sixties, however, efforts were directed towards reforming the existing system.

First Steps towards Reform

IN 1959 the Sister Tutor's Section of the RVCN prepared a critique of the training system and offered some solutions. Nine of the leading sister tutors in Victoria spent six months analysing and correlating material from hospitals and staff.[5] The resulting report was significant because it laid the foundations for future reforms. It found the existing system lacking in teaching facilities, administration, and examination and selection procedures. Many nursing schools failed to cover the minimum curriculum requirements. Lecture methods were invariably used when tutorials were seen as far more desirable, and there were few teaching aids and equipment for practical work. Since the teaching program was not co-ordinated with classroom instruction and ward experience, the link between theory and practice was often separated by many months. At the same time ward sisters were able to find very little time for clinical teaching and their supervision consisted largely of correcting faults in procedure rather than providing actual example and guidance. Little thought was given by administrators grading nursing tasks:

> Many a sensitive junior nurse suffers great anxiety because she is rostered to a senior position, or because of attendance at lectures by the other members of the staff, she is left unexpectedly with overwhelming responsibilities.[6]

The administrators were found to be chiefly concerned with assigning a trainee to a ward where there was a demand for a nurse, giving little consideration to the learning needs of the trainee.

The report's criticisms of the examinations conducted by the VNC were quite scathing, they were both 'inefficient' and 'outmoded'. The first professional examination, undertaken after ten months of training, did not test the abilities of a nurse at that level of training, nor was the final examination after three years 'a valid assessment of her knowledge and understanding'. Moreover, selection procedures were inadequate because many trainees could not cope with the level of the curriculum and were 'completely lost to nursing'. As a result of these inadequacies sister tutors were often forced to resort to teaching through rote learning, rather than linking clinical experience with theory.

Tutors found it difficult to have discussions with ward sisters about their students because the former were so harassed with their workload and their 'exhausting responsibilities'. Nor did some matrons give much support in the area of training:

> With all these difficulties, it is not surprising that many tutors become discouraged and lose satisfaction in their work, that others overwork in an attempt to solve these problems, and others become unimaginative and rigid and produce nurses of the same pattern.

Medical staff often found their role in teaching nurses to be inadequately explained and ill-defined. They became 'irritated and critical', which the report found was 'sometimes justified in regarding nurses as subordinates rather than co-workers in the ward team'. In a similar vein the ward atmosphere was not generally conducive to free discussion with trainees, especially when visiting specialists, medical social workers, dietitians and occupational therapists could provide a total picture of the patients' problems.[7]

Overall, the report presented an extremely critical picture of nurse training in Victorian hospitals. It concluded that:

> the defects of our present educational system are present because many of the principles of learning have not been applied in education ... our students are frequently unable to apply to their practical work what they learn in theory; this is true, not only of nursing skills, but also observation, reasoning, judgements, attitudes and general behaviour, and is, we believe, the major factor adversely affecting patient care, staff relationships, and maybe staff requirements.

The report stressed that 'theory and clinical experience must be properly selected, correlated, and organised'. Appropriate teaching methods were required, 'Those responsible for teaching nurses must know how to teach'.[8]

The sister tutors then put forward a program for basic training which they saw as appropriate for a pilot scheme in one of the hospitals. It is worth examining their proposals in some detail because over the next decade reform of the basic training curriculum was to become a major issue for the RVCN and the VNC and many of these sister tutors were to take an active part in that reform.

They proposed dividing the three year period into three sections — 1 to 6 months, 7 to 17 months, and 18 to 36 months. They envisaged a formidable program for the first period — all basic nursing skills plus the elements of physics and chemistry, anatomy and physiology, nutrition, microbiology, personal and ward hygiene, human relations and the social aspects of disease, as well as recent trends in nursing. Clinical experience was to be gradually increased, building up to seven hours per day, with non-nursing duties excluded. Ideally, there would be a ratio of 1:12 sister tutors to trainees with the one tutor associated with the same group of trainees for the entire period. This all assumed close co-operation between sister tutors and ward sisters in order to ensure a co-ordinated program.

In the second period, which aimed at teaching the 'art and science of basic medical and surgical nursing', the correlation between theory and practice was considered crucial. Medical and surgical experience was to be in unbroken six month blocks with related lectures running concurrently. Work was to be planned so that the students developed the necessary abilities and skills to be able to organise and give 'total patient care', rather than on a 'job' basis. Short periods in junior theatre work, the diet kitchen and district nursing were also considered essential. As ward sisters were to take a leading role in this period, they were to be given more time as well as the opportunity to take a course in improving their teaching abilities.

The last period was to lead to the production of 'professional nurses'. Here the experience of trainees had to be broadened, either within the hospital or in an affiliated institution. The report divided the areas of nursing which were to be included into categories according to order of importance. Essential were children's, gynaecological, ear, nose and throat, isolation, public health, operating theatre, outpatients and casualty.

Learning by rote needed to be replaced by problem-solving techniques which encouraged trainees to search out and use information. Examinations were to aim at testing the objectives of the course. They were to be set to measure understanding and abilities, rather than simply factual information.

Of course all this assumed the existence of sufficient auxiliary staff such as nursing aides to take over the more menial tasks, as well as more sister tutors. It also envisaged a reduction in the supervisory role of ward sisters.[9]

As the sister tutors reported, this was 'not a spectacular change'. It remained well within the training traditions built up over many decades, but it made some attempt to bring the training of nurses up to date with modern teaching techniques and with the radical advances in medical and health practice. Nevertheless, the implications of introducing such changes demanded not only a greater allocation of financial resources by the State Government, but a change in thinking on the part of trained nurses themselves. They were being asked to rethink their attitudes towards trainees. They were recast as educators and advisers, rather than supervisors and directors. Not only was this a difficult role change, but it also ran counter to the whole hierarchical, top down structure of hospitals which had changed little since the 1930s (see chapter 2) As Miss F.M. Peterson, principal of the Nursing Division of the Commonwealth Health Department, commented:

> It is obvious that sooner or later the same serious considera-
> tion must be given to the professional education of nurses as
> is given to other professions. It will require something more
> than the scraps of a hospital's spare time if we are going to
> prepare the type of nurse needed in the future. A nineteenth
> century education is hardly adequate in a twentieth century
> world, with its more exacting demands on intelligence, knowl-
> edge, ingenuity, resourcefulness and social adaptability.[10]

As we have seen, one of the issues which was already being raised in the 1950s was the education of nurses in universities. Many countries provided basic training courses for nurses in universities, for example the United States, Belgium, Canada, Germany, India, Japan, Egypt and Mexico, but these were often there as alternatives to hospital training. In the United States, for instance, only 18 per cent of nurses trained in universities. Nevertheless, it had obvious appeal to some nursing leaders, for it offered an opportunity to raise the whole status of nurse training and education. It would bring it on a par with other professional courses such as medicine and law.[11]

One of the highlights of the Australian Nursing Congress held in Melbourne in May 1955 was a debate for and against university nursing schools. For those in favour it was primarily a question of status and attracting the best quality people into nursing who would be given a broad, liberal education which was 'essential for leadership', together with the subjects essential for nursing. University courses would enable nurses to 'think objectively' and 'evaluate efficiently'. The opponents, on the other hand, were very much concerned with what nursing was all about, that is, 'the proper use of fresh air, light, warmth, cleanliness, quiet, and the proper selection and administration of diet, all at the least expense of vital power to the patient' (Florence Nightingale). What emerged was the dichotomy between the role of a 'carer' and that of a 'medical technician'.[12]

But, apart from other more practical problems associated with the divorce of theory and practice, the reality in the late 1950s was that the University of Melbourne was not interested. It had no problem training doctors, lawyers, architects and engineers, but nursing, like teaching, was not a high status profession. A faculty of education was tolerated, but if it had been politically feasible the university would have readily divested it to a college. Nursing was out of the question, especially considering the existence of a very powerful medical faculty.

Problems of Definition and Opposition

MUCH of the debate on the reform of the training system hinged on what trainees were being prepared for. It raised the whole question of a definition of nursing. At the ICN congress in Melbourne in 1961 (see chapter 3) a resolution concerning generalised training was carried by a majority vote. However, as there was strong opposition, it was agreed that no action would be taken until a study was done of how many member countries really wanted a criterion which limited membership to nurses who had completed 'a generalised nursing preparation in an approved school of nursing' and who were authorised to practise nursing in their own country. 'Such general preparation shall include instruction and supervised practice in order to equip the nurse to care for people of all ages ... in all forms of sickness.'[13]

It is not certain whether the original purpose of this move was to encourage countries to close their special training courses and prepare only general nurses, with post-graduate training being reserved for specialists, or whether it was to get countries to include all the major areas of nursing in their basic training. Neither is it clear whether the general program was to include full training in psychiatric, obstetrical, medical and surgical work, and in public health fields, or whether it was to provide only an introduction to some of these areas, with nurses required to undertake post-basic courses before working in the special fields.

These problems of definition were worldwide in their application, and were highly relevant to any revision of nurses' training in Victoria. As Miss Pat Slater said at a RVCN conference of ward and departmental sisters in 1963, it all depended 'on what responsibilities we will allow her [the exit trainee] to accept on completion of this generalised training'.[14] In Victoria there was nothing to prevent a trained nurse who had, for example, no psychiatric, public health, industrial or school nurse training from her general training, working in these specialised areas, even in responsible positions.

Miss Slater, who was a sister tutor at the College of Nursing, Australia, and later its second director, believed that some form of comprehensive training with theory and practice in medical, surgical, psychiatric, obstetric and community health nursing was the best way to prepare nurses to provide comprehensive nursing care. This would prepare nurses for work under supervision in most areas of nursing, while providing the basis on which future specialisation could be built.[15]

One of the main problems here was that traditional psychiatric training in Victoria was quite separate from training in other areas. Psychiatric nurses did not receive a generalised form of training, but were trained in psychiatric institutions. They were seen as a 'race apart', in common with psychiatric hospitals in general. Many belonged to the HEF rather than the RVCN. As Miss Slater said:

> I believe both trainee general nurses and trainee psychiatric nurses would gain much from each other, if they worked together ... It is hoped that in the future the public and the

nursing profession will stop thinking of these patients as so different from any other, and psychiatric hospitals will be more closely related to general hospitals, and more part of the community.[16]

While Miss Slater did not think that the three year basic psychiatric training course should be discontinued, she felt that 'in the distant' future 'when we have learned more about mental illness and there are many more general trained nurses in the field', basic psychiatric training would no longer be necessary. Perhaps it would wither away, as had midwifery where the basic training program was to be discontinued altogether. Miss Slater felt that a comprehensive basic training program was the way forward, however she did point out that there was no hard evidence in 1963 that it was the best way to prepare nurses. It was what she believed many people thought to be the best form of training from their experiences in Australia and other countries.[17]

But Miss Slater, Miss Jean Murray and the other nursing leaders who were advocating reform of the training system in the early 1960s, were up against some formidable obstacles. Probably the most significant was the environment in which the vast majority of nurses were employed. As seen in chapter 2 it was almost impossible for anyone on the lower rungs of the system to voice criticism. Indeed, the only effective way of protesting against the system was to leave it. So far as training was concerned, matrons at the top of the hierarchy saw this as an important part of their bailiwick. They were loath to give it up, as the experience with the Melbourne School of Nursing had shown.

However, the post-war developments in hospitals had greatly increased the administrative load of matrons. As head of the department in each hospital, a matron employed by far the largest group of staff, of which a large proportion were trainees. The matron, following closely on the example of Florence Nightingale, saw her role as crucial in all aspects of selection and training. But the matron was not a trained educationist, and even if she had been, she would still have faced the constant contradiction in the duality of her role, that is, providing effective care for the patients in her hospital and balancing this with the educational and clinical needs of the trainees. Inevitably, patients had to come first and, as the administrative demands on her increased, she was less able to oversee the training of student nurses.

This put sister tutors in an invidious position. They were mostly ignored when issues concerning the clinical and educational training program were raised. They were not high in the hospital's hierarchy, and there was no question of their intervening to change administrative decisions to favour the further education of the trainees. Besides, there were so few of them, which was another problem facing the reformers. One of the most important requirements in reforming the training system was to dramatically increase the ratio of sister tutors to trainees. But this would require a significant increase in hospital resources. Ultimately, it was up to the Government to provide the finance for a reformed training system. In the early 1960s the nursing profession in Victoria was not united enough on the issue to put pressure on the Government to do so.

A Policy for Reform and the New Curriculum

MANY of the reforms put forward by the sister tutors were brought together in a policy statement on basic nursing education produced by the Education Committee of the RVCN in 1964.[18] The statement suggested a number of significant departures from current practice which challenged the methods of selection, the finance and the control of basic nurse training. It proposed that finance be provided in a separate grant from the Ministry of Education or the Ministry of Health for each hospital's training program. This would be used for establishing and maintaining school buildings, teaching facilities, staff salaries, administration, student allowances and housing and health services. In a direct challenge to the authority of matrons, the statement proposed that 'responsibility for the practical and theoretical programme should rest entirely with the tutorial staff, as they are best qualified to develop, implement and evaluate the programme'. This meant co-ordinating theory with clinical experience using patient assignment methods wherever possible.[19]

The type of three year program envisaged required a minimum of 1500 hours of planned teaching in the classroom and clinical areas. The theoretical material included psychology, sociology, trends in nursing practice and education, selected concepts from the physical and biological sciences and in-depth work on nursing arts and science. The clinical program favoured an all-round generalised training to prepare for 'nursing patients, of all age groups, suffering from diseases common in the community, in all phases of illness, acute, sub-acute, long term and convalescent'. This went with experience in general medical, surgical, theatre, casualty and outpatient nursing.

To carry this through, it was recognised that there would have to be major changes in the provision of support personnel. Each hospital nursing school was to have a director of education (principal tutor) with a ratio of no less than one to 20 students, and all sister tutors would be required to hold a sister tutor's diploma from the College of Nursing, Australia, or its equivalent. Librarians, secretarial and clerical staff and adequate and appropriate accommodation facilities were would also be required. The program also called for an increase in the number of trained nurses in proportion to trainees in each hospital, so that trained nurses could devote time to help and supervise the students. The entailed employing more nursing aides and non-nursing personnel in order to relieve students of 'domestic' and 'non-nursing tasks beyond those required for their education'.[20]

This program advocated by the RVCN was a necessary complement to the preparation of a new curriculum by the VNC. In October 1958 the General Training Working Committee of the VNC commenced its work on the new curriculum by defining the functions and responsibilities of trained nurses in Australia. Early in 1959 the committee distributed a questionnaire to a random sample of general trained nurses in Victoria and found many inadequacies in the existing training. This enabled the committee to define the aims and the broad content areas of the new curriculum. Three working committees were established (Miss L. M. Day, Miss J. G. Murray, Miss P. F. Osborne were the conveners) to develop the 26 syllabi involved. This was a lengthy process and when it all came together in 1963, it was realised that there was still an enormous amount of work to be done in checking and co-ordinating the syllabi. Miss Pat Slater was appointed full time from November 1963 to September 1964 to perform this task. She found that the work of preparing and developing draft syllabi for six of the areas had not commenced, that 13 areas needed complete revision and that seven requiring further work.[21]

The committee was fortunate in having Miss Jean Murray and Miss Pat Slater working on the new curriculum. Miss Murray was a recognised expert on curriculum development in nursing education programs. She was senior staff tutor at the College of Nursing, Australia. Her long experience in the field of nursing education proved invaluable to the committee.[22] Miss Osborne, the Committee's chairwoman, commented on Miss Slater's work:

> I must say the quality of Miss Slater's work was superb, not only the quality but the volume of work she did was equivalent to what would have taken us ten years, if we could have done it ... During the year she spent with us, she gave us four years' work.[23]

Eighty-three people assisted with the preparation and development of individual syllabi and 249 persons reviewed and commented on draft syllabi.[24] The whole exercise proved a mammoth task, and, with so many people involved (mainly nurses), it is not surprising that the implementation of the new curriculum was seen by nurses and their nursing leaders as their main objective in the late 1960s and early 1970s.

It became known as the 1 600 hours curriculum because 1 600 hours over the three year period were to be devoted to 'lectures and revision, testing, examining, orientation etc.'. This was a substantial increase on the existing VNC requirements. Another 4 240 hours were allocated to 'clinical experience which must be educationally planned and educationally supervised'.[25] The 1 600 hours had been recommended as the minimum by the ICN in 1934; it was also about the length allowed in the apprenticeship trades in Victoria for instruction in the employer's time. As Miss Murray explained:

> ... the content of most subjects is very little different from what is required at present, although a few subjects are increased in depth and there are some new subjects included

... many [extra] hours were needed so that more effective methods of teaching could be employed — methods of teaching which would help the students to think efficiently, to learn efficiently and to enjoy learning to become a nurse.[26]

One consideration which was vital for the success of the new curriculum was the relationship between the matron and the principal nursing educator in each hospital. It was intended that 'the tutor was responsible for working out the student's program and the training school was responsible for implementing it as far as possible'.[27] But, of course, matrons had the welfare of patients as their prime consideration. Much depended on how well matron and principal nursing educators could work together.

The *Ramsay Report*

THE new curriculum was presented to the Minister of Health, V. O. Dickie, in July 1965 and 1970 was set as the tentative target for implementation. But the Minister was not prepared to support the curriculum until an inquiry into its implications was held. The inquiry, which was instigated in April 1966, was concerned with the general question of the supply and demand of nurses and this was directly related to the entrance requirements for trainees and the new curriculum. Among other things, the chairman (Sir Alan Ramsay, former Director of Education) and his committee were to investigate 'the effects on metropolitan and country hospitals of the curriculum proposed by the Victorian Nursing Council, including financial implications' and 'to recommend ways in which the training needs of nurses and the service needs of hospitals may be reconciled with the least detriment to either'.[28] The General Training Working Committee of the VNC was very disappointed — they were well aware that an inquiry would further delay already long overdue reforms. However, they went ahead to survey the existing resources and deficiencies in hospitals and supplied the Committee of Enquiry with the results in 1968.

The *Ramsay Report* (Nursing) was brought down in August 1970, over four years after its inception. In considering the effects of the new curriculum on hospitals the committee had two conflicting views before it. Nurse educators emphasised that the new curriculum would produce 'a more knowledgeable and better trained nurse who will be capable of delivering better patient care', and hospital administrators who believed there would be a deterioration in the standard of nursing care by nurse trainees 'who will be working only a three day week in routine hospital work'.[29]

The committee calculated that 1150 additional 'persons' would be required in the teaching hospitals to implement the curriculum. Nor was it impressed with the view that this would be balanced by better care from better trained nurses. The amount of detail in the curriculum was 'more than is necessary in a basic curriculum'. The rapid moves by trainees from one clinical area to another would reduce the standard of patient care. The short periods of experience in many areas would produce a superficial understanding (the curriculum required 16 moves in Phase II over 110 weeks, several, at least, to affiliated hospitals); longer periods in fewer areas would be better. The curriculum would not necessarily ensure that theory and practice were coordinated. These were all serious criticisms which were not related simply to economic concerns, but had sound educational implications.[30]

Much to the horror of the VNC and the RVCN the committee recommended a minimum time of 1200 hours. It did so for 'pragmatic' reasons because the additional staff required were simply not available:

> There could be endless argument as to whether the minimum should be 800 hours [the maximum in most Melbourne hospitals], 1,200 hours, 1,600 hours or even more — and, no doubt, there will be endless argument so long as the present system survives with its inbuilt conflict between the training needs of nurses and the service needs of hospitals.[31]

The committee also stressed that education time should be included in the student's ordinary working week. It also recommended that the number of periods of minimum experience in various clinical areas be reduced. The student was to be given some choice in these areas.[32]

The committee considered that the proposed scale of teaching staff to student nurses was realistic, but pointed out that there were insufficient qualified nurse educators (also termed sister tutors) to meet the demand and that unqualified trained nurses would have to fill the gap.[33] Short courses on 'methods of instruction' for ward sisters, maximum use of non-nurse lecturers and more involvement of ward and departmental sisters in classroom demonstrations were suggested to overcome the shortage of nurse educators.[34]. Even to bring the hospital schools' facilities up to the requirements of the existing curriculum would cost was between $1 and $1.25 million. Altogether, with additional nursing accommodation, the cost was estimated at $3.5 million. A figure of close to $4 million was estimated to pay for the salaries of additional nurse educators and nursing staff.[35]

There was nothing in the terms of reference of the committee to suggest that the Minister was seeking an opinion on the desirability of a college-based education program for nurses. Nevertheless, the committee devoted some time to this alternative and clearly favoured the introduction of a pilot course. It noted that there had been a marked lack of experimentation with other forms of training in Victoria, in contrast with countries in Europe, and in Great Britain and North America. The committee was most impressed with the new Canadian system whereby students completed two years of training in colleges (theoretical and clinical), but were not members of the hospital workforce. It had been so successful that the old 'apprenticeship' system was being phased out, and there had been a rapid rise in recruitment.[36]

College training would aid recruitment. It would reduce wastage and be of more educational value. The committee was concerned that there was a belief that nursing was a profession that required only a low level of academic ability and hence teachers and parents guided brighter students away from nursing into other areas such as teaching, physiotherapy, speech therapy, and so on. In comparison with its position in the 1920s and 1930s the status of nursing *had* diminished, partly due to the competition of more attractive professions, but, according to the committee, a lot to do with the antiquated training system. The system cut into students' social lives, and the nurses' homes which still figured prominently in the life of trainees, were far too restrictive for young women in the 1970s. Hospitals were also sadly lacking in the provision of extra curricula activities which could be expected in any normal multi-disciplinary college, for example sporting, debating and political clubs.[38] The wastage rate wherein 30 per cent of trainees in Victoria failed to complete their training, was far too high. The Canadians had experienced a significant drop in the wastage rate under college training.[37]

Clearly, the members of the Ramsay Committee favoured replacing the existing system with college-based training. They regarded the arguments in favour as 'overwhelming'. The old system could not be abolished overnight and so a pilot project was recommended.[39]

The committee went beyond its terms of reference in examining the training of nursing aides. It found that in 1970 nursing aides made up approximately 21 per cent of the nursing team. The wastage rate was similar to general nurses at 30 per cent. There was also a shortage of nursing aides and this would be accentuated with the new curriculum. The existing nursing aide training consisted of six weeks full time in a preliminary training school and thereafter one hour per week for the remaining 46 weeks of the one year course. This amounted to 286 hours of education time which was approximately 7 per cent of the total time spent as a student nursing aide. It was very similar in fact to the original course established nearly 20 years earlier.

The committee concluded that the course was too elementary and lacked 'challenge' for students other than those of the 'poorest academic ability'. The work itself lacked 'job satisfaction' and this was one of the main reasons for the high wastage rate. There were no minimum entry standards.[40] The Committee recommended that the course should become a more advanced program and that those qualifying should be known as 'enrolled nurses'. The minimum age of entry should be 17 years with a form 3 (year 9) completion as a requirement. There should also be an additional training course for existing nursing aides so that they may become enrolled nurses, just as enrolled nurses should be encouraged to undertake training to become registered nurses, in a period of less than the three years.[41] These recommendations were designed to firmly establish the enrolled nurse as a recognised and legitimate member of the nursing team.

Despite the criticism from the RVCN and other nursing

organisations, the *Ramsay Report* was not lacking in vision. It tackled the fundamental problems of nursing in Victoria and in going well beyond its terms of reference, offered solutions which were to profoundly influence the course of nursing education in the State.

The Reaction to the *Ramsay Report*

E VEN before the *Ramsay Report* was issued the RVCN had begun the campaign to overturn one of its major recommendations — a 1200 hours training course. It took a deputation to Premier Henry Bolte on 22 April 1970, as Miss Mary Evans, RVCN President, said, 'with great reluctance', because 'our approaches within the proper channels have been ignored or deferred or delayed':

> We will not be brushed aside or ignored any longer and so we have sought this interview with you ... this is the first time we have ever sought a direct interview with the Premier ... We nurses are unanimously agreed that a minimum of 1600 hours of teaching during training is of fundamental importance, and we are agreed that whatever other concessions might be made, we will not be satisfied that our problems are understood unless the curriculum is agreed to.[42]

On 13 May 1970 in the lead up to a State election the biggest ever rally of Victorian nurses was held. Four thousand nurses gathered to demonstrate support for the new VNC curriculum, improved working conditions and a 50 per cent salary increase. Miss Jean Murray, vice president of the RVCN, and now curriculum development officer at the College of Nursing, Australia, explained why the 1 600 hours was so important:

> 1600 hours in a 3-year programme represents 27% of the total programme time. This 27% is little more than half the time recommended by W.H.O. in 1961. 73% of the programme time, some 4,240 hours, would be devoted to practical experience ... To devote 27% of the programme to theoretical work does not seem to us to be unreasonable; in fact it is much less than that given in other professional education programmes in this country and in basic nursing programmes in some other countries.

The time was required to permit trainees to receive their class-work in duty hours, to prepare them more adequately for their responsibilities and to meet the demands of increased nursing knowledge and skills.[43]

The new curriculum was seen as a vital step towards building the nursing profession in Victoria. It was believed that it would produce truly professional nurses who were confident and happy in their work. Miss Murray spoke of the growing dissatis-faction and disillusionment among trainees and nurses:

> We are tired of being treated as Cinderellas of the health team, we are concerned, very concerned, at the loss of potentially good nurses through wastage in the early parts of training, and about the great number of graduate profes-sional nurses who do not remain in nursing, and at the small number who pursue post graduate study.[44]

The rally overwhelmingly supported resolutions on the minimum 1 600 hours curriculum and on a minimum teacher-trainee ratio of one to 20.

It was hardly surprising that when the *Ramsay Report* was issued three months later *UNA* carried a 20-page supplement of detailed criticism of the report which had been put before the Minister of Health.[45] The 1 200 hours was unacceptable and the RVCN challenged the report's figures on the number of nurses available. But here the RVCN relied on the number of 'poten-tially available' nurses, that is, the many trained nurses who were no longer employed as such, who could be attracted back to nursing by an active recruitment campaign. The RVCN also challenged the assumption of the report that private hospital accommodation should go on increasing.[46]

Nor did the RVCN agree with the committee's criticisms of the many moves made by students during clinical practice under the VNC curriculum. In a small random sample from metropoli-tan hospitals the RVCN found that under the existing curriculum few trainee nurses had less than 21 moves in three years. The RVCN was also scathingly critical of the committee's suggestion that selected trained nurses attend one or two courses to prepare them for teaching. This was, of course, ludicrous given with the time taken to train teachers.[47]

The RVCN supported the pilot course to train student

nurses under the aegis of the Victorian Institute of Colleges, but wanted it to be a three year course run by the College of Nursing, Australia. It was clear that the RVCN did not regard college training as a likely possibility in the foreseeable future, if ever. The acceptance of the pilot course certainly did not mean that there was any general support amongst nurses in 1970 for a transition to college training.[48]

The implacable opposition of many leading nurses to nursing aides showed up clearly in the RVCN's comments on the committee's recommendations. What the committee was suggesting was another category of nurse which would eventually absorb the existing nursing aides. Moreover, its members would become recognised and qualified members of the nursing team — the [State] enrolled nurse (SEN). The RVCN did not support raising the training levels of nursing aides by revision of the training course , 'The nursing aide has not the necessary nursing educational background to slip into the stream of a professional nursing programme'. It would cause nursing aides 'considerable stress' and contribute to the wastage rate. The RVCN would make no concessions on this issue. Nursing aides were to be kept well away from professional nurse training. There were to be no links which would smooth the transition from being a nursing aide to being trained nurse.[49]

As we have seen in earlier chapters, this approach was typical of the RVCN's attitude to nursing aides. Ever since their inception in 1951 they had been regarded as a threat to the profession causing a dilution of standards. They showed that anyone without qualifications and only a brief training period, could be a 'nurse'

> the scope of duties for nursing aides should not be increased for any widening of the scope would bring them responsibility for decision making, use of judgment, and observations regarding the condition of patients. The basic nursing aide course, conducted over a period of 12 months, is designed to prepare persons with a limited educational background ... The basic general nursing education programme is designed to prepare nurses to function responsibly in these areas. It must be emphasised that nursing aides cannot be equipped with the necessary knowledge and understanding to perform in these areas.[50]

For nearly 20 years the problems of reforming the nursing aides' training program and of ensuring that all untrained nursing assistants took it had met a solid wall of resistance on the Nurses Board and the VNC. In 1958 the council had set December 1962 as the deadline by which all nursing assistants would be required to have the qualifications of nursing aides. But, even in 1966, the VNC was aware that many unqualified nursing assistants were employed in wards across the State. In 1966 Miss Jane Muntz gained no support from her fellow nurses on the VNC when she suggested that the nursing aide training committee which had not met for many years, reconvene to discuss such problems. Further efforts between 1967 and 1970 were also thwarted on the grounds that they would delay the general curriculum reforms for registered nurse trainees.[51]

Success for the 1600 Hours

THE months before and after the release of the *Ramsay Report* were characterised by growing militancy among Victorian nurses over salaries and conditions. Concern over the fate of the new curriculum went along with this surge of activity, and was also part of a general crisis in the hospital system. In the May election of 1970 Vance Dickie lost his position as Minister for Health and was replaced by John F. Rossiter, who proved to be much more sympathetic to the nurses.

But nurses were not fully united on the 1 600 hours. Even on the RVCN Council where matrons still held significant influence, there were members who expressed their doubts that the 1 600 hours could be implemented because of the shortage of staff.[52] The Hospital Matrons Association of Victoria, while supporting the 1 600 hours in principle, felt the 1 200 hours was a more practical figure. As no training hospital gave more than 800 hours in 1970, the 1 200 represented a 50 per cent increase, and matrons felt that in itself would be difficult to achieve because of the lack of personnel, facilities and recruits.[53]

Nevertheless, the RVCN pressed on with its campaign to bring pressure on the Government. Prior to meeting the Minister on 9 November to discuss the RVCN rebuttal of the *Ramsay*

Report, the council discussed further political action, following the success of the May rally. Mr Peter Cullen, a lobbyist engaged by the RVCN to advise on industrial strategies, commented that the RVCN 'was slowly learning the techniques of making itself felt and had the courage to make a strong criticism against the last Minister of Health'. The RVCN was no longer simply ignored, but was one of the groups consulted. Cullen felt that while they might think that marches and demonstrations were 'childlike and silly', 'it was the sort of thing that influences Government'. He advised that a rally be held in the Treasury Gardens followed by a march to Parliament House. After considerable discussion the council took his advice, 11 for and 10 against.[54]

Further political action proved unnecessary, however, because the RVCN deputation to Rossiter on 9 November received a sympathetic hearing. In January 1971 the minister announced that the Government had agreed that regulations would be made to prescribe the 1 600 hours curriculum to come into operation on 30 June 1974. At the same time he announced that the government would provide 50 scholarships in 1971 for nurses to undertake post-graduate courses at the College of Nursing, Australia, to complete the nursing education diploma course. The program for more advanced training of nursing aides had also been adopted, but not the title 'enrolled nurse'. The pilot program for a college course was deferred to a later date.[55]

Nevertheless, the RVCN was to find, as it had so often in the past, that the promises of politicians would soon be forgotten unless the pressures for reform were kept up. In September 1972 when the RVCN took a deputation to the Minister, the president, Miss Mary Evans, spoke of her 'deep distress', at the action of the Hospitals and Charities Commission in instructing hospitals not to allow for any increases for additional staff arising from the new curriculum in their budget estimates. Later the Acting Minister for Health confirmed this action.[56]

It was not until October 1972 that the new regulations were promulgated for the implementation of the new curriculum. From 25 October a training school was free to introduce the new curriculum provided it could meet the requirements of the regulations. At the same time the Minister appointed an expert committee headed by Professor Sir Lance Townsend, and including the chairman of the VNC, the secretary to the Health Department, representatives of the Hospital and Charities Commission and Treasury, and the Medical Superintendent of the Alfred, to oversee the introduction of the new curriculum. Nurses (but not doctors) were conspicuously absent from this committee. Each training school was required to present its plans with estimates for additional staffing, nurse educators and facilities for approval.[57]

In January 1974 the Government announced that $450 000 had been set aside for the implementation of the first stage of the curriculum and that indications were favourable for its progressive introduction over the next few years.[58] It had been a long haul since it was first mooted in the late 1950s. Yet even as it was being introduced moves which would eventually take the responsibility for training nurses away from hospitals altogether and give it to the colleges were underway.

By 1978 there were 15 metropolitan and 14 country hospitals as well as the Northern District School of Nursing in Bendigo with six affiliated hospitals, operating under the new curriculum. There were also ten psychiatric hospitals approved as basic psychiatric nurse training schools and five hospitals involved in nursing training for mental deficiency nurses.[59]

While the *Ramsay Report* on the curriculum had received attention from the RVCN and the VNC, the other recommendations regarding the training of nursing aides had been met with resistance. Although the Government had endorsed the recommendations, by 1975 the VNC had done nothing about them. The Committee of Inquiry into Hospital and Health Services in Victoria (1975) reported that since 1970 the nursing aide had become 'an even more important figure in the health care team'. The growth in the number of registered general nurses holding practising certificates between 1965 and 1973 was only 45 per cent, compared with 152 per cent for nursing aides. The committee regarded the whole question of the role and training of nursing aides as a matter of urgency, and recommended that the VNC and the Melbourne Nursing Aide School do something about it.[60] But when the *Report of the Committee of Inquiry into Nurse Education and Training* (Sax Report) came out in 1978, little had changed. There were ten independent nursing aide training schools and nine regional training schools with which 36 hospitals were affiliated. The course was still of only one year's duration, although the minimum age of entry was now 17 years and the minimum entry requirement the completion of form 4 (year 10) schooling.[61]

Taking Basic Training into the Colleges

THE suggestion of college-centred basic nursing training had come up again and again in the 1950s and 1960s. Nursing leaders were well aware of how college training operated overseas and some, even in the 1950s and 1960s, saw it as the only way forward in terms of basic training and for the achievement of professional status. Nevertheless, many nurses were resolutely opposed to taking control of basic nursing training away from hospitals. This opposition remained strong right through to the 1980s.

Miss Pat Slater, who was appointed director of the College of Nursing, Australia, from 1965, together with Miss Jean Murray, Miss Pat Osborne, Miss Mary Evans and Miss Mary Patten, became the chief advocates for taking basic nursing training in Victoria into the college sector. Building on her extensive overseas experience, Miss Pat Slater had developed some very definite views on the principles which should operate in any such changeover. She was resolutely opposed to combined university/college degree and hospital certificate programs of the type which had been established in New South Wales by 1970:

> It seems to me quite amazing that, with all the literature that is available about the serious consequences of establishing these combined programmes in the United States, Australian nurses would actively promote them. For the effect of programmes, where the non-nursing studies are at tertiary level in the university and the nursing studies are at sub-tertiary level in the hospital is to downgrade nursing education.

Miss Slater believed that in these programs students learnt nursing skills and tasks through practice, but devoted most of their energies to studying specific subjects unrelated, or indirectly related to nursing. Students, she believed, should be devoting all their energies to understanding concepts and principles which had been selected from various sciences because of their relevance to nursing, and to 'developing the ability to apply these principles and to provide comprehensive nursing care at the professional level'. Students also needed to include studies from disciplines not directly related to nursing, in order to develop 'well-rounded' personalities. The essential problem with the New South Wales program was the inherent assumption that nursing was simply performing technical tasks which could be learnt by practice under supervision. The caring side of nursing was seen to come primarily from inborn qualities which would be assisted by study in the humanities. Pat Slater insisted that nurses should study 'the science of nursing and develop skill in making nursing decisions based on that knowledge'.[62]

Another principle which she strongly adhered to was that nurses should be in control of nursing education when it moved to the college sector. She saw a real danger, which had been clearly indicated in a recent New South Wales report, of the control of nursing education being taken out of the hands of nurses and health authorities. In 1969 the Interim Truskett Report had recommended that the whole of nursing education be taken over by the advanced education sector with all control removed from the nurses' registration board, the hospitals' commission and the health department.[63]

Pat Slater favoured moving gradually into the college sector, not only to avoid disruption to nursing services, but also because she knew there were insufficient nurse educators prepared to take on jobs in the college nursing schools. She also felt concerned that faculty members in colleges could be selected on the basis of holding a degree in a discipline other than nursing:

> Unless the most gifted, experienced and dedicated nurse educators (and I make no apology for using this unpopular word) ... are selected to develop and implement the new programmes, the graduates will not be proficient nurses.

Nurses had to be in command of their own education. [64]

As a result of Miss Slater's initiative the College of Nursing, Australia, inaugurated a small basic nursing training program in 1974. By then the college was a member of the Victorian Institute of Colleges (VIC), and the course became the responsibility of the Lincoln Institute of Health Sciences in 1977.

In 1964, the Martin Committee, a federal inquiry into technical education, had opened the way towards federal funding of basic nursing education. It had become clear to nursing leaders who favoured college training that if there was to be any major shift from hospital to college education, it would have to be done at the federal level. For Pat Slater and her colleagues this was the only way nursing could be brought up to the level of professions like law and medicine, which enjoyed prestige and status in Australian society.

Unity in Pursuit of a Common Goal

IT was unity in pursuit of a common goal that won the day. The College of Nursing, Australia, and the RANF had in the past generally gone their own ways, just as had most of the other nursing organisations. While they had occasionally come together, unity of action had not been a feature of nurses' organisations in the post-war period. In fact, it is not too much to suggest that at the federal level it could well have been deliberate policy by the Commonwealth health authorities and some of the leading physicians and surgeons to keep nurses weak by encouraging a multitude of organisations. Nurses in one way or another were told that politics was a 'dirty game' (better left to men) which they would not be able to cope with.[65]

But this brand of paternalism which nurses had always had to cope with was under fire in the mid-seventies in the community at large and in nursing itself, as a result of the growth of a vigorous women's liberation movement. When Pat Slater as Director of the College of Nursing, Australia, and Mary Patten, secretary of the RANF, decided to work to bring the two organisations together in a determined effort to introduce basic nursing training into the colleges throughout Australia, they established a political alliance which was a sharp rebuff to those who had in the past considered nurses of little political significance and who had actively sought to keep them that way.

In 1975 these two organisations, together with the National

Florence Nightingale Committee of Australia and the New South Wales College of Nursing, prepared a report entitled *Goals of Nursing Education*. This was meant as a discussion document and workshops on its contents were held throughout Australia, with trained nurses, nursing aides (also known as nursing auxiliaries), and students all participating. From this a comprehensive policy statement was prepared by a working party representative of the States and Territories and the participating nursing organisations. This statement, issued in April 1976, became the basis for action in the late 1970s and early 1980s.[66]

The document boldly proclaimed, 'The nurses of Australia ...', and indeed it was the first time the nurses of Australia had so brazenly come together to shatter the perception of nurses as lacking in unity and preoccupied with in-fighting.[67] Nevertheless, it was articulate, politically astute nursing leaders such as Misses Slater and Patten who had led nurses to support basic education in the colleges. The opponents remained in the hospitals, inarticulate at the national level, and not convinced.

Three aspects of *Goals in Nursing Education* were of particular significance for nursing in Australia. The first was the clear purpose of the document, that is to phase nursing training into the general education system with programs preparing professional nurses at least at the tertiary diploma level. The second was the recognition of nursing auxiliary/aides as part of the nursing team. The third was the long term implication of the document which was to free the health services from the financial responsibilities for training nurses and, as with the other professions, make these part of the general financial outlay by governments on the education system.

The document recognised two classes of nursing personnel — the professional nurse and the auxiliary nurse: the distinction between the two categories reflecting the different levels of decision-making required. As a result the professional nurse would take her basic education in 'multi-discipline education institutions' at tertiary level, whereas the auxiliary nurse would be in 'multi-discipline education institutions' at the sub-tertiary level. Professional nurses were to be responsible for the development and implementation of courses for both classes of personnel. The document stressed that basic nursing education should aim for both a 'breadth of education and a comprehensive nursing preparation'. No new basic nursing programs were to be established and the current programs were to be discontinued as the colleges took over their functions.

Registration was also to remain firmly under the control of nurses. The nurses' registration authorities in the States were to retain responsibility for the registration of all graduates in both classes of nurses, as well as approving minimum curricula requirements. They were to continue to conduct the examinations leading to registration or to accredit the colleges to carry out their own assessment procedures. At all times nurses were to have majority representation on these registration boards.[68]

By 1978, there were six institutions in Australia offering basic education courses (Lincoln Institute of Health Sciences and Preston Institute of Technology in Victoria) to a total of only 461 students compared with 26 525 in the 268 hospital schools. There were also some 3 000 students in basic training courses in geriatric, psychiatric and mental retardation nursing.[69]

The *Sax Report*

IN September 1977 the Minister for Education in the federal Liberal-Country Party government established a committee to review arrangements for the education and training of nurses. This committee was to report to the Tertiary Education Commission, chaired by Professor Peter Karmel. Dr Sidney Sax, head of the Social Welfare Policy Secretariat in Canberra, was appointed chairman of the committee. Three of the 11 members were nurses, including Miss Mary Patten.

Twelve months later the committee's report seemed more concerned with patching up the existing system of hospital-based training, rather than with recommending a changeover to college education. It suggested various ways in which hospital-based training could be improved, many of which were already part of the 1 600 hours curriculum which had been introduced into Victorian hospitals.[70] It also recommended that hospital-based schools seek accreditation of their awards at the advanced education level.[71] It further suggested that contractual arrangements could be made between hospital schools and teaching institutions whereby payment for the contracted out elements of the hospital teaching program could be provided by the health or hospital authority.[72]

However, the committee did favour expanding existing college programs 'to a point at which each program is large enough to be assessed with assurance'.[73] To achieve this the committee recommended that a target figure of about 2 200 students be set for basic nursing education in colleges for 1985:

> the logistic, educational and financial problems which would accompany a departure from present arrangements suggest that change should be cautious, evaluated step by step, and taken forward only after validation justifies each change.[74]

The members of the Sax Committee knew that in its guidelines to the Tertiary Education Commission for 1978, the Government did not support any new courses or the expansion of existing courses for basic nursing education in the colleges. This meant that even the modest expansion suggested in the report could meet opposition from the Government. After almost 12 months of discussion within nurses' organisations, the RANF put forward its reaction to the *Sax Report*. It accepted the increases in college students as minimum numbers to be achieved by 1981 rather than 1985, and reaffirmed its 'unequivocal support' for college-based training. It strongly rejected any suggestion of accreditation of hospital schools of nursing. This was seen as a move simply to raise the status of graduates of hospital schools:

> a rise in status is but a small part of the profession's motivation in seeking changes to nurse education and training. The most substantive reason for making the change ... is to facilitate the conduct of programmes at a level which enables the rigour of a problem-solving approach to the practice of nursing, incorporating biophysical and behavioural sciences, to be incorporated throughout the total programme including clinical/field experiences ... this is the core of College-conducted basic nursing education programmes.[75]

The Federal Government's reaction to the report took a long time in coming, and in the meantime the National Steering Committee and its advisers for the *Goals of Nursing Education*, together with the task force convenors in the States, kept up the pressure on the Government. A campaign of letters and petitions continued. The annual report of the RANF for 1979–1980 suggested that 'nursing could be transferred to the higher education system ... within a relatively short space of time' if it was a question of 'rational analysis'. What the situation really amounted to, however, was 'health authorities, particularly the hospitals, wanting to retain control over the total socialization process of students of nursing'.[76]

When the Government announced its reaction to the *Sax Report* it endorsed most of its recommendations but placed particular emphasis on a slow schedule for the introduction of college-based training. It also expressed its commitment to improving the existing hospital-based system. There was no indication of general support for the long term introduction of college training.

This response to the report, coupled with the impending federal election in October 1980, provoked further militancy among nurses. Plans were drawn up at a national workshop in August for a nation-wide campaign. Activities included lobbying members of parliament, a rally in Canberra at the opening of parliament with simultaneous rallies in all States, as well as approaches to the media and questionnaires to candidates in the election.[77] Soon after the return of the Fraser government in 1980 the Minister for Education re-emphasised the Government's intention to pursue the matter of contractual arrangements between hospital schools and the colleges. A meeting between the RANF, the College of Nursing, Australia, and the Florence Nightingale Committee replied that this proposal would leave nursing with the worst of both worlds, 'continued employer control of nursing content and a purely 'academic' approach from the higher education system'.[78]

Further Political Action

IN meetings with federal government and the opposition health prior to the 1983 federal election, it was acknowledged that the transfer of nursing education to the general education sphere was inevitable; that there was some acceptance of the feasibility of completing the exercise by the end of 1990.

However, with the election of the Hawke Labor Government, which was more or less committed to taking basic nursing education into the colleges, it was still by no means certain that the plan would be carried through. But nurses saw it as a major step forward when Senator Gietzelt, speaking on behalf of the new Minister for Health, Dr Neal Blewett, declared that one of the most substantial arguments for moving basic nursing to the colleges was to improve nurses' professional status:

> Nurses have traditionally been regarded as the servants of doctors and administrators — performing menial tasks and working at the beck and call of their superiors. The current pyramid structure of the health care system has doctors firmly ensconced at the peak and nurses making up the base. This traditional approach to the roles of doctors and nurses is not the policy of the Commonwealth Government.
>
> We believe in a cooperative, participatory approach to health care, not in a rigid, hierarchical system with doctors making all health decisions. An appropriate sharing of ideas and practices between all health care professionals will lead to better quality care and more informed patient care ... this will be facilitated by educating nurses in multi-disciplinary institutions ... The current system of hospital training ... indoctrinates the current practices of inferior nurse status.[79]

Nevertheless, nurses relentlessly continued their publicity and lobbying campaign. It became very clear to federal politicians and administrators that nurses' organisations were united on the issue, and that they were not to be brushed off with promises, as had so often happened in the past. There were many months of top level negotiations in which nurses' representatives displayed a high level of skill and persistence, leaving the Government in no doubt of the validity of their claims.

A key development in this campaign was the announcement on 7 November 1983 by the New South Wales Minister for Health, L. Brereton, that from January 1985 all basic nursing education would be conducted by tertiary institutions in that State. Finally, on 24 August 1984, the Prime Minister in a letter to all State Premiers announced that the Government had decided to transfer basic nursing education to the advanced education sector. The last intake of hospital trainees was to take place in 1990:

> The Commonwealth expects that significant benefits will accrue from the transfer, including a better trained and more responsive work force, increased employment opportunities for qualified nursing personnel, increased education and vocational opportunities, particularly for women, and an enhanced status of nurses in line with other Health professionals.[80]

Nurses could not afford to be complacent, however, as the editorial in the *Australian Nursing Journal* warned:

> The in-principle transfer decision is only the first, albeit major, hurdle along a path towards total transfer. If nurses feel they can now sit back and allow others to implement the changes, their star will fall as dramatically as it has risen. State Governments have already begun negotiating with public servants and academics ... Nurses must be involved in these negotiations. From now on, it will not be adequate to simply inform nurses about procedural changes.[81]

Politicians had stood up and taken notice. It was now up to the nurses to keep them on their feet.

Post-basic Nursing Education and the Colleges

POST-BASIC nursing education courses in Victoria were conducted at training hospitals and at the College of Nursing, Australia. The hospitals courses were many and varied and fluctuated in their availability from year to year. They could be divided roughly into three categories, registrable, nursing certificate endorsable and others. The *Ramsay Report* listed nine registrable and endorsable Victorian hospital courses in 1970,[82] while the *Sax Report* in 1978 listed 16.[83] They included midwifery, infant welfare, mental deficiency, psychiatric, geriatric, infectious diseases, gynaecological nursing and intensive care. The *Ramsay Report* found that the course content and standard of these courses varied as much as their duration — some lasted 12 months, others only four months. It recommended that the

VNC examine these courses with a view to applying more consistent standards and removing anomalies after the introduction of the new basic nursing curriculum.[84]

Standing quite apart from the post-basic hospital courses were those offered by the College of Nursing, Australia. The college was a national body which initially conducted full-time diploma courses for registered nurses in preparation for positions as matrons, sister tutors and ward sisters. It also offered courses for public health nurses and theatre sisters. The headquarters were established in St Kilda Road, Melbourne, in a building which had been purchased as a memorial to nurses who had lost their lives in the Second World War. Other branches were set up in Brisbane in 1960 and in Perth in 1968. The college was structured in a similar manner to other professional colleges, wherein membership was by invitation. Membership criteria were determined by the college council. In later years fellowship was limited to nurses who had successfully completed a post-graduate diploma course at the college or a similar institution. By March 1977 there were 1 875 members.[85]

The college council established a committee in each State to implement its aims. These included the development of short courses and other study programs, assistance for applicants for diploma courses to complete pre-course preparation, and the raising of funds. An education committee, consisting of six fellows experienced in nursing education (nominated by the State committees), a general education expert, two members of the medical profession and senior members of academic staff advised the council in all matters relating to education. From 1955 an annual grant was made by the Federal Government to the college, but finance also came from membership fees and contributions from the State committees.[86]

In 1964 the Martin Committee in its report to the Australian Universities Commission on the future of tertiary education in Australia recommended that the two existing nursing colleges (College of Nursing, Australia, and the New South Wales College of Nursing) become 'constituent members of the appropriate Institutes of Colleges'.[87] This, in effect, meant raising the post-basic nursing courses in these colleges to the status of courses in colleges of advanced education (CAEs). It also opened the way for increased federal funding of college of nursing post-basic courses, and even basic courses if in the future the colleges decided to undertake them.

Miss Pat Slater, director of the College of Nursing, Australia, described how not long after the *Martin Report* she received a visit from Ian Wark, chairman of the Commonwealth Advisory Committee on Advanced Education. Mr Wark arrived at the Nurses Memorial Centre to find students 'standing in the science labs with their noses in the poisons eating their lunch. There was absolutely no room'. He said the college was exactly the type of institution they wanted to help and he would recommend that the Victorian Institute of Colleges (VIC) 'take it under its wing'.[88] Approval for college students to receive tertiary allowances came first and in 1970 the college became a member of the VIC. Capital funds were provided through the VIC for the purchase of land from the Nurses Memorial Centre, and the new building was completed in January 1970. Recurrent funds were made available to assist in the running of diploma courses which, by 1974, were offered in administration, education, education (midwifery), ward management, operating theatre nursing and management, and public health. By this time there were 270 students.

Miss Pat Slater saw affiliation with the VIC as an important step forward for the college because it gave the college staff and students of the College access to the CAE system. It would help widen the horizons of college staff, most of whom were college graduates and few of whom had had any general experience in Australia or overseas. She felt at the time that nursing needed to mix with other professions, and that this might help break down the deplorably 'territorial' nature of nursing, which was common to all the health professions. She knew that 'nursing had to enter the mainstream' and that college courses had to have 'a stronger input from other courses'.[89]

During 1975, the college commenced discussions with the Lincoln Institute with a view to a merger. Lincoln was then a college of the health sciences affiliated with the VIC. As a result, from 1 January 1977 all the Melbourne college courses became the responsibility of the new school of nursing at the Lincoln Institute. All staff members except the membership secretary became members of the staff of the Institute. Pat Slater became head of the school. The school operated from its headquarters in St Kilda Road, and funds from the Federal Government were allocated directly to the school.[90]

Similar developments occurred in other States, and from 1 January 1978 the College of Nursing, Australia, had no further responsibility for conducting approved tertiary courses. It continued to act as a professional college organising short courses, refresher courses and seminars, and worked closely with the RANF formulating policies regarding nursing practice, education and research.[91]

The School of Nursing of the Lincoln Institute of Health Sciences began in 1977 by offering a wide range of post-basic nursing diplomas built on the old College of Nursing program. Apart from the standard courses in administration, nursing education and midwifery, there were two major course streams centred on the Diploma in Hospital Nursing and Unit Management and the Diploma in Community Health Nursing. The former offered training in advanced medical/surgical, critical care, operating room, maternity, paediatric and psychiatric nursing. The latter in mental health nursing, occupational health nursing, early childhood development, Aboriginal health and welfare, school health nursing, maternal and child health nursing and community health centre development.

It should not be forgotten in considering the general area of post-basic nursing education that a large number of short courses, orientation programs, in-service seminars and the like were run by the hospitals and other health care agencies as part of the ongoing continuing education programs designed to keep trained nurses up to date and to enable them to undertake short courses requiring specific knowledge and skills. In the seventies continuing education was organised in an ad hoc manner with little co-ordination between hospitals. *Goals in Nursing Education* drew attention to the need for health commissions in each state to establish appropriate committees to investigate continuing education for nurses and to draw up recommendations regarding a program, funding and structure through which resources could be rationalised.[92] The *Sax Report* considered these continuing education courses of particular importance for helping married nurses re-enter the workforce or for assisting immigrants to satisfy registration requirements. It also suggested that CAEs, which were providing nurse education courses should move into this field.[93]

Miss Pat Slater

THIS survey of nursing education in Victoria in the sixties, seventies and early eighties would not be complete without some consideration being given to the work of Miss Pat Slater. Her career was devoted to raising the standards of nurses' training and education in Australia. While no one person was responsible for taking nursing training out of the hospitals and into the colleges, Pat Slater provided much of the inspiration, the guidance and the persistence to pursue the campaign to a successful conclusion.

She came from a supportive family background, but because of a shortage of funds only her brother, who was undeniably brilliant in his field, was able to go to university. She decided she was 'dull' and went into nursing, training at the Children's, Melbourne and Alfred hospitals in the late thirties. She gained her midwifery and infant welfare certificates at the Royal Women's Hospital and the Karitane Home for Mothers and Babies, in Sydney. Her political astuteness showed up early in her training, 'My one ambition during training was not to be known by the matron. The day after I finished training the matron asked me my name'.[94]

She spent two years in the Australian Army Nursing Service and was in Borneo when the war ended, where she stayed behind to nurse prisoners of war. She did not join the Returned Servicemen's League and would have nothing to do with the war nurses. 'I belong to an era which rejected a lot of the values of the older generation', she said.

After demobilisation she spent several years working in small hospitals in North Queensland. The turning point in her career came in 1955 when she was appointed a sister tutor. She gained a Diploma in Nursing Education from the College of Nursing, Australia, in 1956, and after a short time working as a sister tutor, was awarded a Centaur War Nurses Memorial Scholarship to study at the University of Washington, Seattle, in the United States. She graduated with a Bachelor of Science (Nursing) and a Master of Arts (major studies in nursing and administration) with the highest honours. She was then awarded a Rockefeller Fellowship for an extensive study tour of the United States, Canada, Scandinavia and Britain studying nursing and nursing education.[95]

As we have seen, on her return to Australia in 1961 she was soon actively involved in the detailed preparation of the 1600 hours curriculum for the VNC. She was Director of the College of Nursing, Australia, from 1965 until 1981, the last four years in an honorary capacity, because in 1977 she had become the first head of the newly created School of Nursing within the Lincoln Institute of Health Sciences. She retired from this position at the end of 1983.

On her retirement as director of the College of Nursing, Australia, it was said:

> I pay tribute to Pat for her outstanding contribution to the development of the College, her dedicated commitment … to nursing education, and nursing, in Australia.
>
> She has worked tirelessly for the implementation of the Goals in Nursing Education Policy Statements. She has lobbied, campaigned, written papers, addressed nurses and other groups within the community, and travelled throughout the length and breadth of this country, in an attempt to see these goals realized.[96]

Endnotes

1 John Lindell, 'Nursing, a Profession', in *UNA*, October 1953, p. 296.
2 Mary Patten, 'Systems of Nurse Training in Victoria', in *UNA*, October 1953, pp. 311–14.
3 'Trends in Nursing', in *The Medical Journal of Australia*, 11 September 1954, p. 437.
4 Jane E. Muntz, 'Nursing — Professional Responsibility', in *UNA*, November 1954, p. 340.
5 'How does Nursing Education affect the Service to the Patient and the Staffing of the Hospital', in *UNA*, May 1959, p. 135. Five of these Sister Tutors were to work later in the 1950s on the 1600 hours curriculum reform. They were Misses G. Berger, L. M. Day, E. N. Hughes, J. G. Murray and P. V. Slater.

[6] ibid.

[7] ibid., p. 136.

[8] ibid., p. 139.

[9] ibid., pp. 139–145.

[10] F. M. Peterson, 'Scientific Progress and the Nurse', in *UNA*, January 1955, p. 24.

[11] Y. Jayawardena, 'Whither Nursing', in *UNA*, October 1961, p. 312.

[12] Debate on 'That Nursing in Australia is handicapped through lack of University Nursing Schools', in *UNA*, October 1955, pp. 302–18.

[13] Education Committee of the ICN, 'Report on an Enquiry, into Basic Nursing Education, 1961–1963, p. 3. Box 55, UM archives.

[14] P. V. Slater, 'Comprehensive Training', in *UNA*, June 1963, p. 203.

[15] ibid., p. 205.

[16] ibid., p. 207.

[17] ibid., pp. 208–9.

[18] RVCN, Education Committee Minutes, 16 July 1964. Box 14, UM archives. Members of this committee were Misses J. Murray (chair), E. Hughes-Jones, L. Day, D. Trethewie, M. Connor, N. Sewell, P. Slater, L. M. Avery, N. J. Chrisfield and J. Dunbar. Six of these were working on the 1600 hours curriculum reform committee of the VNC.

[19] RVCN, Education Committee, April 1964, 'Policies Relating to Basic Nursing Education', p. 2. Box 41, UM archives.

[20] ibid., p. 6.

[21] VNC, general training working committee report to VNC, February 1965. Appendix II, 'The Method of Preparing the Curriculum'. Slater papers.

[22] VNC, minutes of a meeting of matrons and principal nursing educators, 30 November 1965, address by Miss P. F. Osborne, p. 2. Slater papers.

[23] Ibid., p. 4.

[24] VNC, general training working committee. Lists of persons who prepared the curriculum, assisted with the preparation and development of individual syllabuses and reviewed the drafts. Slater papers.

[25] VNC, general training working committee. Report to VNC, February 1965, p. 1. Slater papers.

[26] VNC, minutes of a meeting of matrons and principal nursing educators, 30 November 1965, p. 7. Slater papers.

[27] ibid. Comment from Miss N. Sewell (member of General Training Working Committee).

[28] *Nursing in Victoria. Report of the Committee of Enquiry into Nursing* (Ramsay Report), August 1970, p. 18.

[29] ibid., p. 75.

[30] ibid., pp. 76–7.

[31] ibid., pp. 103–4.

[32] ibid., p. 11.

[33] ibid., p. 80.

[34] ibid., p. 12.

[35] ibid., p. 86.

[36] ibid., pp. 91–2.

[37] ibid., p. 93.

[38] ibid., p. 97.

[39] ibid., p. 92.

40 ibid., pp. 112–13.
41 ibid., p. 14.
42 Transcript of the introductory remarks made by Miss Mary Evans at the deputation to the Premier, Henry Bolte, 22 April 1970. Slater papers.
43 *UNA*, May/June 1970, p. 14.
44 ibid., p. 16.
45 *UNA*, October/November 1970, pp. 9–32.
46 ibid., pp. 13–14.
47 ibid., p. 21.
48 ibid., p. 22.
49 ibid., pp. 26–7.
50 ibid., pp. 24–5.
51 M. K. Minchin, *Revolutions and Rosewater. The Evolution of Nurse Registration in Victoria 1923–1973*, Hart Hamer, Melbourne, 1970, pp. 83–4.
52 RVCN minutes, 28 October 1970.
53 Submission to the Minister of Health, Victoria from the Hospital Matrons Association of Victoria re report of the committee of enquiry into nursing in Victoria, n.d. Box 101, UM archives.
54 RVCN minutes, 5 November 1970.
55 John Rossiter, Minister of Health to Miss Mary Evans, 14 January 1971, reproduced in *UNA*, January/February 1971, p. 1.
56 RVCN, deputation to Minister of Health, 13 September 1972. Box 22, UM archives.
57 *UNA*, October/November 1972, p. 1.
58 *UNA*, January/February 1974, p. 4.
59 *Nurse Education and Training: Report of the Committee of Inquiry into Nurse Education and Training to the Tertiary Education Committee*, Canberra, 1978 (Sax Report), p. 21.
60 *Report of the Committee of Inquiry into Hospital and Health Services in Victoria*, July 1975, p. 110.
61 *Sax Report*, op. cit., p. 31.
62 Pat Slater, address to College of Nursing, Australia, annual meeting 1970, in *UNA*, July/August, 1970, p. 12.
63 ibid., p. 13.
64 ibid., pp. 12–13.
65 See interview, Pat Slater, 26 February 1989.
66 RANF, College of Nursing, Australia, National Florence Nightingale Committee of Australia, New South Wales College of Nursing, *Goals in Nursing Education Policy Statements*, April 1976.
67 ibid., p. 6.
68 ibid., pp. 5–11.
69 *Sax Report*, op. cit., pp. 131–4.
70 ibid., pp. 74–5.
71 ibid., p. 118.
72 ibid., p. 78.
73 ibid., p. 88.
74 ibid., p. 115.
75 *Australian Nursing Journal (ANJ)*, October 1979, p. 11.
76 *ANJ*, June 1980, p. 8.
77 *ANJ*, October 1980, p. 14.

78 *ANJ*, December/January 1981, p. 7.
79 *ANJ*, July 1983, p. 13.
80 *ANJ*, October 1984, p. 26.
81 ibid., p. 5.
82 *Ramsay Report*, op. cit., p. 109.
83 *Sax Report*, op. cit., pp. 141–2.
84 *Ramsay Report*, op. cit., p. 110.
85 College of Nursing, Australia, minutes of twenty-eighth annual general meeting, 28 May 1977. See also College of Nursing, Australia, submission to the committee of enquiry into education and training (Sax Committee), April 1977.
86 ibid., pp. 1–2.
87 *Tertiary Education in Australia. Report of the Committee on the Future of Tertiary Education in Australia to the Australian Universities Commission, (Martin Report)*, vol. 2, AUGUST 1964, p. 123.
88 Interview, Pat Slater, 26 February 1989.
89 ibid.
90 College of Nursing, Australia, *Annual Report 1976*, Melbourne 1976, p. 14.
91 Submission to Sax Committee ..., op. cit., p. 8.
92 *Goals in Nursing Education ...*, op. cit., p. 11.
93 *Sax Report*, op. cit., pp. 112–3.
94 Interview, Pat Slater, 26 February 1989.
95 *ANJ*, February 1984, p. 15.
96 *ANJ*, August 1981, p. 14.

The Struggle to Improve Salaries and Working Conditions

I N 1962, at the invitation of the RANF, Miss Sheila Quinn, director of the Economic Welfare Division of the ICN, undertook a survey of the economic conditions of nurses in Australia. She found bewildering differences in nurses' salaries and conditions and in the various methods of determining them. Nursing awards in Western Australia and New South Wales were noticeably superior in many aspects to other States. There was a lack of uniformity which disadvantaged nurses not only in those States where conditions were poor, but which also discouraged them from moving between States to widen the scope of their experience.[1]

In Victoria, she compared the salaries of nurses with teachers in 1962 and found nurses a long way behind. Nursing was still poorly paid compared with other professions which women chose in large numbers. Nursing was frequently equated with primary teaching and the qualifications required for entry were comparable. Primary teaching attracted a much higher proportion of females compared with males, and the social background of recruits to nursing and teaching was found to be similar.

The allowance for a trainee nurse in Victoria over the three years of training rose from £387 to £468 per annum. During this period trainees provided 60 to 70 per cent of the nursing labour requirements in training hospitals and in their final year they held very responsible positions — girls of nineteen years 'taking responsibility which would make a mature adult hesitate'.[2] Their allowance compared most unfavourably with that of primary teachers in training which was from £500 to £600 per annum, especially as trainee teachers at no stage had to carry similar responsibility. Teaching practice was carried out under the supervision of regular class teachers who retained full control and responsibility. Trainees also spent a significant part of the year in the college rather than in the classroom.

Similarly, graduate nurses commenced work on £811 per annum, compared with a primary teacher on £915. Charge sisters with many years of experience, even at the maximum salary, received only £994 per annum, whereas primary teachers were earning £1490 per annum after a similar length of experience. Even tutor sisters who had to undertake an extra year's college education, and who held positions of greater responsibility, were still £150 worse off than Victorian primary teachers.[3]

The standard working week in Australia was 40 hours, and in nursing as in most other occupations any work in excess of this was paid as overtime. However, in practice the nature of the nurse's work often forced her to work beyond the 40 hours and because this was not officially authorised, no payment was normally made. Indeed, there was a persistent anomaly between the period of the shift for which the nurse was paid and actual time taken to perform the duties required of her during the shift. The net result was a lot of unpaid overtime. The school teacher could expect to work from 9.00 a.m. to 4.00 p.m. five days a week, and even though she may be required to take home work, her hours on the job were fixed and predictable. In many hospitals work rosters were often not known until a day or two beforehand and these difficulties were compounded by the use of broken shifts. Saturday and Sunday work was generally treated the same as any other day. Penalty rates did not apply in Victoria for night work, weekend work or public holidays.

Nurses had no effective superannuation scheme in Victoria in 1962. There was a provident fund which was so unattractive that few nurses participated. When the retiring age for nurses was dropped to 60 years there was such an outcry from nurses that the RVCN succeeded in getting it restored to 65. Nurses could simply not afford to retire at 60. For single nurses who had lived in nurses' homes on low salaries, retirement could be a disaster, and some were left almost destitute.[4]

Apart from the general reduction in working hours across

all sections of the community, there had been little real improvement in the salaries and working conditions of nurses in Victoria since the 1930s, especially when measured against comparable occupations. Nurses had been left behind during a period of unprecedented prosperity and full employment.

Nevertheless, nursing was not the only female-dominated occupation during the 1960s characterised by low wages and poor conditions. Shop assistants, clerical workers, domestic workers, librarians and female workers in the clothing and catering industries all experienced similar problems. It was basically a question of gender, but added to this were two other arguments which hindered the efforts of nursing leaders to improve salaries and conditions. As mentioned in chapter 3, nursing was seen by the public and by many nurses as a vocation. Nurses should be prepared to work overtime for no pay and endure the disadvantages of the job, because they were privileged to be working as nurses. The satisfaction of caring for the sick was the nurse's own reward. Undoubtedly, many nurses were unwilling to actively seek better conditions and salaries because they were happy in this belief. This attitude was to influence the thinking of nursing leaders when linked with the notion of professionalism and the vexed question of penalty rates in the late 1960s.

The other argument frequently used against improving nurses' salaries was related to the question of 'living in'. It was alleged that nurses were given a hidden subsidy by being able to live in a nurses' home for a nominal rate of around £3 2s 6 per week.[5] This worked as an incentive for nurses to live in; if they did not do so the most they could claim was an extra £1 per week, which was granted only if hospital authorities required that they live out. The system was maintained in order to encourage nurses to live in. This had many advantages from the point of view of hospital administrators, but helped to depress nurses' salaries and undermine their independence.

The problem of low wage status was the general problem of women working in a male-dominated society, a society which in the 1950s and 1960s was characterised by a resurgence of male authority after the war years when females had taken over many of the male roles in the workforce. It was a problem related directly to the sexual division of labour which divided work (paid and unpaid) into those jobs which were distinctly 'male' and those which were distinctly 'female'. In the process the status of female work was subordinated to the status of male work. Of course, it was not the actual work which was specifically male or female, but the way jobs were perceived in an essentially male-dominated society. Female work was perceived to be of lower value than male work.[6]

At no stage in the history of the RVTNA or the RVCN struggle to achieve professional status was there any thought or suggestion of a challenge to the male-dominated hierarchy of the health care system. Senior nurses and matrons accepted their role in the hierarchy and enforced this on their subordinates in their everyday work practices. The training of nurses maintained the hierarchical division between nursing and medicine which was based on the subordination of nurses to doctors. Nurses were there to do what doctors ordered, and their work was always open to intervention by the medical profession. Even though by the 1960s there were many practices which doctors left to nurses, these were still subject to medical supervision.

In this scene nurses were always subservient to doctors. They had to grin and bear the chauvinism, the arrogance, the impatience, the mistakes and harassment of many doctors who also often treated them as 'non-persons' and as non-professionals. Most nurses seem to have accepted such treatment without question. It was simply 'the way things were'. Needless to say, this subservience was constantly reinforced and most nurses were probably unaware of this. Of course, there were always exceptions — the charge nurses were frequently referred to as 'Queen Bees' who kept the younger doctors under control, and some nurses took it upon themselves to teach the doctors their jobs, albeit as subtly as possible.

Nurses appear to have exhibited many characteristics attributed to oppressed groups, such as lack of self-esteem and never-ending in-fighting within their institutions and their professional organisations. Contemporaries commented on the contrast between nurses' warmth and sensitivity towards their patients and their relations with their own colleagues:

nurses exhibit self-hatred and dislike for other nurses, as evidenced by divisiveness and lack of cohesiveness in professional organisations. Their lack of interest in participating in professional organisations suggests little pride in nursing and a desire to avoid alignment with powerless others ... These attributes combine to create the submissive-aggressive syndrome ... This aggression is displaced, self-destructively yet safely, within the oppressed group and results in self criticism and infighting known as 'horizontal violence'.[7]

On the other hand, this behaviour may also be characteristic of groups with a strong commitment to an ideal. Being totally devoted to a cause, anyone who deviates from it is likely to attract extreme hostility from other group members. What they have worked for is threatened. A trust has been destroyed. The vehemence towards the heretic is much more than towards an outsider who can be forgiven for her or his ignorance, for that person has not betrayed the cause. A good example here would be the attitude of some nursing leaders to the nursing aides and to anyone within nursing who was seen to support them.

Much of the history of nursing outlined in this book documents internal conflicts, lack of participation in professional organisations and many attempts to define nursing and its future (not that other unions and associations do not have similar problems). These problems point to a general lack of confidence which overflowed into the industrial arena. The low wage status of nursing was intimately bound up with the issues raised above. When linked with the professional aspirations of nursing leaders, it was almost inevitable that salaries and conditions should be pushed into the background.

The main concerns of nursing leaders up until the 1960s were to attain and maintain State registration, to solve all the problems that went with this and to raise the standards of nursing education. The RVCN consistently down-played the traditional concerns of a trade union — the maintenance and improvement of the salaries and conditions of its members. Nursing leaders eschewed these issues by placing them in the hands of the Employees Association. By concentrating on what they believed to be the key determinants of professional status — registration and qualifications — nursing leaders failed to bring the great majority of nurses in Victoria within the ambit of the RVCN. From the trade union perspective most nurses were left leaderless and disorganised. The sources available strongly suggest that had it not been for the HEF constantly knocking at the door, industrial matters would have been thrust further into the background.

Nevertheless, it is not historically productive nor meaningful to lay blame. Nursing leaders were caught up in the net of professionalism. They, like the leaders of many other occupational groups, including teachers, were pursuing a goal which was closely related to the sexual division of labour referred to earlier. The goal of professionalism had been developed by the male medical and legal professions partly as a means of establishing their authority and dominance over their respective fields. They had been very successful in this and it was not surprising that other occupational groups sought to emulate doctors and lawyers.[8] But, for nurses, who were constantly reminded of the 'professionalism' of physicians and surgeons, what they aspired to was essentially a masculine model of professionalism, where all the characteristics generally found in the male were given full play — assertiveness, ruthlessness in pursuit of goals, credentialism associated with careerism, and power over individuals and groups considered lesser in the social scale, which included women. While an alternative to this masculine model existed, which emphasised the caring and nurturing aspects of nursing, in a male-dominated health service it carried little status or prestige outside of nursing.[9]

Penalty Rates

IN July 1950 Mary Harper from Queensland wrote to Marjorie Connor about penalty rates:

> we scream about the domestics getting week end rate, but surely we reduce ourselves to the same level in wanting. It is I think shocking to want double pay for nursing poor unfortunate creatures who are certainly not being ill just for the pleasure of it ... The only times our meetings are attended are when the members want more money ... Nursing appears to be definitely a trade and a means to an end rather than a profession.[10]

Mary Harper's comments reflected the dilemma nurses faced in Victoria over the next 20 years. They knew that the 'professional' physicians and surgeons did not claim penalty rates, but they saw other hospital workers receiving them and in the process gaining higher salaries than the nurses. Did they maintain their 'professionalism' or did they stoop to the level of a trade? It was a problem which raised many of the issues discussed previously linking the low wage rates of nurses and the quest for professional status.

Penalty rates were a recurring problem for the RVCN and the ANFES, VB in the 1950s and 1960s, especially on those occasions when the HEF threatened to lodge a claim for them. In the occupations where they were paid, penalty rates usually applied between the hours of 6.00 p.m. and 6.00 a.m. when the rate was normally time and a quarter, while Saturday work was paid at time and a half. Sundays and public holidays usually attracted double pay. Penalty rates were paid to compensate employees for working outside the normal working hours of most of the community. On the whole, 'professional' people did not receive these rates in the 1950s and 1960s. For example, lawyers, physicians, surgeons, architects and dentists set an all-inclusive fee in which hours of work were taken into consideration. In the 1960s doctors in private practice began charging extra for night and weekend visits.[11]

In this period members of the RVCN had consistently voted against seeking penalty rates. When the matter came up in 1967, after the HEF had again threatened to lodge a claim, it received long and detailed attention from RVCN leaders. The arguments for and against penalties were rehearsed again, but this time it was clear that the unified opposition of previous years no longer existed.[12] The main opposition to penalty rates centred on the belief that they were inappropriate for professional people. When Miss L. H. Durrant outlined her arguments against penalty rates to a meeting of the ANFES, VB in February 1968, she concluded by quoting from Dr Marie Jahoda's address at the 1961 ICN Congress in Melbourne:

> A profession implies that the quality of the work done by its members is of greater importance in their own eyes, and in the eyes of society than the economic rewards they earn.[13]

Closely linked to this concern was the steadfast belief by nursing leaders in the late sixties that nothing should be allowed to hinder the introduction of the new 1600 hours curriculum. Penalty rates would cost the Government money which might otherwise be spent on implementing the new curriculum. They would also take funds away from other areas of need in hospitals and force patients to pay more.

There was also a possibility that penalty rates would upset the nursing hierarchy. As Miss Durrant pointed out, the basic hourly rate for a staff nurse was $1.11 in 1968, for the most senior charge sister it was $1.53. Double time or time and a half for the staff nurse would mean that she would be receiving considerably more than the charge sister when she worked at weekends. This would be an affront to the status of the charge sister. To give another example, a matron of a 200-bed hospital with a basic salary of $2.19 per hour would be 3 cents per hour worse off than the staff nurse on double time. Added to this, the staff nurse would receive the greater salary at a time in the week when there was less to do in the wards.[14]

There was also the invidious example of what had happened at repatriation hospitals in the various States which came under a federal award. Penalty rates had been paid for 15 years up to late 1966. Until 1951 junior staff were discriminated against by having to work at weekends and nights, but when penalty rates were implemented senior staff took over these times. The fact that opponents of penalty rates feared that this would happen in Victorian public hospitals if penalty rates were introduced, said much about their confidence in nurses as professionals.[15]

The argument for penalty rates did not attempt to answer the claim that professionals did not require such rates, but rested on current community practice where penalty rates were widespread. For nursing, they already applied in many other countries and in Australia they applied in the Australian Capital Territory, Western Australia and South Australia, and were likely to be introduced in Queensland. Since it was common practice in many hospitals to roster student nurses on weekends and at night, the application of penalty rates would discourage this and also allow trainees to lead more normal social lives. It would also improve their educational program. Miss Orr, who presented the case for penalty rates at the February 1968 meeting, suggested that if hospitals failed to offer such rates 'wastage will continue and worsen, particularly as there are so many alternative careers.'[16]

In May 1968 Marjorie Connor, in her capacity as secretary of the ANFES, VB, wrote to the president of the RVCN stating that it was of 'vital importance' that the RVCN formulate a policy on penalty rates. The ANFES Committee of Management had to make a decision and it was looking for guidance from the RVCN. Mr W. J. R. Toy, who had been appointed Industrial Relations Officer in 1966, had already submitted the proposition that all nurses be paid time and a half for Saturday, double time for Sunday and an allowance of 7.5 per cent for night duty, except for the night sister-in-charge.[17]

RVCN members were clearly divided on the issue, and delayed making any decision. The Matrons Association, and the Bendigo, Ballarat and Goulburn Valley branches of the RVCN favoured penalty rates, Warrnambool was indecisive and only the Eastern Metropolitan branch and the Nurse Educators were against.[18] The latter saw themselves as being particularly disadvantaged because they did much of their work at home.[19] After many hours of agonising deliberation, the RVCN Council decided against pursuing penalty rates, mainly because they would upset the balance between the salaries of trained staff and senior personnel. Their introduction would also interfere with efforts to introduce the new curriculum.[20] The council agreed that under no circumstances should penalty rates apply to student nurses.

Here the matter rested for some time until, quite unexpectedly, and much to the surprise of many RVCN council members, the Wages Board announced in January 1971 that it had granted penalty rates to nurses other than matrons, deputy matrons, assistant matrons, night sisters-in-charge and principal teachers. The determination provided that work performed on afternoon or night shifts was to be paid at $1 per shift and continuous night shift at $1.50. Work on Saturday and Sunday would be paid at the rate of time and a half.[21]

This unexpected development was directly related to the appointment of Mr Geoff McDonald as Industrial Relations Officer in January 1970, to replace Mr Toy who had joined the Hospital Employers Association. Mr McDonald had had considerable experience working for various trade unions and associations as an organiser and industrial advocate. Early in his career he had been associated with the militant and communist led unions. While he no longer supported them politically, he had retained a strong belief in the effectiveness of militant industrial tactics, especially those which involved rank and file union members. His appointment was a reflection of the growing dissatisfaction of nurses with their salaries and conditions. It came as a surprise to many nursing leaders, and although it was to produce quite a few traumas and long memoranda over the next few years, Geoff McDonald did get results.

In January 1971, nurses were awaiting the completion of a long and drawn out work value case before the Wages Board. Employers were reluctant to make any offers, but Geoff McDonald pressured them to make an interim offer which would help placate the unrest among nurses. The result was that the board agreed to penalty rates. Geoff McDonald came under considerable criticism from nurses for precipitating the issue, especially as the ANFES, VB had deferred a decision on penalty rates pending the outcome of the work value case. What followed was a protracted battle as those who considered themselves disadvantaged by the Wages Board decision sought redress.[22] Senior personnel in the smaller hospitals were particularly incensed and Geoff McDonald received 'innumerable telephone calls' leading him to conclude that penalty rates should apply to all nursing personnel, senior and junior.[23] The ANFES, VB, however, could not accept this proposition.[24]

Nurse educators were especially angered by the decision, which upset the relativity of nurse educators with supervisory sisters with which they had been equated since the 1961 award. Under the new determination, the supervisory sisters required to give supervision over the whole 24-hour period would be able to gain a significant salary advantage by earning penalty rates, whereas nurse educators could not do this, even though, they argued, they took a lot of work home:

> The introduction of penalty rates has grossly disturbed the relativity of take home pay within the hierarchy to such an extent that nurses on a lower level can outearn those placed

above them. Such a state of affairs gives little encouragement for nurses to accept positions of authority and responsibility in both nursing service and nursing education.[25]

The decision also had particular relevance to the introduction of the new curriculum, when it was anticipated that a large number of extra nurse educators would be required.

Worse was to come when the Wages Board finally made its decision on the work value case in September 1971. This provided for a substantial increase in salaries and changed the salary base for principal teachers from bed capacity to student numbers, resulting in a down-grading of principal teachers in many hospitals. It also redefined definitions for nurse educators.[26] Within a week an application was lodged by the RANF, VB seeking a wages board meeting to deal with anomalies concerning nurse educators, even though the RANF, VB had accepted the final offer of employers. This went against all established wages board practice and was done against the bitter opposition of the Industrial Relations Officer.

Nurse educators engaged in a relentless campaign to have the anomalies corrected, which led to the RANF, VB taking the problem of definitions of nurse educators to the Industrial Appeals Court.[27] The RANF, VB engaged a Queens Council for the appeal on 8 August 1972 because they were unhappy about the Industrial Relations Officer being left in charge of the case.[28] On 3 November 1972 the bench of the Appeals Court determined to take no action in regard to the problem of nurse educators' definitions, but gave leave for the Wages Board to re-examine them. Nurse educators gained a $4 per week loading, already paid to charge sisters grade 2, with whom their rates were equated. The Court also ruled that student numbers was an unsatisfactory criterion on which to base the wage rates of principal teachers and recommended that the Wages Board also re-examine this. In the meantime it revised the classification to some degree to correct the anomalies.[29]

This result was a big win for the nurse educators, but the significance of their victory went beyond the issues involved. For the first time the RANF, VB had on its own initiative challenged a Wages Board decision. This action upset traditional practices and was taken even against the advice of its own Industrial Relations Officer. It was a reflection of the growing militancy among nurses who were no longer prepared to meekly accept everything that was handed out to them. It also prepared the way for future appeals to the Industrial Appeals Court. The complicated nature of the anomalies concerning nurse educators also highlighted the need for the RANF, VB to have advocates in the industrial arena who had close links with nurses in various sections in order to provide the advice and expertise which came with 'on the job' experience.

Nurses Move into the Political Arena

ONE of the most important steps towards the growth of militancy in a union is taken when its members move into the political arena to gain support for improvements in salaries and conditions. Nurses had often lobbied politicians, but until the late 1960s this had usually been done by the leading members of the RVCN, and the rank and file were seldom involved. The decisive move towards political action came with the campaign of 1970, which was also associated with the new curriculum. From this time the RANF, VB was to frequently seek to involve its members in applying pressure on politicians, as well as in gaining public support for improved salaries and conditions. The 1970 campaign also coincided with the appointment of Geoff McDonald. One of his first observations in his new job was:

> I must say that the extremely alarming situation of the discontent among nurses is such that I have never seen the like of it in any other occupation that I have had to represent, even in situations where they have been involved in bitter strikes for weeks on end.[30]

This first major political campaign of the RANF, VB was focused on salaries, the new curriculum (see Chapter 6) and working conditions. It began with the RANF Council's decision in early 1970 to impose bans from 18 May 1970 on some non-nursing duties such as mopping floors, cleaning walls, washing dishes and linen, changing screen covers, switchboard duties, messenger services, cooking meals, clerical duties and stoking boilers.[31] This action was associated with a national campaign run by the RANF and coincided with a nurses' strike at the Canberra Hospital.[32] The focal point of the campaign was a rally at the Melbourne Masonic Centre on 13 May, where 4000 off duty nurses met to demonstrate their support for the new curriculum, a 50 per cent salary rise and a ban on non-nursing duties.[33] Much criticism was directed at the Minister for Health, Vance Dickie, who the RVCN president described as having failed to show any real appreciation of the declining standards of nursing in Victorian hospitals, and who had ignored the low state of morale among nurses. He had shown 'indifference' to the problems in the hospitals and she had suggested in a telegram to the Premier that he be replaced. The Premier followed this advice after the election in May 1970.[34]

The demand for a 50 per cent pay rise was the prelude to the work value case which began in June 1970 and dragged on until September 1971 and even then was only partially successful. Nevertheless, by the middle of 1973 Geoff McDonald could claim with some justification that in four years 'taking into account conditions as well as salaries, nurses' take home pay has much more than doubled'.[35] Despite this, as Geoff McDonald would have been quick to point out, nurses had begun from a long way behind the starting line and, while they had made many gains, others in comparable areas of employment had also gone ahead. In the closing years of the long boom improvements in salaries and conditions were becoming increasingly difficult to obtain, as unemployment increased and inflation leapt ahead.

The comparison between teachers' and nurses' salaries was still being made. While both trained for three years, first year three year trained primary teachers received $122 per week compared with $107.60 for first year sisters in 1974. This difference was a key part of a new salary claim based on work value presented to the Wages Board in September 1974.[36] Nurses' salaries had also fallen behind general salary increases. The weighted average minimum adult female wage had increased by 68 per cent from 30 June 1970 to 31 January 1974, whereas nurses' pay had increased by only 56.4 per cent.

The new salary claim was accompanied by another burst of militancy. Negotiations commenced in late September 1974 and prior to this the RANF, VB launched a campaign in conjunction with the RANF and the NSW Nurses Association to bring home to politicians and the public how far behind other occupations nurses' salaries had fallen, and the disastrous effect this was having on recruitment and wastage.[37]

By March 1975 little progress had been made on the new award, and a rally of nurses was organised where various forms of political action were canvassed to highlight the nurses' case. Nurses were urged to write to their local members, and staff in hospitals were asked to decide what work they should cease to do in order to 'promote better patient care'. A further rally, this time on the steps of Parliament House, was planned.[38]

When the Wages Board gave its decision on 3 April 1975 for a 12 per cent salary rise, the RANF, VB immediately appealed to the Industrial Appeals Court against the decision. By the time the result of the appeal was announced the RANF, VB had achieved support from all political parties and the AMA, together with an undertaking from the Premier, Rupert Hamer, that the Government would intervene to state the public interest and what it considered was in the interests of nursing.[39]

The result of the appeal was a landmark in establishing the benchmarks for the salaries and conditions of nurses in Victoria. It was the first time the Court had been asked to arbitrate on the general standard of wages for nurses. There were three grounds for appeal — work value, nurses' salaries in relation to general community salary movements, and relativity with other professional employees, particularly teachers. The Court agreed that there had been some retrogression in nursing salaries, but found it was not possible to assess this with any exactitude. Its key decision was in the area of relativity. Even though the RANF, VB presented a great volume of material comparing nursing conditions with teaching, the Court rejected this in that teachers' salaries had 'an attraction and retention element' which did not apply to nurses. Nor was work value in teachers' determinations argued by all sides and arbitrated upon, in fact the Government which employed teachers remained neutral.

The Court found comparison with physiotherapists and occupational therapists much more attractive. The rates for these occupations were based on the standard of training in a three year diploma course. The Court found that the terms of qualification upon graduation for nurses and physiotherapists were able to be equated. Moreover, nurses upon graduation were already very experienced in areas of responsibility, more so than physiotherapists at the same stage.

The Court rejected some of the evidence given by medical practitioners on behalf of the employers on the ground that it was 'partisan':

> We are not greatly influenced by the suggestion, strongly contested, that nurses are encroaching upon what were formerly regarded as doctors' preserves. But the impression with which we are left is concerned with the constant minute-by-minute care, supervision and attention to the patient which is peculiar to the nurses' duties.[40]

As a result the Court concluded that nursing sisters should be placed at least at the same level as 'physiotherapists and other para-professionals' and awarded a flat 9 per cent increase on existing salary rates.

The Growth in Nurse Militancy

OVER the next ten years nurses gradually became more frustrated with their working conditions and salaries. No longer were they divided on the efficacy of militant industrial action. By now nurses made up an increasingly united body almost inexorably heading towards a direct confrontation with the State Government. In this period it took some time for Governments and the media to shake off their 'handmaiden' image of nurses.

Two developments in the late 1970s and early 1980s form the background to the militancy of 1985–1986. These developments established the RANF, VB as quite a different organisation in outlook and action from its predecessor, the RVCN. Links between the trade union movement were developed and the no-strike clause in the RANF constitution was changed.

But there was one other consideration which was outside the parameter of union affairs. This was the stepping up of the crisis in health care as a result of the generally depressed economic conditions of the period. Government expenditure was being cut in all areas from the mid-seventies and the hospital system was no exception. In August 1977 the State Government imposed a 5 per cent cut in the budget for all health services and this was followed by further cuts in the early 1980s.[41]

The RANF, VB affiliated with the Victorian Trades Hall Council in June 1978, a decision not taken lightly and with much 'soul searching' by older members. It was a measure of the changing nature of the organisation which in the 1950s and early 1960s would not have even discussed such a course of action, for it would have been seen as tantamount to treason.[42]

The next step in clearing the way for militant industrial action was the removal of the no-strike clause in the RANF constitution. An extraordinary general meeting at the Myer Music Bowl in February 1982 voted overwhelmingly for the branch to collect the required number of signatures in order to hold a national plebiscite to determine whether the rule of the RANF Registered Federal Rules (there shall be no strikes by members of the Association) be removed. Over a year later the branch council finally agreed to distribute the petition which needed to be signed by at least 5 per cent of the financial membership. If successful the federal RANF secretary was required to conduct a nationwide plebiscite.[43] In February 1984 the 'no–strike' clause was deleted from the federal rules after a national poll voted 65.3 per cent in favour, with Victoria having the highest percentage of this.

Another development which highlighted the great change in the RANF's outlook was the approach taken to nursing aides. From the late seventies the branch began to take an increasing interest in the salaries, working conditions and education of nursing aides, who became officially known as State enrolled nurses (SENs) from September 1981. Most SENs who belonged to a union were in the HEF, although there was a gradual build up of their membership in the RANF, VB. SENs were by now being fully accepted as members of the health care team and there was a growing realisation that they might be important in any industrial action the RANF, VB might take.[44]

As noted, the main reason behind the moves in 1982 to get rid of the no–strike clause in the RANF rules was the widespread dissatisfaction with salaries and conditions. Ten months after a work value claim had been lodged, in January 1982, the Wages Board awarded an across-the-board 15 per cent increase in salaries. While this seemed to be a substantial increase considering the economic climate, nurses were far from satisfied. Immediately after accepting the increase the RANF, VB lodged a new log of claims on employers in a move which again broke all industrial relations precedents.

The employers rejected the log and on 22 February a meeting of 2500 RANF, VB members unanimously endorsed a program of industrial and political action in support of the new log of claims. Two days later bans were imposed in six major metropolitan hospitals. Nurses refused to collect major hospital statistics, to remake unoccupied beds, to transfer drugs and furniture between wards, to do secretarial work and to run messages. The spark which fired them on this occasion was again ignited by the HEF. The long delay in gaining the 15 per cent rise was in stark contrast to the swift action by the Health Minister in responding to the HEF claim for a 29 per cent increase. As a result the salaries of SENs were only marginally below that of registered nurses. The nurses lifted their bans on 6 March when the case went to arbitration. The result was a $15 across-the-board increase plus an extra 2 per cent for charge nurses and above. However, both the Government and the employers appealed against this decision, particularly as they considered it created a dangerous industrial precedent.

The State elections intervened on 3 April 1982 leading to the return of the Cain Labor Government with Tom Roper as Minister for Health. As a result the appeal was withdrawn and the RANF, VB accepted a 7 per cent increase for all nurses in government funded institutions. Relations between the new Labor Government and the RANF, VB had begun well.[45]

Non-Nursing Duties

THE problem of nurses carrying out non-nursing duties had recurred over the years but it came to a head at a rally of 2000 nurses on 1 June 1984. Among other things, this rally supported a resolution that from 11 June all nurses in Victorian hospitals would no longer undertake non-nursing duties. These were defined as those related to washing and making unoccupied beds, routine cleaning of wards and departments, serving, delivering and returning meals and associated equipment, and clerical duties not related to the nursing care of patients.[46]

The RANF Federal Council in 1983 had declared that nurses should practise nursing and not perform non-nursing duties. At the rally this issue was linked with control over hospital admission and discharge policies, which were not controlled by the nurses. Nurses wanted some say in this area because patients were frequently admitted to wards where there was insufficient nursing staff to cope. This policy impinged on the powers of hospital management and medical staff. It was also related to the nurse-patient ratio laid down by the VNC. The ratio was one nurse to ten patients during the day and one to 15 at night. This had changed little since the 1930s, in spite of all the changes in medical technology since then.[47]

The issue highlighted two ongoing strands in the nurses' quest for professional status. It brought the crisis in health care to the public's attention, and sought to divest nursing of the so-called menial tasks which were seen as standing in the way of true professionalism. The two strands were closely related because part of the crisis for nurses was the increasing number of tasks which were being delegated to them by medical staff in hospitals.

There were an estimated 1 300 vacancies for nurses in Victoria's public hospital system in June 1984, during a time of high unemployment. When jobs were so scarce, this shortage was a measure both of the unattractiveness of nursing as a career, and of the high resignation rate due to stressful conditions. The RANF, VB claimed that between 1977 and 1984 the number of nursing positions provided by the VHC to hospitals and district nursing services had not matched the growth in health services and the advances in medical technology. As a consequence, there was an inadequate number of qualified nurses in hospitals and an ever increasing reliance on nurses to perform the duties of other health personnel. There was also 'completely inadequate supervision of nurses in training'.[48] The crisis was accentuated by another State budget cut of 1.5 per cent in 1983, which resulted in a direct cut in ancillary staff with nurses being directed to perform their duties.

Aspects of the crisis in hospitals were constantly reported in the press during 1984 and 1985. In March 1985 the federal Department of Employment and Industrial Relations indicated that nurses were the 'most wanted skilled workers in Australia' and that the demand was likely to increase.[49] The Vice-President of the RANF, VB, Robyn Millership, reported that 10 000 nurses did not renew their practising certificates in 1984 and a further 8 000 who held certificates were not working:

> They can work in Myers, get less responsibility, less stress, better conditions and the same wage ... in fact, we believe about 800 registered nurses work for the Myer chain.[50]

The management of the Royal Melbourne Hospital contacted the *Herald* early in 1985 to gain publicity about the critical shortage of nursing staff, which had led to the closure of 67 beds.[51]

Another reaction to the crisis was to import nurses from Britain. From the beginning of European settlement in Australia Governments and employers had resorted to overseas recruitment to overcome shortages of labour in Australia. This was regarded as a cheap, quick way of overcoming a crisis. The tradition continued, and in March 1985 the State Government sent off a Health Commission official to recruit 200 nurses from England, Scotland and Ireland.[52] This recruitment continued throughout 1985 and 1986.

The bans on non-nursing duties were carried through and although it is difficult to gauge how widespread they were, they marked the beginning of the sustained industrial pressure which nurses applied over the next three years. It was not easy for nurses to refrain from carrying out work which they had always performed and which was essential for the functioning of the wards. Linda Bradburn, a nurse teacher at Preston and North-cote Community Hospital, described the problem:

> The campaign in Victoria on non-nursing duties has been fought at the ward level. There have been bitter moments of struggling with oneself not to pick up dirty linen bags or remove used meal trays when all those well trained instincts are pulling you to do exactly that. There have been upsetting moments when other staff members have been angry and

unpleasant: our socialisation as nurses and often women has not helped us to do unpopular things (and industrial action is never popular).

The definition of nursing is the beginning of our 'Standards for Practice' adopted by the Federal Council RANF last year. In the 'Standards' we have at last delineated what we expect of a qualified nurse and the general statement of non-nursing duties which have been the platform for our industrial campaign.[53]

Several problems arose which limited the campaign's success. The initiative had not come from the union and as a result it was caught unprepared. It was also the first major concerted 'on the job' campaign which the RANF, VB had undertaken; it was a 'union type' campaign, the idea of which was repugnant to many nurses. Much depended on the ability of the RANF, VB representatives in each hospital to organise the support of nurses and most lacked experience in this type of union action. There was such a diversity of work practices in hospitals that no single list of non-nursing duties could be made applicable to all. Thus there was no clear detailed definition of non-nursing duties, and it was very difficult for nurses to agree on what they should or should not do.

There was also the question of who would carry out the duties which nurses discarded. There was no way the HEF was going to allow its members to pick up the duties and as a result it demanded the employment of extra staff (who would become HEF members!), which would prove very costly for the government.

On 18 July 1984 the Victorian Government Treasurer, Rob Jolly, put forward a $7.2 million offer to the RANF, VB for additional support staff together with some relocation of duties for existing staff. The Government conceded that food plating, the portering of supplies and deceased persons, courier services and the routine cleaning of basic surgical instruments in operating theatres, were non-nursing duties. It suggested that a working party be established to formulate a clear definition of these duties. Once this party had reported, a timetable for the phasing out of non-nursing duties was to be developed, working towards a phased reduction between August and November 1984.[54] The RANF, VB agreed to lift bans except on tasks such as serving patient meals and the routine cleaning of instruments.[55]

Australian Army nurses who served in Malaya arriving in Melbourne 1942. They left Singapore four days before its occupation by the Japanese. Photo courtesy of *UNA*, April 1, 1942.

Nurses for active service. Photo courtesy of *UNA*, January 1, 1941.

Demonstration Room, in the
Preliminary Training School,
Alfred Hospital, 1955

Lecture room, in the Preliminary
Training School, Alfred Hospital,
1955

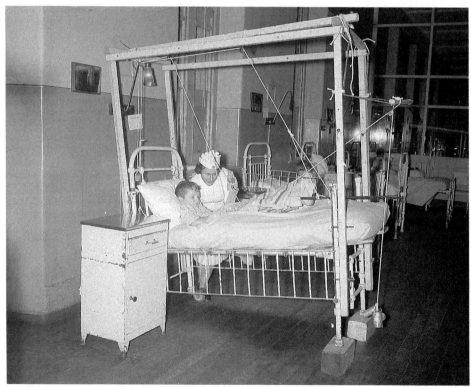

Balkan Frame, 1955

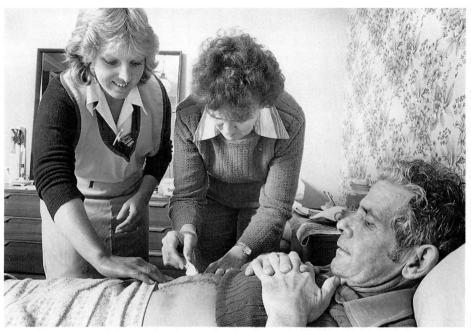

Sister supervising patient's dressing performed by wife, 1985

Ovens District Hospital supplied hospital beds to help protesters make their point in a march through Beechworth, February 1985. Photo courtesy of the *Age*.

Nurses demonstrate in Collins Street, October 1986. Photo courtesy of the *Age*.

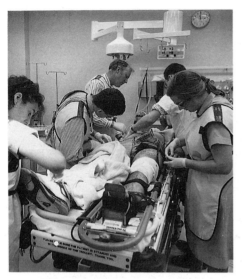

Road Trauma Centre, Alfred
Hospital, 1989

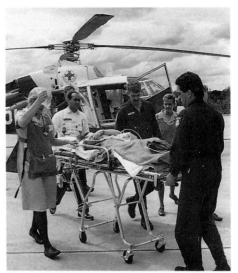

Road Trauma Centre Helipad,
Alfred Hospital, 1989

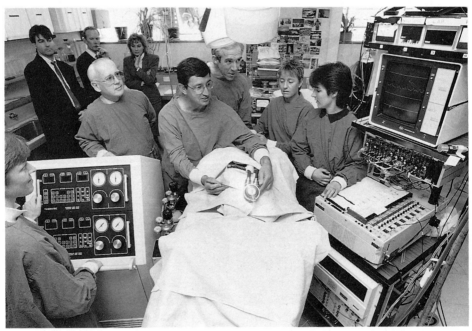

Don Esmore, with members of the Heart Transplant research team,
Alfred Hospital, 1988 conducts a trial of the artificial heart. Photo
courtesy of the *Age*.

As a result of the committee's work the RANF, VB and the Government came to an agreement on 16 August 1984 listing 22 specific duties which nurses would not be required to perform after 30 June 1985. So far as the RANF, VB was concerned the dispute had been settled, and it was up to the Government and the HCV to see that their side of the agreement was adhered to. However, by 30 June 1985 88 hospitals had still not received the additional support staff needed to free nurses from the agreed non-nursing duties, even though some $17 million had been allocated for the purpose.[56] The Government sought an extension to 31 October which the RANF, VB refused to grant. It also gave full support to members who declined to undertake the agreed non-nursing duties.

This dispute presented the RANF, VB with tremendous organisational problems because the bans were meant to cover all public hospitals. There were insufficient field officers and key members. There was confusion over the definition of non-nursing tasks, and the RANF, VB had no fully developed and effective means of quickly communicating with its members. The campaign was an important forerunner to what was to come in 1985 and 1986, in that it involved a large number of nurses and made them aware of the problems involved in an industrial campaign. It represented a major reversal of nurse attitudes towards industrial action. A survey showed that 88.8 per cent of nurses supported the aims of the RANF, VB in this dispute. Even 36.4 per cent of non-members gave support and 93.9 per cent of nurses believed that the dispute was about overwork and stress.[57]

Strike I

THE first general strike by nurses in Victoria took place from 17 October to 22 October 1985. During the strike, in an article in the *Age*, a registered nurse commented:

> When the dispute began it had nothing to do with money. It was over staffing levels, which were inadequate, and working conditions which were dreadful. Its only recently that money has come into it ... that won't solve the original problems. We are understaffed. We are run off our feet. We cannot do everything that we believe and we should be

doing for our patients. And no matter how much money we get, it will still mean that we are not providing the sort of care that we should.[58]

The writer outlined the key to understanding why nurses were driven to strike action in October 1985 and again 12 months later. Salaries were only part of the picture. There were also working conditions leading to stress and sickness, a high number of resignations, and a general feeling of frustration and bitterness as nurses realised that the problems were being exacerbated rather than overcome. Early in August 1982, the RANF, VB, launched a 'Keep Nurses Nursing' campaign, claiming that the shortage of nurses would lead to the breakdown of the hospital system. On 24 September 1985 a general meeting of RANF, VB members resolved to endorse negotiations to obtain wage justice, a new career structure and better working conditions. This was to be accompanied by a campaign of industrial action commencing with members working out of uniform from 30 September.[59]

The Government offered a salary package which it hoped would placate the nurses, to cost some $20 million and with an alleged average pay rise of $50 per week. The Government chose to call this an increase based on work value in order to steer it through the national wage and indexing guidelines. The offer was rejected by the RANF, VB because it claimed that the total involved only a 3.4 per cent increase in salaries over three years. Besides, the other areas were just as important as salaries, and were still outstanding. As a result on 7 October RANF, VB members enforced admission and discharge policies, non-breach of the award patient/nurse ratios (1:10 day 1:15 night) and the refusal to use agency staff to fill gaps in normal rosters.[60] The Federal Government and the Confederation of Australian Industries successfully intervened in the Wages Board hearing to urge that the proposed salary rises be considered by the IRC because of the national implications of an award which might flow on to other areas.[61]

The rejection by the RANF, VB of the Government's offer clearly surprised the Minister and other members of the Government who did not seem to understand that the issues went beyond salaries. On radio Health Minister David White, who had taken over the ministry from Tom Roper after the 2 March election, made it clear that he believed it was simply a question of money, 'obviously in the minds of the RANF exclusively, it is still one of money'.[62] Later he appealed to the nurses as 'professionals':

> Nurses have always been one of the most highly respected groups in the community because of their professional approach. It is not the hallmark of a professional group to go on strike while there are still avenues open for discussion.[63]

Relations between the Government and the RANF, VB rapidly soured, especially when the Minister threatened to stand down nurses and warned of possible criminal and civil action against nurses planning rolling strikes. Bans imposed in public hospitals because of inadequate staffing had forced the closure of more than 400 beds by 8 October, the worst hit being St Vincent's and the Royal Melbourne.[64]

On 11 October a snap strike was called at the Alfred without the consent of the RANF, VB when the Government attempted to force the admission of a patient when minimum ward staffing was not available and White called for volunteers to do the work of nurses. At the time the RANF, VB was negotiating with the Government. Steve Crabb, Industrial Relations Minister, exclaimed, 'It's outrageous: I've never had a strike pulled on me in the middle of negotiations'. David White declared that the nurses' action was 'unprecedented and an act of industrial naivety.'[65]

To add fuel to the flames the patronising remarks by Ministers and some journalists incensed nurses. They were too close to the sort of attitudes they experienced in he hospitals from the medical staff — a pat on the head accompanied by 'now, now, that's enough — take what we offer and go away'.[66] Any trust or respect nurses may have had for the Minister evaporated. Yvonne Barratt from the RANF, VB described the advertisements placed in the press by the Minister as 'patronising, chauvinistic and misleading'.[67]

On 11 October 5 000 RANF, VB members met at the Myer Music Bowl and voted unanimously to strike indefinitely from 17 October. The issues were reiterated. They revolved around salaries, admission and discharge policies, patient/nurse ratios and the use of agency staff. After the meeting nurses marched en masse from the Music Bowl to the HCV offices, through the centre of the city and at peak hour .[68]

The next day the RANF, VB rejected the government's offer of an extra $10 million in salaries. As one journalist pointed out, it was taking some time for the Government to realise that to solve the workload issue was to end the strike — it was not just a question of salaries.[69] The strike went ahead on 17 October. David White remained unimpressed and still appeared to be unable to comprehend the nurses' real concerns:

> We have introduced a 38 hour week, employed over 1000 people to remove 22 non nursing duties and made a pay offer which at the very least means Victorian nurses will be paid $40–50 a week more than those interstate ... and yet they still go on strike.[70]

But as one second year registered nurse said on Channel 2:

> Florence Nightingale does not pay the rent. As a second year junior nurse I've been left to run of ward of 20 by myself ... as a double certificate sister I take home $12,000 ... professionals in other areas get paid almost twice as much.[71]

In the days between the strike decision and the actual strike, the RANF, VB, organised action committees in about 80 hospitals to provide minimum basic nursing care. This was so well organised that hospitals appeared to be functioning normally, leading to the strike being described as a 'Clayton's strike'.

In the negotiations during the strike the Government made no real concessions, although reports in the media suggested that this was not the case. The RANF, VB, leadership built on this at a mass meeting on 21 October when it recommended a return to work. But the decision to return to work was very close. A large number of nurses were angry that the Government's offer did not include any increases for students, first year registered nurses or SENs, nor did it provide a solution to the immediate problem of too many patients and too few nurses.[72] At this time the RANF's main concern was to gain a career structure with an emphasis on improvements for third and fourth year registered nurses and beyond. Some nurses were also concerned that the Government had not put down in writing the terms of their offer to the RANF, VB. Many realised that the strike had failed to influence the government, although it had provided the RANF, VB, with valuable organisational experience, which was to be important 12 months later.

For the RANF, VB, at the crux of many of these problems was the question of admission and discharge policies. This was a major concern which had implications going beyond the current crisis. While the RANF, VB was seeking the implementation of existing HCV policies, (it had no specific policies of its own) the ultimate aim was control by nurses of how many patients could be admitted, depending on the number of nursing staff in the ward, so that a reasonable standard of nursing care could be maintained. As mentioned earlier, this impinged on the authority of hospital management and the medical profession.[73] The AMA was strongly opposed to nurses having any say in this area. The issue ultimately became tied up in hospital committees with much depending on the strength or otherwise of individual nurses in charge of wards.

Strike II

THE October 1985 strike was the curtain raiser for the events which took place one year later. In many respects the second strike of 50 days was a continuation of the 1985 five day strike. The award which the IRC brought down on 20 June 1986 arose directly out of the 1985 strike. It was the State Government's interpretation of that award which did a lot to provoke the second conflict.

But while the issues remained basically similar and the situation in hospitals had shown little improvement, and resignations and shortages of nurses continued, there was a change in the RANF, VB itself. In the intervening 12 months Barbara Carson, the secretary since 1980, had resigned and Irene Bolger had been elected, in May 1985. Irene Bolger had trained at St Vincents and Alfred Hospitals and was a relative newcomer to RANF, VB activities. She had been an organiser for 18 months and a member of the Socialist Left faction of the ALP since 1975.

She certainly brought new vigour and a new perspective into the RANF, VB.

Initially the RANF, VB was cautiously optimistic about the award which gave a new career structure and apparently higher rates of pay to most nurses. Significant wage rises were granted to upper level nurses and the new career structure required the re-classification of nursing jobs. But grade I, first level registered nurses and students in training gained nothing. The IRC argued that the 1975 Industrial Appeals Court decision had given these categories wage justice when it linked their salaries to those of physiotherapists. The commission also rejected the RANF, VB work value claim, basing its decision on anomalies.[74]

Very quickly two major problems with the new award emerged. Under the award the RANF, VB and the Hospitals' Association had to make submissions to the Health Department for coverage of each of the new grades in the restructuring process. It soon became apparent that the Government intended to place most nurses on the lowest grade. This was possible because under the original restructuring proposals put by the RANF, VB to the IRC, definitions of classifications were so loose that the Government was able to use this as a means of saving money. The second problem concerned the qualifications and teaching allowances which were paid to nurses who had obtained special training certificates and/or had teaching responsibilities. By way of example, in the IRC determination, the $17.20 teaching allowance received by charge nurses was abolished and the maximum qualifications allowance was reduced from $54.80 to $19.00 per week.[75] This came as a great shock to the RANF, VB because this had never been an issue in the original negotiations over the award. It later became apparent that the IRC had not realised that such a large number of nurses received these allowances. Matters were made worse by the speed in which these cuts were introduced, within two weeks of the IRC decision.

These two decisions meant that many nurses in the middle and upper ranges would take home less pay per week under the new award. The Minister conceded the 35 per cent of nurses would get no extra pay.[76]

The result was a stop work meeting of 3 000 nurses in the Melbourne Town Hall on 14 August 1986 to protest over these interpretations of the award, as well as the lack of pay increases for students and first year registered nurses. The meeting voted for strict enforcement of the RANF, VB admission and discharge policies, a refusal to wear uniform from the next day, and indefinite bans on all elective admissions from the following Wednesday.[77] Another stop work meeting of 3 500 nurses two weeks later was told that neither the Government nor the employers were giving serious consideration to the problems arising from the award, and, as a result, nurses voted overwhelmingly to continue the bans. Irene Bolger told the meeting that the IRC had postponed awarding the 2.3 per cent increase national wage to nurses because it questioned the RANF, VB commitment to the federal wage fixing principles agreed to by employees, employers and the Government. (The RANF had been the only dissenting voice when the ACTU voted in favour of the wages and incomes accord.) The meeting called for the resignation of the Minister for Health (David White) because of his refusal to negotiate.[78] In response to a request from the Government the RANF, VB put a detailed submission of grievances to the Wages Board, but the employers refused to negotiate claiming that an award had been already made by the commission and therefore there was no room for negotiation. Apart from that part of the submission regarding first year registered nurses and students, it really concerned anomalies and interpretations of the new award. Even though the Government had requested these details, it made out in the media that nurses had now presented a new log of claims. Meanwhile the bans on elective admissions were proceeding and up to 100 nurses had been stood down as a result. As well, 162 nurses at St Vincent's hospital had resigned en masse.[79]

A stopwork meeting of nurses on 5 September agreed to lift the bans to allow a conference with the employers and the IRC to proceed. At the conference the IRC indicated that it had not been the intention of the commission that such small increases should be the result of the award, and leave was granted to the Wages Board to review or alter the award.[80] There was considerable evidence during these developments that the Government was trying to contain the expenditure for the new award within a fixed limit of some $25.5 million as laid down by Treasury, even though it was clear that to fully implement the award costs would be considerably above that figure. Hence the move to cut costs by down-grading nurses in the classification. The IRC had given all employees until 30 October to reclassify their employees under the new structure and when these reclassifications were announced many nurses had been down-graded, that is, their original classification grading based on level of services had been reduced, thus effectively reducing their salaries.[81]

This was a time of financial stringency and the Minister was under considerable pressure to keep expenditure in his department within Treasury limits. Nor were the Labor Party leadership, the left-wing unions and Labor Party parliamentarians at all sympathetic towards any union which sought to break away from the guidelines of the federal wages/income accord. But nurses were in no mood to tolerate restraints. At the stop work meeting called by the RANF, VB on 30 October 5 000 nurses agreed to take strike action from the next day. Twenty outstanding problems, all arising from the new award, were listed as grievances. Following the meeting a march was held to the offices of the Health Minister but he refused to meet a deputation. The main issues were pay rates for first year registered nurses and students, the qualifications allowance, retrospectivity, and numerous problems associated with reclassification involving down-grading. A total walk-out was not planned; critical care units were still staffed and all hospital wards retained a skeleton staff. Nurses in all but one of the major metropolitan public hospitals left their jobs.[82]

Picket lines were established outside the hospitals and some nurses maintained 24-hour vigils in order to keep non-essential items out of hospitals. As well, caravans and tents were set up outside some hospitals for use by the pickets. This was to become one of the more extraordinary features of the strike. The picket lines were more like continuous public demonstrations that the strike was on. They were vital in sustaining the morale of nurses for they kept them together and greatly assisted communication between the leadership and the rank and file. They also gave the public an opportunity to show their support.[83]

The tactics of the Government in the first week of the strike were aimed at convincing nurses who might have been wavering in their support for the strike to return to work. Nurses were threatened with the sack. They were also warned they would lose their 'Melbourne Cup holiday pay'! They would face criminal charges for withdrawing their labour. The Minister (of a Labor government) warned that police would be used to break up the picket lines, but this misfired when Police Commissioner Mick Miller said they would not. Even the use of the Essential Services Act which the trade unions had sought to repeal for many years, was used to threaten the nurses.[84] These threats probably only strengthened nurses' resolve, especially when the Premier, in a public appeal, suggested, 'now it is time for nurses to give a little'.[85]

It soon became obvious, even to the Government which had clearly underestimated the nurses' determination, that there was much public support for the strike. This was reflected in the media coverage and the public reaction to the picket lines outside hospitals. Nor was there any sign that this support would weaken. Indeed, in the early days, it only increased. The uncompromising stance taken by the Minister, coupled with the inability of the Victorian industrial relations machinery to bring the parties together, rebounded not on the nurses but on the Government.

On 5 November an attempt by the Victorian Trades Hall Council to take over control of the strike was abandoned when 2 000 nurses demonstrated at the Trades Hall telling the Trades Hall Council Disputes Committee (controlled by right-wing unions) to keep out of the dispute. The Trades Hall had attempted to enlist the support of the various unions in the health care industry to support the Trades Hall Council Disputes Committee taking over the strike, leaving the way open for that committee to call it off.[86]

In response to a request from the Minister on 7 November the IRC ordered the nurses to return to work. When they did not, it proceeded to arbitrate on some matters in the dispute without the RANF, VB. This time it was the commission's turn to threaten the nurses, suggesting that failure to comply with the return to work order could lead to 'consequences for nurses in law outside industrial law if a patient suffers as a result of a nurse failing to comply with the order'.[87]

A further mass meeting of some 6–8 000 nurses at Olympic

Park on 11 November voted overwhelmingly to continue the strike and demanded that the IRC appoint a commissioner to act as an independent arbitrator on the matter.[88] At this stage the strike had reached an impasse. The IRC adjourned its hearings; the Government refused to negotiate and the strike continued to spread to hospitals throughout the State.

As often happens in a prolonged industrial dispute, sections of the media were seeking out conspiracies and endeavouring to find ulterior motives behind the actions of union leaders. In this respect Irene Bolger became the obvious target. Known for her left-wing sympathies, and friendly with such well known left identities as John Halfpenny and Bill Hartley, she was also female by birth. This latter attribute certainly attracted the media's attention, and it has been argued that the smear campaign aimed at her differed fundamentally from those aimed at other trade union leaders because she was a woman.[89] Her political associations were used by the Government and the media in an attempt to divide the membership of the RANF, VB. As she said before the strike began:

> The minister ... has been travelling around hospitals talking about my political associations. He has the attitude that if he mentions often enough that I'm associated with Bill Hartley (the left-winger recently expelled from the Australian Labor Party), that I go on 3CR (a Melbourne community radio station accused of left wing bias) and that the RANF is like the BLF, my members will start to believe it and rise up against me.[90]

The *Herald* had been particularly vehement against the strike and Irene Bolger[91] and this provoked the following reply from the RANF, VB representative at the Queen Victoria Hospital:

> Irene Bolger has not led us anywhere, she was nowhere near our hospital when we voted to walk out, and she was nowhere near Western General when they voted. The Government has forced us to take this action, not Ms Bolger ... As for professional image, it doesn't pay the rent, neither does your paper's support.[92]

John Kotsifas, the RANF, VB industrial officer, was also vehement in his denial of ulterior motives:

> We have no political agenda here ... Our members direct us.
> The plain truth is the Victorian Government has chosen to
> interpret our new deal in a deceitful way. They have told us
> blatant lies. They are on a money saving exercise at the
> expense of the nurses.[93]

Clearly the members of the RANF, VB were not overtly
influenced (at that time) by the campaign of political and sexual
innuendo that was directed at their secretary. She was the right
person in the right place at the right time. She proved to be an
inspirational leader who was able to enthuse the membership and
encapsulate all the pent up grievances which nurses had endured
over many years as hospitals went from one crisis to another.

Each day, as more nurses joined the strike, the note of
desperation in the appeals from the hospitals for more trained
nurses and volunteers was becoming increasingly obvious.
Indeed, there was no sign of an end to the strike. As one
journalist commented:

> There is no evidence that the determination of the nurses is
> less now than it was a fortnight ago. It almost seems that
> their resolve is becoming harder as the fight goes on.[94]

The IRC and David White were maintaining their refusal to
negotiate with the RANF, VB while its members were on strike.
At the same time the RANF, VB had lost all faith in the IRC's
ability to settle the dispute and saw it simply as doing the
Government's bidding. On 17 November the IRC refused to
direct the parties to the dispute to a private conference and the
impasse continued.[95]

The first indication that the Government was willing to talk
to the RANF, VB came after the strike had been going for three
weeks and after 17 unions had endorsed industrial action supporting the nurses. The unions, located in the La Trobe Valley,
covering the key electricity generating area, endorsed 'coordinated industrial action' from the following week.[96] The IRC
rescinded an earlier decision that the dispute could not be settled
by conciliation and proceeded to convene private talks between
all parties on 24 November, regardless of whether the nurses
remained on strike or not.[97] This was what the RANF, VB had

been seeking since the dispute began, but after three days of talks no progress had been made and the IRC called a halt.[98]

The IRC claimed that the RANF, VB had presented a new claim when these talks commenced and the ACTU president, Simon Crean, rebuked the RANF, VB over its handling of the dispute.[99] But at the same time Irene Bolger had met with the ACTU secretary, Bill Kelty, prior to the ACTU executive meeting in Hobart. As a result a general motion supporting the settlement of the strike along the lines sought by the RANF, VB and including a move towards 'professional rates' was passed by the ACTU executive.[100]

The charge of presenting a 'new claim' only increased the nursing leaders's distrust of the IRC. They claimed that they had only done what the IRC requested, that is, prepared a document detailing the specifics of their original claim. All the major issues which provoked the strike were in the 'new' claim. The 'new claim' appeared to be another invention of the Government and the media and helped to propagate the myth that the RANF, VB leaders were erratic and amateurs when it came to industrial relations — 'the sort of thing you would expect from women'.[101]

Early in December the strike entered a new and crucial phase. Since the IRC refused to meet the nurses, the RANF, VB agreed that the ACTU should put a case on their behalf with the proviso that the ACTU accept the details of the RANF, VB settlement package. The ACTU presented submissions to the IRC and succeeded in gaining a formal decision that a case had been made out for pay rises for students and first year registered nurses, as well as for the retention of qualification allowances. In addition the IRC was prepared to hear further argument on a simplified career structure.[102]

In the meantime, behind the scenes negotiations had commenced between the government and the nurses in an endeavour to thrash out a settlement. These continued for some time until, on Sunday 9 December, Irene Bolger felt 'they were playing games with us' an escalation of the strike was announced.[103] The escalation saw the first total walk-out from one hospital and further walk-outs from critical care, casualty and labour wards in others.[104]

The response of the Minister was to take over the powers of

the VNC and extend the range of duties carried out by the one year trained SENs so they could take over the work of the registered nurses. In this he had the support of Les Butler, secretary of the HEF No. 1 Branch, as well as the AMA, in what was clearly an attempt to break the strike. It was a highly provocative and desperate action. The RANF, VB quickly obtained a commitment from all other state branches of the RANF to take action if the Minister put his threat into practice.[105] There were also many protests from other nursing bodies.

Thus the confrontation between the Minister and the RANF, VB reached its peak with hospitals facing an increasingly desperate situation, nurses standing solidly behind their union, and the public (including some sections of the media), becoming increasingly confused as to why all the industrial relations machinery of the State could not cope with this strike.

Meanwhile in the private talks outside the industrial relations machinery the genesis of settlement had begun to take shape. RANF, VB and ACTU officials met on 11–12 December to negotiate, and a simplified career structure and pay rates were agreed to. These were presented to the government for consideration on 13–14 December. The next day a mass meeting of over 6 000 RANF, VB members voted unanimously to return to work as soon as the Government accepted the ACTU/RANF, VB joint proposal and the Minister withdrew his assumption of powers over the VNC. The following day the RANF, VB recommended that their members in critical care areas return to work and the Government set aside its order regarding the role and function of the SENs.[106]

Still outside the industrial relations machinery, the Government put forward a settlement of its own even though the Ministry had repeatedly said this would not happen. It was quite unacceptable to the RANF, VB. At the same time the Minister launched a media campaign claiming that nurses were returning to work in large numbers. The *Sun* ran a front page headline 'Nurse Strike Crumbles'.[107] But it soon became obvious that this was just another tactic to get nurses back to work. An *Age* survey concluded there 'may have been a 'trickle' returning'. It also published hospital bed occupation lists which showed little change.[108] An HCV employee responsible for the placement of critical care patients said there had been no increase in hospital beds available other than those in the critical care, emergency and labour ward areas.[109]

But then the unexpected happened. On 19 December 4 000 RANF, VB members voted to end the 50-day strike to facilitate the handing down by the IRC of a decision on the outstanding differences between the Government and RANF, VB/ACTU positions. The members warned that unless the IRC recognised the merits of the RANF,VB/ACTU package which contained many concessions by the RANF, VB, there would be further industrial action.[110] Behind the scenes negotiations between the ACTU/ RANF, VB and Government Ministers had convinced the Minister to talk directly to the nurses with a view to framing a joint proposal to be put to the IRC which would be close to the ACTU/ RANF, VB submission.[111] Even though the nursing leaders maintained their strong distrust of the Government, they agreed to get the nurses back to work.

The outcome of the strike was not clear until the IRC handed down its decision on 23 January 1987. Even the *Herald* which had run an uncompromising campaign against the nurses, conceded it was their 'victory'.[112] Those who benefited most from the pay rises were students, grade I and II registered nurses, associate nurses and associate charge nurses. Qualifications allowances were restored to a maximum of $47.40 per week. The IRC also foreshadowed pay rises for nurses in January 1988 and January 1989 in a move to create a 'professional' education-oriented, career structure.

The cost of the IRC's decision was estimated at $100 million — $20 million more than the government had offered to settle the crisis, and more than twice as much as nurses would have received if they had settled for the original award. The IRC had adopted the ACTU/RANF, VB proposal almost in its entirety. For 'naive', and 'inexperienced' nurses it was quite an achievement. The only aspect of the decision they criticised was that which required the RANF, VB to give a written undertaking that it would not make extra claims on issues which had been covered by the decision for two years.[113]

It was ostensibly a conflict over salaries and a new career structure. Yet, because of the gender of the participants — nearly all female — it became much more than this. In the history of Europeans in Australia it would be hard to find a similar event where women had challenged a male-dominated government, a male-dominated industrial relations system, a male-dominated trade union establishment, as well as the media. The nurses did not play the game according to male rules and this infuriated everyone (except the nurses). Hence not only the sexual innuendos thrown at Irene Bolger, but the use of words like 'naive', 'inept', 'unpredictable' and 'emotional', and the deliberate distortion of the facts to make them fit these preconceived notions of women's behaviour. Despite the fact that RANF, VB, as a union went into the strike inexperienced in militant industrial action, the use of these highly emotive terms indicated how gender issues permeated the politics of the strike. They were not terms which would have been used against a male leadership of a militant union.

As Mark Davis and Brendan Donohoe wrote in the *Age*, RANF, VB members suffered under male domination in both workplace and society, and 'seem to have different attitudes towards power and conflict than male unionists':

> This can be seen in the cooperative spirit on the nurses'
> picket lines, in the extraordinary emotion at the several mass
> meetings which have voted virtually unanimously to continue
> the strike, in the nurses' loyalty to Irene Bolger and in the
> way many of them express that loyalty by hugging her.[114]

The strike reflected the frustrations and resentment of nurses which had been building up for many years. It was their demonstration that something was rotten in the state of the public health system in Victoria and that this went far beyond the salaries of nurses. They had seen hospital budgets cut by successive governments, a never-ending shortage of staff and continuing resignations as a result of the stress, the anti-social hours and the poor remuneration which nursing offered. While others in the health care field such as doctors, physicians, surgeons, anaesthetists and radiologists made what seemed to nurses fortunes from their work, nurses had to struggle to get a living wage.

The myth that professionals do not strike took a battering during the nurses' campaign. This was raised before and during the strike in the media and by the nurses themselves. Of course professionals do strike and have done so many times. The most recent, which would have been fresh in the minds of nurses, was the protracted strike by doctors in New South Wales in 1984 to 1985 related to the operation of Medibank and Medicare.[115] Airline pilots did not hesitate to strike, and Victorian teachers had gone on strike countless times since 1965.

As the RANF, VB had discovered, the concept of professionalism could be used in a positive way to advance the cause of nursing, but it could also be used against nurses when they took action that some members of the public and the health system (including nurses) regarded as unprofessional. The *Herald* argued the strike had reduced the 'professionalism' of nurses, and doctors lectured to nurses that if they wanted to be professionals 'they've got to behave like professionals'.[116]

But while worries of 'unprofessional' action probably did not concern many of the younger nurses who went on strike, it certainly would have worried older nurses who had been brought up in an environment where strike action was anathema to nursing. They would have remembered the abhorrence of their mentors in the fifties and sixties to any form of industrial action associated with trade unionism. But professionalism brought its own problems. Were nurses to follow the lead of medical men in their quest for status and recognition? Were they to distance themselves from the bedside in these endeavours or were they to develop their own definition of the professional nurse? One thing was certain in all this, they were no longer 'handmaidens' in health care and industrial relations in Victoria.

Endnotes

[1] 'Australian Nursing Conditions', report compiled by Sheila Quinn, *UNA*, February 1963, p. 54.

[2] ibid., p. 55.

[3] ibid., pp. 55–6.

[4] ibid., pp. 57–8.

[5] ibid., p. 56.

[6] For some discussion of this see Eva Gamarnikow, 'Sexual Division of Labour. The Case of Nursing', in A. Kuhn, A. Wolpe (eds), *Feminism and Materialism*, Routledge and Kegan Paul, London, 1978.

[7] Sandra Speedy, 'Feminism and the Professionalization of Nursing', in *The Australian Journal of Advanced Nursing*, vol. 4, no. 2, December 1986-January 1987, p. 24.

[8] There is an extensive literature on professionalism. More specifically on nurses and teachers, see Etzioni, A., (ed.) *The Semi-Professions and Their Organizations. Teachers, Nurses, Social Workers*, N.Y., 1969; B. Abel-Smith, *A History of the Nursing Profession*, London, 1960; B. Rollins, Socialization Into A Professionalizing Occupation: A Study of Student Nurses, MA thesis, La Trobe University, 1977; E. Palmore, 'Rising and Falling Professions', in *Journal of Social Behaviour*, Autumn 1970; R. Goodman, Teachers' Status in Australia, PhD thesis, Australian National University, 1955; L. Webb, 'The Teaching Profession', in *Australian Journal of Education*, no. 3, vol. 7, October 1963; M. Lieberman, 'The Nature and Significance of the Professions', in M. Lieberman *Education as a Profession*, New Jersey, 1956; M. Jahoda, 'Nursing as a Profession', International Council of Nurses, 12TH QUADRENNIAL CONGRESS, MELBOURNE, APRIL 1961; B. Bessant, A.D. Spaull, *Teachers in Conflict*, Melbourne, 1972, ch. 4; H. Becker, 'The Nature of a Profession', in H. Nelson (ed.), *Education for the Professions*, Chicago, 1962, p. 30.

[9] See Sandra Speedy, op. cit., and Sandra Speedy, 'Feminism and Nursing: From Theory to Practice', in *Shaping Nursing Theory and Practice: The Australian Context*, Lincoln School of Health Sciences, La Trobe University, monograph, 1988, for discussion of the feminist approach to professionalism in nursing.

[10] Mary Harper (Australasian Trained Nurses Association (Brisbane) to Marjorie Connor, 5 July 1950. Box 39, UM archives.

[11] Elaine P. Orr, Penalty Rates. The Advantages of this Form of Remuneration, memorandum, 23 February 1968. Box 19, UM archives.

[12] ANFES, VB, minutes of committee of management, 18 October 1967.

[13] L.H. Durrant, Penalty Rates. Paper delivered at ANFES general meeting, February 1968. Box 124, UM archives.

[14] ibid.

[15] William J. Toy, (Industrial Officer), information obtained regarding penalty rates, memorandum, January/February 1968. Box 19, UM archives.

[16] Orr, op. cit.

[17] Marjorie Connor to E. H. Lang (President, RVCN), 24 May 1968. Box 19, UM archives.

[18] Penalty rates, replies received as at 19 June 1968. Memorandum. Box 140, UM archives.

[19] ANFES, VB, minutes, 19 June 1968.

[20] ibid., 21 August 1968.

[21] ANFES, VB, Determination of the Hospital Nurses' Board, Part I and V — Penalty Rates. Box 101, UM archives.

[22] ANFES, VB, minutes, 9 February 1971.

[23] Industrial relations officer's report (confidential), February 1971. Box 123, UM archives.

[24] ANFES, VB, minutes, 31 March 1971.

[25] ANF, VB, council minutes, 16 June 1971. Letter from nurse educators' section.

[26] ibid., 1 September 1971.

[27] ANF, VB, council minutes, 27 March 1972.

[28] RANF, VB, council minutes, 20 September 1972.

[29] *UNA*, February 1973, p. 25.

[30] Report from industrial relations officer, 2 April 1970. Box 140, UM archives.

[31] Annual report of the RVCN for year ending 30 June, 1970, in *UNA*, September 1970, pp. 4 and 7.

[32] *Australian*, 10 May 1970.

[33] *UNA*, September 1970, p. 7.

[34] *UNA*, May/June 1970, p. 12.

[35] *UNA*, July/August 1973, p. 34.

[36] *UNA*, July/August 1974, p. 19.

[37] RANF, VB, council minutes, 16 May 1974.

[38] RANF, VB, council minutes, 20 March 1975.

[39] *UNA*, May/June 1975, pp. 10–11.

[40] *UNA*, July/August, 1975, p. 17.

[41] *ANJ*, May 1980, p. 52.

[42] *ANJ*, October 1978, p. 78.

[43] *ANJ*, August 1983, p. 93.

[44] *ANJ*, February 1982, p. 57. See also *ANJ*, May 1983, p. 73; July 1983, p. 73; February 1984, p. 83; RANF, VB, council minutes, 8 June 1982.

[45] *ANJ*, November 1982, p. 79.

[46] *ANJ*, August 1984, pp. 27–8.

[47] Heather Gardner, Brigid McCoppin, 'The Politicisation of Australian Nurses: Victoria 1984–1986', in *Politics*, vol. 22, no. 1, May 1987, p. 22.

[48] *ANJ*, August 1984, p. 27.

[49] *Age*, 7 March 1984.

[50] *Ringwood Mail*, 23 October 1985.

[51] *Herald*, 18 March 1985.

[52] *Herald*, 9 March 1985. This was part of a trade off agreement between the Government and the RANF, VB.

[53] *ANJ*, September 1984, p. 5.

[54] ibid., p. 22.

[55] *RANF Victorian Branch News*, July 1984.

[56] *ANJ*, August 1985, pp. 16–17. For a detailed account of this dispute see Carol Fox, *Industrial Relations in Nursing — Victoria 1982–1985*, Sydney, 1989, pp. 71–93.

[57] Gardner, McCoppin, op. cit., p. 26.

[58] *Age*, 22 October 1985.

[59] *ANJ*, December/January 1985, p. 12. See Fox, op. cit., pp. 115–122, for details of the negotiations between the Government and the RANF, VB, prior to the September general meeting.

[60] *Age*, 5 October 1985; *ANJ*, December/January 1986, p. 12.

[61] *Age*, 5 October 1985.

[62] *Current Affairs Monitoring*, Channel 9 News, 6.00 p.m., 6 October 1985.

[63] *Herald*, 16 October 1985.

[64] *Age*, 10 October 1985.

[65] *Age*, 16 October 1985; *Current Affairs Monitoring*, 3DB, 8.41 a.m., 17 October 1985.

[66] See *Age*, 3 and 9 October 1985.

67 *Current Affairs Monitoring*, 3LO Schildberger, 8.41 a.m., 10 October 1985.
68 *Current Affairs Monitoring*, Channel 10 News, 6.00 p.m., 11 October 1985.
69 *Age*, 18 October 1985.
70 *Current Affairs Monitoring*, 3DB, 8.40 a.m., 17 October 1985.
71 *Current Affairs Monitoring*, Channel 2 'The National', 7.41 a.m., 17 October 1985.
72 *Current Affairs Monitoring*, Channel 10, 6.00 p.m., 21 October 1985. See Fox, op. cit., pp. 144–62 for details of negotiations before and during the strike and pp. 179–94 for a general evaluation of strike from an industrial relations viewpoint.
73 See Heather Gardner, Brigid McCoppin, 'Vocation, Career or Both', *The Australian Journal of Advanced Nursing*, vol. 4, no. 1, September/November 1986.
74 *RANF Vic Branch News*, Special Edition, July 1986.
75 *Nurses Action*, August 1986. Published by RANF, VB.
76 *Age*, 6 August 1986.
77 *Age*, 15 and 23 August 1986.
78 *Age*, 28 August 1986; *Nurses Action*, September 1986.
79 *Herald*, 4 September 1986.
80 *Nurses Action*, September 1986.
81 *Herald*, 6 October 1986; *Nurses Action*, October 1986; *Sun*, 8 November 1986; *Australian*, 17 November 1986.
82 *ANJ*, December/January 1987, pp. 13–14; The RANF, VB excluded the Royal Children's Hospital from the strike.
83 Interview with Irene Bolger, 19 June 1990.
84 *Age*, 1 November 1986; *Herald*, 5 November 1986.
85 *Nurses Action*, February 1987.
86 ibid.; Interview with Irene Bolger, 19 June 1990.
87 *Sun*, 8 November 1986; *Nurses Action*, February 1987.
88 *Age*, 12 November 1986; *Sun*, 12 November 1986; *Herald* 12 November 1986.
89 See Judith Bessant, J. Vin D'Cruz, 'When Nurses and Teachers Strike: Public Perceptions of "the betrayal"', in *The Australian Journal of Advanced Nursing*, vol. 6, no. 3, March/May, 1989.
90 *Bulletin*, 2 September 1986, p. 31.
91 For example see *Herald*, 6 November 1986.
92 *Herald*, 13 November 1986.
93 *Weekend Australian*, 15–16 November 1986.
94 *Age*, 15 November 1986.
95 *Sun*, 18 November 1986; *Herald*, 18 November 1986.
96 *Australian*, 21 November 1986.
97 *Age*, 21 November 1986.
98 *Australian*, 28 November 1986.
99 *Australian*, 27 November 1986; *Herald*, 26 November 1986.
100 Interview with Irene Bolger, 19 June 1990; *Nurses Action*, February 1987; *Herald*, 27 November 1986; *Age*, 27 November 1986.
101 *Age*, 28 November 1986.
102 *Herald*, 10 December 1986.

[103] Interview with Irene Bolger, 19 June 1990.
[104] *Herald*, 10 December 1986; *Geelong Advertiser*, 10 December 1986.
[105] *Nurses Action*, February 1987.
[106] ibid.
[107] 18 November 1987.
[108] 18 November 1987.
[109] *Australian*, 19 December 1986.
[110] *Nurses Action*, February 1987.
[111] *National Times on Sunday*, 21 December 1986; Interview with Irene Bolger, 19 June 1990.
[112] *Herald*, 26 January 1987.
[113] *Age*, 24 January 1987.
[114] *Age*, 19 December 1986.
[115] See *New Doctor*, no. 36, June 1985.
[116] *Herald*, 8 November 1986. See also *Herald*, 31 October 1986; *Bulletin*, 2 September 1986, p. 31; *Herald*, 16 December 1986.

8

The Nursing Profession

T HE 1980s saw an accentuation of the crisis in health care, which has been outlined in chapter 4. The persistent shortage of registered nurses continued, with the demand increasing by 44 per cent between 1977 and 1986 in public hospitals. In the same period an extra 650 nurses were required in private hospitals and a further 650 in non-funded nursing homes. Altogether this demand meant 6 700 registered nurses were needed by 1986 simply to keep up with the basic needs of hospitals.

The proportion of registered nurses grew from 56 per cent of total nurses in 1977 to 64 per cent in 1986. This was due primarily to the replacement of nursing students by registered nurses. The introduction of the 38-hour week and the further reduction in the average time patients spent in hospitals, from 8.6 days in 1977 to 6.8 days in 1985, required more staff, although the latter was somewhat offset by the longer stay by patients in nursing homes which required fewer registered nurses.[1]

The nursing workload per acute patient per day continued to increase in the major teaching hospitals. This was accompanied by a general growth, which was difficult to measure, in 'the role, responsibilities and expectations of registered nurses'. This involved the transfer of responsibilities from medical to nursing staff which led to more comprehensive treatment being provided by nurses. Registered nurses also trained other nursing and paramedical staff in the use of new technology. As well, nurses took on new administrative functions created by systems for measuring patient dependency and resource management within hospitals. Added to these extra responsibilities were closer attention to infection control, the continual updating and elaboration of standards required for hospital accreditation, the ordering of medical equipment and supplies, and meeting new government regulations related to drugs, poisons etc.[2]

This growth in the complexity of the work of nurses and the increasing demand for their services was exacerbated by an estimated 5 to 7 per cent leaving permanently and 6 to 8 per cent leaving temporarily each year over the period from 1977 to 1986. In the same period the proportion of Victorian registered nurse graduates declined as a proportion of registered nurses employed from 8.1 to 5.1 per cent. This meant that the output of trainees did not keep pace with the growth in the nurse work-force. Apart from Western Australia, Victoria had the lowest proportion of nurses in this respect than any other State.[3] Thus the ongoing shortage of registered nurses, being one of the most significant features of nursing history since the very early 1940s, showed no signs of being alleviated in 1986.

Apart from the shortage of nurses there have been two dominant, closely linked themes in this book. The first has been the perceived dichotomy between industrial and professional issues as epitomised by the dual structure of the RVCN for most of the period this study has covered. The second has been the quest by nursing leaders from the 1930s to 1986 to raise nursing in Victoria to a status approaching that of the 'higher' professions, such as law and medicine. This quest directly impinged on the first theme because the perceived need to keep industrial and professional matters separate was directly related to the strong belief held by nurses and their leaders for most of the period that an emphasis on 'bread and butter' 'trade union' affairs would damage their quest for professional recognition.

Professional status was to be achieved first by overhauling an antiquated training system and then by taking the initial training of nurses out of hospitals and into colleges of advanced education. By the end of the 1970s gaining a prestigious credential such as a diploma or a degree was emphasised, in contrast to the 'on the job' training certificate of the earlier period. This was also seen as a means by which nurses could go on to gain post-graduate credentials, thus paving the way for more highly qualified nurse educators, administrators, specialist nurses in various fields and researchers.

These endeavours, when looked at over a 50 year period, were highly successful in their immediate aims. Nevertheless, any conclusions on the success or otherwise of the efforts towards gaining professional status depend on the nature of the status nursing leaders were seeking. For some nurses during the period professional status had already been gained in the 1920s with the achievement of State registration. For them professional status was closely related to nursing remaining a recognised vocation. Their way of caring for the sick was professional in itself and did not need the addition of diplomas or degrees to bolster its status. They admired the 'good practical nurse'.

The emphasis on nursing as a vocation is the key to understanding the division of the work of RVCN into professional and industrial spheres. The widespread assumption in the Victorian nursing world that these two spheres had to be kept apart was just as much a means of preserving the professional status which nurses had already achieved, as a means of enhancing it. For those who saw nursing essentially as a vocation, the improvement of wages and conditions, especially by means of industrial action, was in direct contradiction to the notion of a vocation. This was a strongly held belief within the RVCN and was one of the main stumbling blocks to the national unity of nurses in the 1960s.

For others who were more concerned at the association between public image and status, the way to go was to follow the lead of other professions and raise the general qualifications of nurses in and out of training, while keeping industrial and professional issues apart. This second stream became dominant but that does not mean that the former approach was either submerged or washed away. Both approaches reflected fundamental problems with defining professionalism, especially in relation to nursing.

One of the major difficulties which nurses all over the world have had to face in grappling with the question of professionalism has been that nursing, unlike most other professions, occupies a role subordinate to another profession, that is, the medical profession. The doctor decides who shall be the patient, and the doctor is the ultimate authority in law in determining how the patient shall be treated. Throughout the period covered in this book most nurses were female (95 per cent in 1986) and most doctors were male, and as a result the dominance of the medical profession over nursing was compounded by male/female relationships. Many writers have drawn the analogy between the patriarchal structure of the family and the nurse/doctor relationship in the hospital. This must be taken into consideration when discussing professionalism in relation to nurses.[4]

Defining the concept of professionalism has been the subject of many books and articles.[5] Professionalism, however, is not an objective, concrete phenomenon that distinctly characterises an occupational group or its individual members. Professionalism is a broad, dynamic and subjective concept determined by individual and group perceptions which vary according to the different backgrounds and biases of those formulating the notions. Professionalism relates to image, perceptions, status ratings and public recognition of, and the value attributed to, certain types of work. Howard Becker once defined professions:

> simply as occupations which have been fortunate enough in the politics of today's work to gain and maintain possession of that honorific title. On this view, there is no such thing as the 'true' profession and no set of characteristics necessarily associated with the title.[6]

Broadly speaking professionalism can be divided into two categories. The first which is the traditional and popular notion of professionalism, relates to an external image and a set of standards that are projected as the true or real picture of professionalism. This picture is often accepted as an objective reality. Other elements, related to the monopolising of skills, becoming exclusive by legal and other forms of protection, and developing a unique body of knowledge and skills and mystifying that information, all go towards the creation of professions of the legal or medical kind. It is as well to note that both these professions have always been dominated by males. As a result it is not surprising that they have developed practices and characteristics which suit the dominant patriarchal practices of their members.

The second category relates to a desire for what can be described as 'integrity'. Integrity, in relation to their work, develops from within individuals or groups. It comes from setting one's own goals and parameters, and one's own standards and methods of achieving these. Becoming professional in this sense does not rest on receipt of a blue print from others. Nor does it rest on the approval of others, particularly 'superiors'. It depends on the self-assurance of the group or individuals concerned, and their own satisfaction with their performance and behaviour. From that, a tradition may develop with its own symbols, myths and meanings which directly reflect the experiential history of the particular work. In this respect the work of private nurses in the early decades of this century came close to this type of professionalism.

Professional groups of this kind do not need to compete with others to improve their position in the occupational hierarchy. This depends, however, on whether the group possesses a strength and belief in its values, standards and codes of behaviour, which in turn may result in public recognition and acknowledgment. For a female occupation such as nursing it requires that the group have the strength of purpose to break away from the traditional male model of professionalism.

Nurses' struggle to achieve professional status, in the traditional sense, consumed enormous energy, commitment, time and material resources. That effort was directed towards the attainment of a model that developed from other occupations that were very different from nurse's work. This preoccupation with the traditional image of the professional, particularly when hospital nursing took over in the 1930s and 1940s as the main avenue of employment for registered nurses, raised fundamental questions related to their training and work. But in both these areas the parameters of what the RVCN and the College of Nursing, Australia could do were strictly limited by the overriding dominance of the health care area by the medical profession.

Attempts to get the post-graduate education of nurses into the University of Melbourne failed not only because the university was not interested in what it saw, at the time, as a low status, female occupation, but also because the medical faculty which had a dominant role in the university would not countenance a perceived threat to their own hegemony of health care by having nurses with university degrees working side by side with them in the hospitals. At the same time the parameters of much of the work of registered nurses were determined by the medical profession, which meant that the definition of nurses' work was largely out of their control. Nurses were deprived of that independence in determining the nature of their work which is said to be a feature of a profession.

The pursuit of professional status divided nurses in Victoria and ensured that the main focus of attention centred on issues which, it was believed, would raise their professional standing, such as the standard of education and training. Although important, such issues successfully obfuscated some of the more central issues related to professionalism, such as the real nature of professionalism and wages and conditions. The RVCN worked very hard for reform, but it was reform where the nature and conditions of nurses' work were very low on the agenda.

Fixed ideas and a narrow focus on the need to pursue the one model meant that alternative notions of professional identity were seldom considered. Concern with matching up to the traditional professional models meant that opportunities did not emerge to develop a new identity with its own myths and symbols which was based on the female/nursing experience, even though the practice and a rich tradition were there to build on. The political reality was that until nurses' organisations were seen to be actively involved in improving the salaries and conditions of their members, the opportunity to build a numerically strong, united body of nurses which would be able to tackle the fundamental problems of the profession, remained remote.

The shift in the late 1970s and 1980s by the RANF, VB towards industrial action culminating in the strikes of 1985 and 1986, significantly increased the support for that body in Victoria. But it remains to be seen whether the dichotomy between industrial and professional matters will be maintained within the united body, or whether questions such as alternative notions of professionalism, the nature of the work, and salaries and conditions, will be considered one entity, each dependent upon the other.

Endnotes

[1] *General Nurse Workforce Planning*, Health Department, Victoria, discussion paper, 1987, pp. 4–10.

[2] ibid., p. 16.

[3] ibid., pp. 30–4.

[4] See for example Beverley Kingston, *My Wife, My Daughter and Poor Mary Ann. Women and Work in Australia*, Thomas Nelson, Melbourne, 1975, ch. 5; Eva Gamarnikow, 'Sexual Division of Labour: The Case of Nursing', in A. Kuhn, A. Wolpe (eds), *Feminism and Materialism*, Routledge and Kegan Paul, London, 1978; Sandra Speedy, 'Feminism and the Professionalization of Nursing', in *The Australian Journal of Advanced Nursing*, vol. 4, no. 2, December 1986, February 1987.

[5] See note 8 chapter 7.

[6] H. Becker, 'The Nature of a Profession', in H. Nelson (ed.), *Education for the Professions*, Chicago, 1962, p. 30.

Notes on Illustrations

Leitha Mavis Avery, FCNA,
Dip. Nursing Admin.
Nursing officer in Queen
Alexandra Royal Army
Nursing Corps in the Middle
East, North Africa, Sicily, Italy,
India and England, 1939–
1945.
Professional Officer for
Nursing, Universities
Commission, 1945–1949.
Florence Nightingale
Scholarship 1950.
Inaugural Secretary-General of
RANF, 1951–1957.
World Health Organisation
Fellowship 1956.
Inaugural Chief Nursing
Officer of VNC 1958–1967.

Jane Bell, OBE
Lady Superintendant Royal
Melbourne Hospital
1910–1934.
Principal Matron of Australian
Army Nursing Services in
Middle East 1914–1918.
President of RVCN 1931–
1934; 1938–1946.
Founder member of RANF.
Representative of RANF at
ICN Council 1937.

Irene Margaret Bolger
SRN at Alfred Hospital
1969–1972.
Charge Nurse at Alfred and
Austin Hospitals; Supervisor at
Austin Hospital; Deputy

Director of Nursing at
Warringal Hospital; Nurse
educator at Alfred Hospital
1972–1983.
Organiser and Industrial
Officer of RANF, VB
1983–1986.
Secretary of ANF, VB
1986–1989.

Patricia Chomley, MBE
Australian Army Nursing
Services 1940–1946.
Staff, Royal College of
Nursing, London 1948–1949.
Director, College of Nursing,
Australia 1949–1964.

Marjorie Connor, MBE, RN,
FRCNA
Executive secretary RVCN
1945–1973.
Jane Bell scholarship and
RVCN Jubilee scholarship to
study professional nursing and
organisations overseas 1958.
Honorary secretary and
treasurer Florence Nightingale
Committee Victorian Branch
1973–1988.
Honorary Life Member RNF,
VB 1973.
Distinguished Life Member
RANF, 1976.

Helene D. Grey, OBE, FCNA
(Foundation Fellow)
Lady Superintendant Royal
Melbourne Hospital
1934–1957.

President of Royal Victorian
College of Nursing
1946–1951.
President of Australian
Nursing Federation
1947–1951.

Jean Headberry, ADMIN. DIP.
(London)
Nursing officer with the
Australian Army in the Middle
East and Australia
1939–1945.
Dean of Royal Melbourne and
Associate Hospitals School of
Nursing 1950–1963.
Awarded Florence Nightingale
Medal 1961.

Edith Hughes Jones, OBE
Founder member of College of
Nursing, Australia, 1950.
President of College of
Nursing, Australia,
1955–1956.
Honorary Fellowship of
College of Nursing, Australia,
1971.
Honorary Secretary of
National Florence Nightingale
Committee of Australia
1946–1975.
President of RVCN
1961–1967.
Foundation Member and
Honorary Secretary of the
Nurses Memorial Centre.
Honorary Secretary of the
Centaur Trust.
Chair of the Annie Sage
Memorial Nursing Scholarship
Committee.
Instigator of the Clive Steel
Memorial Library 1961.

Betty C. Lawson, OBE, FCNA,
FRCNA
Matron, Royal Women's

Hospital 1955–1977.

Mona Menzies, AM, B.Comm.
Registrar, Nurses Board
Victoria 1951–1957.
Registration Officer Victorian
Nursing Council 1958–1967.
Chief Nursing Officer,
Victorian Nursing Council
1968–1985.

Annie Moriah Sage, CBE, RRC,
Hon. FCNA, FLORENCE
NIGHTINGALE MEDAL
Colonel-Matron-in-Chief of
Australian Army in the Second
World War.
Founder member and President
of College of Nursing,
Australia, 1950.
Matron of Royal Women's
Hospital 1947–1952.
Annie Sage Memorial Nursing
Scholarship established in her
honour.
Founder member of Nurses
Memorial Centre.

Jane Muntz, OBE, FCNA
(Foundation Fellow)
Nursing adviser to Victorian
Ministry of Health
1951–1968.
President of VNC.
Minister's nominee on RVCN,
1953–1968.
Federal President of RANF
1961–1966.

Nurses Memorial
Sculptured by Ray Ewers. The
Nurses Memorial fronts the
Nurses Memorial Centre,
431 St Kilda Road, Melbourne.
The sculpture was unveiled 20
April 1980, with a ceremony of
dedication conducted by Padre
J. T. Benjamin, a former
prisoner of war.

Mary E. Patten, BA (HONS), FCNA
Field Officer, RVCN, 1960–1962.
Assistant Director, Social and Economic Welfare Division, International Council of Nurses, London.
Centaur War Nurses' Memorial Scholarship, 1967–1970.
Federal Secretary, RANF, 1970–1980.

Patricia Slater, OBE, MA, BSc (summa cum laude), Dip. N. Ed., FCNA, FCNA (NSW), FACE, Hon. FCNA.
Nursing Officer with the Australian Army in Labuan, Sabah and Australia, 1943–1947.
Awarded War Nurses Memorial Scholarship, 1959–1962.
Rockefeller Fellowship, study tour of USA, Canada, Scandinavia, UK, 1961–1962.
Florence Nightingale Scholarship.
Director of College of Nursing, Australia, 1965–1977.
Inaugural Head of School of Nursing, Lincoln Institute of Health Sciences, 1977–1983.
Australian and New Zealand Association Award for achievements in Medical Education, 1985.

Bibliography

Archives

The archives of the RVTNA and the RVCN are held at the University of Melbourne Archives. These contain some 180 boxes of material sorted under basic headings. However, the collection needs overall reconstruction and a logical grouping of material.

The ANF, VB holds its own archives from 1970 at its headquarters, plus a set of RVTNA and RVCN council minutes from the early 1930s. Full sets of *UNA* and *ANJ* are available at the ANF, VB and the Victorian State Library.

Official Reports

VPP, 1923–1948, Reports of the Charities Board of Victoria.
VPP, 1949–1979, Reports of the Hospitals and Charities Commission.
VPP, 1979–1985, Reports of the Health Commission of Victoria.
VPP, vol. 2, 1926, Report by Dr Malcolm T. MacEarchern on the Hospital System of the State of Victoria.
Tertiary Education in Australia. Report of the Committee on the Future of Tertiary Education in Australia to the Australian Universities Commission (Martin Report), 2 vols. 1964.
Nursing in Victoria. Report of the Committee of Enquiry into Nursing (Ramsay Report), August 1970.
Report of the Committee of Inquiry into Hospital and Health Sources in Victoria, July 1975.
Nurse Education and Training: Report of the Committee of Inquiry into Nurse Education and Training to the Tertiary Education Committee (Sax Report), Canberra, 1978.

Private Papers

G.N. Burbidge, papers. Held by authors.
P. Slater, papers. Royal College of Nursing, Australia.

Interviews and Material from Correspondents

H. Adair	J. Armstrong	G. Burbidge
A. Anthony*	I. Bolger*	M. Connor*

M. Hanna*   L. Rohricht   N. Spence
R. Henderson   E. Sheldrick   E. Walters*
R. Lockey*   P. Slater*

* denotes tape

Theses

M. K. Benson, 'Revolutions and Rosewater: The Evolution of Nurse Registration in Victoria, 1923–1973, M.A. Thesis, University of Melbourne, 1975.

M. Mackay, 'Handmaidens of Medicine — A History of Nursing in Colonial Victoria', M.Ec. thesis, Monash University, 1982.

B. R. Rollins, 'Socialization into a Professionalizing Occupation: A Study of Student Nurses', M.A. thesis, La Trobe University, 1977.

Articles in Journals and Chapters in Books

Alphonus, Rev. Mother, 'Our Responsibility in Preserving the Essence of Nursing', *UNA*, June 1965.

Archer, S., 'Preparation for Political Participation', *Australian Journal of Advanced Nursing*, vol. 1, no. 4, June/August 1984.

Archer, S. E., 'Australian Nurses' Political Participation', *ANJ*, vol. 14, no. 3, 1984.

Armstrong, M., 'A Brief History of the First 50 Years of the Royal Victorian College of Nursing 1901–1951', *UNA*, Jubilee Issue, 1951.

Becker, H. 'The Nature of a Profession', H. Nelson (ed.), *Education for the Professions*, Chicago, 1962.

Bessant, Judith, D'Cruz, Vin, 'When Nurses and Teachers Strike: Public Perceptions of "The Betrayal"', *Australian Journal of Advanced Nursing*, vol. 6, no. 3, March/May 1989.

Bonowitt, V., Whittaker, Y., 'A Victorian Survey of the Image of Nurses and Nursing', *ANJ*, May 1983.

Bryant, R., 'Power in Nursing — The Australian Scene', E. Jenkins, B. King, G. Gray (eds), *Issues in Australasian Nursing*, Churchill Livingstone, Melbourne 1982.

Burbidge, G.N., 'Trends in Nursing', *UNA*, May 1954.

Bush, M. 'Nursing as a Feminist Issue', *The Lamp*, vol. 38, no. 5, 1981.

Chittick, R., 'University Education for Nurses', *ANJ*, October 1969.

Chomley, P., 'Some Reflections and Projections', *ANJ*, July 1967.

Cole, J., 'In Defence of Training Schools', *UNA*, January 1947.

Evans, M., 'Cooperation Between Medical and Associated Professions in Health Care', *UNA*, May 1968.

Fox, S., 'The Origins of Wastage from Nursing, *Australian Journal of Advanced Nursing*, vol. 5, no. 1, September/November 1987.

Gardner, H., McCoppin, B., 'Emerging Militancy? The Politicalisation of Australian Allied Health Professionals', H. Gardner (ed.), *The Politics of Health: The Australian Experience*, Churchill Livingstone, Melbourne, 1989.

Gardner, H., McCoppin, B., 'Vocation, Career or Both', *Australian Journal of Advanced Nursing*, vol. 4, no. 1, September/November 1986.

Gardner, H., McCoppin, B., 'The Politicalisation of Australian Nurses: Victoria 1984–1986', *Politics*, vol. 22, no. 1, May 1987.

Garmarnikow, E., 'Sexual Division of Labour. The Case of Nursing', in A. Kuhn, A. Wolpe (eds), *Feminism and Materialism*, Routledge and Kegan Paul, London, 1978.

Gillam, R., 'Through a Veil, Darkly; Dilemmas in Nursing Education, *ANJ*, December 1969.

Gray, D, 'Attitudinal Militancy Amongst Australian Nurses', *Australian Journal of Social Issues*, vol. 19, no. 2, May 1984.

Hicks, N., 'The History and Politics of Legislation for Nursing Status', *Australian Journal of Advanced Nursing*, vol. 2, no. 3, March/May 1985.

Howard, K., 'Nursing in the Mid Eighties: Condition Critical', *Australian Health Review*, vol. 8, no. 4, 1985.

Jayawardena, Y., 'Whither Nursing', *UNA*, October 1961.

Katz, F., 'Nurses', in Amitai Etzioni (ed.), *The Semi Professions and their Organization*, Free Press, New York 1969. Lew, Y., 'Trends in Nursing Education in Australia Within the Next Decade', *ANJ*, October 1969.

Lindell, J., 'Nursing, a Profession', *UNA*, October 1953.

Llewellyn-Jones, J.D., 'Educated Nurses', *ANJ*, November 1968.

Martin, J., 'Social Influences on the Nursing Profession', *UNA*, September 1961.

McClelland, R., 'The Need for University Education for Nurse Leaders', R. Gillam, (ed.),*Progress or Retrogression? Realities in Nursing 1969*, New South Wales College of Nursing, Sydney 1969.

McCullock, S. J., 'The Politics of Nursing', *ANJ*, April 1982.

McManamny, S., 'Nurses' Work, Nurses' Worth: Union Struggles Today', *Arena*, no. 77, 1986.

Meredith, L., 'The Doctor Nurse Game: Sexual Politics in Health Care', *New Doctor*, no. 36, June 1985.

Meredith, L., 'Working Our Way to the Bottom: Women and Nursing?', *Labour History*, no. 52, May 1987.

Muntz, J., 'Nursing — Professional Responsibility', *UNA*, October 1953.

Oldmeadow, E., 'The Future of the Nursing Aide in the Health Service', *ANJ*, February 1970.

Parise, I., Meers, G., 'Low Morale in Public Hospitals', *New Doctor*, no. 39, Autumn 1986.

Patten, M., 'The Rights of Nurses', *ANJ*, June 1977.

Patten, M., 'Systems of Nursing Training in Victoria', *UNA*, October 1953.

Paulina, Sister Mary, 'Reflections on the Future of Nursing in Australia, *International Nursing Review*, vol. 16, no. 3, 1969.

Pauline, Sister Mary, 'The Heart of Nursing', *UNA*, June 1968.

Peterson, F.M., 'Scientific Progress and the Nurse', *UNA*, January 1955.

Quinn, S., 'Australian Nursing Conditions', *UNA*, February 1963.

Robson, Professor H.N., 'The Need for a Revolution in the Nursing Profession', *UNA*, September 1954.

Ross, L., 'Sisters are Doing it for Themselves and Us. The Victorian Nurses' Strike of 1986', *Hecate*, vol. 13, no. 1, 1987.

Slater, P., 'Comprehensive Training', *UNA*, June 1963.

Slater, P., 'College Education for Nurses: Object Lessons from North America', *Australian Journal of Advanced Nursing*, vol. 1, no. 4, 1984.

Smith, K., 'Morale: a Spectrum of Attitude Among Nurses', *Australian Health Review*, vol. 9, no. 2, 1986.

Speedy, S., 'Feminism and Nursing: From Theory to Practice', *Shaping Nursing Theory and Practice: The Australian Context*, Lincoln School of Health Sciences, La Trobe University, monograph, 1988.

Speedy, S., 'Feminism and the Professionalization of Nursing', *Australian Journal of Advanced Nursing*, vol. 4, no. 2, December 1986-January 1987.

Westmore, A., 'The Case for Nurses: What all the Fuss is About', *Women Australia*, no. 6, December/January 1984, 1985.

Books

Abel-Smith, B., *A History of the Nursing Profession*, William Heinemann, London, 1960.

Alfred Hospital School of Nursing 1880–1980, Alfred Hospital, Melbourne, 1980.

Archer, S., *Australian Nurses' Political Participation*, College of Nursing, Australia, Melbourne, 1982.

Ashley, J., *Hospitals, Paternalism and the Role of the Nurse*, Teachers College Press, New York, 1976.

Baumgart, A., *Nursing Associations and Unions: A New and Complicated Co-existence*, Thirty-fifth Annual Oration, New South Wales College of Nursing, Sydney, 1987.

Bolton, G., Joske, P., *A History of the Royal Perth Hospital*, University of Western Australia Press, Perth, 1982.

Bowman, G., *The Lamp and the Book. The Story of the RCN 1916–1966*, Queen Anne Press, London, 1967.

Bridges, D., *A History of the International Council of Nurses 1899–1964. The First Sixty-Five Years*, Pitman Medical, London, 1967.

Burbidge, G., *Lectures for Nurses*, Australasian Medical Publishing Co., Sydney, 1954.

Creighton, H., Lopez, F., *A History of Nursing Education in New South Wales: a Comparative Analysis of Australian and International Influences and Developments*, F. Lopez, Sydney, 1982.

Curdhoys, A., Martin, A., Rouse, T., (eds), *Australians from 1939*, Fairfax, Syme, Welden, Sydney, 1987.

Cusack, F., *Lister House: The Story of the Northern District School of Nursing*, Hawthorn Press, Melbourne, 1976.

D'Cruz, V., Bottorff, J., *The Renewal of Nursing Education. A Cultural Perspective of Continuities and Change*, University Health Service, La Trobe University, Melbourne, 1984.

Davies, C. (ed.), *Rewriting Nursing History*, Croom Helm, London, 1980.

Dingle, T., *The Victorians. Settling*, Fairfax, Syme, Weldon, Sydney 1984.

Donaghue, S., *Goals in Nursing Practice. Trends Within the Health Field and their Implications for Nursing Practice*, RANF, Melbourne, 1977.

Doust, J., *The Nhill Hospital, First Hundred Years, 1882–1982*, Nhill Hospital, 1982.

Etzioni, A., (ed.), *The Semi-Professions and their Organizations. Teachers, Nurses, Social Workers*, Free Press, New York, 1969.

Fox, D., *Industrial Relations in Nursing — Victoria 1982 to 1985*, University of New South Wales, School of Health Administration, Sydney, 1989.

Gardiner, L., *Royal Children's Hospital, Melbourne 1870–1970: A History*, Royal Children's Hospital, Melbourne, 1970.

Gardner, H., *The Politics of Health: The Australian Experience*, Churchill Livingstone, Melbourne, 1989.

Gault, E., Lucas, A., *A Century of Compassion: a History of the Austin Hospital*, Macmillan, South Melbourne, 1982.

Goodman, R., *Our War Nurses, The History of the Royal Australian Nursing Corps 1902–1988*, Boolarong Publications, Brisbane, 1988.

Goodman, R., *Queensland Nurses: Boer War to Vietnam*, Boolarong, Brisbane, 1975.

Henderson, R., (ed.), *Alfred Hospital Reminiscences (1927–1947)*, Melbourne, 1990.

Hobbs, V., *But Westward Look: Nursing in Western Australia*, University of Western Australia Press for the RANF, W.A. Branch, Nedlands, 1980.

Hughes, J., *A History of the Royal Adelaide Hospital*, Board of Management, Royal Adelaide Hospital, Adelaide, 1982.

Inglis, K.S., *Hospital and Community: a History of the Royal Melbourne Hospital*, Melbourne University Press, Carlton, 1958.

Katz, F., Mathews, K., Pepe, T., White, R., *Stepping Out. Nurses and their New Roles*, New South Wales University Press, Sydney, 1976.

Kelly, B., *A Background to the History of Nursing in Tasmania*, Davies Brothers, Hobart, 1977.

Kennedy, C., *The History of Heyfield Bush Nursing Hospital*, Heyfield Bush Nursing Hospital, Heyfield, 1985.

Kingston, B., *My Wife, My Daughter and Poor Mary Ann, Women and Work in Australia*, Thomas Nelson, Melbourne, 1975.

Kisler, H., *The History of Occupational Health Nursing in Victoria*, Occupational Health Special Interest Group, RANF, Melbourne, 1984.

Lieberman M., *Education as a Profession*, Prentice-Hall, New Jersey, 1956.

Marshall, N., *The Melbourne School of Nursing 1950–1963. A Chapter in the History of Nursing in Victoria*, Melbourne School of Nursing Past Trainees Association, Melbourne, 1985.

Minchin, M., *Revolutions and Rosewater: The Evolution of Nurse Registration in Victoria 1923–1973*, Hart Hamer, Melbourne, n.d.

Mitchell, A., *The Hospital South of the Yarra. A History of Alfred Hospital, Melbourne, from Foundation to the Nineteen-Forties*, Alfred Hospital, Melbourne, 1977.

National Nursing Education Division, RANF, National Florence Nightingale Committee of Australia, *Survey Report on the Wastage of General Trained Nurses from Nursing in Australia, November 1960-November 1967*, RANF, FNCA, 1967.

Nightingale, F., *Notes on Nursing: What It Is and What It Is Not.* (facs) D. Appleton-Century, New York, 1946.

Nunn, H., *A Most Ingenious Hospital: A History of Sandringham and District Memorial Hospital 1940–1990*, Sandringham Hospital, Melbourne, 1990.

Phillips, P., *A Spirit of Care: Echuca District Hospital. The First Hundred Years*, Echuca District Hospital, Echuca, 1982.

Priestley, S., *The Victorians, Making Their Mark*, Fairfax, Syme, Weldon, Sydney, 1984. Priestley, S., *Bush Nursing in Victoria: 1910–1985, the First 75 years*, Victorian Bush Nursing Association/Lothian, Melbourne, 1986.

Russell, L., *From Nightingale to Now. Nurse Education in Australia*, Harcourt Brace Jovanovich, Sydney, 1990.

Salvage, J., *The Politics of Nursing*, Heinemann Nursing, London, 1985.

Schultz, B., *Founders of the College*, College of Nursing, Australia.

Seymer, L., *Florence Nightingale's Nurses, The Nightingale Training School 1860–1960*, Pitman Medical, London, 1960.

Sheehy, T., *A Hospital for the Bayside*, Mordialloc-Cheltenham Community Hospital, Mordialloc, 1982.

Shryock, R., *The History of Nursing: an Interpretation of the Social and Medical Factors Involved*, 1959.

Slater, P., *The Role of Nursing Organisations in Professional Education: Challenges for the Future*, College of Nursing, Australia.

Smith, F. B., *Florence Nightingale: Reputation and Power*, Croom Helm, London, 1982.

Spark, J., Walkowski, M., *The Geelong Hospital Nurses' League: a History of the First Fifty Years, 1934–84*, Neptune Press, Newtown, 1984.

Templeton, J., *Prince Henry's: The Evolution of a Melbourne Hospital 1869–1969*, Robertson and Mullens, Melbourne, 1969.

Trembath, R., Hellier, D., *All Care and Responsibility. A History of Nursing in Victoria 1850–1934*, Florence Nightingale Committee, Australia, Victorian Branch, Melbourne, 1987.

Walker, V., *Nursing and Ritualistic Practice*, Macmillan, New York, 1967.

White, R., *The Role of the Nurse in Australia*, Tertiary Education Research Centre, University of New South Wales, 1972.

Williams, J. A., Goodman, R. D., *Jane Bell, O.B.E. (1873–1959): Lady Superintendent, The Royal Melbourne Hospital (1910–1934)*, Royal Melbourne Hospital Graduate Nurses' Association, Melbourne, 1988.

Windshuttle, E., (ed.), *Women, Class and History: Feminist Perspectives on Australia 1788–1978*, Fontana Books, Melbourne, 1980.

Woodham-Smith, C., *Florence Nightingale 1820–1910*, Penguin Books, Harmondsworth, 1955.

Index

Matt Fielder is a prolific writer who has already published a poetry book entitled *A Life in a Calendar Year* and previously had work showcased as a food critic, columnist and journalist for The Richmond and Twickenham Times, as well as just about every other local newspaper and magazine in Surrey. He is also a renowned Compere and 'MC' of many events, both large and small, up and down the country, as well as an accomplished kids and adult party DJ. He is, however, perhaps best known for being a rock singer and fronting many bands over the years. He has recently released an EP *Halfway to Hell;* a single – *A Christmas Held to Ransom* and an album *Back to the Boozer* with his current band, Ransom. He has been married for over 30 years to his wife, Alicia, and they have two children – Ryan (19) and Zosia (14) – and they live in Fetcham, Surrey.

To the fallen, the forgotten, the famous and the few…
'Rock in Peace' all my brothers, sisters and folk of a non-binary identification.

Matt Fielder

YOU KNOW YOU LOVE IT

The Story of Hurricane Jane
91–95 (The Glory Years!)

AUSTIN MACAULEY PUBLISHERS™

LONDON • CAMBRIDGE • NEW YORK • SHARJAH

Copyright © Matt Fielder 2023

The right of Matt Fielder to be identified as author of this work has been asserted by the author in accordance with sections 77 and 78 of the Copyright, Designs and Patents Act 1988.

All rights reserved. No part of this publication may be reproduced, stored in a retrieval system, or transmitted in any form or by any means, electronic, mechanical, photocopying, recording, or otherwise, without the prior permission of the publishers.

Any person who commits any unauthorised act in relation to this publication may be liable to criminal prosecution and civil claims for damages.

All of the events in this memoir are true to the best of author's memory. The views expressed in this memoir are solely those of the author.

A CIP catalogue record for this title is available from the British Library.

ISBN 9781398425033 (Paperback)
ISBN 9781398425040 (ePub e-book)

www.austinmacauley.com

First Published 2023
Austin Macauley Publishers Ltd®
1 Canada Square
Canary Wharf
London
E14 5AA

No thanks could ever be enough, but regardless they go in spades to Howard Smith, at No Sloppy Copy for his superlative efforts in the initial edit (I've been back over it a few times since mind you) and for being such a good friend. To the band, Simon, Dave and Jason and all the other musicians who were a part of it in the proceeding or post line ups. To my wonderful wife, Alicia, of 30 years, my son and daughter Ryan and Zosia (my world), my brothers and sisters, Simon, Julia, Andrew, Kate, Louise and Rebecca, and to all my extended family, my sadly departed mother and elderly father. Karol and Krystyna Suszka (RIP), To my best mates, Conn, Vicky, Steve, Tom, Andy, Nick, Mandy, Brian, Simon, Jane, Karen and Jack, Steph, Shirley, Tony, Anne, Dave and Sandra, Dave, Zach, Zippy and all the Ransom family, Brian, Pete, Mike, Andy, Adrian, Dean, Pete, Gina (my absolute bestie), N&D Blanchard, Jo, Sandra L, Hannah, Nick London, Marek, Andrej, Chris, Karl, Pete G, Andy, Lusia and all my Polish family and friends, Alan Goff, Danny, Scott, Alec, Victoria and all at Crazy Cowboy, Nigel W, All at MMH, HRH, Geoff L, Charlotte, Glam rat, Steve H, Andy S, Tina, Caz, Mike P, Max P, Paul's C& D, Letty Rock, Marcin (RIP), Hugh McIlvanney Rob, Tony, Alex, Jai, Woody, Elizabeth Regina (RIP) and a supporting cast of literally thousands far too long and numerous to mention! But you should all know who you are by now, what you did, or what you are currently doing and what you will always mean to me... So thank you, all of you... And yes, surprisingly enough, even YOU as well!

To all the musical legends I have either met or who have helped or influenced me, Bon, Ozzy, Lemmy, Phil Lynott, Biff Byford, Freddie, Axl, Chris Cornell, Dee Snider, Brian Johnson, Bernie Torme, Dave Lee Roth, Bruce Dickenson, Dio, John Lydon, Steve Jones, Paul Cook, Dave Grohl, Roger Daltrey, Pete Townsend, Dave Meniketti, John Nyman, Lea Hart, Steve Hopgood, Paul D'Ianno, John, Paul, George and Ringo, Elvis, Mick and Keef, Joel O'Keefe, Baz Mills, Laurence and Reuben Archer, Mike Dyer, Matt Tuck, Pete Jupp, Lee Mark Jones, Mike Edwards and to all those other folks who either accidentally, innocently or even deliberately got in the way. There are no hard feelings. You have all helped shape this story one way or another, either willingly or unknowingly and ultimately contributed to this, continuously, amazing and incredible journey…

Rock hard and Ride free my friends. See you all on the other side!

Introduction
Through Hell and Heartbreak

"Don't give up, you got to keep on believing, burning ambition, don't ever let it go."

The Nightmare after Christmas! Big Dave and I sharing the 'hallowed' stage with Simon and Jay, a couple of days after our crash course in Christmas catering, The Marquee, 27th December 1994

Trying to write an introduction to this book was never going to be an easy task. It was always going to be coloured by my own personal reflections, imperfect recollections, perceived misjustices and the distorting effects of my not-so-rose tinted goggles. What I once may have regarded as past glories have, over the years, morphed into a series of hilariously deluded past tragedies.

And this account is, of course, only told from my perspective, from my diaries. Others in the story naturally have their own versions – which, a bit like the four gospels may differ ever so slightly from mine. And just like that Jerusalem Carpenter fellow, whichever way you want to look at it, I'm still going to end up getting crucified, well…in some quarters at least!

That said, every event described in this book happened one way or another. Not only that, but they also account for a period in my life that has ultimately affected me personally, professionally and emotionally right up until today. Now, some 27 years on, it's finally time to get this story off my chest and out there to you lovely people!

I initially wanted to open with a meaningful quote, something profound that engaged and set the tone, thereby compelling you, dear reader, to want to read on.

I searched long and hard for something appropriate but in the end, the best I could come up with was multi-millionaire and tantric sex god Sting's response to receiving his lifetime Brit Award by claiming: "Music was in fact its own reward." Great quote, Gordon, but perhaps ruined a little by the somewhat smug smile that accompanied it.

In Sting's defence, he did record the wonderfully pretentiously titled, but also brilliantly executed debut album, *Outlandos d'Amour*, with his band The Police in my (recently adopted) hometown of Leatherhead in 1978. If you've ever stood outside Tesco's there on a cold, wet, grainy Monday afternoon, you'll certainly see the irony in all the romantic 'imagery' created by that particular title.

Another option I toyed with was Rudyard Kipling's likening of 'Kissing a man who hadn't waxed his moustache' as to 'having egg without salt'. The problem with that one however was that I have absolutely no idea what he was on about (or smoking at the time), it just sounded quite profound and out there.

I digress. The lesson is basically to just stick to what you know. Feed your own soul, fill your own boots, do it for yourself. Imitating others or faking it just to impress people is the route to inglorious failure. It's far better when you can hold your head up high and say you did it your way and died with your boots on, fully filled. That's what we did, and we failed gloriously...or did we?

Okay, so let's set the scene for you for the main part of the book shall we, It's the early to mid-1990s. Grunge has taken root, Kurt is King. Nu and alternative metal bands are coming to the fore. Korn, Ugly Kid Joe, Extreme, Faith No More and, Red Hot Chilli Peppers are the big international acts.

In the UK, Brit pop is on the rise. 'Madchester' and all its happy pills are in full swing, and Oasis and Blur are taking chunks out of each other. Football and comedy are part of the deal, too: Indie music, Baddiel and Skinner, Chris Evans, The Big breakfast, The Word, Men Behaving Badly – this is the zeitgeist as I approach my 30th year.

Prestigious London gig venues were becoming franchised as night clubs from 11.30 pm onwards. If you came to see the band and were still kicking around after the gig, you had a choice: Pay the entrance fee again or fuck off. The other side to this non-daylight robbery was that the 'dancing around their handbag's types would have to wait until the band had finished before they could get in.

The upshot was the soul-destroying grind of playing to an audience of approximately 50 or so of your 'mates' before exiting the venue just as a queue of at least 500 people were being let in. This was also the time of ruthless promoters and the 'pay to play' culture.

This was our landscape and our battleground. Apathy, alienation, ignorance and indifference.

Okay, so now you are all hopefully up to speed, totally on board and ready for this journey?

Good, then without further ado, "Ladies and gentlemen, please take your seats, switch off your mobile phones and welcome onto the stage, still stuck in the eighties, playing their own brand of dated hair metal, the one, the only, Hurricane Jane!"

Chapter 1
Head in The Clouds

"And you'll wonder who your friends are when you've left them all behind."

Adrian, Pete and me as Hurricane Jane MK 1 on safari in black spandex and leg warmers, Shepherds Bush 1984

I arrived into the world on Sunday, 5 April 1964 at 8 am, my point of entry being 16b Tudor Gardens (off White Hart Lane), Barnes, London SW13.

Fire of the dragon, Diamond my Stone, Mars my ruler, And I Rock to the bone. Horn of the Ram…Yeah…Okay, I think that's probably just about enough of that.

Anyway, I'm an Aries in case you hadn't guessed it.

I was in my mother's womb when President John F Kennedy was assassinated and so my mother decided to Christen me with John as my second name in his honour, I think Lee, Harvey or Oswald were names probably off the table at the time. Mind you book depositories and Grassy knoll's aside Catholic families generally named their offspring after biblical figures or Saints in those days. That process continues right through your religious development and upbringing. I know that as when I was confirmed I was allowed to adopt a third name.

I initially wanted Clint after my acting hero of the time. But again, I was told it had to be a Saint, so I opted for Roger (Moore) after the TV show. However there seemed to be an apparent sense of humour bypass for the Monsignor in charge at the time of Our lady Queen of Peace, East Sheen, who as it turned out, was sadly neither a fan of spaghetti westerns or suave sixties TV thieves and instead 'Instructed' me that David would be a far more appropriate and befitting name for someone like me.

I never use it, but I believe I can if ever I wish to do so, for illicit hotel trysts, marriage annulments or tax evasion purposes.

The middle child of seven – I have two brothers and four sisters who I love and admire deeply – I am the son of an English dad and an Irish mum.

As I said we were raised as a strict 'Catholic family' but none the less my childhood was a very happy one and I thank my loving parents for instilling in me the good values, virtues and attributes I hold dear still to this day.

In a family as large as ours there were always going to be many challenges to face, but my parents never shirked their responsibilities and as in fact you can quite clearly see, my dad never pulled out of anything.

Most of my childhood memories are idyllic though, the sun always shining, playing happily in Richmond Park, going to the beach at Boscombe for summer holidays. But maybe time just does that to you and filters out all the bad ones.

In fact, the only unpleasant memory that I can recall as a toddler, was being strapped virtually 24/7 to a wooden potty commode on wheels.

Looking like some sort of Baby 'Davros' from the Dr Who and the Daleks TV series. The unfortunate aftermath of this 'Soiled' nappy saving exercise, would be on being released from its constraints.

You would be left with a leather belt strap and buckle mark across your stomach, a 'raw' red ring around your buttocks and backs of your upper thighs and leaving behind you a plastic container full of the ejected deposits of the days' various drinks and meals which you had been riding around with for most of that day.! Social services would've had a field day with this today I'm quite sure!

Mind you there were also times when I wondered how devout my folks were. Indeed, while I was growing up, I used to babysit for a family across the road from casa Fielder which was now in East Sheen, Richmond. Late one night as I was saying goodnight to my employers on their doorstep, our eyes were all suddenly drawn to activity over the road, where two sinister shadows were moving behind a Venetian blind in our new loft conversion. There was certainly some strenuous exercise going on up there for sure. Mum, I was later told, was putting a duvet cover on the bed while Dad was having a go at pull-ups on a wooded beam. I was never convinced, and neither were my employers.

"Looks like you may well be babysitting a little closer to home very soon Matthew," they both said at once. Funnily enough they were both quite possibly right, as my youngest sister Rebecca was born roughly about nine months later!

Of course, having a large family can get complicated at times. You forget who you've told what to, sometimes with disorienting results.

One night circa 1989, after a heroic bender in Richmond, when it seemed easier for me to crash at Ma and Pa's rather than negotiate the complexities of public transport back to my own pad, I turned up at my childhood home at around midnight.

I'd been drinking in 'The Old Ship' a haunt we all frequented a lot from our college days, and which had become a rock'n'roll hang out for quite a few bands and their entourages during the eighties.

Anyhow, I banged for some time on the door, confident my parents would be up, possibly even conceiving yet another addition to the family.

What I wasn't expecting, however was to be greeted by a salad cream-stained dressing gown or the perfect stranger inside it. And he certainly wasn't expecting me, either.

He didn't invite me in but was polite enough to explain that he'd bought the house from a Mr and Mrs Fielder and had recently completed on the purchase.

Mum and Dad had moved to a new house down in Wiltshire and had apparently' forgotten' to tell me.

Middle of the family I was always going to be a misfit I suppose. I mean the warning signs were there way back as young as six years old when our mother broke the news that her Irish father had passed away, I asked quite innocently, "Who shot him?" And was in fact quite horrified to discover that some awful disease I'd never heard of called 'natural causes' had taken him.

I went to two Catholic schools. The first was St Mary Magdalene's Primary school in Mortlake. I loved it. (Sandra, Mary… Where are you now?)

The second was an all-boys secondary comprehensive establishment in Gunnersbury, near Brentford. I hated it and was in fact asked 'Not to return 'by the School's Director for my second year of sixth form education there!

In fact, my all-abiding memory from there was on the first day of the summer term, April 5th, 1976. It was the start of the cricket season, and this was when I realised what it truly meant to be at a comprehensive school.

I had turned up, on my birthday at Gunnersbury Park for games, wearing my full cricket attire and it was obvious I was the only one that got the memo. "Fielder are you some kind of total cunt" I think was the opening gambit as I stood there, in my dad's flared white flannels, hobnail boots (from the fifties) a public-school sweater and cap from St. Benedict's (my older brother's private school) and an old linseed oil-stained Cricket bat with lots of white tape around it, badly cracked and quite possibly once owned by WG 'Fucking' Grace himself! No one else was wearing anything even remotely white!

As a result of this public shaming, I briefly dropped out and the next week, took up athletics instead. But we had a very strange teacher taking that (weren't they all?) who started off by giving us a lecture about this annual event called 'The London Games' which we should all be aiming to take part in, but generally making it sound more like the Colosseum in ancient Rome. Describing in salacious detail, how some poor sod the previous year had got a Javelin through his neck and had died "screaming for his mother". Another child who had received a shot-put throw straight into their chest and as a result their heart had stopped beating and despite some desperate and frantic resuscitation attempts to revive him had also died right there on the field.

Then finally and perhaps most tragically, A young girl who got a stray discus to the head which took nearly half her brain out, rendering her an almost virtual vegetable at the time. Thankfully I did hear that over time she made sufficient recovery to become a Comprehensive School games teacher herself and by all accounts is doing very well at it!

Anyway, the result of this meant that reluctantly after weighing up the lesser of two evils, I decided to go back to the Cricket and suffer all the abuse and ridicule of having a surname like mine in this sport.

"Bowler's name please?" would be the cry from the 'scorers-box, from whatever other school we were playing at the time!

"Fielder," I would reply.

"No, Bowler's name," would come the very obvious response back, "Or are you just trying to be some sort of total cunt mate?"

Sanctuary eventually came, however, when I enrolled at Richmond College (which was, in fact, in Twickenham) aged

17. It was here that I met most of the people who continue to be some of my best friends today.

To be fair, I did get thrown out of this place as well after eight months or so (Mostly for alcohol related issues and generally for being a constant pest in lessons), but I did manage to secure a drama 'O' Level at least to add to my other six!

My best mate here (and am happy to report still is today) was Conn McIlvanney. A year after starting college, Conn and I eventually managed to secure a tenancy on a one-bedroom flat on Richmond Hill.

This period comes very much under the term 'A learning curve'. Officially, Conn and I were the named occupants, but no way could we afford the monthly rent between us – my job at the Total petrol station being not exactly congruent with an address in one of TW10's most select roads. We couldn't even scrape the deposit – Conn's dad, the late great, famous sportswriter, Hugh McIlvanney put that up for us.

So, to hold things together, we got a third flatmate, Mark Dalling, in on the quiet. He's the cousin of another great friend, Howard Smith, who's currently helping me edit this text (very well).

Countless mates and college buddies came and crashed in this flat during our tenure, fellow 'Richmonders', Gianni Malpelli and Aidan Doyle (sadly taken way too soon from us) among them. Domestically, we were a hopeless bunch. There was a double bed and two camp beds in the bedroom and the only house rule ever observed was 'whoever gets the girl, gets the bed'.

We lasted six months in that flat and not once did I get the bed. And I was there for a good full month on my own after the other two lads left.

Why only six months? Differences of opinion between us and our neighbours over what constituted a polite interval between parties really. One, on Christmas eve which as I recall half of South-West London came 'uninvited' too, was probably the final nail in our already made-up coffin.

Nevertheless, that half-year was a fertile time for me creatively. I wrote songs I'm still proud of today and even squeezed in the odd rehearsal with my fledgling band there – which probably hastened our eventual departure.

This then was the early beginnings of 'Hurricane Jane'. The line-up would change dramatically between now and the period this book mainly covers – the 1990s. I often read books by various musicians and look at where their love for music originated from. Currently reading Dave Grohl's 'The Storyteller' and there always seems to be a common theme of hardship or some unfortunate incident that triggered their various creative streaks. Most all these guys had their legends and idols, and I am no different. Growing up in the late sixties and seventies, my earliest memories are of The Beatles running away from screaming girls in the film 'A hard day's night'. Followed by 'Glamsters' Slade, Sweet and dare I say it Gary Glitter.

We all wanted to be in his gang then, whether we admit it now or not. It was mostly "C'mon feel the noise, girls grab the boys" back at primary school!

But it was one night in December 1976 that it all changed for me. When I really connected with something.

Back in my house switching over the TV from BBC to ITV was a crime punishable by 'bed without tea' or worse having to eat up all your greens! But that night for some reason (I remember not why?) I found myself on my own and switched channels just in time to catch the end of the 'infamous' Bill Grundy/Sex Pistols interview.

My outlook and perspective on life literally changed, right there and then. As shocking as it was exciting, these guys just didn't give an actual fuck!

It was as though all I was going through, a misfit, and black sheep of a very middle class family, not 'rough or tough' enough for the 'Mockneys' of my West London comprehensive school, but also dropping far too many 'h's for my parents liking, was reflected in the angst of these guys…This, yeah this was a bit of me alright, this was perfect, now where's that guitar with only one bottom 'E' string on it?…I'm gonna go and write a 'punk rock' album, see you in about ten minutes!!

This was not my first foray into the music world. I did record an album with my Gunnersbury school choir 'Music from all Saints' (Gaudeamus recordings) a year before in 1975. Which also included spending the night at London Colney with three teachers (later all alleged paedophiles). But thankfully, not one laid a finger on me (I was obviously a very ugly child), so I can neither deny, substantiate or collaborate any of these rumours. But yeah, feel free to look it up, the album is probably lying in some old antique shop somewhere gathering dust (or spunk) next to 'Fly fishing by JR 'fucking 'Hartley'.

As a footnote to this ill-advised 'arse threatening' venture, it was also sadly the night that Grand Prix legend Graham Hill crashed his plane and died less than a mile from where we were recording it! He must've heard us singing!

I decided however, not to tell his son Damon this, when we met recently at a 'Go kart' charity event, I was hosting at Daytona Sandown Park, especially after he'd just been black flagged twice!

But as far as actually playing rock music goes, that started when I began jamming with a guy called Adrian Cumber who I met through my older sister Julia and his younger brother Pete at their Teddington house sometime in the summer of 1981. It was mostly AC/DC covers and never really went anywhere as we didn't have a bass player at the time.

Then an ex-school reunion band from Gunnersbury we called Epitaph (a suitable name for ending any potential aspiring career) I mention this in passing as I have just recently been contacted by the drummer Alan Trevisani, (who also funnily enough sang on that choir record) and he shared on social media some photos of our first gig at the 'spaceship' community hall in Greenford!

Although it was nothing to set the Rock world alight it was certainly a good fun night and planted the seed for what was to follow. Even got a plug on Capitol Radio back in the days when it still played Rock music and it was cool hearing the late great DJ Roger Scott say our band name live on air!

Which did also make me feel more nervous. So much so that I spent the next hour listening to Iron Maiden's new album 'Number of the Beast' to get myself fired up. It worked, for as nervous as I was to face this (surprisingly) packed West London Suburban crowd. I knew deep in my heart that "Hell and Fire" had been "Spawned to be released" so I dually obliged.

Hurricane Jane itself was formed primarily from the ashes of a band called PSO, which stood for Primate Social Organisation (don't ask). PSO comprised of Teddington brothers Adrian and Pete Cumber on guitar and drums respectively (who I'd already mentioned I had initially been jamming with the previous summer) and they were joined by talented art student Dean Rose on bass, with yours truly on lead vocals.

My guitar ability had now at least stretched to playing all six strings and just as many chords E, A, B, C, D and G, so most of the songs we wrote were still pretty basic. They also (as I was the lyricist) would be about things I knew a little bit about, i.e.) Getting pissed, Girls dumping me, schools excluding me, jobs sacking me and nobody really liking me.

We started off playing a lot of local gigs. Richmond College, the Ad Lib Kensington and the Derby Arms, East Sheen (now a block of flats) all of whom were lucky enough to witness the unforgettable primacy of our social organisation and all things considered, and as Mrs Jones might agree, we had a good thing going on.

I also played a lot of sport in those days – Sunday league football, tennis and lots of cricket. I did eventually become quite a talented fast bowler (trials with Middlesex, yes indeed!). I supported Spurs (the White Hart Lane mistaken birthplace thing (i.e., SW13 as opposed to N17), loved punk and metal and adored female company. Still do.

I used to take the number 33 bus from the top of my road in East Sheen (when my parents still let me crash there that is) having saved up my dinner money all week to go and see bands at Hammersmith Odeon. Special times from 1979-1984,

I think I saw just about everybody, well everybody that mattered to me that is, AC/DC, Maiden, Lizzy, Motorhead, Ozzy, Saxon and one band from San Francisco which became mine and Conn's firm favourite's and still are to this day Y&T!

According to the ancient Chinese proverb, a coward dies a thousand deaths, a hero only one. Now I'm neither a hero nor a coward, but I suffered more than a thousand deaths on stage fronting PSO I can tell you!

One of these occurred at the Derby Arms, when a after one gig a Swedish 'pisshead' calling himself Rocky Caberman (you never forget a name like that) asked me for my autograph. The warm, ego-boosting surge this gave me was cut brutally short the following day when I discovered the same scrap of paper, I'd scrawled my name on sticking proudly out of a freshly laid dog turd outside the pub.

On the plus side though, I'd started dating a nurse from Whitton called Jane and home for me now was the Cumber's attic at 161 Kingston Road, Teddington. My new gaff was also our rehearsal studio. Life doesn't get any more rock 'n' roll than that.

Naturally, the neighbours banging on our door complaining about the noise (or waft of weed) was a constant. We attracted the attention of the local constabulary on more than one occasion – which almost put an end to Pete's codeine experiments.

He was 14 ffs.

He was also hot-headed. I can't forget the time our dear neighbour, Ron dropped a note through our door late one night asking if we could please refrain from rehearsing for a few days as his mother was very ill.

Decent fellas that we were, we duly obliged. However, on day four of our amnesty, Ron's and his mother's silence was rudely and unceremoniously broken, by an impatient Pete banging on their door and enquiring sympathetically, through their letterbox. "Oi, is she fucking dead yet or what?"

There was one neighbour we were fortunate to have though. Living opposite us was Reuben Archer, lead vocalist with Stampede, a band who'd just played Reading and were signed to Polydor Records. He and his guitarist stepson, Laurence Archer (later of Grand Slam and UFO) heard our noise and took an interest in us.

To be specific, they were interested in Pete. Their band was on standby for the Monsters of Rock festival at Castle Donnington that summer and their drummer had just broken his hand. They didn't get the gig, but we'd become mates by then anyway. They gave us some great advice and helped us out with our first Porta studio demo (Keep Holding On, Candle in the Wind and Something More to Love) and gave us the support slot at their next gig.

Ironically, as it turned to be their final one at the time, as Laurence was joining Phil Lynott's 'Grand Slam'. This gig took place at the Red Lion in Brentford (now a Drive Thru McDonald's).

In all honesty, PSO was doomed from the start. Sibling rivalries, girlfriend arguments, extreme naivety and musical differences all took their toll and we inevitably split up (as I did with Jane) in the spring of 1984.

I had reason for optimism, though. In the summer of that year, I had visited a gypsy queen fortune teller in Blackpool

Tower whilst staying with a female friend Susan in Accrington. The fortune teller was adamant that I would have a successful career in the music industry. But then she also said she was coming to London to hold a series of psychic nights at a local pub that summer and that we would meet again, very soon. We didn't.

Despite my belief in myself, I was still a mess: 20 years old and homeless, jobless, band less and girlfriendless. I spent my days and nights 'spunking' my dole money on Special Brew and whisky depth chargers, dossing at strangers' houses and shagging anything that moved (if it would shag me). To my shame I even took a mate of Pete's, 16-year-old Tom Wan (though he looked about 30) with me on this destructive path.

It's not something I'm proud of. But Tom saw and did stuff others of his age could probably only dream about with a 'tube of lube' and a box of Kleenex in their respective bedrooms. Which reminds me of the few nights he kindly let me stay at his parents' house (without telling them) sleeping on a mattress fortified by a multitude of '70s' porn mags (apparently, they were all his older brother's).

I apologise unreservedly to anyone who encountered me during this period. I wasn't good to be around. In fact, I was a complete asshole. However, in retrospect, I did learn a lot about myself, which, hopefully, I have used to become a better human being (the jury's still out on that one).

I don't claim to be an angel these days either – as my self-destructive streak has reared its head on a few occasions since – but my episodes are nowhere near as frequent or anywhere near as cringeworthy as they were back then.

The lowest point being on my 20th birthday where I stood outside, on the ledge of the first-floor window of 'The Old

Ship' pub in Richmond (after a day of downing approx. 32 bottles of Special Brew (and four whisky depth chargers) and conducting Friday night's revellers in the street below as some 'bright spark' put 'Jump' by Van Halen on the pub's jukebox!

Thankfully I didn't, but it was one of many truly 'idiotic' things I did and indeed 'run ins' I had with various establishments and Police at the time.

The most famous of which being when I organised a game of 'impromptu' cricket (after hours) on the grass of the Richmond Circus (A316) Roundabout with total strangers, as stunned drivers drove around 'blasting' their horns in sheer disbelief at our utter stupidity!

It was probably a good job they didn't see the sightscreen we pulled out into the middle of the road from Kew bridge cricket ground a little later either I suppose.

For self-reflection, and to counter act these moments of 'Matt Madness' I'd sit on Richmond Hill, gazing out at the view of the Thames from a concrete plinth over the road from the Roebuck pub, a scene painted many times by artists down the centuries (though perhaps not all of them with a Special Brew in both hands). I needed to get straight, get a job and get my life back on track.

Many people have asked me about where I got the name Hurricane Jane from. Was it a reference to my ex-girlfriend that I'd made such a dick of myself getting over? Was it a nod to an album by Stampede? Or was it even a tribute to the unsung planes that defended our skies in the shadow of the legendary Spitfires during World War II?

A bit of them all. There was a distant but lingering memory of an early Friday evening spent lying in bed with

Jane in Teddington before a gig at the Ad Lib club in Kensington. We were listening to Laurence playing lead guitar on our demo. Stampede's album at the time was called Hurricane Town. And that afternoon we had just watched the film, The Battle of Britain on TV. In the actual Battle of Britain, Hurricanes scored the highest number of RAF victories, accounting for 1,593 out of the 2,739 total claimed (source: Telegraph.co.uk) and a lot of them flown by Czech's and Poles for the record!

From there, the song, *Hurricane Jane* started writing itself in my head:

It's Friday night you're ready to go,
Rock 'n' rolling to another show…

The legend was born.

Nowadays I think about the creation process of that song as a massive turning point in my life. Triumph over adversity. Being able to laugh at unfortunate periods of your life and be able to reclaim your pride and dignity.

Whenever people ask for it either at a gig or I hear it played at someone's house, it reminds me of exactly why I wrote it and what it means for not only me personally, but also, I'm very proud to say, for a lot of other people too. It was our anthem, our song and…There will never be a Hurricane, like Hurricane Jane!

For all the dreams I had before
I'm gonna fight for evermore

It just had to be the name of the band as well. And the logo would have wings on it. Yes folks, I was back in the game again by October 1984.

Chapter 2
Lipstick Lies

"Killing time working nine to five, you just don't seem to understand!"

Bedlam in Brentford. Roaring at the Red Lion (now McDonald's)
"You want fries with that, son?" February 1991

This was going to be the start of something special. We would all acknowledge our naivety, apologise to each other, hold hands and skip happily together down the musical meadow of merriment and melody.

Bollocks, would we. This was rock 'n' roll, not The Sound of Fucking Music. Forget Edelweiss, this was more 'idle vice'.

Adrian, Pete and I did at least get the band back together though and back on some sort of track. Armed with a new name, new logo, some new songs (it's amazing how creative you get when your strung out and your life's a complete mess) and two new members. Guitarist Bob Williams joined us from Rough Justice while Sean West of Sweet Revenge took on temporary bass duties.

The revolving door that was our bass berth would next be occupied by Jon Shankster and then Ian Clements, with cameos on guitar from Messer's Gianni Malpelli and Steve Whilton (best get their names in as they are all bound to be reading this at some point).

I cleaned up my act too and got employed at Outmere Direct Mail in Wimbledon. The job description suited me to the ground: To supervise elderly ladies whose job it was to stuff envelopes, moist flaps being vital to the execution of the role.

Run by the Blanchard family including two brothers, Dominic and Nick Blanchard, Outmere Direct Mail was a rock for me. I'd go on to spend 15 of the next 22 years working there over three separate spells. These stints set the parameters as to what I believed (rightly or wrongly) to be acceptable and appropriate behaviour in the workplace – and indeed on stage…and it's got me into so much trouble since!

Carry On references, Benny Hill slapstick, 007 style double 'entendres', innuendo and one liner's abounded here and the Outmere ladies loved it. Nothing fazed these lasses, many of them old timers who'd lived through at least one world war, some both and one or two quite possibly even rooting for the other side.

If fact on that very topic if ever there was a nice way to be compared to Adolf Hitler, Inga at Outmere achieved it. She told me that when she was a child in 1930s' Austria, the visiting Fuhrer had patted her on the head and given her a sweet. "You are a schmoozer just like him, you know," she said to me, one day.

My place in Anglo-Austrian relations assured (this would prove useful some years later), I moved back home for a while towards the end of that year. There were six of us in the house – my parents, my three sisters and me. Life was hectic but good – especially when the bathroom was free.

Hurricane Jane knocked out some great gigs, too. We created a bit of a stir playing at The Wellington in Shepherds Bush and had an absolute screamer at the Guildford Royal. We were supporting Dumpy's Rusty Nuts, whose following were mostly bikers. Thanks to Nick at Outmere, who'd organised a works coach outing that night, our following was mainly the grannies of direct mail.

The collision of these two demographics didn't just make for an interesting night, it smashed the venue's attendance record (and a few windows too, though I'm convinced the bikers were innocent).

Another great memory from that period is 'Ear Feed'. Our version of 'Feed the World' which gave new meaning to the term 'Waxing lyrical'. We performed it at my old school in Gunnersbury, Brentford, which I have to say was very satisfying personally. Some of my old teachers were there and the sense of closure the occasion gave me was strangely cathartic…In fact apart from pulling the microphone out of its lead with my less than classy entrance from through the school Canteen doors. I had been attempting to try and replicate Dio's classic 'from the cave' entrance under the raised drum kit, first song. I also split my zebra spandex trousers (yes really) halfway through the set, to reveal a pair of my dad's brown, yellow and purple seventies style Y-fronts, I'd hurriedly borrowed on the way there!

But these moments stand out because they were the exceptions. In almost everything else we did we had a kind of reverse 'Midas' touch affliction going on. In fact, anything we seemed to try or attempt just turned into complete and utter shite…A sort of 'Shidas touch' if you like?!

The good times were just too few and far between. So again, after a couple of line-up changes, including ditching me for a couple of gigs, Hurricane Jane disappeared into the abyss.

This was around the time of 'Live Aid', and I remember witnessing what I still think is the greatest 24 minutes of live musical performance ever. I'm talking about Queen's set at this historic event, not anything my replacement as Hurricane Jane's frontman did, good as he may have been.

Over the next four years or so, I kept trying to get a decent band together, but in truth only two other line-ups among my various attempts really stand out as being worthy of any mention.

Firstly, in the spring of 1986 Andy Burgess (now of Praying Mantis fame) got in touch. His band, Stateline were looking for a singer, so I met them at Tweeters studios in Kingston one Sunday afternoon. Tweeters was then run by

Nigel Wade, a close friend still to this day and someone I've worked with many times since at festivals up and down the country comparing and crewing.

I turned up with low expectations, however the minute Stateline started playing my jaw literally hit the floor. They ripped through a couple of Honeymoon Suite and Foreigner numbers. Shit! How good were these guys? Mark Kirkland (who now works for Yamaha guitars) alongside Andy on guitar, Kevin Wakeford on drums and Alan Holden on bass comprised a truly awesome outfit.

Time to flex the internationally renowned Fielder schmooze.

It took a while, but Stateline eventually agreed to become Hurricane Jane Mk 2. After what seemed like only a few months of rehearsing, our first gig was to be at the Wellington, Shepherds Bush on the day of Prince Andrew's and Fergie's wedding. 'Rock 'n' Royal', we called it.

Despite us not having played anywhere, word had somehow got out that Hurricane Jane Mk 2 might be 'quite good'. That and the proposition of an antidote to 24-hour media coverage of another 'Royal wedding' meant that we got a better-than-expected turn out for our debut gig.

I'll never forget the reaction as we finished our first track, 'Do or Die', and launched straight into 'Head in the Clouds'. The crowd was literally bouncing off the ceiling.

At last, Hurricane Jane had finally arrived. Hurricane Jane was going to rule the world. As it turned out Hurricane Jane Mk 2 wasn't even going to last the rest of the summer! Still, what a night. Prince Andrew may claim to have been 'perspirationally' challenged, but we certainly weren't. It was hotter than hell in there and I may have been a bit ring rusty to start with, but I must've felt and smelt like a Slovakian boxer's jock strap by the end of that night I can tell you. (Please don't ask me to explain how or why I am able to verify that particular sporting analogy, but believe, me sadly I can).

A few days later I went on holiday to Crete with some friends on a high. Amusingly, I met the late great Rick Parfitt of Status Quo in the duty-free shop at Gatwick Airport before flying out. He told me he was off on a well-deserved holiday, exhausted after their extensive world tour (Reborn after Live Aid). I must admit my one gig at The Wellington did seem a little tame in comparison.

This holiday was spent with Conn, Tom, Brian a Scottish lad we'd met at a UFO gig (who has since emigrated to Australia and time has not mellowed him one bit) and finally Steve a lad fresh down from Lancashire and who now runs a very successful gift shop in Scotland.

It was a trip I could write a book about in itself (and who knows maybe I might one day), suffice to say the word 'Raki' and leave the rest to your vivid imaginations (trust me you won't even get close).

While I was soaking up the Greek sun and beer and the odd appearance at the local Crete Police Station. Yeah, we all got arrested on our third night, after a fracas in a local bar when attempting to play air guitar to U2'S 'Electric Co'.

Unfortunately, Brian's hand strumming gestures far more resembled self-gratification than any intense dextrous finger picking.

It was just a simple misunderstanding. which naturally escalated quickly into the usual embarrassing mele of beer glasses smashing, chairs and fists flying. Followed up by the usual testosterone and alcohol filled volley of accusations, threats and insults (in many various dialects) coming from here, there and everywhere. Not just the guitar solo then, we were all now on 'Edge'!

It was all settled quite amicably in the end, common sense prevailed, oh yeah and one of the local cops drew his pistol and pointed it in our direction and telling us that he could quite easily help us 'Disappear from the island' and that "nobody" would really miss us.

We were good boys after that, well almost. Anyway, back in Blighty old grudges going back two years amongst the rest of the band were resurfacing. Apparently, the band had been talking about a split before I came along and, in my absence, they'd made the decision to enact it. Not the sort of homecoming I was expecting after the euphoric 'Wave of the Wellington'.

The band did agree to fulfil one last gig at The Wellington (our second), though, which gave the attending media an opportunity to rub more salt into my wounds. They relished it.

The Kerrang guy liked the song, *Hurricane Jane*, but not my 'horribly one-dimensional voice' apparently, while a local female hack who clearly preferred the pre-Fielder Stateline took offence to my 'In between song 'banter', particularly when I allegedly 'lied for effect'.

The lie in question centred around Brian May, legendary Queen guitarist, astrophysicist and animal rights campaigner. As I was introducing our next song, May, or a bloody good impersonator of him, entered the venue and glided through the crowd smiling at people as he walked towards the stage.

"Brian, May's here!" I shouted nonchalantly. As if it was a regular occurrence.

"Okay, here's a song for him entitled, *Hair in the Crowds.*"

'Lying for effect or not' If I could track her down today, I'd show her the business card the PA guy Steve Hopgood (Persian Risk) gave me at the end of that night. It has a signature on it that says Brian May quite clearly written on it.

Mind you she also wrote that the band didn't need my "garbage rhetoric" either… To be fair, she may have had a point there!

This line up did also manage to record a single though, a track I'd penned called 'Written in Your Eyes', it was paid for by my boss (and granny coach trip organiser), Nick Blanchard. Laurence Archer produced it and we recorded it over forty-eight hours at Fair deal Studios in Hayes, Middlesex. This is where punk band 'The Ruts' recorded their debut single 'In a Rut' for music buffs.

Looking back, it's somewhat taken on the hue of a parting gift, but you can still hear how bloody good those guys were as a band. I say over 48 hours, but thinking back, about four of them were taken up by a desperate mission in search of a 'Gallien Kruger' amplifier, which was the current 'rad' sound at the time. According to the newly founded 'Guitarists Club' and its honorary members of Messrs Archer, Burgess and Kirkland the single could not be completed properly without it! To be fair in the end, they were probably right as it was a nice guitar sound.

It did however reduce my singing time at the end of the recording a touch and I was under a bit of pressure to get it finished. But the upside of it was that it at least gave me time to work out and record a nice keyboard melody over the chorus. Which I did whilst they were all out hunting somewhere they could hire this confounded thing!

The second memorable line-up eventually arose from a four-year partnership with my younger brother, Andy who managed me from 1987 to 1991.

It all began with me galivanting on a trip down to Newquay to go and visit a New Zealand barmaid I had been seeing in Richmond, who had now been working down in Cornwall for three months or so.

Again, in the days before mobiles, letters were the only real way of communication and there was nothing in her letters to suggest anything other than how much she was missing me. So, I decided to get a coach down and 'surprise her' on her birthday (big mistake).

With hindsight I should have got off in Plymouth where I had a kind of 'Sliding Doors' moment with a pretty blonde girl. She was dressed in faded double denim and red suede ankle boots and standing at a bus stop as the Coach refuelled and passengers disembarked at the station.

Gazing into her eyes we had a connection for 10 to 15 minutes or so we smiled and laughed and made gestures through the window to each other. I remember, I had the song 'Playground' by the Outfield on my headphones, and as the coach was leaving, she beckoned me to get off... I really wish I had!

On arriving in Newquay on a sunlit Friday night, proudly armed with my Birthday present, Suzanne Vega's latest album, I made my way excitedly to my 'betrothed's' place of accommodation and yes you guessed, it she lived on the second floor.

However, it wasn't so much the four hours from 7-11pm that I waited patiently for her, sitting naked on her bed, with a red ribbon tied lovingly around my knob, or indeed the fifteenth hundred time I reset 'My name is fucking Luca.' on her cassette player that was the worst bit.

But the arrival of a big tanned blonde surfer dude looking very much like Patrick Swayze from the film 'Point Break, called Joe coming into the room and saying (not the slightest bit taken aback), "Oh you must be Matt," and then reaching out to shake my, well hopefully my hand, I guess that really hit me hard… "Fuck me, she'd been living with this guy for nearly four months and still writing me romantic letters!"

It was only then that I noticed the large boots, Y-fronts on the floor, shaving foam, condoms and Slick Willy's 'Wax and Board' polish on the sideboard.

He was a decent fella to be fair, as he explained that the lady in question was still out at work, and he even got me a beer from the fridge. However, it did mean a very long lonely weekend in Cornwall ensued as my return coach ticket wasn't valid until Monday!

When I returned to London I went straight out on the piss and got absolutely bladdered, I was a complete mess and my brother Andrew who luckily had been cabbing in town, came very kindly, to pick me up. I remember him bundling me into the back of his cab and as we drove through the brightly lit lights of London and along the Thames, Kate Bush's 'Running up that Hill' came on the radio. It was, as I recall very comforting to me through the haze of alcohol, drugs, disillusionment and heartbreak.

I mention this now as I have just watched an episode of the Netflix drama 'Stranger Things' with my daughter, where the song is used for one of the characters to escape the clutches of a demon and head back into the light and all her friends and I just started crying for apparently 'no reason', in front of my bemused daughter.

Incidentally on a lighter and much happier footnote to this escapade, I have now incredibly got in contact with the girl from the coach station in Plymouth. Through a bizarre and chance coincidence on social media. It is ridiculous how things like that can sometimes happen in life. Only thirty-five years too late…eh? Anyway, A big 'Hello 'goes out to Catherine and "Yes, I really should have got off that coach".

Anyway, back to my brother and after this 'mission of mercy' Andrew decided we should put a band together and formed a management company called Trick or Trust, a line from a song I'd written called, *'Love not Lust'*.

He also changed his name to Andy Rich so we could pretend not to be related. (It came in handy for him after some of my more sub-optimal vocal performances later.)

Anyway, bro and I decided to form this new band from the ground up. I will also never forget the meal we sat down to discuss how we would go about it either.

Complete with my new girlfriend in tow, we all sat down at a beautifully set candlelit table at his house, as my brother presented us all with our starter.

It was a bowl of freshly made alphabet soup, mine with the letters lovingly and beautifully arranged to spell the words 'YOU R A CUNT!', it really was a nice touching sentiment from my bro.

The meeting went well though and we arranged to start advertising in 'Loot' and 'Melody Maker' for prospective band members. All seemed a doddle, until we got to the actual audition process that is.

Andy set up a hidden camera in his house in Twickenham, the idea being for us to capture me having one-to-ones with an assortment of guitarists, bass players and drummers etc that we could view and discuss afterwards. Not sure of the legality of this process nowadays, but we asked each applicant beforehand, and no one objected.

We would hopefully then assemble a band free of 'previous': agendas, or old scores to settle. Sound good? Data privacy rules and ethics aside, it was a great concept marred only by one thing.

Each day Andy would leave a decanter of whisky in the room. This would lubricate conversations between my auditionees and I about serious stuff such as song structure, rehearsal planning and the band's growth trajectory. But as the Scotch went down, so too did my credibility. Pretty soon, talk of local support slots would give way to our first gig at Wembley Stadium, our debut album, American tour, that sort of bollocks.

If you were on the receiving end of one of these endless 'wishful whisky wittering's of wonderment and wank', I whole heartedly apologise. My brother keeps threatening to unearth these videos one day. Lord help us!

It did drive it home to me though that the music biz really is a bastion of self-delusion. These days, of course, social media demonstrates this constantly where narcissism is rife. But back then, the self-deluded were just as numerous, just less visible.

And it wasn't just me. I met a bassist who'd never played his instrument before the audition. He arrived with an 8 string

Shergold, a Marshall stack and a 'how hard can it be to learn it from scratch?' Attitude. I had a non-audition with a drummer who possessed not even sticks, let alone a kit, "I thought it came with the position," the fella said with all the intellect of a… well, er…a drummer I suppose.

I also shared my 'brother's' whisky with a guitarist who would happily gig anywhere but he couldn't 'do nights' because he drove a taxi. What was he expecting? High-decibel, alcohol-fuelled hellraising and womanising at birthday parties for eight-year-olds?

He'd also say things like, "Your music is very 'loose windscreen' you know what I mean?" I had no idea what he meant, so I reached out for the decanter again and was ultimately never 'blinded by his light' but maybe he was just 'Born to Rum' instead.

However, If I'm going to be totally honest, my favourite audition was the large breasted female keyboard player who turned up in a very tight fitting, cropped Playboy bunny T-shirt, who kept asking me between jams, in a kind of breathy Marilyn Monroe voice, "If I would like her to use both hands…" But we'll leave that one there for now.

Don't ask me how, but apart from one hurriedly put together Christmas gig in Richmond along with guitarist Gary Davis (later of 'Cry Wolf), Alex a part time postman on bass and a drummer who looked very much like ex Russian President Gorbachev. My barren 'proper' gig run finally came to an end in the summer of 1990.

After nigh on two years of what seemed (at the time at least) like an eternity of trying, we finally managed to put a line-up together that was good enough to play on a regular basis. Hurricane Jane Mk3 had finally arrived.

In it were Karl Bruce on lead guitar, his mate Pete Goffin on drums and Justin Deary on (two handed) keyboards, a first for the Jane. On bass was another Andy, who's surname sadly escapes me for now but who at the time was also playing with Ivor Biggin, aka Doc Cox. If you're unfamiliar with Ivor's work, The Winker's Song is good primer.

I wouldn't say Andy was awkward or ugly, just that perhaps his image and love of Star trek (Next Generation) and all things 'IT Bites and 'Marillion' wasn't quite right for our band. However, that said, I do seem to recall we made him wear sunglasses and a baseball hat and stand behind the PA for one gig. Not long after this, Chris Wilson took his place.

We went big in those days. Andy (bro) and I forked out for extra lights and a dry ice machine, and we laid on explosive pyrotechnics. Our first gig was at the Red Lion, Brentford, where I appeared on stage in a Red Circus ringmaster's outfit. I reckon Hugh Jackman came to that gig and decided there and then exactly what he'd wear in The Greatest Showman, but hey 'this is me'.

Though big on ideas, we weren't so great on forethought. This was an August Summer Holiday Weekend with temperatures in the 90s, even after dark.

But one thing led to another, and our extravagance would open an unexpected door for us. The venue was heaving that night and our sound and lighting guy Alan Goff was getting nervous. All those lights, smoke and pyros in the high ambient temperature made higher by our target-rich environment of denim and leather-clad head bangers – Alan wasn't liking it one bit. So, he got the Red Lion's assistant manager to call the fire brigade.

Who on arriving took one look at the scene and wanted to shut the whole thing down before it'd even got going?

Which in turn drew the attention of one Brian Peters. Brian owned the Red Lion so came down to see what all the fuss was about.

Brian surprisingly (to us at least) liked what he saw. True, there was a packed crowd, a half decent performance by the band and the ample cleavage possessed by the beautiful wife of our manager (Hi Maureen).

The upshot (no pun intended) was an invitation to play at the other venue Brian owned.

Only the London fucking Astoria!

On a Friday Rock Club night with none other than DJ Nick London. He of local rock nights at The Clarendon, Jesters and The Pit fame. Nick deserves a special mention here as being the first DJ to ever play our PSO demo tape, *Keep Holding On,* back in 1983 and to this day still playing our 'Ransom' stuff on his Monday night Rock Show on Hayes FM in 2022.

Back to my bro again, Mr Andy Rich was now on fire, his blagging skills honed to perfection and as if this wasn't enough, on the back of the Astoria revelation he then managed to get us a gig at the Mecca of all aspiring metal bands. The London Marquee!

The Marquee gig was to be the week before and supporting some band whose name, I cannot for the life of me remember. However, I think one of them was related to Billy Gaff, Rod Stewart's ex manager and now the current co-owner of the prestigious venue. Anyway, regardless this meant two huge box tickers in as many weeks.

This first Marquee gig does get an extra special mention for two reasons really:

Firstly, the venue had moved from its iconic Wardour Street address to its new home on Charing Cross Road. Nevertheless, the Marquee name is synonymous with many great acts down the years. Which made it even more astonishing that the dressing room was such an utter shithole. Filthy, grubby and bespattered with the graffiti of bands that had played there before us – and many more that hadn't and wouldn't. Naturally, we added a contribution of our own to this unlovely collage.

My second abiding memory of that gig, however, was more Spinal Tap than Hurricane Jane. Even though we were the support act, the Marquee still gave you a proper band entrance. So, there we were, dry ice pumping out, the lights dimmed, Terminator theme segueing into Justin's opening bars of 'Written in Your Eyes', me grabbing the mic and screaming, "Good evening, London Marquee. We are Hurricane Jane!"

And Karl behind me shouting, "Where's my fucking guitar?" We didn't have guitar roadies in those days.

We were lucky though. The dry ice gave Karl the cover he needed to return to the dressing room, where his guitar was waiting patiently for him. The crowd meanwhile was being treated to an extended intro to the song as I introduced the other members of the band – twice.

As for the Astoria gig, deflating is how I'd describe it. Especially after all the hype and expectation leading up to it. There was a decent enough crowd but apart from our own mob, few of the regular club members were expecting an actual live band and they seemed a bit put out when we took to the stage.

They also seemed unimpressed by both our appearance and our performance. This was my first inkling that our more melodic rock style was being side lined by the grungy scene developing around us.

I was even spat at that night, which isn't great at the best of times. I've had a few altercations down the years. I've been attacked, punched, threatened with a shotgun, abused physically and verbally, and had many an insult and beer thrown at me. But the stage is my ground to stand, and few things phase me once I'm up there. It's usually long after the event that I reflect on it and realise that things were a tad scary. But I was particularly disheartened on this occasion as the gob dripping from my face originated from someone I knew.

He has since apologised and said it was just meant as a 'Jokey, punk thing' revenge for me throwing up on his carpet at a party when I was only 17 which was fair, I suppose.

Especially as it was my best shot at nailing my first 'true love' Alison, who I'd played with as kid. We then met ten years later at a Youth club, by chance and now in our late teens I fancied her like mad and there she was sitting on my knee, I was totally in, but I 'blew it' by getting nervous, drinking too much whisky and then throwing up. Finesse! (We're quits now Julian and I still love you mate.)

The only real highlight or actual bit of 'Euphoria at the Astoria' was watching my brother Andy steam into the crowd and lamp an annoying drunk guy who'd spent most of his evening doing the 'wanker sign' in my face. It was sensational stuff from my bro, and I had the best seat (well standing position) in the house for it.

Allegedly, seven record company A&R guys came to see us that night. None of them followed up.

'Mutiny on the Bandy' followed. The other guys in the band talked about financial issues and a new musical direction. Justin was the first to leave, opting for an afternoon playing Frisbee in a park somewhere in Marlow rather than rehearse. His replacement was a young friend of Karl's. I can't remember his surname. Let's just call him Carl with a 'C' for now.

The next stage of this tailspin saw Andy and I (well mostly Andrew to be fair) get monumentally pissed and stoned with the sound crew in advance of a gig at the White Hart in Kingston. Naturally, this did little for the sound quality or my performance and both Andy and I were ousted by the other 'mutinous' band members in quick succession shortly afterwards. 'Not quite cutting it' was their verdict on my attitude to the band's new melodic and experimental direction. Jazz Odyssey anyone?

Funnily enough about four years later and by sheer coincidence, Carl with a 'C' shared a taxi in London with two guys, Simon and Dave, (spoiler alert) who were at the time unbeknown to him current band members of Hurricane Jane mk4. In conversation he told them how he'd once joined a band called Hurricane Jane, and that they'd got rid of the singer due to his 'musical deficiencies' but sadly the band had fallen apart soon afterwards anyway. They didn't let on, but while this little trip down mutiny lane; was going on, the taxi drove past the Marquee. Outside it was a neon sign displaying the name of the band that was playing there the following night… 'Hurricane Jane'. He saw it.

I'm not into vendettas or revenge, because life at the end of the day is all about opinions and just like arseholes, everybody seems to have one of their own. In any case, the water has long since passed under that bridge and I bear no grudges towards anyone. Life is way too short for that! Indeed, Chris Wilson has stayed in touch (bless him) and we often chat and laugh about it all.

Okay, so finally all the groundwork has been laid for the main part of our story. You may think you've heard it all before but believe you me you've heard nothing yet and this ride is about to get bumpy, real bumpy. Even worse, as ye gods of rock are about to bear witness too. It's the truth, the whole truth and nothing but the truth…with maybe just a small smidgeon of artistic licence 'thrown in' for good measure.

Chapter 3
Boys Don't Cry

"I'd given up on you, but still, you make me wonder."

'The three amigos' Jason, Dave and Simon, at the White Swan, Fulham, 1994

There was only one thing for it. After mine and Andy's ignominious exit from Hurricane Jane Mk3, I really had no other option other than to form…Hurricane Jane Mk4.

This was eventually (after naturally another couple more line-up changes) to be the Jane's final and defining line-up. Simon Woodley, Dave Rocker (a shoo-in for his surname alone), Jason Lee Porter and yours truly. However (you know the drill by now) this soon to be legendary ensemble didn't exactly fall into place either – it took a bit of cajoling and a fair bit of outside help.

Summer 1991. *Terminator 2* was smashing it at the box office, Guns 'n' Roses were still bossing it on the stadium tours and Metallica weren't far behind. Matt Fielder, meanwhile, was once again unemployed and pretty pissed off with life in general. From the highs of securing the Marquee and Astoria gigs in quick succession to 'Our Drinking Hell' at the White Hart in Kingston, things had turned pear shaped in less time than it takes to say 'Run to the hills'. For brother Andy (no longer rich) and me it left a nothingness in our lives and something similar in Andy's finances. He filed for bankruptcy!

I'd once again moved into a flat share with Conn, this time a ground floor one-bedder in respectable Manor Road, Twickenham. It was our third shared address in a decade. From there, most days I'd wander into Joanna's Polish Café and chow down on a 'Jumbo' breakfast over the morning papers before submitting myself to the warm embrace of one of two welcoming taverns, The Cherry Tree or The Prince Blucher. Usually, Andy would join me.

We drank Newcastle Brown Ale. Lots of it. So much that I would usually fall asleep or pass out in the pub's garden or, if I could make it that far, Twickenham Green. On the days I managed to stay awake, I'd stagger into the local video shop to flirt with Jan, the leggy blonde who worked there. Video?

I hear you younger readers ask. Yes, that nefarious medium that once killed the radio star.

After one such sojourn, Jan let me take home from the video shop a life-size cardboard cut-out of Dolph Lundgren, a promo for the film, The Punisher. At the time I congratulated myself on a romantic breakthrough with Jan. Only in retrospect do I see it as Jan's way of getting a randy pisshead out of her workspace.

Cardboard Dolph was my contribution to home security. Conn and I placed him by the front window of the flat as a grim warning to would-be intruders.

But Dolph's big moment wasn't about who he deterred; it was about who he attracted. Driving around the neighbourhood one day, a location manager from Twickenham Film Studios clapped eyes on our unorthodox interior design statement. From that sighting alone he guessed we'd be up for having our place 'Blown up' in the name of entertainment. And he wasn't wrong.

The Good Guys was a TV show starring Nigel Havers, Keith Baron and Sarah Crowe ("Chives"). The idea was that Nigel Havers would knock on the door of the flat in which Sarah Crowe would be unconscious, having left the gas on. Unable to get a response, Nigel would go to a phone kiosk (a prop placed outside) and call Sarah. At that point, the flat – our home – would burst into synthetic flames.

It didn't go quite to plan. Assured that it was all done with special effects and that any damage would be minor and cosmetic, we looked on in horror (as did most of respectable Manor Road) as the flat became the epicentre of what looked, sounded and smelled like a crudely executed terrorist attack.

The explanation the techies gave us after involved references to the science of suction and the physics of combustion, stuff like that. The bottom line, though, was that we had to live in a fucking bomb crater for two weeks until the reinstatement team arrived.

Mr Havers – Nige, as he was to us now – was every bit as charming and nice as he comes across as on telly. Which is why I was only too glad to rush out a potential theme song for the show. It was an upbeat, Minder-like sing-along number called, *A View from the Hill* which I wrote and recorded overnight with Jon Sweigler, an amazing guitarist (Kiss fan) and old college buddy whose beautiful sister Daniella, so tragically died, way too young whilst on holiday in Marbella. But she will never be forgotten, and I have included her in a photo at the end of this book.

I didn't realise it at the time, but I was 'Out Dennis Water manning' Dennis Waterman with this effort. 'Write the theme tune, Sing the theme tune'. Sadly, Nige didn't see it that way or simply just decided not to take us up on the offer. Again, equally sadly as I write this, I hear dear Dennis has just passed away as well, gone to join Uncle Jack Regan for more episodes of 'The Sweeney in the Sky!

Things come in threes, right? So, perhaps, I should've been prepared for the next two incoming explosions in my life.

The first of these, was meeting my future band members.

It was an early weekday evening in May. My routine at this point in the day would normally be to sit outside the ruin of the flat and await Conn's return from work, which in turn would mean more beers and sometimes, fish and chips, too.

Most days around this time a high-heels-and-stocking-clad lass would enter the flats opposite our wreckage where, I speculated, a pre-aroused gentleman friend would then enter her. Seeing the two of them emerge from the building looking more lived-in than our gaff just 30 minutes later only added weight to my idle speculation. About four years later, however, I, by complete chance, became great friends with the young lady in question when we bumped into each other in a bar and were introduced by my 'less than subtle boss at the time's introduction "Oi love, did you know, he used to well fancy you". Anyway, we got chatting and she quashed my idle speculation – and all the imagery that went with it. She did also however begin following the band around our London gigs for a while, so I'd best not name her. But for the record I fancied Sammy-Jo like crazy and some part of me probably always will.

Anyway, on this night, as I was deep in my reverie, a light blue Capri, pursued by three police cars, sped past our building, 'dough-nutted' expertly, then outrageously 'wheel spun' (like a boss) at the end of our cul-de-sac road, then came back and drove past me at top speed in the opposite direction. As quickly as it had arrived, it went out of sight and earshot.

Two beers later and our modern-day Smokey and the Bandit returns to respectable Manor Road – minus his pursuers. As he cruised past, he accepted the appreciative gesture of my raised bottle and approving nod before pulling into the forecourt opposite. Turned out the reprobate only lived down our road as well.

A couple of days later I saw him again, this time with a mate. With their long hair, ripped jeans and inverted baseball hats they looked like a sort of Bill and Ted's Excellent Adventure / Wayne and Garth hybrid.

I just had to introduce myself.

Paul (Capri man) and Jai were apparently also musicians. Along with two other fellas, Simon and Dave, they'd started a band but as luck would have it, yet to find a singer. I gave them what, in today's mangled language, was my elevator pitch. They seemed to like it, so it was all over to Paul's a few days later for a chemistry meeting with the rest of the 'Wyld Stallions'.

Now I've done a few auditions over the years with varying degrees of success. I've put myself forward for local bands as well as TV shows such as The Voice and some ITV show, the name of which I've long forgotten. But none of them felt more like an interrogation by the Stasi than this supposedly, friendly 'get together' in the flat over the road.

Perhaps some of my original conversation with Paul and Jai got lost in translation when being relayed to Simon and Dave. Something wasn't quite right, because I had the unmistakeable feeling of a certain distrust and animosity directed towards me. Over the next half hour (unintentionally as it later transpired) they made me feel like an egotistical megalomaniac living off reputation and past glories. As I mentioned I've since spoken to Simon and Dave about this, and they both categorically deny that was what they were intending, but at the time they could've fooled me.

It felt like they had just given me the third degree from start to finish, seemingly doubting every word I had said as complete and utter bullshit (to be fair some of it probably was) and I left with my self-confidence in tatters and not expecting to hear from them again. However, a few days later the 'Wyld

Stallions' did get back in touch with me having listened to my material, particularly the old single 'Written in your eyes' and agreed to have a jam.

Ram studios in West Drayton, where I'd rehearsed with previous line-ups, was the venue. It was a shithole within a shithole, a dislikeable structure in a scuzzy industrial estate – but it was priced accordingly. It was also an opportunity to hang out again with its then manager Marion, wearer of a pencil skirt, seamed stockings and Christian Louboutin's at our Astoria gig. Colour me both a cheapskate and a part time 'perv' but that was the currency I worked in back then.

As fate would have it, my old band was rehearsing that very same night in the studio room next door. This led to an encounter in the car park beforehand that was as awkward as it was amusing. We hadn't yet made our peace in the weeks and months since 'Our Drinking Hell' and although things weren't quite as competitive and intense as in the Run DMC vs Aerosmith, *Walk This Way* video. It was a little bit weird when both bands were playing the same song at the same time.

Our rehearsal didn't get off to the best of starts. There wasn't a lot of horseplay with the 'Wyld Stallions' at first and they weren't the easiest of individuals to communicate with. But Dave and Simon were one hell of a rhythm section, and the potential was there. Even better for me was when they both left the room in the break, to check on Simon's car radio for the latest football scores, at last fellow band members who liked football!

They were all younger than me. Simon Woodley, the 'Pale Face of Bass' was a quiet, brooding kind of guy. He came across shy and introverted yet had no doubts about what he wanted to do musically. That steely determination was underpinned by a dry, sarcastic sense of humour. Excellent. He supported Liverpool.

Dave Rocker (unbelievably his real name) or 'Big Dave' as he liked to refer to himself, was originally from Nice but had been raised mostly at his grandma's house in Aix-en-Provence. Dave was wild and funny but serious when it came to music and spoke with a turn of phrase that was both Gallic and 'Sarf' London. We called it 'Frogney'.

Dave supported Chelsea. The story goes that upon his arrival in London, he got off the plane and went virtually straight to Stamford Bridge where the Blues subjected my beloved Spurs to a routine 3–0 seeing to. Whenever he told this story, he'd conclude it with a 'Frenchified Forsythian'. "Now let's take a look at the old scoreboard." It would be another 11 years before Spurs would get a win against Chelsea, in which time, Dave's story wore tiresomely thin. But when it did eventually come in 2002, the victory was glorious: a 5–1 hammering. Sadly, 'Big Dave' went missing for a month…only to pop up again when they beat us 4-0, twice in the space of a week, or 'normal service has resumed' as he texted me!

Like Simon, Dave was loyal, confrontational and a fantastic musician. The pair of them shared a flat in Acton and were obviously close. But certainly not in that way or "Nah, nah, none of that". As Dave would often retort 'I think you've got the wrong punter son' (not very PC by today's 'cotton wool, woke society' standards), but nonetheless this was an advantage for a rhythm section, and I grew to love them both and still very much do to this day.

Paul and Jai were in it for the crack. Guitarist Jai, who now lives in the US with his American wife and child was a happy-go-lucky soul. His image was pure long-haired rock 'n' roll cliché. Musically, he had his limitations but was a seriously great guy to hang out with. He was like 'Bez' but with a guitar!

And finally, there was our dear old 'boy racer' Paul Karner. A troubled soul from a broken home, he was a great guitar player on his day. He displayed keenness on the outside, but I was never convinced his heart was really in it. A genuinely nice guy who probably deep down wanted to be playing the Whisky a Go-Go on the Sunset Strip. I believe he eventually got a scholarship at the guitar institute in LA so probably got his wish. However, while researching for this book I also learned sadly that a few years ago, he died of a drug related illness. RIP fella, you won't be forgotten.

Hurricane Jane Mk4 was ready for its first gig by Christmas 1991. The venue? The legendary Durrell Arms, Munster Road, off Fulham High Street. You know it? No, neither did we!

Chapter 4
The Life and Soul

"And not a word of a lie, Ain't gonna change, until the day I die."

With Bill and Ted (aka Jai and Paul) during our most Excellent Adventure in Fulham. What time's the raffle again? December 1991

No band had ever played there before to our knowledge, there were no stories, true or otherwise of it ever being trashed by any true disciples of rock 'n' roll, no one had ever heard of it and, as it turned out, it didn't even have a music licence.

So, why the Durrell Arms, Munster Road, off Fulham High Street?

The short answer is because I'd been doing some casual labour in the area. A teammate at Sheen Park Rangers, my Sunday League football club, needed help for a painting and decorating job in Fulham and having no other gainful employment at the time, I stepped up. And as you know, it is a truth universally acknowledged that a man in possession of an income must be in want of a pub.

I say income, however, this was 1991. Likely, the earliest you'll be reading this is 2023 – and yet I still haven't received a penny from this assignment.

Nevertheless, the Durrell Arms was our adopted local for the duration of the project. We were there most lunchtimes and early evenings.

The governor of the pub was an Irishman called John (weren't they all were back then?). Naturally, I put it to John that Hurricane Jane could be just the act to put the Durrell on the map. After a few more beers, John warmed to the idea and even came up with a ruse to circumvent the music licence (or lack thereof) hitch.

There'd be a raffle and a whip round to buy beers for the band. In other words, it would be a charity night.

My football teammate, who now I think about it, could have inspired Jay's 'completed it mate' character from the TV hit show, The Inbetweeners, was also seduced. He lavishly promised crates of whiskies, vodkas, brandies, gins – whatever I wanted – as he'd been given loads of the stuff off the back of a lorry. Suddenly, the unveiling of my crack new line-up for Hurricane Jane was starting to look like a dubious knees-up for Del and Rodney et al at the Nag's Head. Actually. On that note I was saddened to hear of the recent passing of the actor John Challis 'Boycie' from that iconic TV series 'Only Fool's and Horses'. A man whom I had the absolute pleasure of working alongside at the Far Forest Countryside show in Callow Hill a few years back, a truly top fellow and he will be sorely missed.

I mention this now as around about the same sort of time as this gig, I had been drinking in the Racing page (The Cobwebs) in Richmond when his on-screen wife, actress Sue Holderness, who had been starring in a play over the road at Richmond theatre, walked into what, I have to say, was a very respectful silence. Actors and actresses liked this pub as they could drink there normally without being hassled. Anyway, she was no more than halfway up to the bar with her real-life husband, when who should walk in the pub, behind her, (with his own real-life wife) but none other than dear old John himself, they were friends, so he'd obviously been there to watch her. Again, there was the initial same respectful silence, but this time probably only for all of about three seconds and then in almost telepathic unison the whole pub all joined in, at the same time, in a very low, but very audible mumble "Marleeeeeeene".

His face was an absolute picture…it was at the time and still is, to me at least, a very funny moment! I think, mainly because everyone joined in so spontaneously,

In fact, the only other time I have ever witnessed anything remotely similar in spontaneity, was on a Sheen Park Rangers football coach trip back from Brighton once in the eighties. When a posse of Lambrettas' with parker wearing 'mods' on the back of them, overtook us on a tight corner and without hesitation or consultation everybody on board (including our driver) immediately jumped up and gestured furiously out of their various windows, in complete and total unison and shouted 'Wankers' all at the same time!

But anyway, back to Fulham, I mean seriously, what could possibly go wrong? Seemingly nothing. Rehearsals were going swimmingly, and raffle ticket sales were buoyant.

Then out of the blue, 'Big Dave' broke his arm. He did it playing 5 a side football somehow and called me up to declare that 'The gig was off'.

"Well pardon me all over the place" to coin a phrase from Robert Mitchum in the Cape Fear remake, but no, "Off" it most certainly wasn't, not after all the shoe leather I'd worn through flogging those sodding raffle tickets.

But whatever, the fact remained, 'Big' Dave not going to be part of it. We were Hurricane Jane, not Def Leppard: We didn't have the resources to adapt our hardware for a 'Crocked Rocker'.

With a final rehearsal scheduled three days before the gig I sent out an SOS to my old PSO/Hurricane Jane drummer, Pete Cumber. Dave's arm was broken but I managed to twist Pete's with the offer of hard cash.

Pete had done well since the PSO and Hurricane Jane Mk1 days. He was now a session drummer of some repute and had been touring with my older brother Simon's band, Buddy Holly and the Cricketers, a kind of tribute act made up of former actors and musicians from the hit West End stage production, Buddy.

Being close to 'Big' Dave, Simon 'The Pale Face of Bass' was initially down on the idea but came around because 1)

Pete was up to speed with a lot of our set as we were playing a lot of the older Hurricane Jane songs, and 2) money was at stake. He knew it made sense.

And it could have been worse. The incident reminded me of a similar situation when we lost the services of a bass player with just four hours' notice in PSO days. That time, my older brother Simon had graciously stepped in and managed to learn up the whole set before we took to the stage. Consummate musician and pro that my older bro is, this probably speaks more about the simplicity of our songs rather than his ability to learn them.

So, drummer crisis averted, I felt confident as I stepped out of the cab outside the Durrell Arms on the night of the gig.

Pulling up alongside me however was my footy teammate, bang on time. Which was a relief as he'd been ignoring my calls all day.

But there was no evidence of the promised spirits that had fallen off the back of a lorry. All he had was bottle of Bells falling out the back of his rucksack.

He started on some long, meandering explanation about how he couldn't stay, and I immediately zoned out, concerned instead on how the raffle I'd worked so hard to big up would go down among my hard-won base of ticket holders. I only zoned back in when he said something along the lines of: "…And I'm not being funny, Matt, but there was fucking claret everywhere…The geezer was definitely brown bread!"

And with that he was off.

Ever so slightly unbalanced, solitary bottle of whisky in hand, I went inside. There, our stage area was in a slightly raised section of the bar occupied by some inebriated lads looking alarmingly like members of Chelsea FC's notorious

'Head-hunters'. There was a pool table on the floor and money on the game in progress.

Could it get any worse?

Yes. At that moment two fellas drifted in. They wore ripped jeans and cowboy boots. They'd made themselves up in pink lipstick and black 'Guyliner. And they were quoting lines from Bill and Ted. Oh Christ.

'Head-hunters, meet Jai and Paul, guitarists in the band'. I almost said out loud. I had visions of us all getting a right good 'kicking', right there and then to be honest.

Next to appear was my Polish girlfriend (the third of the three explosions I mentioned in the previous chapter, more on whom will be spoken about later). To be exact, I heard the cat calls and wolf whistles that signalled her arrival before I saw Alicia. With her leather jacket, stockings and heels, she looked for all the world like a Russian hooker and the Durrell Arms regulars loved it. (Sorry darling).

Alicia, less so and I take full responsibility. In a moment of Fosters-fuelled Fielder flippancy, (the 'Newky' brown was having a night off) I'd told her that this was exactly what the rock chicks wore to our gigs. She was only 19 and until then, believed everything I said. Not anymore or since.

More positively, my sense of intimidation proved unfounded. The locals didn't beat us up or give us a hard time, perhaps because half of them didn't have a clue as to what was going on while the other half were strangely fascinated by the car crash playing out in front of them. It was Christmas time and even the Head-hunters got into the spirit of it, willingly surrendering their pool game and table to our makeshift stage and allowing people to get close to us.

By the time we got to play I was mentally exhausted. I think I was just relieved that after everything, the gig was taking place at all. It went okay – we had a decent turnout and no musical hiccups. I'll remember it most for Jai and Paul smoking brown cigars with their pink lipstick and adopting a camp high kicking routine to the Hurricane Jane chorus.

The following day, Alicia and I set off to spend Christmas in Eastern Europe, where I would make plans for 1992 – the Year of the Jane!

It wouldn't be the last Christmas that I'd plot the 'Year of the Jane'. The phrase would become an annual New Year's Eve rallying cry – my 'This time next year, Rodney, we'll be millionaires!'

In case you're wondering, the raffle at the Durrell Arms didn't happen either. I clean forgot all about it, so I kept the ticket money and drank the Bells in the back of Simon's van on the way home from the gig.

While I'm down here on the moral low ground, I didn't follow up on what my football teammate was saying about all the 'claret' and 'brown bread' fellow either. But I did emulate him in one way. As I never paid Pete for his services that night either… Sorry Pete!

So, roll in 1992, the year of the biggest event of my life so far. And it had absolutely nothing to do with the band.

Chapter 5
The City at Night

**"I've got dreams I'm living for, they're something you
may not see, but can't take away from me."**

*The Jane at our local, The Red Lion, Brentford showcasing our
unique 'twin clitarist' sound, October 1993*

1992 began like most years: High hopes, big ideas and Great
Expectations. And if we're talking parallels with Dickens'
characters, we had the sex appeal of Miss Havisham and the
spending power of Bob Cratchit.

I was still living in respectable Manor Road, Twickenham with Conn and still going steady with the young, beautiful Alicia. I was also still on the run from Interpol over 'raffle gate' the illegitimate proceeds from which were being modestly topped up by temporary work for a labouring agency called 'Munelly's' who seemed to quite enjoy sending me to Irish building sites.

There, you'd typically find me, gloveless and midway up some frozen scaffolding pole steadying a tube through which concrete would be cascading into a wall cavity somewhere beneath me. If not up in the air, I'd be sub-terra, tasked with digging endless – and quite useless – trenches. If the foreman was in a good mood, he'd let me unblock a sewer.

I love the Irish, probably because my Irish grandma (maternal) took me under her wing when I was a kid while my parents cracked on with growing the family. Just as well, as my paternal gran took a justifiable dislike to me when the three-year-old rock star in the making pissed all over her award-winning rhubarb patch. She was a proud lady, my paternal gran. Bit of a WASP too, mind.

Her husband, Freddie 'The fingers' Fielder, a promising jazz pianist, had died in the war after a German shell hit his tank in Normandy in 1944. Granny Fielder made it to 106, by which time she barely knew who I was. Cue some cynical rewriting of the family history in which I emerge as the favourite grandchild. Nothing doing though – she'd finalised her will yonks ago.

To lighten my mum and dad's load, Maternal Irish gran would take me for weekends. Friday nights for me went like this: Bingo and alcohol at St Osmund's Church in Barnes, unsuitable Hammer House of Horror Film when we got back, then sherry or ginger wine nightcap at around 2 am. Pretty rock 'n' roll for a nine-year-old, no?

For everything it frowns upon, the religion I was born into is refreshingly tolerant of alcohol, an observation I joyously pounced upon.

I love the Irish humour, too. Some years later after the transsexual Dana International won the 1998 Eurovision Song Contest, my site boss Declan at the time approached me and in his thick brogue accent, said, "You're a music man aren't ya, Matt?" I nodded, and he continued, "Well did ya see that Jewish fella win the Eurovision thingy on Saturday night…? Well, they went a little bit heavy-handed with the old circumcision on that one, didn't they?"

He often made me laugh my boss, which was good as the work was tough. But the rest of the builders on the site were a little less welcoming and came across at times as a bit exclusive. But in their defence. they were particularly supportive of their own up and coming musical artistes and were in fact, often seen wandering around the site with collection buckets requesting, "Money for The Corrs!"

While work was a craic, cracks were appearing in the band. In Dave and Simon, I had a solid foundation and a great rhythm section. However, I could see Paul was getting itchy feet, so it was no surprise when he quit after the first couple of gigs of the year. Jai followed him soon after. So, by the summer we'd gone from a five-piece to a trio *sans* axeman. We were three musketeers searching for our six-stringed D'Artagnan.

Appropriately enough it was a compatriot of D'Artagnan who rode to our rescue, albeit temporarily. When Big Dave first arrived in the UK in 1990, he'd done so with his brother, Michel.

Michel, later Mike, then eventually 'Mon frère Michel', was a lead guitarist with both a good reputation and a decent band. He couldn't make a full commitment to the Jane, but Mon-frère did agree to record a demo with us to help us recruit for our vacancy.

Whilst we are on a Gallic theme, it does remind me of the time some years later when my seven-year-old son Ryan came running out of his first French lesson after Junior school and in front of all the waiting parents in the playground proudly exclaiming, at the top of his voice, with almost uncontrollable excitement, "Daddy, Daddy I can count to three in French, listen…Un…Deux………TWAT!"

To be fair his English, unlike his guitar playing, is not a lot better…even now!

Studio 125 in Burgess Hill, West Sussex had a great setup. Over 48 hours they helped us record our tracks, fed us and put all four of us up at a rate that even we could afford.

That didn't mean it was a tin pot operation, though. Between them, Studio 125's owners, the affable Geordie, Ian Clarke, and his lovely wife, Sue ran a slick business and made a bloody good chicken curry. I didn't know it at the time, but UFO – now with my old mucker Lawrence Archer in the line-up – had been there just before us to record their 'High Stakes and Dangerous Men' album.

The three tracks we recorded were once again, *Written in Your Eyes*, *City at Night* and a new song called, *Life and Soul*. This was a tongue-in-cheek tale about a surprise birthday party Conn and Alicia had sprung on me earlier that year. It must have been a surprise to the invitees as well as I only recognised about five of those who turned up, two of whom were an ex and her new fella.

Also pitching up that night were four pissed up gate crashers, there to cause harm both to the flat itself and those of us inside it. They succeeded.

My abiding memory of the night is shutting the door behind a vanload of departing policemen and holding a bucket out for a bruised and battered Conn who immediately put it over his head while he simultaneously drank the rest of his Stella and puked, all at the same time.

Happy fucking birthday indeed. Still, we got a half-decent song out of it.

The recording went well. We used our time like the pros we were and were even able to slip a few bars of the 'Hurricane Jane' chorus in to finish it off.

As all this was going on the Summer Olympics were in full swing in Barcelona. I remember going to the local pub to watch Linford Christie taking gold in the 100 metres final. It was very inspiring, and confidence was now running high in the band.

So high that we were even capable of tolerating the Olympian bullshit being spouted by the locals at the pub we spent the Saturday evening in. I had no idea that Burgess Hill was such a hot spot for 'garbage rhetoric' but by Christ they talked some shit in that pub. It put me in mind of that scene in Trains, Planes and Automobiles where Steve Martin says to John Candy, "Here's a tip for you. Try and have a point to your stories, an amusing anecdote or two…Your stories have none of these." Thank God I'm not like that.

My French was improving too, thanks to my proximity to Big Dave and "Mon-frère Michel" over those 48 hours. Okay, it was more '*Deux jambes mortes* 'than '*Je m'appelle Matthew*', but their teaching methods were impeccable. I'll never forget falling like a sack of spuds after Dave and 'Monfrère Michel' gave me a 'dead leg' with their respective outstretched knees in tandem, taking out a thigh each, after a session at the pub. Wow, those childhood days back in the backstreets of Nice must have been a hoot!

Still, it proved useful for my trip to France around this time to visit my sister Julia and her husband Steven at their French property in Belfort, near Strasbourg, where my sister had been teaching English on the Eastern side of this beautiful country.

When you were back at school you generally learnt about the French language via slides that depicted things like the bakery being next door to the butchers and the local school opposite the town hall or just around the corner from the local brothel!

So, coupled with this background knowledge and Dave and "Mon-frere Michel's" more practical lessons off I set to practise 'for real' on a jolly gallic weekender of my own.

I will go into a little bit more detail later, but around this time I was suffering from Ulcerative Colitis, (A chronic bowel disease) although I was unaware of its medical name at the time as I hadn't yet been properly diagnosed.

However, the upshot (or down shot) of this was lots of frequently being' caught short' moments when I was out somewhere or spending long boring hours in assorted bathrooms 'Basooning' farts like 'The Brighouse and Rastrick Brass Band' (look 'em up, they charted) performing under a Doncaster railway bridge!

Anyway, one day, whilst I was out there, desperate to prove to my sister that I could go down the road and order a loaf of bread in French, pay for it successfully and then return home in time for breakfast ("le petite dejeuner") I decided to get up early.

I left the third floor of my sisters' apartments and strutted off down the road passing the local school, the mayor's office (and the Brothel around the corner) and 'Voila' sure enough, right there, next to the butchers, was the patisserie.

I went in and smiled broadly at the French girl in the shop took a deep breath and opened my mouth, "Bonjour, Je voudrai du pan s'il vous plait mademoiselle," I paused nervously half expecting either a bemused look or maybe a disapproving frown, but instead, amazingly she smiled back. She then walked over to the counter and handed me a baguette the size of a baseball bat. "Merci, Combien de?" I asked, getting more and more confident now.

I have absolutely no idea what she replied with, but just to be on the safe side I just gave her all the francs (pre the euro remember) that I had in my pocket. Which could've been ten pounds for all I know, I then smiled, said "Merci, au revoir" and skipped happily out of the shop, waving and blowing a kiss to the large breasted 'madam' shaking dust (or sperm) from a rug out of the Brothel window.

Mission completed successfully, I was suddenly completely overcome with the sheer intoxication of the irresistible smell from the freshly cooked bread and just had to rip off a piece and have a 'cheeky' nibble.

Almost immediately I did so I regretted it, as that (soon to become) regular feeling of a stirring, tremor like rumble from down below began and the horror of knowing that I was still at least 100 metres from my sister's apartment.

So, you think Linford Christie was fast? Well, believe you me I reckon Usain Bolt's world record would've been under threat if my 'dash against splash' run up la rue de Belfort was being officially timed.

I got to the front door just in time and panickily ran up the four flights of stairs, happy in the knowledge that my sister never locked her front door and that there was also a mini bathroom just inside it on the left.

I made it to 'Sanitation Sanctuary' dropped the bread by the door outside, undid my ''kecks' and gratefully hit the throne with all the grace and dexterity of a hippo on ice!

But alas nothing came out, other than those constipated 'bassoon' sounds I had gotten so accustomed to.

Only this little bathroom was made of wood, making every fart sound like the QE2 'horning' it's way out of Southampton harbour. It was getting so loud that not even my acutely timed coughs were covering it. So, I decided the best course of action was probably to start commentating on it just to hide my embarrassment.

Thinking of Test Match Cricket, especially Richie Benaud's distinctive early morning Australian drawl, I began in earnest.

"Morning Geoffrey, morning everyone, beautiful day here at the Oval, a slight breeze coming in from the Surrey stand end as Bob Willis starts his twisted, mazy, meandering run in, for the first ball of the morning…and it's a Wide, as signalled by umpire Dickie Bird."

Now math's probably isn't my strongest suit and some of you may have already picked up on this, but as I looked around the bathroom, I suddenly noticed that I didn't recognise anything, and I mean anything, my toothbrush, deodorant, after shave, just wasn't there and who's teeth were they, in that jar?

It was also round about then that I became more and more aware of some French speaking voices outside the door whispering and muttering, sounding very much like the Norman soldiers receiving 'The Trojan Rabbit' in Monty Python's Holy Grail!

And then it dawned on me. I'd gone up one too many flights of stairs...I was in the wrong fucking Maison! "Merde," I thought or rather the lack of it!

I guess I'll never truly know what that elderly couple thought as I exited their bathroom, grabbed my bitten off 'baseball bat of a baguette', smiled sweetly, said "Bonjour" and, "I'd probably give that 'Cinq minutes' if I were you."

But my sister has been far too polite to ever bring it up again, but hey I think I left a favourable enough impression... certainly on one of their bath towels at least!

Anyway, back to Burgess Hill, Big Dave and I went back to Studio 125 the following weekend to remix the demo. It didn't go so well this time. A liquid lunch at the Bullshitter's Arms slightly impaired ('Beered' I think they call it) our finely tuned hearing capabilities and I think we did little to improve the finished product.

Never mind, the demo was good to go, and it gave us a great recruiting tool.

Next up, I got a full-time permanent job. From now on, I would bring my knowledge of the direct mail industry and trench-digging skills to bear in the making of in-car entertainment. No, not strip shows in the back of a Fiesta, just workaday radio cassette players, makes like Phillips, Kenwood, Pioneer and Blaupunkt for a company in Wandsworth called Sextons!

Life was good again. That was until one never to be forgotten night at Gatwick Airport in October that is.

I was there to meet Alicia off a plane home from a visit back to see her parents in what was still at the time, Czechoslovakia.

There's something weird about arriving at an airport terminal and hearing your name – or a version of it – being blared out on the public Tannoy system. As I passed through the glass doors to Arrivals, the message boomed out asking for a 'Mr Matthew Fiddler' to please report immediately to the immigration desk.

Was my first thought, *oh shit, is Alicia, okay? Had the folks at the South Terminal received a call asking them to relay bad, urgent, news to me about my family? Did they want my autograph?*

None of the above. The first thing to enter my mind on being publicly addressed as Mr Fiddler was Sid James and Peter Butterworth from the Carry-on Camping film. Or more accurately the former's filthy laugh. When you're meeting your teenage girlfriend off a plane from Czechoslovakia, and you're summonsed by the immigration people you're not supposed to laugh.

But that's what I did. So much so that had I not been passing a WC at the time, I probably would have pissed myself. Anyway, I went in.

"WC? That'll be a pound, sir!"

"You don't say. Get away!"

I often wonder if that announcement was retribution for a prank, I'd played at a summer fare on Richmond Green a few years earlier. It was a sunny day, turnout was excellent, and people were enjoying themselves on bouncy castles, roundabouts, coconut shies etc. The Cricketer's Pub was doing a roaring trade and local MP Alan Watson, now Lord Watson of Richmond CBE, was 'MCing' the whole thing.

Desperate for a piece of the action, particularly as there was a microphone involved, I approached the honourable member and told him I'd lost my brother and could he put a call out please.

Alan was an affable man (and I was also of voting age now), so was happy to oblige. He asked me for my brother's name.

"Mike," I replied.

"And the surname?"

"Hunt."

"And what's your name?"

"Isaac."

I re-joined my friends just as Alan put the call out.

"Isaac Hunt," he boomed, "has an important message for his brother, Mike. Will 'Mike Hunt' please come to the stage where your brother 'Isaac Hunt' is waiting for you. That's Mike Hunt to the stage please. Thank you."

Poor Alan was totally oblivious to what he had just 'boomed out' to the whole of Richmond!

Oh, how we imbeciles laughed.

Anyway, back to the matter in hand (so to speak) I emerged from the airport loo and duly reported to the immigration desk.

But to fully grasp the real significance of what was about to happen when I got there, maybe it's time you all took a bathroom break yourself before we move on.

Chapter 6
Written in Your Eyes

"Rain's falling, but still, we rise and heaven's closer in your eyes."

Nigel Havers proving you can't stop rock 'n' roll. Manor Rd, Twickenham, Beirut, July 1991

It was in fact an unusual chain of events that initially brought Alicia and I together in the first place, so it's probably best to get a little bit more background here for some better understanding and perspective.

About a year before 'Fiddler on the hoof' a work colleague of Conn's from the old Our price records shop in Hounslow by the name of Dean started living with us in our one-bedroom flat in respectable Manor Road, Twickenham.

Now Dean was a big strapping lad from Barnsley. A proper Yorkshireman, he was very set-in-his ways and a fry-up fanatic. He rode a British motorbike (loudly), loved indie music and loved watching movies (and not all of them of his old band). When he wasn't indulging in any of these pastimes or asking me if I had any 'decent filth' to watch, he'd be soaking and smoking in the bath and constantly requesting me to 'Stick the fookin kettle on Matt, there's a good lad'. We were providing Dean with a temporary home as he'd just split with his girlfriend, and we were like that. From our earliest flat sharing days anyone and everyone was always welcome at our pad, with or without a sob story, just so long as they brought beer!

One night however, neither Conn nor Dean made it home from work.

In fact, I didn't see either of them until the afternoon of the next day, when they returned home in stony silence, looking distinctly dishevelled and sheepish.

And both were wearing cheap, lurid white plimsolls, the kind you wore for PE at primary school when you forget your kit and had to do the exercises with your nylon vest tucked into your pants.

When my laughter subsided, I found out why. Conn's and Dean's shoes had been confiscated by the police, as they were now to be used as evidence, Exhibits 'A' and 'B'. Apparently, on their way home from work the previous day they'd both got very drunk. So drunk that when passing a used car dealer's forecourt, they saw not cars but trampolines – and decided to play.

Which caught the attention of a nearby curtain twitcher, who in turn called the police. Who duly turned up and arrested the drunken bouncers in mid-air?

Second-hand car dealers are instinctive situation exploiters, and the Arthur Daley of this establishment was no exception. Pretty much every fault and defect on his cars was the result of this 'outrageous intrusion'. Court – and possibly even prison – beckoned.

Caring flatmate that I was I spent the next few weeks creating a reassuring atmosphere in the flat in the only way I knew how, by taking the absolute piss. My banter took on a 'Pick up the soap, boy' or 'By the time I'm finished with you, you ain't gonna shit right for a month' kind of tone.

They didn't really need that. What they did need was a good defence lawyer and quickly. As Johnny Cochran wasn't available and soon to be rather preoccupied by some American geezer called OJ Simpson we plumped for the lesser known, but far more local and affordable Mr George Keppe.

To be honest I wasn't that confident for either Conn or Dean's hopes. I'd seen a copy of the police's transcripts of their interviews. Conn had held his hand up and admitted his guilt as the numerous eyewitness accounts and charges were read to him.

Dean, on the other hand, didn't. Taking his cue from the movies he watched, he demanded his right to a phone call, refused to say anything until he'd spoken to 'his brief' and even claimed his name was not Dean but Dwain.

To deepen the sense of impending doom, the felon up before the beak in the case before us was 'led down' in handcuffs shouting and screaming. "It was a fit up! I'm innocent." We had no idea who he was or what he was supposed to have done but the psychological effect of his exit from the courtroom on us was none too good.

But Keppe was a keeper. He was great. I watched in awe as, having trousered my flatmates' cash, he looked the magistrate in the eye and said, "This was a prank that got out of hand. These are decent lads who just couldn't handle the amount they had to drink. I 'll put my hand on my heart and am entirely confident, in fact I would stake my whole career on it, that these two boys will never be in trouble with the law again." Or something like that.

Looking back, I think the magistrate just wanted an early lunch. Either that or he had filled his jailing quota for that day. Because he yawned through Mr Daley's impassioned plea for the two 'menaces of society' to get the incarceration they deserved and handed Conn and Dean an £1,800 fine each, to be paid over 12 months.

Result. Off to The Blucher, where brother Andy would join us too.

Conn and Dean, though relieved were still wounded. As mentioned, Conn is the Son of the late, great sportswriter, Hugh McIlvanney, a man who enjoyed many a legendary late-night tipple in the various watering holes of Fleet Street. Dean's old man, from what I could gather, was your typical old school, no-nonsense Yorkshireman. He may have even been an ex-coal miner and owned a whippet.

Neither patriarch had been made aware of the case and the boys wanted to keep it that way. No way did they want their dads finding out that a lawyer had stood up in a public forum and told all within earshot that their sons 'just couldn't handle the amount they had to drink'. The headline which graced the front cover of the following week's Richmond and Twickenham times, 'Pair Who Just Couldn't Handle Their Drink', was also as far as I know never seen by either parent.

For the record they both more than can.

As we entered the 'Den of Destiny', I clocked three sullen, pasty-faced individuals I hadn't seen there before.

My 'Bevoir of choice' currently at the time was still Newcastle Brown Ale. I can't remember now if it was a tribute to Gazza for the free kick, he scored against Arsenal in the FA Cup Semi Final that year, a tribute to Brian Johnson of AC/DC or because Clint Eastwood had recently shipped an ocean's worth of the stuff over to Carmel, California. Not that it matters – I mention it because I hold the beer responsible for the following life changing events.

As the barmaid sorted our drinks and my mates disappeared towards the beer garden, I leaned towards the pallid trio and enquired as to their origins.

Two of them stared blankly back at me, the third broke into a smile and said, with an accent I couldn't place, 'Nigeria.'

At which point I came over all Biff Byford, the gruff Yorkshire frontman of metal band, Saxon (Wheels of Steel, Dallas 1 pm, etc.).

"Well, I was only fookin' asking, d'ya know what I fookin mean?"

I didn't. I gave her my sweetest smile, lifted my tray of celebratory ales and joined my mates in the beer garden.

I like to remember it that I said to Conn, "I think I may have just met the girl I'm gonna spend the rest of my life with." But I'm pretty sure what I said was possibly less romantic, probably more Anglo-Saxon (just like Biff) and more of a short-term arrangement.

But even I know a spark when I feel one and 'Nigeria' and I had made a connection right there. Her name was Alicia. It still amazes me that even today people struggle to get her name right, so don't even start me on her maiden surname. Which is 'Suszka' or 'Suszkova' as it was at the time, as she wasn't yet married then.

Anyway, Alicia was 18 and of Polish descent. She had grown up just over the border in what was still at that time Czechoslovakia.

She was in Twickenham visiting her mother (who was already working over here) and had travelled To England with her brother and best friend, Magda. Mum, it turned out, worked at Joanna's café, so had been serving me breakfast three times a week (insert your own sausage gags here) for at least a couple of months.

Alicia told me a lot of things at the start of our relationship, and I believed them all. It was exciting stuff to be dating a girl who'd been locked up by the KGB for protesting communism. And I'm not at liberty to discuss the African nationality claim.

Tall stories aside, I loved having her around and her English was getting better all the time. But the real clincher – and the reason I begged her to move in with Conn and I – was her cooking.

Take the day, for example, when we had no food or drink in the flat and payday (or benefit day) for either of us was a good full week away. Well Alicia came over and, from a bag of old flour, some old potatoes, salt and water she performed a miracle.

It was called 'Platzki' and it was a revelation. A kind of potato pancake that was out of this world. They say you can't make a silk purse out of a sow's ear. Well, I must admit Alicia certainly managed it here!

In fact, I think there is an old Polish expression I've heard many times since, which roughly translated goes along the lines of, "If you want your man to stay faithful and true, keep his stomach full and his balls empty."

Well, I have to say over the years I've never been hungry, although since the birth of my kids, my balls have swollen up to the size of space hoppers on the odd occasion.

Anyway, it was decided, she was going nowhere.

At least not until October 1992 when she went home to see her dad and friends back in Eastern Europe. Alicia's visa would expire in six weeks but having applied to go to drama school in London, she was hopeful of both an extension to her visa and a grant.

Two flaws: One, drama school term was already underway and two, there was no grant or potential provider of one in play.

And it was these two flaws that the immigration people at Gatwick Airport had in mind when they put the call out for Mr Matthew Fiddler!

Chapter 7
The Wrong Side of Love

"Hole in my pocket, heart on the floor and this long and winding road."

Team photo with l-r Paul Karner, a great guitarist and an even greater loss, Big Dave Rocker, yours truly and Simon Woodley, the 'Pale Face of Bass', January 1993

That's how the Matt/Alicia backstory begins. But there's more. Much more of this. Three chapters worth in fact, so if you don't want to know the score (or love interest stuff just isn't rock 'n' roll enough for you), look away now! – as they use to say on the BBC Saturday evening news before 'Match of the Day' or "Go and put the kettle on" and we'll see you all in Chapter 10.

Although Alicia and I had only been an item for a year, thoughts of popping the question to her were taking up more and more of my time. So much so that I'd moved from 'Shall I?' To 'how and where shall I do it?' I was loving her company almost as much as her cooking.

When 'Mr Matthew Fiddler' arrived at the Carry On (Not) Stamping scene, the setup was pretty much as predicted. Joyless jobsworths with epaulettes, a guy who looked like a chemistry teacher (and may well have been buggered a lot at school) and a brassed-up lady from Dan Air.

They took me into a holding cell away from Alicia, (who Incidentally, I still hadn't been allowed to see yet) and laid on the time-honoured good cop, bad cop routine. Clearly, they wanted to see if my answers tallied with what Alicia had told them. Having seen the Gérard Depardieu classic, Green Card, I knew this game, so I played along with their pointless charade. But after an hour and a half, they went and told Alicia that I was intending to ask her to marry me. Yes! The egregious bastards did that. It was the second time my gaff had been blown in as many years. (You have read the previous chapter, right?)

Eventually, they allowed me to see Alicia. Not surprisingly she was in bits. The contents of her suitcase (which for some strange reason also included a huge, wooden 'phallus' given to her by a 'friend' as a joke) had been callously strewn across the table in front of her and her makeup was running from her tears.

But I didn't rise to the bait or react to the wisecracking over my rock 'n' roll hair "Which one of them are we refusing entry to, again". For the first time in my life, I suppressed my Arian temper and adopted a more 'Yes sir, yes madam, you're so right. Absolutely, of course' approach.

Andrew my brother had finessed this technique over several years of overstepping the mark with his Glaswegian wife, Maureen. As I sat there, sucking up this nonsense at Gatwick I remember how, one day after he had been half the night on a complete 'bender' Maureen had laid into poor old Andy, all effing this and jeffing that and hurling plates, ashtrays and other smashable at him. And there was Andy, unflustered as he gathered up the shrapnel, doing his best Sergeant Wilson voice from Dad's Army. "Yes dear, I totally agree, as usual you're right. Let's bring this up for discussion at our next AGM."

Lovely lady that she is, it used to properly piss her off.

But even this tactic had limited success with the epaulette's men, chemistry teacher and the Dan Air dame. Despite some nauseating sucking up on my part, Alicia was still refused permission to re-enter the UK.

However, I knew my rights (or some of them) so, inspired by what I'd seen from George Keppe I declared proudly 'Your Honour, I can honestly put my hand on my heart...' and yeah, well you can guess the rest.

It bought us five days at least. Alicia was released into my supervisory care on the understanding that I would return her to Gatwick at the end of that period to produce either proof of her permission to remain in the country, face arrest or assist with her deportation.

We explored every avenue. I contacted our local MP, made countless phone calls and fired off a blizzard of letters. At one point I even considered contacting 'Jim'll fix it'. Thank Christ I didn't. But in the end, all I managed to achieve was a one-day extension to the rapidly expiring five.

So, try as I might and after a labyrinth of dead ends eventually there was the dawning realisation that no matter what I did there was only ever going to be one real way out of this. Go to Czechoslovakia and get married.

So, my meticulously thought-through, *how and where shall I do it?* Plans weren't to be. Time and cash were more important commodities than grand romantic gestures now. Our engagement had to be actionable and affordable. Right now.

Which is why the next day saw us on Sheen Common, me down one knee proffering a £45 Elizabeth Duke engagement ring.

(Elizabeth Duke: Brand of Jewellery favoured by the chav. Rarely exceeding nine carat and exclusively found at Argos. Thanks a bunch, Urban Dictionary.)

Not exactly Gone with the Wind but it was our moment, and it was beautiful in its own way. And Alicia said yes, which was as helpful as it was nice.

Next up was to plan and budget for a marriage that would be recognised as legal in the UK. But first I had to get Alicia back to Gatwick. We made it to Dan Air's check in desk with just about enough time for an argument between the airline and me about who'd pay for Alicia's ticket home. I won that one, but Alicia still had to go. They printed the ticket, took her baggage and after an emotional hug, she was gone. As it happens, Dan Air has gone now, but Alicia is still very much here. Karma, eh?

We set the wedding date for 29th December, three months away. Three months without being able to see my fiancée. Three months in which Sexton's in Wandsworth enjoyed an unexpected uplift in my enthusiasm for my work. It's amazing how getting yourself 'Balls deep in Blaupunkt' in-car cassette players can help take your mind off things.

But. Three months is also a long time to go without a leg-over. Few people who witnessed my outrageous nightly flirting with The Cherry Tree's barmaids believed it was possible, but I did succeed in keeping it in my pants for the duration.

Sort of.

I didn't want to misbehave but needs had to be met. And remember, we didn't have the internet or mobile phones back then. We did have phone sex lines though, so I called one up from the landline in the flat.

'Sarah' was a sweet-sounding girl with a deep Mancunian accent. As soon as I got through, phone in one hand, something else in the other, all thoughts of filth deserted me. If Sarah was hoping for 'what colour thong, are you wearing, love?' She was disappointed. Because what she got instead was chapter and verse on my intended's emotional deportation, my looming marriage abroad and my rationalisation that by phoning her I was avoiding the physical act of infidelity.

At which point 'Salford Sarah' became 'Samaritan Sarah'. She told me that it was the ''sweetest thing' she had 'ever heard' and then went even further. Informing me that I could call her up any time say 'Hi' put the phone down then her or one of the other girls would call me back and chat with me about 'whatever I wanted' for ten minutes, thus saving me the 95p per minute charge.

They were a lovely bunch, the phone sex girls, even the one who sounded like Jim Bowen from the darts-themed TV quiz show Bullseye who kept asking me if I had a moustache and was all 'muscley'. I think we may have shared a few of bully's special prizes during these calls for sure.

Inevitably my song writing took on a sentimental hue and much of what I created was way too slushy for the band. That said, one song from this period would see daylight a few years later.

It wasn't all romance, though. I was also working hard to recruit a guitarist. 1993 was going to be the 'Year of the Jane' so we had to hit the ground running.

So 'no', in case you are wondering, I wasn't one of those 'Self-righteous, "It was a fix, nobody understood what they were doing, let's have second referendum." 'Re-moaners' but after this little episode, I certainly wasn't ever really going to be a Brexiter come voting time in in 2016.

Whilst we are on conspiracy theories. It is funny, to me at least, how it always seems to be the same kind of people who think there's some sort of secret, overseeing world order constantly trying to suppress the truth and keep the masses down. You know the sort, we never went to the moon, Princess Diana was assassinated, 9-11 never happened, Biden rigged the polls. These folk are almost always anti-vaccinations, anti-masks, anti-Europe. When they're in Italy Anti-pasta and in the winter possibly even anti-freeze... But to be honest, just so long as they're not anti my book, I'm really pretty much okay with most of that, because deep down I love them all dearly, and this 'Flat Earth' would be a very dull place without them!

Incidentally just going back to that Princess Diana theory, in 1997 (the year she died) Al Fayed's son, quite literally threw me out of Harrod's, for larking about on some Arabic Bean bags, one sunny, Saturday afternoon.

"Did he?" I hear you ask. But you'd be wrong... as it was in fact Dodi!

Anyway, I'll get my coat and move on with the next chapter before Howard realises, that I've snuck that gag back in!

Chapter 8
If You Still Believe

"Nobody feels the pain, as a tear drops from my eyes, just can't stand and watch, as this dream slowly dies."

Simon and Jason in 'heads down see you at the end mode'. Meanwhile, I'm off to phone Jim Bowen to claim Bully's special prize. The Red Lion, Brentford, 1994

Between the farewell at Gatwick and Christmas, a one-night tryst with Alicia in Calais at the end of October was the only physical contact I had with my fiancée. To get there, I hitched a lift with her mum who was making the 17-hour journey home from Twickenham by car to help arrange and plan the wedding.

Remember, we didn't have Facetime, WhatsApp, Zoom or any of the other communication essentials of the Covid-19 era back then. Long distance romance in the early 1990s was still all about letters and badly connected phone calls from landlines or red boxes on the streets. And it wasn't cheap.

I often laugh at how easy all these 'Gen Z' and 'Millennials' have it these days. Swipe left, swipe right, an emoji here, a 'lol' or two there, add in a few PMSLs for good measure. Or indeed for the more bolder and brazen of them, a slyly sent 'dick pic' or 'flap snap' and then bingo!

Within minutes they're either being 'noshed' off or 'fisted' in the back of a Vauxhall Corsa in some dimly lit Lidl car park. The Lucky bastards!

In my day you schlepped to a graffiti-covered phone box. You felt the eyes of the neighbourhood boring into you as you opened the door and snuck inside. You recoiled from the acidic perma-stench of cidery piss. You dialled the number with your ten pence piece delicately poised for it to go one of two ways. If your sweetheart answered, you pushed it into the slot before the pips finished. If her dad answered – and you prayed that he wouldn't – you kept your money and scarpered.

I hate to say it but if I hadn't kept a photo of Alicia think Kyle Reece in Terminator "I travelled back through time for you, Sarah", I would've probably forgotten what she looked like.

Getting psyched up for your wedding is quite stressful. More so when it's in a foreign country and you're not involved in any of the arrangements. So, in the end I just decided to leave my worries and concerns in the 'fuck it' bucket and just went with the flow.

The plan was that we'd get married in a registry office in Trinec, which is close to Alicia's hometown of 'Cesky Tesin' in the northeast of then Czechoslovakia. The area is home to a decent ice hockey team but is more famous for its steel production industry and the pollution that comes from it.

I was nervous about the journey as I'd been there once before. How could I forget the 23-hour coach trip with no toilets on board and the four new-born babies crying their little hearts out and soiling their nappies every half an hour?

The Berlin wall had fallen (with some help from David Hasselhoff and the Scorpions) and millions of people were breaking free from the chains of communism to find out what capitalism and (so called) democracy could offer them.

But that sort of change doesn't happen overnight. Much of what I saw was still very 'Funeral in Berlin' or 'The Odessa File'. Guards still goose stepped along the Polish/Czechoslovakian border and the queues outside basic food shops were like those at the Apple Store on iPhone launch day. And Putin wanted to go back to this?

However, on the plus side they did have some very strange customs, if a new coffee shop opened, there'd be strippers. Where lorries queued up at the border, there'd be fur coated hookers. But still nobody smiled and (or possibly because) nobody used deodorant.

But trust me they could put their vodka away though. In Twickenham, I nurtured my reputation as a bit of a boozer. Here, I was a virtual teetotaller in comparison.

Local shopping tax laws threw up some fun stories, too. If you crossed the border from 'Cesky Tesin' into the 'Polish

Ciesin', the tax you paid on your purchases was determined by how many people travelled with you: The bigger your party, the lower the tax. No, I didn't understand it either.

However, we did hear of a family who were shopping for a sofa bed for their grandma so she could stay over more often. They'd arrived in Polish Ciesin with a borrowed trailer and a tiny car crammed with Mum, Dad, three kids and dear old Grandma herself.

The excitement of it all proved too much for Grandma. Just moments after Dad had paid for the sofa bed, she had a heart attack and died, right there and then on the shop floor.

This was a 'bummer' as it meant there would be investigations involving police forces of two separate countries and the expense of repatriating a corpse – a real concern now that hard cash had just been laid out on the now 'seemingly' redundant sofa bed.

Then 'someone' suggested. Why not hide Grandma in the sofa bed and drive home without informing the authorities? Sure, there'd be a risk of a spot check at the border, a heavy fine and a possible life prison sentence, but worth a go, surely?

The family agreed. And made it back over the border incident-free. But they didn't go straight home. They stopped at the first opportunity to toast the 'stiff in the sofa bed' with a stiff vodka in a pub.

I quite like that the Polish and the Czechs confront distress head-on by throwing more alcohol at it. If only it solved things, though. When the family returned to their car, the trailer was gone. The region was renowned at that time for its large Romanian gypsy population and, statistically at least, a member of that community was probably the most likely culprit.

As the effects of the vodka faded, gruesome reality set in. With the trailer, had also gone the sofa bed and its decomposing occupant, Grandma.

They were never found. But I still wonder sometimes how that evening went for King Gypsy Giorgi and his wife as they relaxed on their new piece of furniture, the atrocious waft of death rising from beneath them. "Not fish again tonight, Andrea. Please for the love of God no!"

Czechs celebrate Christmas on 24 December, so there were no seats to be had on any flight to Prague on the 23rd. Plan B was for me to fly to Vienna where I'd be met by Alicia and Michael, father of Magda. From there, Michael would drive us across the Austrian border and into Czechoslovakia. We'd continue our journey through Bratislava, taking a break at a barn in the middle of nowhere to choose the wine for the wedding. Assuming all went to plan, we'd be in Cesky Tesin in time for a nightcap.

Before I left Twickenham to make this life-changing journey, Conn, being unable to attend the wedding, gave me a great send off.

By getting me absolutely 'shit-faced'. No surprises there.

In fact I don't recall making it onto the 216 Bus to Heathrow at all, but I do have a hazy memory of telling anyone and everyone on board who couldn't avoid me that I was riding out on my white horse to rescue my 'Beautiful Eastern Princess' from the injustices of Dirty Dan Air and the Beastly British Immigration officials. They knew they loved it. They even applauded me as I was getting off the bus. Partly because of my Quixotic mission but mainly because I was at last getting off their bus.

Perhaps not surprisingly, not all my mates were fully behind what I was committing to. Friends and family from both sides were telling me I was making a mistake. 'She's too young' or 'you're a fucking arsehole', that sort of thing.

Conn was an exception, which was why I was sad he couldn't make it. Given our track record together in pubs, however, I probably dodged a bullet. (A few years later we would famously miss a flight for a wedding after a lock-in at my brother's pub, which was just ten minutes from Gatwick Airport.)

I met a delightful lady in the queue for the loo on the flight to Vienna. She was 75, Jewish and quite specific about why she was standing aside to let me go ahead of her. She told me she wanted to be absolutely, 100 percent sure we were directly over Germany before she took a 'damn good shit!' What a delightful picture.

On arrival in Vienna, immigration wanted a word with me. My image – long hair, sunglasses, Hurricane Jane T-shirt, leather jacket, ripped jeans and cowboy boots – didn't quite stack up. Nor were they any the wiser when I tried to explain my presence while still under the influence.

We had one of those conversations where the more you stick to the truth, the more far-fetched it sounds. Almost mirroring the famous John Candy/Macaulay Culkin breakfast exchange in the Uncle Buck film.

Immigration Guy: Why are you here?
Pissed Bloke: I'm getting married.
IG: To an Austrian citizen?

PB: No, Polish.

IG: You are getting married to a Polish girl in Vienna?

PB: No, Czechoslovakia. It'll be the Czech Republic next week. Will that make me a free man?

IG: Why is she not with you?

PB: She got deported.

IG: Where are you meeting her?

PB The other side of that curtain, I hope.

IG: There is no Iron Curtain anymore. Then what?

PB: We're going to go to what will be soon Slovakia to do some wine tasting for our wedding…in a barn.

People who threaten a country's national security are usually sober, compos mentis and anonymous in their appearance. I ticked none of these boxes. He let me go and in so doing, left my standing as the greatest exponent of Anglo-Austrian relations the world has ever seen (remember Inga) intact.

Which was good news for me – but not so great for the Hurricane Jane T-shirt I was wearing. In the years ahead, it wasn't unusual for me to leave items of clothing in the wash over in the Czech Republic. That T-shirt became one of them and while hanging out to dry one day suffered the same fate as dear old Grandma from the sofa bed episode. It was nicked and, like Grandma, gone forever. Possibly.

Then, by pure chance one day after we'd been married a few years, Alicia and I were out walking in 'Cesky Tesin'. When we came across this down and out, hairy-arsed man taking a piss against a lamppost. AND HE WAS WEARING MY HURRICANE JANE T-SHIRT.

It reminded me of that day a few years before when my autograph had been dropped unceremoniously in some dogshit. Was it symbolic? Poignant? I don't know, but it did make me laugh though. A lot.

It was so great to see my intended when I finally got through to the arrival hall. Three months of separation (Calais notwithstanding) evaporated in two minutes. But before my hard-on could subside, we were on our way from the 'Bone of plenty' to the 'Barn of plenty' to choose some wine.

This wasn't so much a wine tasting as a syphoning. There were no glasses, just rubber hosepipes. Nor was there any ambience. The winemaker's client presentation area was a dimly lit straw-strewn structure. Imagine a nativity scene thrown together by a desperate wino. I loved it. Amazingly (considering my state) I think I got the red choice right. The white perhaps less so.

So, anyway I'd landed, made it to Czechoslovakia and played a vital role in the wedding preparations. There were just six days to go.

Six days of celebrating Christmas with my fiancée's family.

Chapter 9
If I Could Go Back

"If I'd stayed with you, would you still be there for me?"

After lots of shots of vodka at the wedding to end them all. Trinec, Czechoslovakia, 29 December 1992

As I mentioned, families – or at least the one I was about to marry into – on the Czechoslovakian / Polish border go big on Christmas. The fun starts on 24 December, the day they call

'Wigilia' the Polish term for Christmas Eve supper, and it continues for a further 12 days and nights.

That supper is a seven-course meal. Soups, 'Pierogi' (a mushroom-based pasta) and other side dishes too numerous to mention comprise an exquisite support act. The headliner is carp – slaughtered and battered at home as per tradition – and cooked in a variation of ways.

This was my second Christmas with the 'Suszka' family, so I was aware of the carp slaughtering tradition. You don't forget darting into the bathroom after a heavy session on the vodkas and finding three fully grown cyprinid splashing around in the tub right next to you, as you are trying to conduct business.

This year we would spend our pre-wedding Christmas with Alicia's grandparents who lived in the Polish town of Rzeszow. Rzeszow is nearer to Ukraine than the then Czechoslovakia and this year it was under four feet of snow. As I write this my heart goes out to these brave folk and all they have and are enduring. I won't comment anymore on what's happened to that beautiful country, as by the time you are reading this whatever I say about it now will be out of date. Still, it was my first proper white Christmas in a while (if ever) and the first one I'd ever experienced at minus thirty degrees.

It was so cold you felt your insides burn when you breathed. Which made things a tad uncomfortable when the family's 'passed down through the generations' Trabant decides to break down and you must get out and push it. At minus 30 degrees I felt a right twat in Alicia's dad's 'long johns' – featuring detachable nappy flap – pushing this crocked vehicle for over a half a mile in a cold I never knew existed. Achtung Baby my arse.

Excellent though that Christmas was, the wedding was imminent, and nerves, stress and tension were starting to creep in. With this in mind, we took a detour on our way back to 'Cesky Tesin' from Rzeszow.

To a cheery little destination called…Auschwitz!

Alicia's grandad had been a prisoner there during the war. The stories he has relayed about his time there in his diaries shocked me to the core. I really did sense that trauma when I was there too. Visiting Auschwitz is harrowing and deeply disturbing, yet it's also salutary. I think it's somewhere everyone should go and visit at least once in their lives.

We also visited the thirteenth-century salt mines in nearby 'Wieliczka' afterwards, which helped to lift the mood. Slightly.

As the big day loomed, I started getting cold feet (it was minus thirty, remember). If there was a plane on standby with clearance to take off, I might well have boarded it. Thankfully, the arrival of five great friends from home calmed me down.

Nick and Mandy West, Simon and Jane Coggins and Tom Wan Tsy were on site.

Which meant the combined stag and hen night was on. Not that the presence of my wife-to-be moderated the worst excesses of my behaviour. After a boozy night at Partika, a bit of a dive in downtown 'Cesky Tesin', I woke up the next morning at Alicia's auntie's house in bed with a couple of her German girlfriends. A simple case of everyone crashing out anywhere and everywhere. Honest.

The sun shone on the morning of the 29th and the temperature had risen to a relatively tropical minus fifteen. I had breakfast with Tom, Alicia's auntie and my two bedfellows whose names I now knew were Belinda and Anjelica. I got dressed into my wedding suit (a Moss Bros job with salmon cravat and matching hanky brought over by best man Nick as I'd only hired it for three days) before being summoned to the 'House of Suszka'.

The concept of not seeing the bride on the day of the wedding didn't apply here, but no worries, Alicia had been to the hairdresser. At this time, western fashions and styling techniques had still to make it to 'Cesky Tesin', so there was a bit of 'touching up' to be done at home on Alicia's hair. Plus, there was vodka in the house, so I was able to uphold the no contact, no peeking tradition and leave the house before Alicia resurfaced. Either that or I hadn't cottoned on that the chick with the Bonnie Tyler coiffure trying to hide in the corner of the room was in fact the girl I was about to marry. Indeed, if she had been 'holding out for a hero' he was already hallway through a bottle of 'Wyborowa'!

As Tom, Nick and I crossed the town square in our matching top hats 'n' tails, the locals must have thought a film crew were in town for a Czech take on 'Downtown Abbey' or whatever the latest BBC Period drama was at the time. My own thoughts, however, were far closer to the bone. I'd selected a particularly fetching pair of Indonesian silk boxer shorts (thanks Hannah) with my wedding night in mind and as the sub-zero wind blew through them, I kind of regretted it.

In fact, I was regretting it so much that I failed to spot my shiny, ribbon-adorned wedding carriage and peak-capped chauffeur (Michael Magda's dad) and boarded the grubby coach hired to transport the 'less important' members of the wedding party instead.

Now disoriented, I was thrown into further confusion when the bus pulled up outside a steepled church right opposite the steel factory in Trinec. I'd been told we were getting married in a registry office.

Then I learned that:

- the registry office had been double booked.
- our translator had pulled out the day before having taken a job at the BBC.
- the paperwork from the British Embassy that would validate our marriage in the eyes of the British government hadn't materialised,
- our gold wedding rings (not Argos this time) had mysteriously disappeared.

Where to start? Well, Karol, Alicia's dad, was friendly with a local Evangelist priest. Some ecclesiastical palm greasing had obviously taken place because, at the last minute, my pop-in-law's priest pal allowed us to 'borrow' his church in Trinec and, even better, preside over the service himself. Meanwhile, Alicia's mum had a friend who shared a place with an American translator who was also game and stepped in at the eleventh hour. The paperwork arrived with seconds to spare but we had to take our vows using borrowed jewellery. Three out of four. Not too shabby.

The service was relatively straight forward. My bride glided down the aisle to Gilbert O'Sullivan's Claire. No idea why – maybe it was still number one in the Czech hit parade.

Her dress was as beautiful as her, WOW! she looked amazing! It was a white and black number based on a creation Gina Davis had worn at the Oscars that year. It had a fluffed up unzippable tail and black shoulder straps (and matching black stockings) and was made by the costume department at her dad's theatre.

It was a work of art but is sadly now history. Some years later it got destroyed by exposure to the elements because I stored it in a cheap large suitcase in our garden shed while we had some building work done. I will never be forgiven or allowed to forget this; I know that.

Funnily enough she was also wearing a pair of beautifully crafted earrings and neckless, which perfectly matched and complemented her outfit as well (she still has these by the way). Amazingly chosen by her drunken 'husband to be' and bought at the Heathrow airport Terminal 2 duty free shop on the way over. All this without any prior knowledge of the dress that they were too 'incredibly' match so well. It was, in all honesty, just a hastily guilt, ridden, Christmas present afterthought. Serendipity…or was 'Aphrodite' truly at work here?

Whatever, the whole ceremony only took about 45 minutes and thanks to my American translator I even understood some of it. I wasn't sure about the bit when the priest said what sounded like 'stench trench' to describe my beautiful bride and I was still 'Corpsing' when I fluffed my lines and messed up my vow in the Polish tongue.

Then, as we emerged from the church, we saw our rings hanging from the door by a piece of string. We have no idea who found them or where, but if you are our ring returner and you're reading this, thank you. A cold vodka, but warmer welcome await you if you're ever lost in Leatherhead.

So, this blissful union of East and West took place in a country that politically no longer exists, with rings we've never worn and based on a vow I uttered incorrectly in a language totally foreign to me, I mean does that give me an out? Take note Mr Jagger!

Once outside, we posed in the freezing cold while someone took pictures – not the official photographer as he was another no-show. We often get the polaroid album out and relive the romance of that moment: Blissful newlyweds kissing and hugging as the steel factory behind us belches out Clouds of toxic waste into the air above us. Put it this way, I perhaps won't ever be showing them to Greta Thunberg, if she ever happens to walk from her home in Sweden to come and see us for 'Kale cake and Nettle tea' one 'Carbon free' afternoon.

Next stop, the Classic night club for the reception. It was literally just across the road from the church, but having missed the limo experience on the way, I insisted on taking the car this time.

The reception was upstairs at the Classic and it was total mayhem from the minute we walked in. No one had a clue what was going on and even fewer people cared. There were two dinners, impromptu speeches from people neither Alicia or I had ever seen before, me addressing the crowd in my beginner-level Polish and a seemingly endless series of toasts washed down with vodka and cheap Champagne. For some reason, we both got carried across the dancefloor on chairs. Plates got smashed and so did we.

At one point, Alicia and I snuck downstairs to the night club for a private dance away from the Birdy Song, Gary Glitter numbers and other naff /inappropriate choices of our DJ.

There, a blue, fluorescent light illuminated Alicia's dress beautifully. Both totally immersed in the spirit of the occasion we became oblivious to the crowd of onlookers building around us. It was here that we had 'our moment' and Alicia looked me in the eyes, with a smile very reminiscent of Jennifer Gray's in Dirty Dancing. It was suddenly very clear to me that she was indeed having 'The time of her life'.

In fact, it was only when my new wife whispered in my ear that maybe the reason that the crowd had gathered so enthusiastically was not perhaps to celebrate our union, but that maybe they all thought that we were a speciality 'striptease' act instead, that we decided to make a swift exit back upstairs. Just before anyone had any ideas about putting my baby in the corner and where Whitney was now in full flow promising. "Iiiiiiiiiiii will always love youuuuuuuuuuu."

And then the final surprise. Out of nowhere a three-piece band started setting up. Nobody I'd spoken to knew anything about it, but I liked the opportunity it presented.

For an hour, the band bashed out traditional Polish folk songs. All very nice but not the rock 'n' roll they seemed itching to play, so I approached the guitarist, who without a hesitation, handed his instrument to me. Music is an international language, no words needed to be spoken, but to this day it is still the only time a guitarist in any band I have been as ever handed me their guitar!

There was a Bosch distortion pedal on the floor in front of me, so I pushed it down, turned to the bassist and said,

"Follow my lead." As I said music is a universal language and he got it straight away. We were off.

For about twenty minutes, we rocked the Classic. Whatever riff sprung to mind, I played it, and the rhythm section didn't miss a beat.

That was until I got the 'Paddington' stare from Alicia which I have come to recognise over the years as 'enough!'. It probably was, to be fair. A bit like the Prom dancers reacting to Marty McFly's floor gyrating, finger tapping climax to his solo in the 'Back to the Future' film, this Eastern European audience perhaps also, wasn't quite ready for 'Improv Jane' yet, but deep down I knew, and so did they, that their kids were just gonna love it!

After ten hours of partying, Alicia and I made our way to the aptly named Steel Hotel around the corner. Where hopefully there would be just enough juice left in the tank to consummate our marriage.

A few days later, when I left to return to the UK (alone, as Alicia's paperwork still needed to be finalised) Czechoslovakia had now become the Czech Republic and its borders were being patrolled by a new breed of less Moscow influenced 'goose steppers'. However, around this time there had been an horrific IRA attack somewhere in England and the main culprit was on the run. Eager to make their mark, these new but still, 'very keen' Czech border control guards got excited about my brand-new GB and Northern Ireland passport, they took one good look at me and convinced themselves that I was an absolute dead ringer for the grainy black and white photofit of 'a person of Interest' all the international news agencies were currently pumping out on their various channels in the aftermath of the aforementioned atrocity and promptly called Interpol. Ah well, I mused, just so long as they don't connect the dots to 'Raffle gate' in Fulham I should be okay.

As you know, this wasn't my first assignation with border patrol types, nor would it be the last. In another memorable incident some years later I had a pair of brand-new Caterpillar boots, a Christmas present from Alicia, confiscated by armed guards at Prague airport. Without any preamble, the guards placed my Caterpillars on a protective bomb disposable tray and sprayed them with a white powder. It looked like they were planning a controlled explosion right there for the benefit of our fellow passengers. And all the time Alicia was shouting. "Hey! I bought those in Millets, and I still have the receipt!"

Then, when we got home, we heard about some guy called the 'Shoe Bomber' and it all made sense. As for the boots, they didn't make it back. I keep them at my father-in-law's place deep in the Moravian mountains where they get plenty of use. Just like most of my clothes, passed around the village for communal use. You remember that scene in' Coming to America' where Eddie Murphy and Arsenio Hall see all the locals in Queens, New York suddenly wearing their clothes? "Yes, Yes, FUCK YOU TOO."

With the (Non) honeymoon period over, it was back to the grind in wintery London. Car cassette players needed assembling and Alicia's paperwork needed ratifying.

A Christmas wedding guaranteed that we'd now spend every anniversary ever after in the Czech Republic, so difficult to forget. On the fourth of these happy occasions, Alicia surprised me by taking me to a restaurant that also doubled up as a brothel. The story went that one hot summers evening, when all windows were open, all that 'grunting, groaning and grinding' was keeping my mother-in-law awake. So complete with hair curlers in, dressing grown on and slippers, over she went to complain to the madam in charge. Well, naturally apologies were very forth…er coming and she got invited in

Then of course out came the champagne, vodka etc (you know the drill) and they became the best of friends.

I have to say the menu certainly made my mouth water. Starters, main course, inter course, afters. I now love our Christmases and anniversaries in the Czech rep, Hi Simona!

So, another year over and a new one had just begun. 1993 was surely going to be the 'Year of the Jane!'

Chapter 10
The London Heartbeat

"And If you really care? Then girl I'll find you there."

Mr Rocker aka Big Dave getting into the groove at rehearsals,
January 1993

Once back in dear old Blighty it hit me how much I'd missed
gigging. We needed to play again and soon. So, five minutes
after I got back to the flat in Twickenham, I went straight back
out, crossed the road and put it to young boy racer Paul that

he should re-join the band, if only to get back into the gigging scene. I took a no-pressure-just-see-how-it-goes approach. I didn't see a long-term future in it, but as he was still living right opposite me, the idea appealed as a potential quick win. I hit him with the demo, he liked it, so agreed to 'help us out' for a while.

Still euphoric from the wedding and now slightly pissed from the beers I'd treated myself to following my successful meeting with Paul, I called up The Red Lion in Brentford and booked us in for a gig on 2 February.

Then I thought I'd better let Simon and Dave know. At this point, they weren't even aware I was back in the country, let alone that I'd re-recruited our ex-guitarist and committed us to a live performance in just four weeks' time. Woops.

Worse, the timing coincided with Alicia's long-awaited return to England and what she assumed would be a joyous, romantic reunion after a gruelling twenty-hour coach journey from 'Cesky Tesin', Czech Republic to Victoria Station, SW1E. As she stepped off the bus with all her belongings in a suitcase the size and weight of a Trabant (non-runner), I broke it to her that we needed to get a wiggle on as I had rehearsals that night.

The gig was on the following Tuesday. Bad timing. Few classic rock 'n' roll songs celebrate Tuesday night, even fewer when the one in question follows the first weekend payday after Christmas. We weren't exactly sharp either, a fact not lost on the fella Andy managed to drag down from the record label, Arista. Well, he said he was from Arista. We never found out if he really represented a record company because we never heard from him again after that night.

We opened our set with 'Written in Your Eyes' and from the word go I knew something was wrong. There was this strange, breathless voice coming through my fold-back monitor on every chorus. Imagine Inspector Clouseau on a treadmill. It got so bad that I started singing, *Written on my ears!* Instead for the chorus.

At first, I assumed it was my brother Andy getting hammered with the PA guy, as was his recent MO at gigs. Then it dawned on me. The band that had opened for us that night was a Genesis tribute act called 'Penesis' (I possibly made that up). If you know your Genesis, you'll know that their drummer post Peter Gabriel was also their lead vocalist AKA Phil Collins. And so, it had to be with 'Penesis'. So, doing a bit of Clouseau tribute acting of my own, I deduced that the breathless (and aptly French) heavy breathing was emanating from our drummer, Big Dave. I hadn't realised he could even sing (the jury is still out on that one too).

Not that muting Big Dave would've saved us that night. The gig was summed up when, as I shook the hand of the Arista enigma, some slob puked all over my boots and jeans.

Rumours circulated afterwards that the up chucker in question was in fact my newlywed bride. It's never been proved either way, but I'm told there's a 'smoking gun' photo somewhere. If this is true then it is unlikely to ever see the light of day, unless of course that fucking 'ruined wedding dress' ever gets mentioned again.

The final insult came a few weeks later though, when I phoned The Red Lion again to book another gig. Owner Brian Peters himself took the call and mistaking me for Andy, immediately launched into a scathing tirade against the band's lack of potency and its singer (namely me) was in for less than favourable praise. "Hurricane Jane was a 'load of old rubbish the other night, their singer has lost it as a frontman," he told me. "The band should get rid of him."

I didn't, couldn't, let on. I agreed that he (I) was a spent force and thanked Brian for his forthright views.

Back to the drawing board for Hurricane Jane. Again.

And back to The Cherry Tree pub for me. Not just for its three glorious barmaids (you still know who you are and were) but also because Sean, it's Geordie owner, was a top fellow and the clientele were becoming like family to me.

So, when Sean asked me to 'help out' at a charity fair at the pub one Saturday in March, I didn't hesitate. I readily agreed to put myself at his disposal in any capacity he saw fit for me, which as it turned out, was to be supervising the bouncy castle. Out in the garden, tucked away behind the pub, safely away from everyone else and perhaps more importantly. the bar and its clientele. What could possibly go wrong?

Well, you know those moments when time sort of seems to stand still. When you're seemingly powerless to stop yourself acting out what feels at the time, to be like a pre-written and scripted farce? Almost like you're an observer, rather than an actor, in your own little comedy play? Yeah, that.

On the day of the fair, the weather had started off quite dull and dingy, typical March really. Not like the one we had recently at the start of lockdown in 2020, When it was hotter than Ibiza and we were all furloughed at 'pissed o' clock' from ten in the morning every day. Only after we'd all done our Joe Wicks family workouts of course! So naturally by mid-morning the inflatable fortress had seen only two takers.

As the clouds got even darker and we started preparing for torrential rain, along a came a lady with a large young girl in a dress many times too small for her. The girl quite obviously had Down's syndrome, but what was most noticeable (although you tried not to look obviously) about her was how 'blessed around the chest' area (or 'balcony' as 'Big Dave' would describe it) she was.

The lady, who I learned later was the girl's carer, asked me if I would mind the girl on the bouncy castle while she went to the bathroom. I reluctantly agreed, but my instinct immediately told me that this was going to be a very bad decision.

My instinct was spot on. As the bouncy castle's third punter of the day started furiously pogoing, her bra loosened itself to the point that it came off. Did she put it back on? Nope. She lifted her jumper right up, flashed her tits at me and started shouting. "Do it! Do it! Do it!"

I dread to think what 'it' was and more worryingly, I didn't have a clue what to do.

The next few moments happened in slow motion. I don't know why but I kicked off my shoes, mounted the large, inflated object (the static one) and reached out to get this poor girl's bra and jumper back to where they should both be (covering her dignity). All while she was still jumping up and down exhorting me to 'do it!'

Not a great look. It's one thing to slip a girl's bra off – it comes with practice – but it's quite another to put one back on a moving target.

Which is exactly what I was trying to do when the girl's carer, Sean the manager, the Mayor of the London Borough of Richmond upon Thames, his wife, a photographer from the

Richmond and Twickenham Times and Uncle Tom Cobbly and all, suddenly appeared all at once by the bouncy castle.

As the mortified carer took in the scene, she broke down. "Oh my God. Oh my God," she cried. "I'm so sorry, I left you." I, meanwhile, had visions of a day in court that would make Conn's and Dean's experience look like a bouncy car sale frolic.

As the dignitaries and the pap looked on, I heard myself say, "It's not what you think, I was trying to put it back on." I still shudder at the inadequacy of that response.

Still, the Cherry Tree family had a good laugh about it at my expense that evening. My own personal 'Storm in A D Cup' or 'faux pas with a bra', was the catalyst for many gags like 'it's a fit up, your honour' and 'where's Matt? At the bra struggling to get a round' set the tone for the whole of that session.

I tell you what though, my first pint of Courage 'Breast' went down well that night.

As I was revelling in that newfound infamy, I got chatting to a regular called Gordon who had found the whole thing utterly hilarious, which to be fair it really was. Gordon was always immaculately turned out, was undoubtedly minted and liked to surround himself with young lads.

And he drank shit loads.

We chatted away, eventually getting onto the subject of music. It turned out he loved Guns 'n' Roses and was involved with a theatrical agency that was working with one or two well-known folks. One thing led to another (not like that) and I played him my demo (I always carried a C90 cassette tape in my pocket just in case) and told him we were also on the lookout for a new guitarist.

Then bang, just like that, he wanted to manage us and help us find one by placing an advert in Sounds or the NME!

One thing I didn't openly discuss with this fella was his sexuality. But it was blatantly obvious to me that, as a cricketing legend once put it, that he "Preferred to receive his bowling from the pavilion end".

Not that I had a problem with that, but I knew it might take some smoothing over with Big Dave. Today, while we are still some ways from perfect, most civilised societies do embrace sexual diversity and gender fluidity much better than they did back in the early 1990s. Thank God.

You see here was your typical Frenchman who couldn't comprehend that any man could ever be truly homosexual and then me telling him that the person I wanted to become our next manager was possibly of that persuasion.

To help convince him, I told him about a French movie called Les Nuits Fauves (Savage Nights). It's about a camera man and aspiring film director who is HIV positive yet still has lots of unprotected sex. With people of both genders.

It sort of worked and Gordon became our new manager.

With Paul's second stint with the band nearing its end – he would soon depart for the bright lights of LA – and the Jane finding its Epstein (Brian, not Jeffrey) there was a sense of renewal in the air. We stepped up our search for a new guitarist, or 'Clitarist', as Simon's French girlfriend Chantelle use to pronounce it. During this period, to get my childish giggle of the day, I'd often steer any conversation I had with Chantelle onto this subject just to get her to say it. "'ave you found your new 'Clitarist' yet?"

Next, we organised a series of rehearsals and auditions at Survival Studios in Acton, expecting day after day of drudgery and an endless flow of 'drongos', misfits, wannabes and other ne'er do wells. But fuck me, what happens? We go and sign up to two prime candidates on the first night.

Jason Porter was from near Beckton Heights in East London. He loved all things American, especially Bon Jovi. He was a great lead guitarist and with his long hair and double denim, rocked the Jane look. He kept changing his surname from Porter to Lee to Pride Fuck knows why but anyway we christened him the 'Leytonstone Cowboy'.

Also excellent was Woody. Not Allen, Harrelson or Sheriff Woody Pride, just Paul 'Woody Woods' from New Malden. Woody was a little bit timid and totally overpowered by his domineering girlfriend, Alida, but give him a 'Clitar 'and he'd turn into a beast. I mean he could properly tear it up. He looked the part, too.

So rather than decide between the two, we tried out the twin 'Clitarist' format. It was bloody excellent – to start with, anyway – so Hurricane Jane (summer 1993 vintage) started plotting its two-pronged, twin-axe attack on the rock venues of southwest London.

Happy with my recruitment of a new manager and not one but two guitarists, I left the band to its own devices and buggered off to Antigua with Alicia for a better-late-than-never 'proper' honeymoon.

Chapter 11
Finding Your Way Back Home

"Heading down this road that goes on forever."

Jason Lee Porter Pride showing us all the way home while Simon
sits this one out, March 1994

I promised Alicia I wouldn't go into too much detail about the
honeymoon. It is, though, the holiday against which we've

judged every trip we've made ever since. And we've made a few.

We stayed at a guest house in the town of St Johns and spent most days taking a minibus to Turners Beach on Antigua's western coast. When not sunbathing, we'd find ways to immerse ourselves in the Caribbean culture, a habit that won us many new friends among the locals. They called us 'Snowflake' and 'Pussycat'. No prizes for guessing who was who?

It was the perfect trip but for one thing. By the end of it, I'd had enough steel drums and Bob Marley to last me a lifetime. One night, for some light relief I borrowed a cassette player from 'Mein Host' and, from our balcony, tried the locals out with Icon's 'A Far Cry' from their album 'Between the Eyes'.

'He was born in New York on a subway train'

Get a load of that, reggae fans!

Unfortunately, the only reggae fan that engaged was a horny black goat. In fact, it got attached to us to the point where our very religious hostess rushed out of her office brandishing a wooden broom to chase the 'cloven-hoofed follower of Satan' away.

So, 1–0 to rock 'n' roll. But it wouldn't last. The steel drum rules supreme in the Caribbean and even the cassette player reverted to type and defaulted to 'Jammin' when I wasn't looking. 1–1.

Another highlight – or low light – was Alicia knocking the electrics out for the entire street when she fused the toaster. We took our bread raw that morning but the German fella next door who we left powerless mid-electric shave wasn't so easy to placate. "Vot is going on? ...Hey you in zere!" We lay low, giggling uncontrollably as he knocked on our door aggressively as we ourselves pictured in our heads the asymmetric facial 'Herr' on the other side of the wall.

We then sneaked out to a party on the Jolly Roger cruise boat. Having been on board for a while awaiting to depart, the captain advised us to go easy on the rum punches as they were 'very, very strong'. Too late, mate. We'd had four each already and there would be several more. By the end of the night, we were into our first full-blown barney of our fledgling marriage. Great times.

Incurable romantics that we are, we were making up almost straight away. Then remembering that someone had told us Whitney Houston and Bobby Brown were holidaying on the island at the same time as us, we spontaneously broke into 'And Iiiiiiiiiiiiiiiiiii, will always love Youuuuu' as we staggered back from the dock. Again, none of the locals were impressed. Not even the cloven-hoofed follower of Satan, this time although we did set a few stray dogs off howling in the distance.

Probably my crowning glory from that trip (the one I am allowed to share) was blagging seats on the BA staff-chartered flight that got us there. An old college friend, Tom Deszburg, knew a bloke called Mark who we both went to college with who worked at BA. Tom got Mark (thanks Mark) to pull a few strings for us and get us on the 'posh' plane. Boarding a half empty charter aircraft to the Caribbean made for a great start to the flight. Telling the cabin crew that we were honeymooning got us treated like decadents for rest of it.

We've pulled the newlyweds act off a few times since, to great effect. It's not so easy these days, mind – not with two teenage kids in tow!

Tom D was of Polish origin and thoroughly approved of my marrying into his kind. He loved AC/DC (just like me), revered Bon Scott (just like me) and was highly intelligent (ahem). Having done the dirty BA deed dirt cheap for us he expressed an interest in getting involved in the management of the band. So, before we left for Antigua, I introduced Tom D to Gordon at The Cherry Tree. They got on famously so agreed to work together for the good of the Jane.

Once back from honeymoon, I was ready to 'find my way back home', home being the stage. But home in the literal sense needed addressing, too. Now married, it was far from ideal for us to continue our 'ménage a trois' with Conn, so Alicia and I took out a rental on a one-bed flat in Larkfield Road, around the back and up the hill from Richmond Station. Our first marital home!

I was as excited with the band's new line-up as I had been with the Mk 2 line up of '86 and itching to see what Gordon and Tom had cooked up in my absence. I couldn't wait to unleash the new Hurricane Jane on an unsuspecting public.

Hurricane Jane Mk4's assault on the world – twin 'Clitarists' an' all – was booked for its first ever gig by Gordon… at…wait for it… 'The Cock Inn', in Edmonton. to be precise…What a fucking surprise!

The name of the pub alone (chosen at random) should have set alarm bells ringing. But Tom and Gordon were proud of what they'd lined up, Gordon especially so, so we went with it.

Until we got there.

The pub was slap bang in the heart of a 'tough' social housing development comprising of several tower blocks. In one of its windows was a sheet of white paper on which someone had handwritten in pen:

Hurricane Jane…Tonight…It's Heavy metal maaaan!

Was that really the best they could come up with? Seven words, an ellipsis and a piss take of an exclamation mark. They made the event look like an afterthought and us look like a bunch of hippy dropouts. "Oh yeah," it mattered. "Some band who are like Neil from the Young Ones will be here later." It really got my goat (and not my Antiguan buddy).

It got worse.

Inside, tables were being set for dinner right in front of the miniscule stage by an elderly guy who had ears sticking out like the 'FA Cup 'and didn't even bother saying 'Hello' to us.

Where proper venues have a PA system, this joint had two tiny speakers. And the saloon bar next door was full of pissed up 'swearing' skinheads in bomber jackets and DM's 'larking about playing darts and pool – a kind of warm up before getting stuck into some long-haired 'hippies' like us, just for the hell of it I suppose.

The provocative stares started the minute we walked in, and I made the decision there and then. No way were we playing this shithole. They can fuck right off.

Gordon was annoyed by our point-blank refusal to play, so we took a vote. As a group we were overwhelmingly in favour of us pulling out of playing with his Cock Inn. (You knew I'd get there eventually, right?)

We hadn't unloaded any of our gear, so we went straight to Survival Studios in Acton for a rehearsal instead.

Not my proudest moment but some 30 years on, the Cock Inn cock up remains the only gig commitment I've personally ever failed to fulfil on the day. Ironic really, given that, geographically, it's the closest to my beloved Spurs I'd ever had the chance to play.

I think we dodged a bullet, though. I've since played to countless audiences of a similar profile to The Cock Inn's clientele and nine times out of ten the nuanced wit and sophistication of Hurricane Jane's lyrics is lost on the boneheaded boozers who stand there calling out for Ska, Two Tone, Weller or Oasis.

We had little time to dwell on the episode because in almost no time, we were slated to appear at the Royal Standard in Walthamstow, again not too far from Spurs!

We were there to support some indie band who had just been on telly and had a single out called Tourniquet. Don't ask me who they were as I've forgotten. I haven't forgotten what an arrogant fellow their singer was, though. I took an instant dislike to him when I caught him sniggering dismissively at us, as we wrapped up our allotted ten-minute soundtrack. *Okay, so you're an indie band and we're rock outfit*, I thought inwardly as I scowled sweetly in his direction. *We're still gonna go for it, though.*

And we did. We gave a bloody good account of ourselves too. Woody's blistering guitar solo on Through Hell and Heartbreak will live long in the memory. We picked up a couple of new fans and, best of all, the venue wanted us back!

They offered us a choice. Headline or support act for Suzi Quatro. I say a choice, but the decision was kind of taken out of our hands when I shared with the promoter that I'd had my first ever wank over sexy Suzi*. I mean not literally obviously!

So, just to be on the safe side he diplomatically put us down for the headline slot instead. So, there's some good advice for any aspiring young band s out there, reading this. Take it from me. If you ever want a headline slot anywhere, just admit to being a total wanker and you'll get it for sure!

*It was a lie anyway. It was over Debbie Harry, but I didn't envisage Blondie hitting Walthamstow any time soon. Or ever reading this, for that matter.

Chapter 12
In Through the Back Door

"You kiss ass before you kick some too, you bite your lip before you cut a few."

Living 'Alida' Loca, the five-piece Jane with Woody shredding like a 'mofo' under orders from his missus, October 1993

It was great to be back up and gigging again. We were loud and proud once more. So much so that even Brian Peters softened his stance and welcomed us back to The Red Lion in Brentford. This time, I could see he was impressed. We'd pulled in a decent crowd and were bossing it on stage in front of loads of new followers. "Even the singer" had apparently regained his 'Mojo' according to Brian!

It wasn't all good that night though. For some reason, about halfway through our set, Woody's guitar lead started malfunctioning intermittently. But rather than style it out and replace it at the end of the song, he stormed off stage in a strop. Immediately I was thankful for Alida's overpowering influence over him. Like many in the audience I watched in awe as she pinned Woody up against the wall and, I assume, ordered him back on stage, an instruction he duly obeyed.

Alida's fury clearly had a similar effect on the guitar lead as well because it too behaved itself for the rest of the gig. Both finished the set strongly.

I was on a high, but deflation was imminent. When the gig was over, Gordon and Tom ripped into me about my on-stage image.

I couldn't understand it. What was wrong with standard denim jeans and American NFL or baseball shirts? It wasn't like I was still in my 80s' mode, where, okay, maybe I overdid the zebra striped spandex, cream leg warmers and boxing boots look once or twice. And the blond hair dye, obviously, which started as a stunt for my 21st birthday party. My sister, Kate, helped me out with it and applied the colour but something went drastically wrong. The following day, a Sunday, as I awoke the sun reflected off my lurid orange 'Barnet' and lit up the flat, Conn went into paroxysms. At football that day, they called me Ronald, as in 'you want fries with that?' I wasn't lovin' it.

Not only did Tom and Gordon not approve of my clothes, but they also took a dim view of the frequent exposure of my gut. They advised me in no uncertain terms that it was time for a sartorial makeover.

To prove they meant it, they took me to some swanky store in Covent Garden, from which a reinvented and admittedly classier new me emerged. They picked up the tab between them as well.

From now on I'd be all about black silk shirts, mauve and black velvet waistcoats, black cowboy boots and a black leather biker jacket to arrive at venues in. Get me.

I debuted this new look at a Battle of the Bands competition at The Swan in Fulham. I hate the reductive format of these things. Music is about individual taste, which in turn is influenced by a person's mood at any given time. Sometimes I want heavy metal, other times classic rock, or maybe even a bit of punk. They all do great things for me but just don't ask me to decide between them.

In my experience, a Battle of the Bands winner is usually the entrant that best aligns with the various biases and musical preferences of the judges present at the time, not necessarily the act demonstrating the more thoughtful song writing, great musicianship or performance and stagecraft, etc. (stick around – I'll prove this later). To Simon Cowell I say, big respect for what you've achieved for yourself and all the wannabe mirror-and-hairbrush performers. But mate, that isn't where it's at as far as I'm concerned. Incidentally, Simon's brother Nick who owns the Bike Shed in London is a top fellow though and really into his rock!

Anyway, we'd been signed up, so we played our part. We didn't win the competition (how could we when one of the judges had entered his own band?) But we did win the crowd. Which was gratifying as many of them were quite a few of my own work colleagues. Even better, some of them who weren't that into Rock initially, began following the band around for some time afterwards, too.

This even spawned a couple of 'Rock 'n' Rave' gigs (one at the Red lion in Brentford) where we hired a friend, DJ Paul to play his own hypnotic mix of 'Dance and Trance' music in between our sets, it never quite caught on, but both nights were a lot of fun.

One of these new followers was 'Dangerous' Dave, a delivery driver and as such a familiar face around goods inwards at Sexton's. People told me to avoid him like the plague because he was apparently a right 'bullshitter' and a diabolical' timewaster'.

So, naturally I sought him out. And we got on like a house on fire (Havers again). He wasn't just a bullshitter; he was a *highly advanced* bullshitter. He packed his stories with impeccable attention to detail, involving real life events and verifiable references.

They were all still total, utter bollocks, but each in their own way, uniquely brilliant in their conception and creativity, though. Like the one about how he got former West Ham and Scotland striker Frank McAvennie arrested after fisticuffs over a dalliance with his two-timing girlfriend. None other than British Olympic gymnast, 'Bond' girl and television presenter, Suzanne Dando.

And the one about how he was Robert Plant's hospital carer when the legendary singer broke his leg. Dave told me he accidentally got Plant's plastered leg stuck in a lift door, and through some circuitous route, inspired the Led Zeppelin song, *Trampled Under Foot*.

And (my favourite) the one about how Dangerous Dave's dad singlehandedly contained the great 1950s' East London rat infestation – a crisis I didn't want to appear ignorant of then but on which I've found no record or mention of since.

Nevertheless, the story goes that Dave, then a mere toddler, accompanied his dad via 'piggy backing' his shoulders, one foggy night to the riverbanks of the Thames on the eastern part of Old London Town. On request, young Dangerous would pull dynamite sticks from a canvas bag and pass them to his dad, who would then light them from his pipe and hurl them into strategic locations alongside the fetid-smelling Thames. "No word of a lie, Matt, the problem cleared up overnight," said the son of the legendary 'Pie (and mash) Piper from Tower Hamlets'.

Course it did. I was fond of Dangerous, though and when my kids were young, I never told them a bedtime tale without judging myself against his prodigious storytelling talent. I liked him even more when one night he made the journey across London to support the band at The Royal Standard in Walthamstow.

I lost touch with Dangerous after leaving Sextons but some ten years later I asked after him when I met a Target driver from the same depot. He paused for a moment, not knowing who I was on about. Then I mentioned the 'rat bombing' story and his face lit up briefly, then turned sad. "He's brown bread mate. I never met him personally, but I heard he was decapitated in a multiple car crash."

I was shocked and saddened by the news, but also reminded of yet another Dangerous Dave yarn. In this one, he'd bought a cut and shut, a vehicle in which the front end of one car is welded to the back end of another. This abomination had the nose of a Porsche and the arse of a Ferrari. If you believed Dangerous, the two sections parted company at the M25/M40 intersection, the Porsche and Dave heading towards Oxford while the Ferrari (with his wife and kids still on board) continued to orbit London.

I couldn't shake the suspicion that, somehow, Dave had perhaps managed to bullshit his own death. In a strange kind of way, I hoped that maybe like at the end of The Shawshank Redemption he was perhaps on a beach somewhere in Mexico painting a boat…Or just maybe blowing up more rats!

Well, if you are reading this Dave, wherever you are? Please get in touch, you never finished your 'Lord Lucan riding Shergar' story…

With a new sound, a new image and a growing following, the time was right to record another demo. We chose our set opener, Through Hell and Heartbreak and two from the previous demo, Written in Your Eyes and City at Night and got to work on Jason's Porta studio.

Unfortunately, the recording coincided with a deterioration in Jason and Woody's working relationship. With Jason taking the lead on the production side of things (because it was his Porta studio) Woody felt relegated to the role of guitarist number two. The overall result was a bit of a hotch-potch or 'Hudsput' as I believe the Dutch call it and there was more than a whiff of 'I told you so' about the result.

It was by now almost Christmas, so to lift morale in the band, I floated the idea of a band members' Christmas dinner party with wives and girlfriends…RAGS!

If you're in a band and you've toyed with this idea? Please, take my advice. Just don't!

Big Dave, the band's sole singleton at that time, took a rain check and in so doing made an excellent decision.

What we effectively did that night was throw a young Polish woman (still at loggerheads with immigration over her right to live in the UK despite being married to me for a year), a tempestuous French femme, a fiery redhead and highly strung overpowering English lass into a melting pot and doused it with alcohol.

Nobody died, but as the couples retreated, arguing and bickering, to their respective beds that night, a whole new world of grudges and gripes was born.

The first casualty was Woody. Shortly after our 'party' he quit the band citing musical differences and a yearning for a new musical direction. I was sad, I liked him a lot and admired his talent.

The second casualty was our musical identity. It was 1994 and the music scene had changed beyond recognition during the years I'd spent getting Hurricane Jane going. We were the product of AC/DC, Def Leppard, Van Halen era influences strutting our stuff while the likes of Nirvana, Soundgarden, Rage Against the Machine, Korn and Green Day were taking over. Lines between indie, alternative rock and post punk were blurring. Oasis and Blur were staging their media-fuelled 'Battle of the Bands' and in so doing, ushering in Brit Pop.

It was a thriving scene, and the Jane was nowhere near it. Our 'balls-out' eighties rock style suddenly felt antiquated and against the grain. And we were now reduced to a four-piece.

Just as well then that I had a cunning plan.

Chapter 13
Shake the Sugar

"Alright, it's late at night, my head's shaking 'cos it don't feel right."

Jason showing off his fancy fretboard skills without a Kleenex – or a red dress – in sight, February 1995

As well as being a man short in the band, we were short of commitment at management level, too. Gordon, now drinking more heavily than ever, was losing interest and Tom, whose chemistry with Dave and Simon was never great at the best of times, was finding himself more and more immersed in his day job, which must be said, he was very good at and still is today.

A malaise had set in, so once again it was time to hit the reset button on the Jane.

The first decision we made was to get a change of scenery, which we accomplished by moving our rehearsals from Survival Studios in Acton to Westbourne Studios in Paddington. It made sense as Dave had now moved to East London to be nearer his work at HMV so he could travel in with Jason, who lived there already, and Simon was based in Acton, so it was only a short hop for him. I commuted by tube from Richmond, sometimes being picked up by Simon on route.

The next step was to generate some new material. So, as I began jamming out some new ideas and riffs, everyone else joined in as well. It was energising and the start of what was to be the most creative period for this version of the band. Lipstick Lies, for which I already had the lyrics for, came together very quickly, with Simon and Dave laying down a solid rolling rhythm, Jason adding his 'Riff-tastic' guitar lick and myself overlaying the whole thing with the required raucous vocals about my Lancastrian phone Sex worker friends.

That's how you make great rock 'n' roll, out of pre-marital phone sex in an area made famous by a 'Royalty approved' marmalade eating, bear from Peru!

In fact, the organic and cathartic nature of the song writing process behind Lipstick Lies became the template for how we'd want to write future material. As for the song itself, it was so powerful it became our new set opener.

Then Jason came up with two new songs. The first was a slow ballad about finding your way back home, which I wasn't sure If he meant metaphorically speaking, or he genuinely was just into navigating and orienteering! Essentially it was Poison's 'Every Rose has its Thorn' at a slightly different tempo (and less prickly flower stems), but it worked. We needed a lighter-held-aloft ballad in our oeuvre, and this was most definitely it!

The other one was a stonkingly good up-tempo track that he called 'Shake the Sugar'. I couldn't be one hundred percent sure, but I think it was all about hand jobs. Whether or not it was conceived that way, I followed my instinct and reworked the lyrics accordingly. If indeed it was about something other than self-gratification, I don't think many people would've got it.

But that said, why should Ivor Biggun and The Vapors have the 'wank rock' genre all to themselves, great track though that *Turning Japanese* is?

'Shake the Sugar' also became a great live number for us. Not so great, however was Jason's third contribution to our creative explosion. It was about a girl who kept slipping in and out of a red dress but none of us really fell in love with it. We ditched the track, but I don't think Jason ever let go of that dress. Funny that current NWOCR heroes Massive Wagons (A big shout out to Baz their singer by the way, top fella he is) seemed to have resurrected the idea on their brilliant 'House of Noise' album recently, so maybe Jason was just ahead of his time!

Not to be outdone, Simon pitched in with a funky, catchy rhythm bass line upon which we constructed another favourite. It was a power ballad that I decided to match to some lyrics I had written about believing in something you were in danger of losing, such as a young Eastern European girl who made great potato pancakes for instance. We called it "If you still believe" and again it was a song that seemed to go down very well live.

Then finally there was my own contribution, which as always, had a story behind it.

With our management in limbo, I'd decided to step up and try my hand at getting the band the gigs, the exposure and the PR it desperately needed and, in my opinion at least, deserved. Over the years I'd become quite well connected with promoters, venues and established musicians, so nothing ventured...

Gut Reaction, a promotion company and label, had shown interest in the band when Andy managed us back in early 1991. However, the timing back then was bad. We were reeling from the Astoria gig and Justin, our keyboard player, had left us to play frisbee in Marlow, so we'd put the rep off from coming to our rehearsal.

Time to renew contact and see if there was still interest. So, in my capacity of player-manager of Hurricane Jane, I booked a meeting with Gut Reaction's founder and owner, Guy Holmes and arrived at his office in Maida Vale at the appointed time armed with the band's two demos.

As I was walking up the stairs, two baldies in shades were walking down. I watched them leave the building and climb inside the limo that was waiting outside for them.

That'll be me if I play the next hour right, I thought to myself, (The Limo ride that is, not the bald heads, obviously).

I had no idea who the baldies were. I wasn't massively into the pop scene – if they weren't in Kerrang, Metal Hammer or Rustler magazine they didn't exist to me. So, if Gut Reaction can get that sort of vibe going for a couple of boneheads in sunglasses, they could do the same for the Jane. That was my thinking as I sat down with Guy and hit him with my demo, my passion, my enthusiasm and my unshakeable faith in myself and the band.

It got me nowhere.

As Guy's secretary showed me to the door, she pointed to a picture and framed gold disc on the wall and said to me without a hint of sincerity. "Sorry, it didn't work out but if you come up with something as quirky and cool as these guys, you might be able to get another shot."

It was the guys I'd passed on the stairs. None other than Right Said Fred.

Of course, I'd have to be 'deeply dippy' to believe that having Justin around at that rehearsal in '91 would have made any difference, but I was a bit pissed off. When I got home, I ripped off the shirt (I was obviously far too sexy for) plugged in my guitar and started bashing out some chords to let off steam.

Before long I had come up with a very, dirty, heavy riff that seemed to reflect my current mood. Then I started mumbling random lyrics over the top of it. Some stream of consciousness shit, about walking the streets where everybody knew my name and letting rip because secretly everybody, whether they admitted it or not, knew that they wanted to 'rock' really! I was saying stuff like "You know

you want it; you know you need it" and "You got to have it".
But just couldn't find the pay-off, line on the chorus.

I put the telly on. Channel 4 was showing The Comic Strip
presents…The Yob. It was about an arty music director and
Arsenal hooligan who, being the subject of an experiment in
a public toilet, switches personalities in a scientific matter
transportation contraption setup. A bit like 'The Fly'.

It was just a few minutes in before Keith Allen's character
slapped his posh girlfriend's arse and snarled, "You know you
love it." I bloody did love it! And I knew I had to have it. My
mind wandered. My thoughts turned to The Sweeney, Ray
Winstone and then Bob Hoskins in The Long Good Friday.

I let it all incubate and decided that 'You know you love
it, you "schlaaags"'! My angry Finger in the air response to
the music industry, was my chorus 'pay-off' line. In fact, all I
had to do now was convince the rest of the band to play it.

Once David and Simon had stopped laughing and picked
themselves up off the studio floor, Jason had exhausted all his
American alternatives ('Shmucks and Jerkoffs' just didn't
fit) they went for it and the result was utterly glorious.

Although Dave himself didn't contribute any new
material as far as the song writing process itself went, His
powerful drumming was paramount and played a key role as
the songs evolved from their embryonic stage and
underpinned just about everything we did.

We were also all getting on well personally,
professionally and socially together. We shared a lot of
private stuff too with each other. I remember one rehearsal
where we played truth or dare. One of the guys (I will not let
on who) let slip that he enjoyed being interfered with anally,
particularly with suitably shaped inanimate objects.

Dave was naturally appalled. Placing one drumstick horizontally between his teeth and holding the other vertically up to his face, he effected a mock crucifix sign to prevent the notion getting anywhere near him. The confessor then shared that those inanimately inserted objects even included drumsticks and Dave visibly wilted. That was when we learned that Dave had indeed borrowed some sticks that very evening from Hurricane Jane's 'anything goes' bum fetishist.

I should perhaps mention at this point) especially as the band 'member' in question (who shall remain anonymous) having read a draught of this manuscript, wanted it pointed out that the act was never actually carried out alone but always in the presence of his girlfriend!

Gross though it may be to some, this shared intimacy was the catalyst for a new' *Us against the outside world'* mentality that was starting to grow. It was a *'they-don't-like-us-we-don't-care'* kind of vibe.

Hurricane Jane. 'The Millwall of Metal'.

So, we had some great new material and, for the first time in years, real esprit de corps. What we needed now was gigs. I had quite a wish list of venues I wanted us to play and a goal of getting back to the Marquee. My big handicap at this time was that I still hadn't learned to drive, I do now thankfully! so getting around to meet promoters and venue owners like a proper manager should was more problematic than it really should have been.

Enter Mr Tony Willet, plumber and fellow Larkfield Road resident. Tony kindly agreed to drive me around the pubs and clubs of Southwest London. With his help I managed to secure slots at places like The Rock Garden, The Borderline, The Kings Head, Fulham and The Half Moon, Putney. My strategy at this point was to offer the band up as a support act. It took away the pressure of trying to drum up an audience and we were confident our killer 40-minute set would leave people gagging for more.

We weren't disappointed. Many a headliner regretted allowing us to open for them I can tell you.

We christened Tony, The Road Manager and always referred to him as such in a deep post-apocalyptic Australian drawl. Think the closing scenes of Mad Max 2. "We never saw the road warrior again." Writing this post Covid-19 lockdown, it feels vaguely apt all over again. And, I haven't seen The Road Manager for a while, so I'll try and put that right soon.

We had an arrogant swagger about us now. We were going into other bands' backyards and wiping the floor with them. And we didn't care whether their fans liked it or not. But it still wasn't enough to convince the Marquee's promoter to put us back on.

I had no choice but to enact that cunning plan. Now, call me conniving, call me clever or just simply call me a cunt, but whatever the plan worked.

David Hoyland, an old friend, was the drummer in a band called Crocodile Smile. Robin Yates was another musical mate and played the bass in a band called Trash Ville (formerly Jokers Wild). I'd met up with them a lot over the years, played with them at various venues and seen them around various Rock clubs like The Clarendon in Hammersmith, Jesters in Kingston and The Agincourt in Camberley.

I started a conversation with them about how our three bands should maybe do some kind of 'Dinosaurs of Rock' or

'Triple Trouble' Tour. Well, that or maybe just one-off gig at least.

They were up for it. The only questions were around who would headline and where this 'Monsters of Metal 'event might take place. "Leave it to me," I said.

The next day I spoke to the Marquee's promoter. I outlined the 'dinosaur' concept and then relayed to him the absolute fiction, that whilst Crocodile Smile and Trash Ville both had decent enough followings, both bands were adamant that they'd only take part if we (Hurricane Jane) were the headline act, as we obviously had the biggest pull (which was so not true).

He 'hummed and erred' but eventually agreed to give me a date with us as the headline.

Over beers with Robin and Dave a day or two later, I affected part three of my cunning plan an impulse brainwave. "Guys actually, I just remembered something. I don't know if this will work but we've got a gig coming up at The Marquee next month, we booked it ages ago and the support band has just pulled out. Why don't you guys join us on that… I mean if the Marquee agrees to it that is… I can phone and ask at least…It would save us looking for another venue."

Their eyes lit up, just as mine had done three years before. The Marquee. The mecca for all aspiring bands. It was a no brainer. They knew they loved it. Okay, now you can really call me a cunt but, we and they, were back at the Marquee and that's all that mattered…For now at least!

Maybe 1994 really was going to be the 'Year of the Jane'.

Chapter 14
Hurricane Jane

**"Open your heart, but don't give it away, and you will
live to fight another day."**

*Headlining the Marquee with a very
'Trashy Crocodile Smile', 1994*

Or maybe not.

I think it was the comedian and TV presenter Michael
McIntyre that said the only unwritten justifications for waking
your other half up in the middle of the night are for either the

fall of snow or the death of a celebrity. I was there when he said it because when Adrian Cumber, (aka Rox), our guitarist from the early days of PSO and Hurricane Jane became a comedy promoter (rock 'n' roll can do that to a man), he actually gave McIntyre his first ever paid, stand-up gig.

Anyway, it was the first week of April. There was no snow but there was a celebrity death. And not just any old celebrity. On 5 April 1994, Kurt Cobain, vocalist in Nirvana, pioneer and figurehead of grunge took his own life.

I was livid. It was my 30th birthday and I took it personally. I'm not sure why he did it but obviously his life was in more of a 'hole' than his wife Courtney's was. (See what I did there?)

I despised grunge at the time, but have learnt to like and appreciate it more over the years It was Just at the time it seemed to be the enemy and total antithesis of what we were trying to do. And now this. Don't get me wrong. If a man is so tortured that he feels his only option is to kill himself, I can only sympathise with his plight. He alone knew what he was going through, and my thoughts really were with him and all those he left behind.

I felt especially sorry for his young daughter then just two years old. Daughters trust their dads unconditionally.

Well at least mine used to. When my daughter, Zosia, was five, a bloody great pigeon flew into our big pane glassed windows, breaking its neck and collapsing in a bloody heap at her feet.

I had to think quickly. I took the pigeon and buried it at the bottom of the garden. I then handed Zosia my 'magic' watering can and told her that if she closed her eyes, watered the ground and said 'Abracadabra', the pigeon would grow back.

And it did. Sort of. As Zosia went through the motions (as instructed), another pigeon soon appeared on the scene.

"Open your eyes, darling," I said. Zosia's eyes opened and then lit up as she saw what she presumed to be the newly resurrected bird, "Thank you, Daddy! You saved him!"

Good Daddy.

The payback sadly came less than a year later, at a friend's house gathering, when all the parents were inside drinking and chatting merrily one Easter Bank Holiday, suddenly we all became aware of a huge commotion coming from outside, where all our children had been playing (up until that point at least) very happily. Soon after, Zosia came inside hardly able to contain herself and grabbed me by my hand and asked me to come outside where all the other kids were now lined up in a circle around a small mound of freshly piled earth and asked me to 'repeat my magic trick',

It soon became obvious the kids had found a dead mouse (fatally savaged by a cat) and had buried it in the garden. By the time the rest of the adults arrived outside, the makeshift grave was now complete with two sticks laid out horizontally in a makeshift cross on the top of it.! Handing, me a watering can, Zosia, with all the excitement and anticipation of a miracle about to be repeated written in her eyes, said, "Okay, now everyone, close your eyes. Daddy, do your Harry Potter thing."

Bad Daddy.

Anyway, going back to Mr Cobain's tragic demise, this was also a big blow for the Jane. Overnight, people who'd probably never even heard of Nirvana before, were suddenly claiming to be life-long fans who behaved like they'd lost a relative or limb. Almost anyone who owned a guitar and shoulder-length hair was forming a Nirvana tribute act and the band's album sales soared.

It did really feel like the final nail in the coffin for our form of hair metal.

Not that we were willing to grasp this reality. We'd secured the headline slot at the Marquee (heh!) Remember. It would take a lot more than simply being out of whack with the zeitgeist to knock us off our stride.

As I said I did make my peace with grunge and its followers many years later. At a Foo Fighters gig at Wembley Arena, about five songs into their blistering set, I raised my arms and beer glass in respect to the band. Then out of the blue, Dave Grohl suddenly picked me and my Superman T-shirt out of a crowd of around 14,000.

He said, "We know who our true fans are." Just as a reflected light shone off a glitterball on to my beer glass revealing the 'S' Crest on my T-shirt, about fifty rows back. Then, I absolutely know, without a shadow of a doubt, one hundred percent, that the self-styled 'nicest man in rock' dedicated the next track, *My Hero,* to me and said, "I'm also sorry. Kurt ruined your birthday, like forever!"

Great bloke that Dave Grohl and his book is truly awesome by the way!

However, it's tragic to report as I write this, that there has been another close death to him, That of his friend, Foo Fighters' drummer and 'brother in arms 'Taylor Hawkins, a terrible loss and one more for that ultimate gig in the heavens!

Back then when you played the Marquee, you did the sound check around mid-afternoon, leaving you free to hang out in London for a few hours before your performance. It was fun. You'd have a few beers sitting outside The Cambridge Arms on the corner of Charing Cross Road, see your name on the giant billboard outside the venue and then watch people strolling past looking at it and thinking, 'Who the fuck are those cunts?'

On the day in question, we got there at about 2.45 and found Crocodile Smile had beaten us to it. They were already setting their kit up on the main stage. They had quite an entourage too, if the multitude of 'Crocodile Smile Back at The Marquee' T-shirts were anything to go by. People who were 'with the band' were wandering around like they owned the fucking place. I must admit, we did get a bit of a kick out of watching the Sound guys and house management reminding them that that they weren't the headline act so could they please remove their kit and wait for the 'headline' act, (namely 'US') to complete our sound check, first...if they didn't mind?

After we had done the soundcheck and had our customary 'few beers' at the Cambridge, Big Dave decided to go 'walkabout' and promptly disappeared. In fact, he cut it so fine that as we prepared to go on stage, he still hadn't turned up, and we were still wondering if our set would go ahead at all.

Apparently, returning to the venue, Dave had taken a piss in an alleyway around the back, unaware of the policeman watching him. There was talk of a trip to Snow Hill Police Station, something about a caution and a lot of apologising as Big Dave zipped himself up. 'Oui, oui, monsieur,' he must have surely said at some point for sure, which is probably the only time anywhere in the world where this affirmative Gallic phrase had been uttered quite literally as a form of justification and defence.

Thankfully, he made it inside with about five minutes to spare. From that moment on, we had a great night. Some Crocodile Smile fans did 'their duty' and walked out in protest at their boys not being the headline act after the very first chord we played. All very petty and predictable but ultimately of no consequence to us at least. The place was still packed.

Trash Ville loved it though. They joined us on stage for our Hurricane Jane anthem and went on to support us many more times afterwards even getting a headline of their own later in the year.

The venue promoter loved it too. Whatever he thought of the bands, the 'kerching' of the tills behind the bar that night was the real music to his ears.

And we loved it. We were 'in' and I think we played there a further eight or nine times over the following 14 months or so. This might even be some sort of record for an unsigned band I don't know.

Other doors opened for us, too. As conquistadors of the Marquee, we were welcomed with open arms at venues that had routinely dismissed us in the past. We were bucking the trend. We were a force to be reckoned with.

We started spending more time in London and drinking in pubs favoured by the wannabees of our era. In places like The George on Charing Cross Road and The Intrepid Fox on Wardour St, I shot the breeze with musos like Tyla from The Dogs D'Amour and the guys from Therapy? Spike from The Quire boys who as I write this, coincidentally enough I will be supporting with the 'Ransom' boys (or will have supported by the time you read this) at a festival in October 2022. Proper 'Pirates' the lot of them!

Around this time, Jason also got us a gig at The Ruskin Arms in East Ham. It may sound like just another pub, but The Ruskin Arms was the venue that helped launch the careers of the Small Faces and more recently – and more significantly for us – Iron Maiden. Apparently, Judas Priest and Black Sabbath were also visitors during this seminal era.

The pub was now owned and run by an Indian fellow who also ran an Indian takeaway business next door. The deal was we'd be paid a tenner each and could choose anything off the menu for free after the gig. It was a better offer than most of the others we were attracting at the time, so we bit his Keema Naan off!

At one of my networking drinking sessions, I'd met an Italian girl called Lorenza. She'd just arrived in London and told me she was a big Maiden fan and was going to be living near The Ruskin Arms. So, once we'd sealed the tenner-and-takeaway deal, I let Lorenza know we'd be playing at her local.

She came along and she loved it. She also promised to come to our next gig and bring her boyfriend along too.

Lorenza was as good as her word. When we played the Half Moon in Putney a week later, she was there. With her boyfriend…none other than Paul Di'Anno, original lead singer with Iron Maiden.

And what a guy he was. Although he did spend most of our set telling the resident sound guy of 20 years there, Doon (now sadly passed), how to do his job and indeed what levels were best for my voice. "Use 23, yeah? That's what I fucking use anyway…" I had absolutely no clue what he was on about but as I was 'already 'Running free' with alcohol and as he was a living legend to me' I just nodded in agreement with him whilst also sporting a completely vacant expression across my face.

Not a namedrop alert. I've met and worked with a lot of famous people on my travels over the years, from all areas of TV, sport, stage and screen and am rarely fazed by it or them, in fact If was to start mentioning them all we'd be here all fucking night and you wouldn't believe half of them anyway.

From the Dalai Lama to Michael Caine, David Attenborough to Cher, Joe Wicks to Lemmy, there's quite an eclectic mix. But I was determined not to mention too many in this book because I think it just sounds needy and a bit naff. But suffice to say I've either met, drank or at least exchanged brief pleasantries with most of my musical and sporting heroes over the years, so I got on with Paul well, in fact I think he's even given me a dedication on one of the Killer albums.

By now we were regularly playing good London venues. Hurricane Jane had real visibility across the capital and given plenty of mentions in the Kerrang gig guide which apart from two crap reviews is about all those useless 'K-k-kunts' have ever done for me over the years (however they still have time to put that right, If the bridges aren't totally burned of course). It was an exciting time even though none of the music media or record labels seemed particularly interested in us. In fact, I recall one gig at The Borderline where the 'aforementioned' magazine had one of its freelance writers in attendance and despite us absolutely 'wiping the floor' with the headline act (who I won't mention) I mean literally destroying them. In fact, to the point where their singer lost his way so badly in their set, that he wandered around like a frightened 'deer in the headlights' when his guitarists amp momentarily packed up, Not even saying a word to his adoring fans. It was like being stuck on a packed tube train waiting for the driver's announcement to explain why the train had stopped for so long in a dark tunnel. The silence and confusion only interrupted briefly by 'Big Dave' shouting out anonymously "Get on wiv it" which under the circumstances was quite a reasonable shout to be fair.

What was worse was that he was supposed to be a frontman of some repute and yet he turned his back completely on 'his audience' for the whole duration of the delay! Yet, sure enough, they still got a five-star review in the magazine, and we didn't even get so much as an "Oh yeah and Hurricane Jane were there as well" mention as an afterthought from our dear friend the 'Kerwank stain' as we later Christened him after this obvious and incomprehensible (to us and most of the punters there at least) snub.

A few nights later I was having one too many tequilas in The George with Lea Hart, former guitarist with Fastway. Lea ran the Limelight Rock night at the Wag club in London and I suggested he give us a slot. Any slot. Indeed, it was 'A Slot for a Shot', Hi Lea.

Whether it was the tequila or my smooth talking I don't know but either way Lea, true to his name was all heart and gave us the gig. We were given the One am berth on a Wednesday night / Thursday morning.

Obviously, everyone in the audience was so pissed. We could have been The Wombles for all they cared. And our slot was the earlier of the two gig places. But we enjoyed it and went on do it a few more times. On one of these, I developed a crush on Beki Bondage of Vice Squad, who'd played after us and joined us for a drink before some annoying promoter interrupted our little 'tryst' and whisked her away with the promise of an appearance in the latest video for The Almighty. Beki still looks great, today by the way 'Big up to Paul and Vice Squad.' We have also become connected on Facebook at least and have chatted occasionally from time to time on there.

Being married at this time, I'm not going to deny that I found some of these situations quite challenging. There was no shortage of temptation in the circles I was now moving in and once or twice things got, shall we say a little awkward. But as I've always said, a gentleman never tells. Well not his wife, anyway especially if he wants to wake up in the morning with his balls and manhood still securely attached!

I think it's probably worth also pointing out here, (and sorry to disappoint some of you) that there are many stories (as I'm sure you can quite imagine) centred around the female species that I could mention. Some hilariously funny, some perhaps, less so.

However, what may appear an amusing or salacious anecdote to me is also someone else's life and that needs to be respected. I have been very careful in this book not to mention some surnames with this in mind and I also believe quite strongly, a private moment is a private moment and that needs to stay that way…just between the three of us……and possibly the Octopus!

Also, I read and hear a lot of stuff said or written about me on social media and ill-informed gossip via various friends, musicians and work colleagues. It does make me laugh how far from the truth some of these opinions and accusations are. True, it took me a while to realise that when you try and flirt or joke about online with some folk that with the lack of emphasis (or punctuation) it doesn't always come across in the harmless, cheeky, frivolous way in which it was intended.

However, my heart and soul have always been (mostly) in the right place. I genuinely just want to make people smile, laugh or feel good about themselves and I make no apologies for that!

I do however, often wonder sometimes, away from the up front and over the top bravado act I put on, whether people honestly believe that I could possibly have been married for over thirty years (to the same woman) if I really was acting out (or upon), this tongue in cheek, self-deprecating innuendo and cheeky flirtatious banter?

Anyway, back to the story, we were getting to the end of yet another year, but this time with a string of gigs booked over the festive period, including the Marquee on 27 December. Our good mates Trash Ville would open for us that night, which we dubbed 'The Nightmare after Christmas'. Alicia would travel alone to spend Christmas with her family back home in the dear old Czech Rep.

Brother Andy and his wife Maureen were now running a pub at Beauchamp Place in fashionable Knightsbridge. Having invited myself to spend Christmas with my bro, this would be my base while Alicia was away.

As I was idling away the afternoon of Christmas Eve, Monsieur Rocker called. He too was at a loose end and wanted to drink some beers. I obliged; Indeed, as I recall we also took things a step further by indulging in some nasally ingested stimulus.

It's fair to say I was pretty much 'fucked' by the time I arrived at Andy and Maureen's for Christmas with an equally incoherent Big Dave in tow.

Andy was cool about it, Maureen less so. But hey, it was Christmas, but little did we know at the time that it was to be a Christmas none of us was likely to forget it in a hurry.

What's the worst unscheduled wake-up call you've ever had with a hangover? Workmen with drills outside your window? Someone running the vacuum cleaner around you. Two Yorkshire Terriers licking your arse? (Actually, the Jury's still out on that one) Or maybe an unattended alarm or an unanswered phone ringing incessantly?

Mine was hearing my brother say, "Fuck, both my chefs have blown me out and I've got thirty plus covers coming for Christmas dinner in just a few hours. Boys, I need your help."

At my most ambitious in the kitchen, I'd only ever been capable of rustling up beans on toast, maybe with grated cheese if I was out to impress Alicia. My cooking rarely went beyond 'pierce film lid in several places'.

Yet here were Dave and I, fresh from a cocaine and alcohol-fuelled bender, donning chef whites and preparing to plate up lobster bisque with coriander, toast with liver pate, turkey, roast potatoes, pigs in blankets, sprouts, peas, carrots, and gravy followed by apple strudel and custard to the Smyths, Forbes and Fortescue-Ponsonby's of SW3.

Given our rank unsuitability to the task we made a decent fist of it too. We got a full proof system going and Dave injected some gallic flair into it. We looked the part too, in white aprons and hats, hair tied back. Under no circumstances were we to leave the kitchen in this gear. The denizens of Beauchamp Place must not suspect that one of their most anticipated meals of the year was being thrown together by the singer and drummer of a big hair metal band called Hurricane Jane. If we needed the loo, the uniform had to come off first.

Well, of course we'd need the loo. For every two plates we sent down the service lift, two pints of beer would come back up. It got to the point where I felt – and looked – like Mrs Doubtfire forgetting what to wear when she grappled with the costume related needs of being in two places at once.

In the end, it does have to be said, we did a bloody good job. There were only two minor complaints from customers, and I couldn't help thinking that was a better average than a typical Hurricane Jane gig.

Even more impressive though was that I remembered Alicia's 12-digit Czech telephone number (which I'd inadvertently left written down on a piece of paper at home, quite possibly used in some recent nasal injective activity) and that I had the presence of mind to dial it at 10 pm to wish her a Merry Christmas.

So, all in all, 1994 was a good year for the Jane after all. As the last guest left the pub that night Dave and I agreed we'd give the band our all in 1995. We'd throw everything, including the kitchen sink, at it. Once we'd got the dirty dishes out of it, that is.

Chapter 15
You Know You Love It

"Don't you get up tight or hang on any words I say, it's just A Hurricane Jane that's gonna blow you the fuck away."

The money shot. Say you don't want it, The Marquee, London, June 1995

Before I could throw a kitchen sink at anything, I had a few work and personal problems to deal with first.

Like health and housing. Firstly, health I was beginning to (as I mentioned in my French exploits earlier) suffer from a bowel disease now fully diagnosed as Ulcerative Colitis. Who knows what caused it, my years of excessive drinking possibly, 32 special brews including (four whisky depth chargers) on my 20th birthday probably helped set the tone and path for this delightful little 'Bowel bashing beauty'! The 'end' result (no pun intended) being that I had to go into hospital for colonoscopy i.e.) a camera shoved unceremoniously up your rectum and then followed by endoscopy (one down your throat). Thankfully, they washed it in-between trips.

Even though I was under mild anaesthetic I could still see it clearly all unfolding on the big screen opposite, it was just like watching Raquel Welch in that classic 'B' movie 'The Fantastic Voyage'. Where she is shrunk to the size of a peanut with some fellow doctors, and they set off to cure some guy's cancer in a miniature submarine…Only this time the sequel was set inside my arsehole and cavorting up my 'Colon canal'!

Incidentally I've got Raquel's autograph somewhere, wishing me a happy birthday, written on that Iconic film poster 'One Million BC' (Before Colon).

Back to housing, our lovely landlord at Larkfield Road had sold the property and it had completely slipped his mind to let us know this (not just my folks then). The upshot of this was that we moved into first one, then another tiny bedsit, as our priority was to stay in the Borough of Richmond-upon-Thames.

It was hard living in such reduced circumstances and more than once Alicia and I came close to killing each other (she's tried many times since). Our endurance paid off, though. Eventually we were offered a one-bedroom garden flat near Richmond Park at way less than the market rate. Our landlord would be the amazing Richmond Parish Lands Charity, the organisation that was also paying for Alicia to study at Richmond Drama School.

On the work front, I'd left Sexton's. The company had relocated to Hack bridge, which was an absolute bugger to commute to by public transport from Richmond at the time.

I'd moved on from assembling car cassette players to purchasing computer consumables for a company called 'Kyotek' in Kingston for about a year. Then, out of the blue, first thing on a Monday morning the boss called me in and, without any warning, fired me. "It's nothing personal, Matt, it was purely a business decision." He mumbled as I left his office. I wouldn't have minded, but the fella had only just awarded me a pay raise the Friday before!

When a girl dumps you, you generally try and shag her best mate or arch enemy in revenge. When 'Kyotek' dumped me, I went to the business next door and got a job with their fiercest competitor. Would Sol Campbell have crossed Seven Sisters to join Arsenal from Tottenham without the precedent I set? I doubt it.

Tony, full-time plumber and our ad-hoc road manager, his then wife Anne and their three children also had to move out of Larkfield Road. I feared we'd lose touch. But no, Tony was still thinking of the band.

Anne was Swedish and she and Tony had spent some time living with her family in Sweden. Tony had made some connections over there and one day he dropped by our one-bedroom (boxing ring) flat to tell me about these four motorcycle clubs he was in touch with. They were based in Norrtälje, an area northeast of Stockholm and had a stake in couple of music venues.

He'd had recent contact with Sweden and cooked up a plan. The way 'The Road Manager' saw it, we would fly to Sweden on a Thursday night and play one of the venues on the Friday and Saturday. We'd then move on to the second venue and play there on the following Tuesday and Wednesday before heading home the next day.

We wouldn't be paid but all our board, food and expenses would be covered. The bikers' clubs would split our air fares between then and some vague family connections of Tony and Anne would put us up. The venues, Tony assured us, had all the backline and kit we would need – all we had to bring was ourselves, our guitars, picks and sticks, a bit of beer money and a bunch of 'let's 'av it' attitudes.

Oh, and a pen and 'poop scoop', just in case Rocky Caberman turned up and wanted my autograph again.

So, I started casually dropping it into pub conversations that Hurricane Jane had a Scandinavian tour lined up. "Lock up your daughters," I'd say. "We're gonna avenge all the raping and pillaging done to our ancestors by the Vikings. We're gonna turn Norrtälje into Whore-tälje etc.!"

I'm not sure exactly if geography was one of Dave's strongest subjects at school as to me, he didn't seem to quite get where we were going. As for the next few weeks, he would spend most of his days mimicking vocalists like Klaus Meine (Germany), Don Dokken (America) and Bruce Dickenson (England) and screaming, "Good evening, Reykjavík. Mwaaaah!" (Iceland) at every opportunity!

It was vintage Dave in a social context. Miles off point, but charmingly hilarious. He since tells me he knew exactly where it was and well, I for one believe him.

The tour would be mid-February, which gave us a few weeks to hone the set and learn a few covers. Among these was Saturday Night's Alright for Fighting, which we assumed would go down well with Swedish bikers. Another was Knock on Wood, for no reason, other than a lot of the stuff Ikea sold was wooden.

We went into central London to have some expensive publicity shots taken (such as the one on the cover of this book).

We gave Tony our passport details and told everyone who our bragging hadn't yet reached that Hurricane Jane would be 'doing stuff overseas' for a while.

Yep, we were properly excited and as ready as we would ever be.

And then, the night before we were due to fly, Tony phoned me.

"Bad news, Matt. Sweden's off."

The details were sketchy but from what I could glean, one of the biker groups had gone bankrupt, two of the other three had fallen out with each other, a lot of shit had gone down in the aftermath and the 'thing' with the English band had fallen through the chasm that now divided them.

I sometimes wonder now if Tony had even booked the flights. I never asked him as I didn't want to know the answer. I still don't. It would be too much of a plumber's wrench.

My big problem now was how to get the message to the rest of the band before they all set off for the airport. I couldn't reach David or Jason, but I did get through to Simon. He, like me, was gutted, but also like me, no stranger to disappointment. Together, we dealt with it with the stoicism of the philosophical.

At one point he started giggling uncontrollably. "David and Jason are on the piss in the East End tonight. I bet David's standing on a table in some run-down shithole in Leyton screaming 'Reykjavík we love you! Mwaaaahhh!' At a load of bemused cockneys."

So, another downer in our perpetual game of snakes and ladders. A defeatist mood took hold and, worse, we all had a week off work to wallow in it.

I recall this low feeling being even further validated and reaffirmed when Jason, Simon and Myself went for a beer in Richmond at The Old Ship pub (my old stomping ground). As we were leaving there were three very 'brassed up' forty something ladies by the door with make up running and obviously a little bit worse for wear checking us out.

As we went through the door onto the street outside, we heard of one of them reluctantly say with a sigh, in almost resigned desperation, "Oh c'mon they'd do... wouldn't they?"

As we wallowed in self-pity it did seem like this had been a once in a lifetime experience, (Sweden not the brasses) a bit like a sighting of a comet! Indeed, I always thought Bill Haley was so lucky to have one named after his band!

Funnily enough I have seen one in real life! Which brings me onto a nice little aside just to break from all the 'doom and gloom' here and is worthy of a mention as it could only really have happened or made sense in this place and at this exact juncture of time and space.

It was a few years later but around 1997 I had been drinking with my Wife and her cousins at a pub called The Running Mare in Cobham, Surrey. After a while I'd noticed, as it was getting dark that all these bespectacled nerdy looking guys were setting up on the grass field over the road with Telescopes pointing up at the night sky. It soon transpired that apparently the 'Hale-Bopp' Comet (I'd never heard of that band) was due imminently to be visible soaring high overhead the starry Surrey sky. Quite a rare event as the next time it would be visible in our orbit would apparently be in 4083…So yeah quite a few pints later. Well anyway as me and a few locals wandered over and contemplated being born again astronomers suddenly there was an excited shriek from one of them. "I see it!" he exclaimed sounding like he was on the point of ejaculation!

"Where?" I asked getting quite caught up in the moment.

"It's over there between the Plough and the Bear," replied our new friend.

Now I was no Patrick Moore or Brian Cox but even I knew he was referring to the two-star constellations. However, the guy behind me, pint in each hand was less informed and looking completely bemused and confused, staring in totally the opposite direction to everyone else. It then dawned on me (hence why the importance and previous reference to our specific location was so important) As where we stood was exactly equal distance between two other Cobham 'dens of iniquity' AKA, yes, you've guessed it, 'The Old Plough Inn' and 'The Bear' public houses!

Anyway, back to Kingston and the aftermath of 'Scandigate' I called my new boss, Mr Rob Jones, to let him know what had happened and asked if I could possibly cancel my leave and come into work instead? He was having none of it. His brother dabbled in the music business, tuning out white label dance mixes for DJs. He immediately understood how distraught we all were and tried to find ways to save the tour.

There was, unfortunately, nothing doing Sweden-wise, but Rob really wanted to help us, so he offered to fund the cost of a demo. He asked me to come over to his flat in Kingston that evening to discuss options.

I bring this up now as somebody recently asked me about the rudest welcome or lack of hospitality I'd ever received. Well other than the other day when I asked the lady in the Coffee kiosk opposite Tower Hill tube station if she knew where Dawson House was and got the reply, "Do I look like a fucking map?"

The award goes hands down to Rob's flat mate Glyn! Rob was out when I knocked on his door and when I asked Glyn what time he might be expecting him back he seemed firstly to be a) very uninterested in his co-habitué's existence let alone whereabouts and secondly b) as to who I even was or why I might be there, so he just left the door ajar and walked away. I presumed I was supposed to follow him and enter. Soon after I did, I found myself almost immediately in their lounge (as there was no real hall to speak of). I sat down on a wooden chair in silence as Glyn preceded to roll himself a 'spliff', pour himself a beer and stick on some hardcore porn (which with hindsight he might well have been in himself) without so much as offering me a cup of fucking tea…or a Kleenex!

Rob eventually made it back thankfully as I was beginning to feel unwanted and dare, I say it a little soiled (Some half an hour later) and we started making some calls before he drove me about to check out a few studios around London. Sadly, almost all of them charged extra for an engineer. The only one that didn't was a grubby little shed behind a shabby block of flats in Camden Town. From the word go, Rob and the studio's owner, Pete Lorentz, got on famously. I could see where this was going, but as Rob was paying, I could hardly put my foot down.

Crescent Studios, Lorentz proudly declared, was available on the following Monday, Tuesday and Wednesday. No surprises there. Rob looked at me and said, "Let's book it!"

How could I refuse?

Pete Lorentz was barking. He was like a mad professor who, having been cloistered in his laboratory for far longer than is healthy, cannot recognise the norms of the world he has re-entered.

I liked him. He spoke his mind and had none of the fakery or superficiality that defined the London music scene as we knew it.

In truth, it proved to be a very long three days, but we got what we came for. We laid down Lipstick Lies, our trusty opener and still relevant in the era of a thriving phone sex industry, If You Still Believe, Simon's composition and my ode to coping with Alicia's deportation, In Through the Back Door (not what you're thinking or maybe it is) and our new anthem and now title of this book, You Know You Love It…You Schlaaaags.

It was a good demo to be fair but, in all honesty, not a great one. Maybe some of the residual disappointment from the Swedish fiasco shone through, and maybe the choice of studio failed to give us the lift we were looking for. Still, I'm forever grateful to Pete's uber-posh neighbour for her spoken contribution of "I say, I think you've got the wrong hole". She was referring to something technical to do with leads and speakers and nothing to do with a reference to a friend's alleged rear-guard encounter with a student from the Royal

Ballet school in Richmond Park! We mixed it into the intro for, *In Through the Back Door*, and it seemed to fit quite nicely (her line that is).

Once mastered and formatted onto cassette, we sent the demo out to do its work and, happily, it got us some new gigs. Off the back of our three days with 'Prof' Lorentz, we got to play The Orange in Kensington, The Garage in Islington and The Mean Fiddler in Harlesden.

Thus emboldened, Jason and I and we even pitched up – cassette in hand – at Virgin Records' London HQ.

There we met a rock A&R guy who repeatedly told us that our sound was 'right up his alley, yet while he loved what we 'were cooking' and was totally 'on our side', the rest of his label wasn't and that included the people that made the signing decisions. I know what I wanted to cook and shove sideways up his alley that was for sure.

From there we headed to Redditch, where a small independent label had made enthusiastic noises about having one of our tracks on an upcoming rock compilation album. We were greeted by an oleaginous redheaded rep in an ill-fitting pin-striped suit and over polished shoes. He explained that, naturally, we'd have to pay to appear on the album by way of an upfront fee. Standard practice and all the other bands had readily agreed. To sweeten the deal, he offered us some tea and biscuits. We returned south, our expletives still ringing in his ears.

Another return on Rob's investment in our demo was selection for a 'prestigious' Battle of The Bands tournament at The Redback in Acton in conjunction with TNT magazine. The prize was studio time and a label-backed single release.

You already know my views on these things. And sadly they weren't about to change.

Chapter 16
Unfinished Business

"And when it comes, you just won't feel a thing."

Way out West. The Redback looking more like a Texas brothel (or Czech restaurant). Just ripe for some Thrush Jam wouldn't you think?

We'd often driven past the Redback Tavern en-route to Survival Studios in Acton. There always seemed to be crowds of Saffas, Aussies and Kiwis in and around it and our general feeling was that whatever they were into, they'd probably give us a fair crack of the whip even if we did have to dodge the odd beer glass hurled our way.

We'd read it well. At the first night of the Battle of the Bands, we blasted through our first heat, destroying our five rivals. The antipodeans lapped us up almost as greedily as they did their Fosters and Castlemaine XXXX. We'd never experienced anything quite like it.

TNT magazine however somehow saw it slightly differently. Reporting on the event, it barely mentioned us, apart from the obligatory sentence that we had been 'Judged first'. They even managed to make that read like a putdown. No doubt about it. The people in charge of this event did not want us to do well, let alone win it.

But we'd made the semi-final, there were to be three of these so I guess it was really a 'Tremi-Final', where only the first two bands would go through from each. Again, we felt we did ourselves proud. The judges put us second. Again, we felt a bit bruised, but second was still a pass to the final. That said, it still niggled as we could see that there was a lot of disagreement among the judging panel.

Proof of that observation came when one of the judges, who claimed he was a session drummer with Steppenwolf at the time (we can neither deny or corroborate this fact) came over to us at the end and said, "I've no idea what competition those other three judges were watching but I just couldn't ignore you guys. You were awesome."

And then with that and perhaps just like a 'true nature's child' he promptly rode off into the night on his Harley Davidson. where I think he quite possibly 'fired off all of his guns and then exploded into space'

TNT magazine however, remained unmoved. According to their reporter who wrote our performance up, we were nothing more than a novelty act or 'Thrash Glam' outfit as he described us. Irked beyond my breaking point, I fired off an open letter to the editor of TNT. In it I said, "We actually saw ourselves more as 'Thrush Jam', a sort of soothing remedy for irritating cunts such as their reviewer". Or as my Scottish friends would say, 'I really 'Canesten' people like that… I really canna.'"

It felt good. I'd developed a liking for the cutting riposte a couple of years earlier when a record company executive described our music as 'so out of touch it was almost prehistoric'. I reminded him that the biggest grossing movie currently at the box office at that time was in fact 'Jurassic Park' so we were actually on point.

A week before the final, Steve the promotor at the Redback called me. They'd apparently 'just' had the draw to decide the running order of the band slots and, surprise, surprise, Hurricane Jane been allocated the second slot before 9pm. The tumbleweed slot.

TNT magazine came out on that same day, and it featured the full running order as part of its Battle of the Bands update feature. So that must have been one speedy print job to include that.

The final itself would take place on 27 July, slap bang in the middle of a Hurricane Jane tour.

On 26 July we were playing at the Cartoon in Croydon. The audience was sparse and largely indifferent to us. The feeling was mutual, and it resulted in one of the poorest performances we ever delivered.

It was so bad that halfway through it, I lost it. I turned on the band mid gig and said to them, "If we're as fucking shit as this tomorrow night we are gonna come last." Simon later told me that if it had come from anyone else, the band would've downed tools and broken into a full-on ruck there and then. I believed him. In fact, I think Big Dave was already off his stool and ready to steam in as I returned to the mic.

We made our peace after the gig and decided on our set for the final of the Battle of the Bands. Deep down, it felt futile as the competition was so obviously rigged and we only had 20 minutes. But, taking Queen's Live Aid performance as our template and inspiration, we chose our five best songs of four minutes or under and factored in a bit of time for my trademark onstage banter Aka garbage rhetoric.

We went with:

1. *Lipstick Lies*
2. *Boys Don't Cry*
3. *In Through the Back Door*
4. *You Know You Love It*
5. *Hurricane Jane*

We had a good attendance along to support us that night, which was a real boost, given our poxy 'teatime' slot. Alicia's parents were over from 'Cesky Tesin', and they came along. So did my sister Louise and...Fuck me sideways! There was Doctor Who! Louise had brought Peter Davison of that and 'All Creatures Great and Small' fame along. They were good friends and not destined to be lovers. Louise would soon be 'Tempted by the fruit of another' (sorry Sis) and marry Chris

Difford of Squeeze instead. Who incidentally is a brilliant lyricist! Typical really, I rate myself as a bit of a poet and a 'wordsmith' but now I'm not even the best poet in my own family!

Peter Davison was a lovely guy though and even better, being a former Time Lord, he wouldn't give a rat's arse what era our music came from.

In fact, the 20-minute set we played that night was one of the finest live performances I've ever been a part of with this or any other group.

The band was sensational. Jason shredded like Ritchie Sambora, Simon's bass rumbled and thundered like a steam train and Big Dave beat the skins like a demon possessed. I even managed to stay in tune and keep the 'bants' and 'garbage rhetoric' to a minimum.

From somewhere, I summoned up some humility and urged the audience to be fair to all the bands that were playing that night whoever they themselves were there to support. That went down well with rival bands and fans alike, but not so much with the judges. We noticed the Steppenwolf guy wasn't part of their panel tonight so, despite a great performance, we weren't hopeful. It felt like we were 'Born to be riled'.

When the band that followed us took to the stage, the first thing their singer magnanimously said was, "Second place is still up for grabs, isn't it?" I applauded him, nodded and raised a beer glass in his direction (he knew at least).

When the remaining four bands had finished, we waited by the bar for the result. I asked the Doctor if I could borrow one of his hearts as mine was working overtime.

The way the judges read out the results still baffles me. They began by announcing third and then second place. Neither one was us. An enormous Aussie slapped my back and said, "Well done, mate, you guys were fuckin' awesome tonight." Conn, who'd lived through nearly all my ups and downs over the years thus far, clenched his fist and yelled. "Fucking Yeeesss!"

Then the announcer continued, "And the winner is…The Jackdaws."

I couldn't believe it. Nor could the audience (and possibly not even The Jackdaws, themselves either). An audible groan just like the one in School of Rock when 'No Vacancy' won broke out across the whole pub.

Essentially, the last band to play was the winner, the second from last to play was the runner up, and so on all the way down to sixth place. We, however, bucked the system by playing fifth from last, yet ending up in fourth place (if that makes sense).

It felt like they'd constructed the format to crush us.

I was even more downtrodden when I was shown the scorecard. I'm a performer. This means I create a persona on stage. It's an act. It's only a part of who I am or what Hurricane Jane was about. So, I took exception to cheap shots like 'Singer loves himself' and 'Like Bon Jovi on speed' and the breathtakingly sanctimonious, 'Too much fun to be considered seriously'

This last comment particularly rankled with me. Which is again why I hate these things. Music to me is a form of personal expression and interpretation, but when it's played in front of a live audience, primarily it should mostly be about Entertainment!

Indeed, when I gig with Ransom these days, I'm often seen standing with arms held triumphantly aloft parodying Russel Crowe's Maximus Decimus Meridius character from the film Gladiator, loudly questioning an appreciative audience with the words: "ARE YOU NOT ENTERTAINED?"

With only four points separating the winner and the fourth place (us) the Battle of the Bands, was a close-run thing in the end. But it sent a clear message to me. Entertaining people had no place in rock 'n' roll in the eyes of these judges.

This was the final straw for me. In front of all my friends, my family and the seventh Doctor Who, my humiliation was complete.

The Jackdaws to their credit, were gracious winners. They were generous to us in their victory speech. And TNT, with the event wrapped up, had nothing to lose by reporting that the audience had 'greedily devoured [our] set with delight'. But even that implied that to enjoy Hurricane Jane was to commit some sort of cultural crime.

We were deflated. Again. On a real low. In our minds we were the equivalent of 'musical leprosy'. We knew now that no record company would ever open its door to us, no matter how hard we knocked.

So, right there and then we promised ourselves one thing. If we were going down, we were going down with all our guns blazing.

Chapter 17
The Storm Over London

"It's time to unleash hell upon everyone."

"They don't like it up 'em, Mr Mannering!" Levelling the Marquee, August 1995

If this book was a western, this chapter would probably be best described as 'The last sundown'. 'The final shootout', 'One last stand', 'holed up at the pass' with no escape, the Apache hollering all around us, vultures circling overhead. With no late cavalry charge to save us. We were now very much on our own. For our 'Alamo, our 'High noon', our own 'OK Corral'.

The only ammunition we had left was our spirit, our pride, our stupidity and our songs. Well that suited us just fine, so, let's fucking do this shall we.

But perhaps, just before we do, let's go back slightly in time, to earlier in the year, to 8 May 1995 to be precise, the 50th anniversary of VE Day (a bloody long time ago – But poignant as I've just got off the ladder right this second from putting up some bunting to celebrate the Queen's Platinum Jubilee). Actually, Strike that as just now (on final edit day) September 8th, 2022, she has sadly now just passed away at ninety-six years of age. So, she didn't get to send herself a telegram on her one hundredth birthday after all, but still what an impressive lady and what a legacy.

Anyway, at this point the Battle of the Bands debacle was still yet to happen, and the boys and I were in the Cambridge Arms right in the heart of theatre land, our pre-gig watering hole, pre-hydrating for a show somewhere that night in London.

A two-minute silence was being respectfully observed by everyone in the pub apart from a table of Japanese tourists. They seemed oblivious to their surroundings and merrily chuntered on while everyone around them remained mute.

This incensed the landlord, a royalist. When the two minutes were up, I saw him stride towards the Japanese party to remonstrate. I stood up and politely blocked his way. Telling him that maybe he should cut them a little slack as I pointed out, that for them the war did continue for another three months after.

But it planted a thought in my mind. As a band, we'd been nurturing something of a bunker mentality recently and the time was now right to plot our own VE Day – Victory over, well everybody really.

Over the following days I hit the phone hard. By the end of them I'd booked us 17 gigs in 14 different venues over a period spanning ten weeks.

We called it 'The Storm Over London' Tour.

So, I thought for this upcoming career defining, 'Tour of London' that I would need a bit more energy and perhaps it would be a good idea to get myself into better shape. So, I decided that maybe it was high time I joined a gym.

Cannons of Richmond in Old Deer Park (Fuck knows what it's called now) was where I eventually settled on to get myself fit. It was here that I met a very nice guy who was, as I recall, originally from Jamaica, called Paul. I think he was a stockbroker or something as he was always very smartly dressed and drove a Ferrari. I think he also played Rugby for Richmond.

Regardless, he was built like a fucking 'brick shit house' with fully ripped arms, a six-pack torso and legs like tree trunks. However, we got on like a house on fire and he also had the most infectious 'booming' laugh that I just loved.

Anyway, one day he finished his work out a good twenty minutes before me, so I was a little surprised and I dare say it, a tad unnerved to find him not only still in the building but also still shampooing his hair in the communal showers when I finished.

It's always a little awkward talking to another man when you're naked (unless you are in the porn industry I guess). It is universally acknowledged that always maintaining eye contact, is paramount!

Luckily this wasn't too much of an issue initially, as he had his back to me. Until suddenly he didn't, and he turned around to speak to me, fully 'soaped up'

However, it wasn't his 'Sud-laden' dreadlocks (and I don't mind admitting this) that I was transfixed by, but the sheer size and girth of quite possibly the biggest, most impressive 'man piece' that I have ever been privileged to see or probably ever likely to see, in my lifetime!

As I tried to hide my own insecurity, regain my composure and self-confidence, Paul spoke to me and said in his deep, rich 'Barry White' like tone.

"Ok Matthew so tell me, what are your actual goals here, I mean what are you hoping to gain or trying to achieve for yourself physically?"

I paused for a few seconds... then broke the unwritten rule, I lowered my gaze and pointed quite unashamedly at the 'elephant in the room' and replied,

"Well how much do I have to fucking bench press to get one of those?" I think I can still hear him laughing now to be fair.

Anyway, these were tough times for bands trying to get noticed. Many venues operated a 'pay to play' system. You, the band would pay the venue to use its PA system and sound engineer. The payment would be deducted from the takings, of which the sum attributable to you would be a calculation based on the number of people turning up bearing a flyer with your band's name on it.

Which meant for every gig, you'd have to print – at your own expense – reams of flyers, get them into the hands of potential punters and then hope to God that a) they'd turn up and b) remember to bring the flyer with them.

We did our best but our usual haunts like The George were increasingly a waste of time. Invariably the clientele would be other bands, musos and their hangers-on pontificating about their next 'project – a kind of fusion of alternative grunge and hybrid nu-metal, man' while nursing a single Jack Daniels and diet coke throughout an entire evening.

With a straw.

We needed help and got it from a couple of unlikely sources. Sammy Jo, the be-stockinged stunner from my Twickenham days, and her mate Wendy sacrificed some serious shoe leather for our cause, as did the two Pakistani sisters, Farrah and Suraiya. They took great delight in reminding perfect strangers that they knew they loved it in a highly suggestive tone of voice. Both sisters are happily married these days and their (I presume) Muslim spouses probably know nothing about their wild rocker and Hurricane Jane tour promoter days…until now.

This was also the era of franchised post-gig DJ nights where, as the band finished its set-in front of 50 people, there'd be about 500 plus outside waiting to come in. Anyone already inside who wanted to hang around was obliged to pay the entry fee a second time.

Never was there a concessions policy that allowed punters to pay for both sessions upfront at a reduced rate. I never understood why. It was always a bit gutting when the DJ who replaced us on the stage to spin records after had an audience ten times the size of ours.

Rob Jones, my boss at work, had given me a mobile phone and that helped me work through the endless negotiations with venues. Not many people had mobile phones back in those days. I remember taking a call from Rob on the 71 bus in Kingston, one evening. Everyone turned around to watch, including the driver. It was an expensive form of communication back then too. Call charges were outrageous, so I used it sparingly.

Rob also managed to add You Know You Love it onto a telephone sex chat line. Punters would pay £1.50 a minute and get a blast of the track as they waited for the business part of the call. We'd get a cut of the takings. To help the initiative prosper I had a bulk job of mock prostitute call cards made up. They featured an image of a thigh-high booted lovely with 'You Know You Love it' written in a speech bubble coming from her mouth. The call to action (or header) in big suggestive type face was 'Get Blown Away' by Hurricane Jane above the number to call. Once printed, I placed them in strategically chosen phone boxes around various seedy rock joints in London. They didn't generate much revenue – few calls lasted beyond ten seconds.

There were some memorable stand out moments during 'The Storm Over London Tour'. Like the one at The Swan in Blackheath where some Millwall supporters got disproportionately offended at the presence of a West Ham fan and it kicked off mid-gig. However, just as the heroic band on the Titanic did, we played on, an almost comical sideshow as tables, glasses and chairs went flying everywhere until the police arrived to calm it all down. Think they even stayed on for a couple of numbers themselves.

And the night at the Orange Club in Kensington when a 'sassy' blonde woman allegedly from Sony Records, Australia came along. She told us we were great and would be interested in seeing us again but wouldn't be able to come to any further gigs on this 'tour' as she was flying back to Oz in the morning. I then spent the next six weeks trying to track her down with midnight phone calls to Sony's offices from Sydney to Perth. But she was beyond reach, even with my state-of-the-art mobile.

Incidentally Kula Shaker had played The Orange Club the week before us and I'd been to check them out as I remember meeting the band's frontman, Crispin Mills, son of the actress Hayley Mills. He made quite an impression on me when he told me that, while spending time in India, he'd become fascinated by the mystical powers of the letter 'K'. It gave Crispin a different perspective on life that I quite fancied for myself.

So much so that years later during the recent covid pandemic I borrowed the idea but opted instead for the letter 'V'. I've since embraced veganism, vodka (and other vices), various vaginas and, more recently, Viagra. But I'd appreciate it if you keep that last one to yourselves.

Just going back to the pandemic, it's relevant because most of this book has been written during it, in the spare time most of us have had off. Where we've all had nothing much to do but drink or moan about MP's flagrantly flouting the same rules that they themselves set.

But I have now got a newfound respect for two things. Firstly trees, did you know that they can communicate with each other underground and send moisture and positive vibes through their roots to other trees that might be struggling in their immediate vicinity...! How cool is that?

And birds, I mean again, I never knew how fucking noisy they were, but you can learn a lot from their 'dating and mating' rituals, especially pigeons, who seemed to like using my new garden fence, like it is some sort of 'dogging' hot spot (RHS Wisley car park, eat your heart out). But mostly you have got to have the most profound respect for anything that can just shit on you so indiscriminately, at any time, from any height!

Anyway, back to the Storm tour, another 'highlight' was the night I and my driver for the night (a work colleague called Steve) unfortunately, spent at Snow Hill Police Station. We'd hung around after our gig at The Borderline (the one with the Zero bants from the headliners singer) to get on the piss with a couple of cute Goth chicks and got in the car afterwards. DR10. Breathalysers and 16 cups of coffee aside, the thing that sticks out the most about this incident was the pearl of wisdom (I took from a totally unexpected source) that I still pay close heed and attention to still to this today.

As I was waiting for Steve to give the police various samples of who knows what, blood, Saliva, faeces... Sperm (I cared little which). A new suspect was brought in for processing at the front desk for selling class A drugs. The officers had him firmly in handcuffs, but at one point he still managed to briefly wriggle free and attempt to make a dash for the door and freedom. Alas, our wannabe escapologist didn't get very far, and they managed to pin him down on the floor without too much fuss. As he lay down on his stomach, broken but unbowed, on the cold concrete floor, with a policeman's knee firmly engraved into his back, our eyes momentarily met.

He must've noticed I was sitting rather uncomfortably on my wooden chair. Indeed, it was a hot summer's night, I was in leather pants, sweating from the gig and I must admit there had been a fair bit of chaffing, squirming, fidgeting and squelching going on.

"Talcum powder mate," he said "Preferably Johnson's, you 'll thank me for it one day. trust me!" And with that, he was whisked away unceremoniously down to the cells for what possibly was either a bit of a good 'Shoeing' as the All-blacks rugby team used to describe it as, that or an undignified, prolonged, rectal cavity search at best.

I'll probably never know what happened to that fellow but today Friday the 17th of June 2022 is that day, so wherever you are, whatever police cell you may or may not be in today? "Thank you for your priceless tip." In fact during the summer months nowadays I never leave home ever without first heavily 'powdering my privates'!

Next morning as I recall, things got even worse when we were eventually released and I dialled the phone number, one of the goth girls had given me, just to check that they'd got home, okay. What I wasn't expecting, however was her spectacularly Glaswegian dad answering the phone and informing me she'd already left for school!

Indeed, put it this way if I'd been back in one of those piss-stained phone boxes of my troubled youth, I would certainly not have inserted my ten pence piece at this point, in fact I decided to leave that one well alone, it was probably for the best.

Another cool but perhaps more of a "I could've possibly done with just a little bit more notice" moment, came when Alicia arrived backstage at The Marquee to surprise me with the news that she'd just been accepted into the Guildford School of Acting.

I was naturally delighted for her of course. But trying to explain to her who the four provocatively dressed Swiss rock chicks, I was currently 'entertaining' at the time in the 'dressing room' Or indeed what they were doing there (especially as none of them spoke any English), was perhaps a little less of a reason for celebration and maybe more of one for hibernation.

The gig itself coincided with Gay Pride in London and some folk from the march had made their way into The Marquee as we were playing. Apparently, they saw the name 'Hurricane Jane' over the door and assumed we were a drag queen act. Fortunately, I found this out with a few tracks still to go, so time enough for me to parade my best Dale Winton on crack routine.

Then there was the gig a bit earlier at the Mean Fiddler in Harlesden this was on the same night as the Cup Winners Cup Final. Arsenal v Real Zaragoza. Our PA man was a mad 'Gooner', and he'd set up a portable TV behind his desk. I happened to look over at the exact moment that former Spurs legend Nayim lobbed Seaman, that of the David 'safe hands' variety (and a top bloke by the way) from about the halfway line. His face! Our sound.

Then there was the day we made a pizza and pasta bar regret its 'All you can eat for £3.99' offer after our sound check at the Rock Garden. Four skint, starving blokes with a long night ahead. We got through so much food that the restaurant had to bring the sign in and shut up shop for the rest of the day after we cleaned him out.

I also learnt quite a big 'life lesson' as well, one that I still adhere to this very day. We had played a gig at the 'Flicker and Firkin' pub in Richmond. It was a pub next door to The

Racing page and the owner of the latter was stopping people from going next door out of some sort of jealous competitiveness.

He needn't have bothered as the acoustics were so bad in there, I think we did a pretty good job of clearing out the regulars on our own.

Anyhow, one such guy who did cross the embargo was a guy called Matt who worked at Twickenham film studios. Apparently, he came to say 'Hello' to me after the gig and was greeted with a very insincere "Yeah cheers, thanks for coming" for his troubles, I then completely blanked him and carried on talking to the two young girls I was trying to impress at the time.

I know this because I met the fella a few days later in another pub and he came over to me and said, "Mate, can I just tell you something?"

"Sure," I said, "Sit down," not initially recognising him from the gig.

He then proceeded, "Last week, I had been working all day at the Film studios, have you any idea what my job entails?" I shook my head and he continued,

"Well sort of listening out for any rogue sound that isn't meant to be there in a film or TV production, i.e., a 747 flying over The Battle of Hastings, or a dog 'barking' on the moon, that kind of thing."

Anyway, I'd had enough for the day and popped into The Racing Page to have a pint and heard the manager 'slagging' you guys off and stopping folk from going next door to see you play! So, I thought, 'that's out of order' and even though I had a headache, I decided to go and give you boys a chance.

Well, to my surprise, I was totally blown away by your band and really loved your connection with the audience, A 'Proper frontman' I thought. Indeed, initially I was only going to stay for a couple of songs but ended up watching the whole gig.

So anyway, I came up to you afterwards to tell you how much I enjoyed it and your performance, and you just totally blanked me for two 'slappers' and I thought, "What a cunt!"

Since that day I now stop and chat to everyone and anyone after a gig, however tired I am, however many 'slappers' are around me or however pissed or annoying that person might be! Young, old, male, female, non-binary, whatever, I stay and chat because you never know what sort of day they are having or what is currently going on in their life at the time.

As for Matt, well we became good friends after that and 'Hey buddy thanks for the pointer'.

But if I'm truthfully honest the one 'Moment' or abiding memory that stands out for me from all those 17 gigs, came at The George Robey on the Seven Sisters Road.

It was a Monday evening, and our support act was a student indie band. They were, young, callow and so nervous they could barely tune their instruments themselves.

We'd been there and remembered how daunting it was, so we took pity on them and decided to help them out, especially as they seemed to have brought half their college with them to watch them play. We chatted with them, put them at ease and helped them set their gear up. Well, I didn't obviously I'm a singer, we never help set up gear, that's our MO.

I think Dave even lent them some drumsticks as they'd forgotten theirs. In fact, as they'd brought a massive crowd of students with them, we assumed they'd observe etiquette by letting their followers know what jolly decent fellows we'd all been and how fitting it would be for them to show their appreciation when we took the stage after them.

Not a bit of it.

From our very first chord, these snotty nose kids turned their backs on us and the stage and behaved with nothing but utter contempt for us. Even the indie band members themselves were joining in with the mocking, mimicking and general piss-taking. Not once did they even applaud us.

Over the years we'd all met some right 'Tossers' dealt with rude, ignorant, deluded people (some even more so than us) self-entitled, narcissistic folk, some who, like this mob were just downright disrespectful. Who 'rightly or wrongly' seemed to regard us as some sort of relics from a bygone age?

All this resentment started welling up inside me as I watched these smug 'little bastards' in front of me throw the kindness, we'd shown them back in our faces. Thinking about how we were slogging our guts out all over London and No cunt wanted to hear us play. So, after about four songs I just lost it and let rip.

"Okay, that's fucking enough! You ungrateful little cunts! We've been respectful to you guys, even showed your boys how to wipe their own fucking arses. But you lot are just fuckin' rude. You've probably all got fucking school in the morning, anyway, so why don't you just Fuck off now and save us all the trouble."

I don't think I've ever seen a room empty so fast before or since… well apart from maybe when I'd played my first college gig back at the end of 1982. In fact, even the one drink they had between the lot of them, was left behind, still half full, on one of the tables. I turned back to the band, fully expecting a full-on mutiny, but they were all right behind me on this one and nodded in the affirmative.

Apart from our gang, Well I say gang, but in all truth only really comprised of three people Lorenza (Paul Di'anno's now ex-girlfriend), Tony, the road manager and one of his sons, Anders. In fact, there was only about one other person still left in the pub – the landlord. "Good job, Matt," he said appreciatively. "They were all underage anyway."

We then launched into a blistering "You Know You Love it" and even though there was virtually nobody left in the audience, I've never enjoyed performing a song more or indeed since. It was almost as if the song had been written just for this one specific 'moment in time'. It is also why it is the title of this book too.

Ok so now the gloves are finally off, I'm going to alienate a few of you, and I am sorry but in truth, I always have and always will hate what the term 'Indie' music' (in all its pretentious forms) stands for in my eyes. Or indeed anything the 'manipulative' music media in this country tries to force upon on us as 'gospel'. Whether it be mainstream or Independent!

Be it by the medium of TV, radio, magazine, social media platforms or word of mouth by so called 'influencer' student types like these 'cunts', who think they decide what's 'in' and what isn't. Seriously, fuck 'em all! Music is and should always be about freedom of choice, and this is just mine!

'The Storm Over London' tour thundered its last at around midnight on 30 August 1995 at The Bull and Bush in Richmond. That was when we finally called time on Hurricane Jane. We'd given it everything we had, but in the end, we just had to accept that we were either, just the wrong band, in the wrong place, at the wrong time or that quite simply we just weren't good enough.

I did actually manage to have one day out during this period and it was in truth, quite a day out. Just before the end of our 'tour' on Saturday, August 26th to be precise.

Now I'm often asked about the time I allegedly 'roadied' for Paul Weller. Well, true; I was a massive fan of the earlier Jam stuff. 'All around the world' was a particular favourite. But yes, I guess I sort of did, really. He certainly owes me a pint, that's for sure.

I had gone to the reading festival as a guest of his old guitar tech, David Liddle, who had recently became stepdad to a mate of mine from my Sheen Park Rangers Sunday league football team, Paul Turney.

David (no longer with us sadly) was a fantastic guitarist in his own right but often mistaken for looking like Uncle Albert from 'Only fools and horses' with his big white beard…but boy he could play and indeed went on stage with Weller that night.

The only drawback to this 'dalliance with the stars' was that we had to hump all the amps off stage after the performance and take them back in Dave's van to Nomis Studios in Kensington, where they had been hired from.

Luckily, I was completely wired by this time, as backstage at this show were some scantily clad girls, promoting a new drink called 'Red bull'. Nobody told me it wasn't alcohol and really just an energy drink, until after I had drunk about eight of them (I was obviously blinded by the blue hot pants); I was up for about four days straight after that! Still, at least it meant I was full of endeavour and enthusiasm for the humping of those fucking amps during Bjork's set! "Sup up your beer and collect your fags."

Anyway, back to the Bull and Bush in Richmond so as the last chord was struck, the last symbol crashed and last orders were called, we knew in our hearts that this was finally it.

However, I wasn't at all despondent. Everywhere I looked I saw smiling and happy faces. It felt good to be bowing out in Richmond, my hometown, surrounded by my dearest friends and my family. In Richmond, where, as a kid, I'd first picked up a guitar in the garage and dreamt of becoming a rock star.

And right here in The Bull and Bush where, back in the sixties when it was then The Craw daddy Club, The Beatles had come down in their flash new suits to cast an eye over their fiercest rivals, The Rolling Stones. Richmond, where Pete Townsend and Mick Jagger still lived at the time.

True, there was to be no glorious, Hollywood style ending for Hurricane Jane. Just a few beers, a few hearty high fives, solid handshakes and a self-congratulatory pat on the back. We wouldn't be headlining Glastonbury or Download anytime soon and no one from Virgin or Sony would be calling Rob's mobile.

But nor would we have to conform anymore to the demands of the most fickle, shallow, industry I've ever known. Whatever we'd done or not done, we'd achieved it on our own terms. Not many bands can say that.

So, if you're reading this and you have a passion, whatever it is, follow your dream. Don't listen to all the people who tell you that you can't.

Because even if, like us, you don't quite make it to the top, In the end, it doesn't really matter. Just do it for you, for your own soul. It's surely far better to fight for something you're passionate about than die on your arse for absolutely nothing at all.

I honestly believe, hand on heart that there's no better feeling in life (apart from maybe marriage and childbirth) than doing 'your own thing, your own way' putting it all out there, leaving nothing behind and having no regrets about any of it…Well, maybe only a few.

In the end, perhaps, Sting was right after all. Music is its own reward. You can forget that Kipling quote though. I'm not growing a moustache for anyone, any time soon, let alone waxing it. In fact, if you ask me, I think he should maybe have just stuck to making those exceedingly good cakes!

Music having its own reward

Epitaph for Rock 'n' Roll

"Some took a Stairway to heaven; some took the Highway to hell."

The 'final finale' at my brother's pub in Knightsbridge, Simon and Dave and a state-of-the-art light show, January 1996

That wasn't quite it though, I mean I don't want this book to finish up having about three different endings or encores (if we are using a band analogy). Or indeed an over extended climax for that matter, like they did in that third 'Lord of The

Rings film. Where I was left holding in my bladder for dear life for over half an hour at Esher Cinema that time.

Incidentally, I once had a dream that I wrote the whole trilogy of those books. Sadly, when I awoke, I realised that I had only been 'Tolkien' in my sleep (last one I promise).

But yeah, we did reform to do one more final gig. Andy my brother had asked us to play a reunion at his pub in Beauchamp Place, one night in January 1996.

Having gotten pissed there quite a few times over the previous twelve months and even cooked a Christmas dinner for 30 plus covers, it would've been churlish not to.

I've also played with Simon and Dave a few times since. We've done the occasional covers gig and we even rolled back the years and rocked out at Dave's wedding (less said about that one the better though). But we have also reminisced and chatted about this book just to make sure I've got most of my facts and (soiled drumsticks) straight!

We've all done different things since Hurricane Jane. I returned to Pete Lorentz's 'Wrong hole' studio in Camden the following year with an assortment of musicians and recorded an album entitled "Rock is Just a Four-Letter Word" or "When you shat on us" as Big Dave so eloquently puts it!

The money for this project was very generously put up by another good friend Danny Toffel and hopefully one day I will be able to make good on his investment and he can at least get some of his money back.

I had a crack at Eurovision in 2014 and almost got the gig, my song, '*We are the United Kingdom of Rock*, was a tribute to all the great British Rock acts of yesteryear and aimed at reminding the rest of Europe, (who'd been giving us Nil points for a few years) of our Musical heritage.

Despite a great campaign and some well-placed publicity, the BBC decided that the rest of Europe wouldn't get it and went with a girl called Molly and her highly sanitised 'Children of the Universe' song. She came 17th. But who's to say I'd have fared any better against the 'Bearded lady'?

Oh, and guess what? I even got to play in Scandinavia! Copenhagen. Denmark to be precise. Somewhere in cyberspace is some footage of me and the HJ21 boys, Mike, Pete and Brian (the band I formed after 'The Jane') and a fridge full of Tuborg Christmas Lager (The best payment and rider ever by the way).

I then produced an album of remastered 'rough demos' entitled '21-gun salute' with my good pal Nigel Wade, which also included a magnificent cover design by another buddy, Scott Ebbz, this was my own personal tribute and thank you to all the wonderful and talented musicians that I've worked and played with over the years. A sort of 'Greatest Shits' album if you like!

I also managed twelve years as a party DJ for both kids and adults. I was pretty good at it too. Got the nickname 'DJ Matt' locally and I often get stopped in the street today by big lads in groups, shouting at me from across the street "Oi mate, you did my eleventh birthday party" as if they are about to attack me or falsely accuse me of some heinous child abuse, before they thankfully follow up with a much more validating "Yeah you was good as it goes…do you still do it? Only it's my cousins, uncles, sons, stepbrothers, twenty-first birthday in July… next year and I think they were looking for a 'cheap' DJ".

For the record I don't. I still compare some festivals and events around the country though. But all they really do is make me hanker for rocking out with a band on stage again,

So, in 2018 I joined a cover's band called Ransom, initially an amazing 70 gigs a year rock covers tribute band. Set up by the fantastic guitarist Dave Barlow and his very talented son Zach on bass. It was later joined by the brilliant 'Zippy' Lee on drums to complete the line-up.

However fun as this still is, the originals bug soon kicked in again and over the Covid 19 outbreak, we started writing and recording our own material (under covert conditions) when we couldn't play anywhere. We are currently promoting our Christmas single, *A Christmas Held to Ransom*, (out on the Heavy Metal Records label) after our very successful debut EP entitled, *Halfway to Hell*, recorded during the summer of 2020 brought us to everybody's attention.

We have also just been added to the Hard Rock Hell 15 festival bill for 2022 and 'Call OF The Wild' festival in 2023 in Lincolnshire (plus quite a few others) and indeed now have an album out aptly called 'Back to The Boozer' available on Spotify, iTunes etc.

However, more of that in the sequel to this book…Oh yes dear reader there's a whole twenty-seven years' worth of stuff to catch up on in between!

Indeed, like the fact that in 2018, I also wrote a book of poems, A Life in a Calendar Year. Which If you haven't seen (or bought) yet do keep an eye out for it as it's been released through the same wonderful publishers as this one.

With my nephew Chris at the final Hurricane Jane gig. He's a bit bigger and a lot hairier now. January 1996

But the question I know you are all secretly asking?

Could Hurricane Jane ever make a comeback?

Well, I did get a call from Simon, recently. He's uncovered a live recording of us at The Orange during our 'pomp'. It's going to need a bit of work to bring it back to life but it's a great representation of us at our best. A bit of TLC and a skilled engineer is all it needs. Simon certainly sounded up for a reunion and last time I spoke with Big Dave, he also had the fire back.

As for Jason, according to his LinkedIn profile, he now works in anti-terrorism, specialising in forensics and biometrics. He'd certainly get some interesting samples off those drumsticks Dave borrowed on that night we played truth or dare.

Anyway, we have finally tracked him down, chatted and he's given his approval for this book. At the very least he's alive and well and we are all hoping to meet up for a beer soon, once he's free from the constraints of CSI Salisbury (where he now lives) that is.

The last time we saw Jason (biometrically speaking), January 1996

As for me... right now? Well, despite having ulcerative colitis as already discussed, I've have also added a 'Hiatus hernia' and a lung condition called 'Bronchiectasis' to my collection of life-threatening illnesses and diseases,

But I have them all under control and despite them, I'm still a very active fit fifty (maybe nearer sixty by the time this book eventually gets released) something.

I've also recently turned vegan, kept myself in decent shape. Still, playing football, tennis and squash. My hair is long and bottled blonde (blends nicely with the grey), and now post lockdown I am gigging at least once or twice a week with Ransom. The singing also helps to clear my lungs out. So, I genuinely really can't live without rock n' roll.

Family is everything, though! As I write this I am still very happily married to my gorgeous, long suffering wife Alicia and my two kids have both grown up into wonderfully creative Individuals.

Both now teenagers, my son Ryan (in his own right) is now an exceptionally gifted guitarist of some repute and gigging with his own college band. Might even get him and his equally talented mate Jack to play with Simon and Dave one day.

My beautiful daughter Zosia is street dancing playing for her local football team and coming with me to watch Spurs! Seems, the apple never falls far from the tree in this house!

So, at last could 2023 finally be the Year of the Jane Rodney?

Well, who knows what the future holds, Ransom is currently doing well right now and getting lots of attention and high-profile gigs at various festivals, so it's not all over and done with on that front just yet!

Not bad for being just a bang average 'Pub band'. But no matter what happens or doesn't, one thing is for sure, there will always be a special place in my heart for Hurricane Jane.

Anyway, as you can hopefully tell, I don't take myself too seriously and I am not too precious about anything. I just wanted to tell my story, my way! In the end, the best revenge in life is always to be happy!

Thanks so much for reading this and for sharing in my journey. I really hope that it strikes a chord with some of you and just as I would say to any Ransom audience on any given weekend gig!

"ARE YOU NOT ENTERTAINED?"

Oh, and just one more final thought before I go, and I'll leave this one with you...To any hardworking, gigging bands or performers currently out there, reading this, right now or in the future, wherever you are, whatever your level, whatever your genre The next time someone gets in your face, heckles you, or gets on your case about your talent or musical ability, just think of me, look them straight in the eye, smile and say... "You know you love it, you Schlaaaaaaaags!"

THE END

THE STORM OVER LONDON TOUR

HURRICANE JANE

Venue	Date	Time
The Swan, Fulham	12.6.95	9:00
The White Swan, Blackheath	17.6.95	10:00
The Borderline, Charing Cross	19.6.95	10:00
The Swan, Fulham	22.6.95	9:00
The Marquee Club, Charing Cross	24.6.95	9:15
The John Bull, Chiswick	28.6.95	9:30
The Rock Garden, Covent Garden	1.7.95	4:30
The George Robey, Seven Sisters	3.7.95	11:00
The Flicker & Firkin, Richmond	5.7.95	9:15
The Red Back, Acton - Battle of the Bands semi final	12.7.95	9:00
The Orange Club, West Kensington	19.7.95	9:45
The Cartoon Club, Croydon	25.7.95	10:00
The Red Back, Acton - Battle of the Bands final	26.7.95	9:00
The Mean Fiddler, Harlesden	9.8.95	9:00
The Marquee Club, Charing Cross Road	17.8.95	9:15
The Kings Head, Fulham	22.8.95	9:00
The Bull & Bush, Richmond	30.8.95	9:00

Please come to any of the above

A good time is guaranteed for all.

You have now been conscripted into the Jane Army whether you like it or not.

Your band needs you !!

This is the story of an aspiring band's out-of-control, flat spin and predictable nosedive into rock 'n' roll obscurity. It's a torrid, tragic, yet hilarious tale that will strike a chord with many a band out there both young and old.

These guys weren't going down quietly either. They'd kick and scream with a defiant swagger and a firmly raised middle finger directed towards the tide of indifference – both musical and cultural – and the perceived prejudices of the times. If not for these barriers, they'd have been bigger than Zep. For sure.

But it wasn't to be. Hopes, dreams and ambitions crashed and burned, then sank without trace, buried for all eternity…Or so it appeared.

Now, like an unearthed fossil uncovered after well over a quarter of a century, the real story can, at last be told in all its salacious detail. The filth and the fury, the divisions and the dirt, exposed and retold in all their glory.

It's a personal, honest, warts an' all account, drawn from the diary entries of the band's frontman and lead vocalist, Matt Fielder.

What emerges from these memoirs is the ups and downs of a rock 'n' rollercoaster ride through the tears, beers and ironic cheers of life in an outmoded but still gigging heavy rock band in the 1990s.

And like all good stories, there's even a little romance in it. Something for everyone.

The story begins in a world untouched by mobile phones, the internet and, by definition, social media. 'Pay to play' was the norm, cutthroat promotors called all the shots and French drummers thought Reykjavik was the capital of Sweden. (Well, ours did.)

The memories are still fresh, the heartbreak still real and the wounds still sore. So, plug yourselves in and follow Hurricane Jane across the London gig circuit from 1991 to 1995.

From its humble beginnings to its ill-fated 'Storm over London' tour and inevitable demise, its raw, it's raucous, its rock 'n' fuckin' roll…and

YOU KNOW YOU'RE GONNA LOVE IT!

Ingram Content Group UK Ltd.
Milton Keynes UK
UKHW020923160323
418667UK00015B/1248

9 781398 425033